Instruments *of* Empire

Instruments *of* Empire

Colonial Elites and U.S. Governance in Early National Louisiana, 1803–1815

M. K. Beauchamp

Louisiana State University Press
Baton Rouge

Published by Louisiana State University Press
www.lsupress.org

Designer: Laura Roubique Gleason
Typefaces: Whitman, text; Village, display

Cover image: *A Plan of New Orleans,* c. 1804, by John L. Boqueta de Woiseri. Courtesy
of John Carter Brown Library, Brown University.

Library of Congress Cataloging-in-Publication Data
Names: Beauchamp, M. K. (Michael Kelly), author.
Title: Instruments of empire : colonial elites and U.S. governance in early national
    Louisiana, 1803–1815 / M.K. Beauchamp.
Description: Baton Rouge : Louisiana State University Press, [2021] | Includes bibli-
    ographical references and index.
Identifiers: LCCN 2020033837 (print) | LCCN 2020033838 (ebook) | ISBN 978-0-
    8071-7428-9 (cloth) | ISBN 978-0-8071-7496-8 (pdf) | ISBN 978-0-8071-7497-5 (epub)
Subjects: LCSH: Elite (Social sciences)—Louisiana—History—19th century. |
    Statehood (American politics) | Imperialism. | Louisiana—Politics and govern-
    ment—1803–1865. | Louisiana—History—1803–1865. | Louisiana—Race relations.
    | United States—Territories and possessions.
Classification: LCC F374 .B43 2021 (print) | LCC F374 (ebook) | DDC 976.3/04—
    dc23
LC record available at https://lccn.loc.gov/2020033837
LC ebook record available at https://lccn.loc.gov/2020033838

In Memoriam
Margaret Augusta Beauchamp
1918–2016

Aux yeux des fondateurs des grands empires, les hommes ne
sont pas des hommes, ce sont des instruments.

In the eyes of the founders of great empires, men are not
men, but instruments.

—Pensée #209, *Maximes de Guerre et Pensées de Napoléon,*
  edited by Honoré de Balzac

Contents

Acknowledgments

Like any work of history, this project benefited from numerous librarians, archivists, readers, advisors, editors, amateur psychotherapists, emotional support dolls, etc. April Hatfield at Texas A&M University read the roughest versions of the manuscript, all while providing professional guidance and mentorship, along with James Rosenheim. My debts to them rise to the level of an obligation. Walter Kamphoefner and Colleen Murphy provided notes and advice on improving the draft, as did Troy Bickham and Rebecca Schloss, who read selections and versions of it much later. The input of all of these individuals greatly improved the final product, as did the anonymous recommendations from the reviewer at Louisiana State University Press. Any errors in the knowledge of particulars or of interpretation are wholly my own. In addition, others at Texas A&M University—R. J. Q. Adams, Terry Anderson, Joseph Dawson, Arnold Krammer, Linda Radzik, Adam Seipp, Phil Smith, David Vaught, and many others—provided valuable lessons in and out of the classroom.

The staffs at the Historic New Orleans Collection, the Hill Memorial Library at Louisiana State University, the Louisiana State Archives, and numerous parish archives in Louisiana happily and professionally helped me locate and access documents, as did the staffs of Evans Library at Texas A&M and the library at Texas A&M University in Qatar. A conversation with Jeremy Black in Doha convinced me to send the manuscript to LSU Press. Some of the initial research was funded by a Texas A&M History Department Research Fellowship and a Melbern G. Glasscock Center for Humanities Research Graduate Student Stipendiary Fellowship.

A visiting assistant professorship at Texas A&M University in Qatar gave me the time and resources to finish the initial draft thanks to the national leadership of Qatar and the Qatar Foundation for fostering a cordial and supportive environment in Education City. My new home, the History and Political Science Department at Rogers State University (our motto: the least dysfunctional department at RSU!), is a pleasure to work in thanks to Paul Hatley, Jane Johansson, David Ulbrich (who has decamped to greener pastures), David Bath, Sigismond Wilson, Ken Hicks, Steve Housel, Carolyn Taylor, and Quentin Taylor.

My personal debts are as great as the professional. Brian and Margaret Beauchamp; Brentt, Elizabeth, Wyatt, and Zoey Brown; Alexander, Annie, and James Beauchamp; and Lyanna and Andromeda Beauchamp have supported and encouraged me in all endeavors. Pat and Michelle Beauchamp wined and dined me on numerous trips to New Orleans, as did Dick and Denise Chopin. The incomparable Lee Daub, Stephen Frisbie, and Kamran Omidvar provided friendship and advice. Most importantly, Sudina Paungpetch read draft after draft, offering editorial advice and accent marks, but also her love and support, which makes everything worthwhile.

Instruments *of* Empire

Introduction

Portrayals of Louisiana, and New Orleans in particular, cast the region as exceptional, outside the American mainstream. This is unfortunate because Louisiana provides a crucial context for the history of U.S. expansion. Anyone who travels the region certainly comes away with the same conclusion—Louisiana is unique. Except its history is decidedly not. Louisiana is not an exception to the American experience; its history offers insights into the history of American expansion and the interplay between class, ethnicity, race, and colonialism, as well as the nature of republics, democracy, and empire. Placed in an imperial context, the history of the territorial period in Louisiana can reshape perceptions of American expansion and the complexities of manifest destiny in the nineteenth century and beyond.

With the Louisiana Purchase in 1803 the United States confronted new issues of expansion that involved the transfer of sovereignty of a territory that contained a large population who by birth, language, and religion differed substantially from inhabitants of the United States but who had been promised full citizenship rights. Federal officials failed to put the Territory of Orleans on a quick path to statehood over doubts as to the loyalty of the local population and their capacity for self-government. Consequently U.S. officials looked to other supporters within and outside the territory. Free people of color, Native Americans, and recent immigrants found themselves well positioned to negotiate for greater privileges. In essence, U.S. administrators, despite claims to impartiality and equality before the law, regularly acted as imperial agents in applying different rules to different peoples. Most importantly, the U.S. territorial government in its appointment practices co-opted local elites through prominent positions within the parishes. The methods utilized by the United States in governing Louisiana demon-

1

strated commonalities with European colonial practices elsewhere on the North American continent, and accommodation between federal officials and local elites in Louisiana served as a crucial national experience for the United States as it expanded over the course of the nineteenth century and encountered other Creole elites in Florida, the Southwest, and California. Local elites and U.S. officials operated as the middlemen who oversaw the implementation and at times obstruction of national policy as they integrated the territory of Orleans into the American nation. Louisianan elites encountered a federal administration that chose to be accommodating in some areas but in others implemented policies through Anglo-American or foreign newcomers. The transfer in sovereignty to the United States offered many individuals, both local elites and outsiders, new pathways to power. Local cooperation played a pivotal role in the success of the U.S. exertion of sovereignty within Louisiana.

Acquiring Louisiana placed U.S. administrators in Washington and on the ground in New Orleans in the odd position of governing a foreign populace, even as they espoused an ideology that maintained that all individuals possessed natural rights and all free male citizens equal political rights. At the outset of the Louisiana cession, Federalist senator William Plumer of New Hampshire framed the problem: "The constitution of the United States was formed for the express purpose of governing the people who then & thereafter should live within the limits of the United States as then known & established. It never contemplated the accession of a foreign people, or the extension of territory. . . . I know authority is given to Congress to make *new states*; but this authority from the very language which gives it, is necessarily limited to the territory then within the boundaries of the United States."[1] While several legislators opposed the formation of what they identified as an unrepublican government for the territory, others feared that Louisiana's eventual inclusion within the union as an equal partner might alter the nature of the nation's demographics and its values.

As historian Peter S. Onuf points out, "The history of Jeffersonian statecraft was one of ruthlessly exploiting regional power imbalances according to the pragmatic precepts of reason of state diplomacy—and of the hypocritical denial or, worse, the convenient self-delusion that republicans operated on a higher moral plane than their corrupt European counterparts."[2] Regardless of the Jeffersonian ideology based on a rejection of European models of universal monarchy or empire, in Louisiana the "empire of liberty" encompassed a populace who could not be conveniently removed or left out of the ideological framework created by the Constitution. In Louisiana a national compact model eventually won out with concessions that provided for a territorial legislature and, in 1812, statehood and political equality within the federal system. None of this sequence of events, however, was foreordained. The inconsistencies rendered Louisiana's territorial experience republican in theory but imperial in practice.

Louisiana's local population had to adjust to a new system of law based on trial by jury, a republican form of government that offered local representation in decision making, a stricter slave code that reduced emancipations, and freedom of religion under law. In addition, U.S. territorial policy maintained that once a territorial population reached 60,000, it could apply for statehood, and the purchase treaty obligated the United States to follow such a course in Louisiana as soon as practical.[3] The population of the territory of Orleans at the time of the transfer in 1803 was predominantly Francophone and remained so well into the 1830s. A census of 1806 suggests that more than half of the white population of twenty-six thousand (free people of color and slaves amounted to over twenty-seven thousand) were native Louisianans, mostly of French ancestry. The governor of the territory, William Charles Cole Claiborne, estimated in 1809 that around two-thirds of the new immigrant population of three to four thousand persons between 1806 and 1809 came from the United States.[4] The French-speaking majority increased by approximately another ten thousand individuals as Saint-Domingue refugees expelled from Cuba in 1809 arrived in Orleans. Historian Paul F. LaChance, in a more thorough examination, estimates that within New Orleans in 1809 at most 10 percent of the white population spoke English and 60 to 80 percent spoke French.[5] As a result of the influx, the 1810 Census recorded over seventy-six thousand persons in the territory (approximately a third of them in Orleans Parish), with over thirty-four thousand of that number slaves and over seventy-five hundred, or nearly one-tenth, free persons of color.[6] Ten years later the population had more than doubled to approximately one hundred forty-three thousand.[7] New Orleans dominates the historiography of Louisiana given its large population and position as the economic and political capital over the course of the early national period. Yet the parishes outside New Orleans that made up the majority of the population affected territorial politics and posed challenges for U.S. governance, in part because of their distance from the center. Each parish contained internal dynamics, which U.S. officials struggled to understand. Local elites wanted the United States to address security concerns involving the Spanish, Native Americans, and large slave populations. Parishes also requested assistance in assuaging the more stringent requirements of the new system of U.S. law and administration. When U.S. officials met these needs, parish elites proved far more cooperative.

The give-and-take necessary for cooperation resembled earlier imperial systems in Louisiana. In a survey of empires, Jane Burbank and Frederick Cooper contrast nation-states with empires: "The nation-state tends to homogenize those inside its borders and exclude those who do not belong, while the empire reaches outward and draws, usually coercively, peoples, whose difference is made explicit under its rule."[8] Regardless of the U.S. rules for the path to statehood, as in any other empire, ethnic and racial minorities in Louisiana continued negotiating practices in which they had engaged under the Spanish, lobbying for greater equality to safeguard their own interests against a hostile majority. The United States in turn identified loyalists whom it could use to hedge against a potentially disloyal majority. Empires often allow far greater latitude for racial, ethnic, and religious minorities, as Charles S. Maier notes in contrasting the prerogatives empires grant to groups, particularly elites, with national commitments to universal equality.[9] In Louisiana Native Americans would eventually be excluded and free people of color marginalized, but it became easier for U.S. officials to act in such a manner once convinced of white loyalty. In the meantime, federal officials employed imperial methods as they constructed the not so homogenous national state. U.S. control in Louisiana was not a matter of prefigured exclusions but analysis of who desired and was capable of inclusion. As opportunities opened for some communities and individuals, they closed for others.

The first historians of Louisiana fashioned a nostalgic historiography of their section before the Louisiana Purchase, which portrayed Anglo-American immigration into the territory after 1803 as that of a hostile, uncultured, and colonizing population. For much of the twentieth century, scholars wrote little about Louisiana politics in the territorial and early state periods, but historians of the Jacksonian period such as Joseph G. Tregle perpetuated an ethnic understanding of political divisions that originated with the Anglo-American influx.[10] Scholars of the Jacksonian era have represented the two-party politics that arrived in Louisiana after 1824 as a more mature form of political development. This interpretation assumes that parties are less self-interested and more ideologically centered than smaller factional groupings and thereby more democratic and efficient vehicles for the advancement of policy agendas and the expression of the popular will.[11] Territorial Louisiana's politics proved more complicated than an ethnic dichotomy suggests. Neither ethnic groups nor parties alone guided voters or officials in the territorial period. In addition to local Creoles, the Francophone community included Acadian families, many of whom had spent time in France or the United States, as well as the foreign French (refugees and immigrants from the Caribbean and France).[12] Louisiana also contained a white population made up of Germans, Spaniards, Irishmen, Britons, Canary Islanders, and other communities whose members could claim U.S. citizenship. A personal system of politics that dealt with advancing individual and community interests provided greater opportunities than a party system both for those who sought accommodation with the new territorial government and for U.S. officials seeking allies. This system facilitated territorial policies in Louisiana that introduced U.S. law and government while curbing practices that upset locals. Interethnic cooperation occurred frequently as economic interests and evolving racial and national identities bridged ethnic divisions during the territorial era, because politics were not primarily democratic.

The lack of confidence in locals' attachment to their new nation occasionally moved U.S. officials to adjust U.S. law in practice and, in some cases, ignore it altogether. This use of situational legal practices was another manner in which U.S. administrators acted as imperial agents.[13] U.S. officials and locals retained their own internal divisions, which advanced the territorial project by allowing both to more easily relate to other groups.[14] Accommodation became a consistent practice of U.S. administrators in other territories.

The first works that launched a move beyond the ethnic conflict paradigm explored processes of negotiation and accommodation between Creoles and recent Anglo-American arrivals. George Dargo in 1975 viewed the cultural clash between the Anglo-American and Creole populations through the prism of whether U.S. common law would replace civil law. The creation of a system of Louisiana civil law within the United States demonstrated both limitations to and degrees of tolerance within U.S. imperialism.[15] More recently Peter Kastor refutes the filiopietist interpretation by arguing that ethnic divisions during the first two decades under American control were always more apparent than real and links Louisiana politics in its themes to the larger issues facing the early national United States.[16] Kastor's argument reorients Louisiana history during the early national period away from ethnic discord to a more complex system of politics.[17]

The period between 1803 and 1815 represented the formative years for American governance in Louisiana as an older colonial elite adjusted to U.S. law, government, and immigration, while territorial officials came to terms with the older colonial population. This process required accommodation on both sides. At the same time, however, there was a clear power dynamic at play. For all the examples of cultural continuity, there was an expansion of power on the part of the United States inherent in the annexation. As Jack Greene offers in a brief essay that surveys changes of sovereignty in North America between colonial powers and cultural perseverance, "As early modern Americanists lovingly construct histories of the many worlds we have lost, they need to keep in mind the disproportionate role of power in the creation of the Americas."[18] Concessions and accommodation should not be interpreted as presuming equality. There is a voluminous historiography on American empire from 1898 to the present but fewer works on the nature of American empire in the eighteenth and nineteenth centuries. The neglect is understandable since continental territories entered the union as fully represented states. Still, a few historians have forthrightly argued for the first phase of U.S. expansion as an imperial project.[19] The differences between the first and second phases of U.S. imperialism demonstrated important changes within the American nation, both positive and negative. The nature of early American expansion that brought earlier European colonial populations into the nation points to continuities, as well as processes of inclusion and exclusion, that were far from unique. Territorial expansion can serve as a bridge linking the U.S. early national and colonial periods.[20] The early national United States engaged in a process of colonization across the western frontier, but this colonization differed in Louisiana and other areas where it encountered European populations. Certainly, some Americans of the time recognized this as a colonial process. William Plumer recorded how John Quincy Adams believed the first territorial government of Louisiana smacked of colonialism: "This is a Colonial system of government—It is a bad precedent—the U.S. in time will have many colonies—precedents are therefore important."[21] Although the ostensibly more democratic Jeffersonian Republican Party oversaw the acquisition of Louisiana, a few Federalists quickly grasped and criticized the nondemocratic elements of U.S. governance, even if more to point out Republican hypocrisy than to advocate a solution.

The U.S. government instituted a territorial government in Louisiana in 1804 to which the previously Spanish- and French-governed population adapted. The United States created a new judicial system and militia regiments, both manned at the higher levels for the most part by recent immigrants from the United States, the Caribbean, and Europe. At the same time, notwithstanding adaptation, Louisianans of various stripes also resisted the new system. Both Anglophones, the established Creole community, and émigrés from the Caribbean frequently violated the 1807 U.S. embargo on foreign trade and federal prohibitions against the international slave trade. U.S. sovereignty also afforded the potential for greater freedoms for marginalized communities, which U.S. authorities proved willing to explore.

The manner in which the United States initially acted after the cession of the territory by France exacerbated these issues. The United States took control of the administration of the Louisiana Purchase in December of 1803 and vested territorial governor Claiborne with executive and legislative powers.[22] Immediately after the transfer of sovereignty, the United States established its authority at the local level outside of New Orleans through the appointment of commandants for existing communities, who served until their replacement by judges ten months later. The commandants exercised executive and judicial functions, and Claiborne selected them based on their social position within their communities and their attitude toward the United States, except in parishes along frontiers with Spanish territory, where he turned to U.S. military officers. Many of the men appointed had held analogous offices under the Spanish government, denoting continuity in local politics.

In October of 1804 the newly created Legislative Council divided the territory into twelve counties. In some cases, a county in its boundaries replicated an already existing parish, but in other cases it might contain two or three parishes. The county system attempted to make Louisiana conform to institutions found in the rest of the United States. Each county had a judge, sheriff, clerk, treasurer, and justices of the peace. This system replaced the government by commandants, though in several cases commandants became judges under the new system. In theory, all these appointments from judges to justices of the peace came from the governor, but in practice Claiborne often made lesser appointments on judges' recommendations. In March 1805, in reaction to complaints by the inhabitants of the territory over the lack of representation, Congress allowed citizens of the territory of Orleans to elect a lower house that could propose a slate of ten candidates for the Legislative Council, from which the president selected five to be confirmed by the U.S. Senate.[23] The lower house in Orleans, the House of Representatives, was made up of just twenty-five members and together with the Legislative Council constituted the territorial legislature.[24]

The county structure proved short lived; the scattered populations hindered the formation of a sense of community, whereas parishes could be replicated in their jurisdictions in the political realm to greater effect, as they had under the French and Spanish. In 1807 the legislature recognized nineteen parishes and granted each parish a judge and organized five Superior Court districts. This new system replaced the county court system for local police and judicial functions, although the counties continued to be electoral districts and used as the basis for taxes on land and slaves. As with the county system, in addition to judges, parishes contained sheriffs and justices appointed by the governor. An advisory body to the judge made up of local prominent citizens, the police jury, also came into existence. The judges' powers lessened over time, notably in 1811 when police jurors became elected rather than appointed. After statehood, police juries increasingly took on the powers of a city council with control over public safety, internal regulations, and appointive powers for the parish treasurers and road overseers. The shift back to parishes reflected the influence of the prior political infrastructure and a willingness on the part of the territorial government to cater to local wishes. Parishes relieved many of the problems of the county court system by reducing the number of cases for judges and the court costs for litigants. Only after statehood in 1812 did the parishes fully begin to supersede counties for tax purposes, although the fourteen-member state Senate (which replaced the Legislative Council as the upper legislative body after statehood) continued to be chosen from senatorial districts that mirrored the counties, with Orleans divided to receive two seats.

These were not the only changes made with statehood in 1812. The earlier franchise for the territorial House of Representatives had been based on Mississippi's voter qualifications. The Louisiana state constitution of 1812 allowed voters a say in the election of the governor for the first time, though it kept limits on the franchise. Only white males at least twenty-one years of age who had resided in the state for a year and paid state taxes six months before an election could vote.[25] The legislature elected the governor from the top two candidates selected by the electorate at large, and the governor retained broad appointment powers.[26] As in much of the rest of the nation, the electoral system benefited the elite, and in particular the landed elite, who paid taxes on land and slaves. Economic and political elites essentially represented the same class, overcoming ethnic differences and places of origin to form a socially coherent leadership group.

This study will examine the ways in which the U.S. territorial system functioned in an imperial context. It will begin with a chapter on the United States' Spanish predecessor and other imperial competitors in Louisiana, which will explore U.S. officials' fears of foreign influence within Louisiana and perceptions of the Spanish external threat. The following chapter will cover U.S. policy in Louisiana for Native Americans. Territorial officials found themselves in the odd position of attempting to forge better relations with Native Americans in the West to counter Spanish influence and securing living space for tribes migrating from the East, even as American settlers continued to appropriate tribal lands. The third chapter will explore the slave regime erected in Louisiana under U.S. auspices and reactions. The existence of a large slave population prompted locals to adhere to U.S. governance, as the federal government offered not only security in the event of a rebellion but a legal regime attuned to planters' interests. The impetus for much of this legislation came from local planters rather than federal officials. The first three chapters examine external and internal threats to Louisiana that inspired elite fears and demonstrated the need for U.S. sovereignty.

The fourth chapter will focus on the free people of color caught between the interests of planters and U.S. promises of individual rights. Like the history of Native Americans, the history of the free people of color within Louisiana demonstrated one of the great tragedies of the antebellum United States in that despite the language of individual rights, free people of color increasingly became marginalized under U.S. control. Even so, during the territorial period federal officials, in part because of doubts regarding Creole loyalty, proved receptive to greater political involvement by free people of color. The fifth chapter will examine the ways in which the U.S. government won support at the local level from white Louisianans, frequently by subverting or ignoring policies set in Washington. It was just as much what federal officials chose not to or conveniently failed to implement as what they did implement that secured adherents. The sixth and final chapter will deal with the appointment practices of the U.S. government. In predominantly Creole parishes of southern Louisiana the territorial government regularly appointed and co-opted Francophone locals, while in the less settled parishes of the West it generally appointed Anglo-Americans to the most prominent positions. Recent immigrants, particularly those with knowledge of French, also regularly secured appointments. The chapters are ordered in this manner to illustrate a sense of the threats and challenges U.S. officials faced and the manners in which different groups attempted to manipulate the new regime for their benefit before coming to the means by which the U.S. government attempted to govern Louisiana at the local level.

Louisiana, like future acquisitions in Florida, Texas, Utah, California, and New Mexico, contained a large population whose inclusion within the new nation as citizens required that they shift their allegiances but also adjust to different legal and political systems. This period of expansion linked the United States with the decidedly colonial past of North America, with multiple legal systems, languages, and allegiances, where populations and sovereignty frequently changed hands. Louisiana underwent this process multiple times, with transfers of sovereignty from France to Spain and then briefly back to France before annexation by the United States. By viewing the U.S. effort in Louisiana from the point of view of the appointees who actually made the system work, one can discern how the United States approached governing a colonial population and how it both differed from and resembled its colonial predecessors. With the Louisiana Purchase, the United States gained a territory with a population similar enough to its own in culture and makeup that it was willing to grant citizenship but different enough to require significant adaptations from both the incoming government and the local population. Much of this process has been described from the perspective of policy makers in Washington or from the perspectives of marginalized groups hurt by these policies. Rather than viewing the process through the lens of high policy makers in Washington or disenfranchised local groups, this study aims to shed light on the territorial elites who allowed government to function.

1

Frontiers and Colonial Loyalties

As a Federalist advocate of expansion, James Workman avidly supported the Louisiana Purchase, despite its occurrence under Thomas Jefferson. Indeed, he wrote a play, *Liberty in Louisiana: A Comedy,* celebrating the transfer, which went into production in Charleston (and later staged in Philadelphia and New York). Workman had served in the British army, studied law, and worked as a journalist, publishing pieces with the *Monthly Review.* He immigrated to the United States most likely because his Irish birth barred him from work as a solicitor, and his political opposition to the war with France and advocacy of Irish political rights became increasingly unpopular.[1] Workman lived in several cities on the eastern seaboard, became active in Federalist politics, and advocated filibustering expeditions whether mounted from Britain or the United States. For Workman, the purchase advanced the rule of law and civilization, and he wanted to be a part of it. Consequently, after the play closed he moved to New Orleans in 1804 and quickly became a clerk for Governor Claiborne and later secretary of the Legislative Council, where he drafted legislation, including the criminal code for the territory. In 1805 Workman secured an appointment as a judge of Orleans County.

In the final act of Workman's play, a U.S. general dispatched to oversee the transfer informs the character Don Bertoldo de la Plato, a corrupt Spanish judge who wishes to abscond with his ward, the romantic lead, that "LIBERTY IS NOW IN LOUISIANA!—The government which now rules here will not admit your rank as the testimony of your innocence; nor suffer it to shelter you if you have acted wrong. Our laws confer no privilege which justice may refuse to recognize—the humblest are shielded by their protection." The general, in concluding the play, declares: "The confederated states of which our commonwealth consists, compose an IMPERIAL GOVERN-

MENT, sufficiently united for national defence and those objects for which union and uniformity are requisite; and MUNICIPAL GOVERNMENTS sufficiently numerous powerful and divided to adapt regulations suitable to the circumstance of each state."[2] Workman held no doubt as to the superiority of the American system. Even so, he did not dismiss Spanish jurisprudence so much as the corrupt manner of its application.[3] Workman believed in the impartiality of law and the virtues of the U.S. federal system that would bar abuses common under corrupt monarchical regimes. Caricatures of Spanish governance in the New World had become commonplace. The British traveler Francis Bailly observed of Spanish governance in Natchez in 1797: "They depend in all their civil and criminal affairs upon the *whim* or *caprice favour* or *folly* of an upstart Spaniard who is set over them as their governor, and who, through pique or malice, or in a fit of drunkenness or insanity, has it in his power to sport with the lives and property of those persons over whom he is placed for the ostensible purpose of protection."[4] Consequently Bailly found it unsurprising that most inhabitants welcomed the cession of Natchez to the United States under the 1795 Treaty of San Lorenzo. Foreign observers regularly reported the same phenomenon of incompetent and corrupt governance in Spanish Louisiana and assumed that the cession to the United States would be welcomed.

Workman did not just theorize. Over the winter of 1806–7 he found himself in a position to enforce the law impartially. During a period of national emergency brought about by a purported conspiracy by Aaron Burr that aimed to either separate portions of the West from the United States or to conduct a filibustering expedition into New Spain, General James Wilkinson with Claiborne's tacit approval instituted martial law, made military arrests, and suspended habeas corpus. Workman publicly voiced his opposition to these measures and then moved to counteract abuses. After he ordered the release of three men arrested by Wilkinson in the city, it resulted in his own arrest along with his friend Lewis Kerr. Despite Workman's beliefs in the impartiality of U.S. law and the virtues of a federal system that barred officeholders from abusing their authority, he became a clear victim of exactly that in the name of public order.

Workman resigned his judgeship and in opposition proved an embarrassing critic of Wilkinson's violations of civil liberties and Claiborne's negligence in failing to prevent them. More importantly the behavior of public officials during the incident belied the U.S. rhetoric over its superiorities. Workman addressed Claiborne in 1807, accusing him of cowardice in the face of a military tyranny, and asserting that Wilkinson's acts "have in great measure blasted the hope which the Louisianians began to entertain of the permanent freedom and prosperity of their country."[5] Due to their opposition to Wilkinson's measures and alleged support for Burr's expedition, Workman and Kerr were put on trial for violating U.S. neutrality laws, with the U.S. attorney for the territory, James Brown, leading the prosecution. Kerr's first trial ended with a hung jury, and when he was tried again the jury returned with a not guilty verdict.[6] Though he was acquitted, Workman's judicial and political career in the territory was finished. He continued to practice law and criticize the administration as an editor of the newspaper *La Lanterne Magique* for two more years; this too came to an end. In an argument before the bench with Philip Grymes, the district attorney for the district of Orleans, over the batture case in which Workman represented Edward Livingston, who attempted to claim private ownership of a batture (the land between a river and levees) in New Orleans, Workman responded to allegations that he opposed the government a falsehood. Incensed, Grymes threw an ink well at Workman, spraying several surprised observers. The judge, Joshua Lewis, ordered both men to appear the next day, whereupon they were fined and incarcerated for eight hours. The incident resulted in challenges to duels from Workman, which Grymes declined, and acrimonious pamphlets from both men. The handbill war led to Workman's disbarment when Judge Lewis felt Workman misquoted him as to Grymes's misconduct. Without a source of income, Workman left New Orleans in 1809 and did not return for eight years. He then reestablished a law practice and began to participate in the social and public life of the city until his death in 1832. Workman's experience strikingly demonstrates the capability of the U.S. government to operate in a manner contrary to the ideals it espoused. Workman, an Irish Briton and capable ally of the governor until 1807, could be removed in a flagrant violation of the very principles he believed to be at the heart of U.S. administration.

Federal officials justified the extraordinary measures undertaken during the Burr conspiracy in the name of national security and public order. The internal threat represented by Burr coincided with an external threat from Spain that manifested itself on the Sabine. U.S. officials worried that a separatist plot could appeal to the French-speaking populace of Louisiana. The irony was that Creoles remained unmoved by the appeal of separation, and the men targeted by Wilkinson were generally Americans or British immigrants like Workman rather than Creoles. During the Burr conspiracy, which raised the specter of both a potential Spanish conflict and an internal secessionist threat along the American frontier, constitutional safeguards and the men committed to upholding them, such as Workman, would be sacrificed at first in the name of public safety and then later for political expediency.

For all the importance of the last two generations of scholarship that treat frontiers as zones of economic, social, and cultural exchange (which they certainly were), frontiers are about power. Charles S. Maier writes: "The point is that frontier defines authority, and those who govern lose legitimacy if their frontiers become totally permeable." Federal authority on the frontier created by the Louisiana Purchase mattered a great deal as the United States justified its rule not just to the international community but to the foreign-born populace of Louisiana. In examining frontiers Maier draws a useful distinction between peer competitors and asymmetrical threats: "Call the one function *anti-adversarial* and the other *anti-incursive*."[7] Louisiana contained western and eastern frontiers that fit both categories, and the territorial government strove to establish its authority in the face of threats from other nations as well as a series of nonstate actors: Native American tribes, bandits, smugglers, filibusters, and pirates. This chapter will deal with the antiadversarial frontier and the following with the anti-incursive, though it must be kept in mind that in Louisiana the two frontiers until the resolution of the War of 1812 regularly would be linked in the thinking of U.S. officials, all the more so given the foreign nativity of the population and the plasticity of national attachment.

At the onset of the transfer many Americans, both Republicans and Federalists, harbored doubts over the loyalty of the populace of Louisiana, an assessment complicated by external threats. Senator William Plumer of New Hampshire reported that President Jefferson desired to pass a bill to distribute land to encourage immigration into Louisiana, since so much of its population could not be depended upon in the event of a threat.[8] The federal union created by the founders and advanced by the Jeffersonian Republicans fundamentally opposed the European concept of a balance of power, but in Louisiana imperial competition played a key role in binding the local population to their new nation.[9] With the monarchical empire of Spain in close proximity, the United States could demonstrate its value by offering greater opportunities for advancement than those across the border, while continuing to protect against outside aggression.

Worries over local loyalties in combination with outside threats were nothing new for the young republic, nor for previous imperial occupants of the Mississippi valley. The United States encountered challenges of governance in Louisiana remarkably similar to those earlier encountered by France, Spain, and then France again in dealing with Native Americans, slaves, free persons of color, and the local European population. Spain earlier struggled with the same fears throughout the Mississippi basin when it came to exercising control over non-Spanish populations.[10] Nor was the United States unique in the anxieties brought about by the presence of geopolitical competitors that might threaten the nation's seemingly tenuous control over the region, and these issues recurred elsewhere.[11]

The United States succeeded in Louisiana for three key reasons. First, geography and the fact that Louisiana lay contiguous to the United States eased control and promoted immigration and economic ties in a manner that Spanish and earlier French control had not. The United States as a nation on the continent found it far easier to project power despite the weak state of the federal government. Indeed, that weak government because of its federal component proved highly attractive to national ethnic and religious minorities, which might constitute local majorities. The federal system allowed for greater local control over a host of issues that facilitated U.S. empire, as long as territorial officials acceded to local prerogatives. For European states the maritime nature of New World colonies posed significant costs for administration, defense, and reconquest. Where other nations had to make difficult decisions in terms of encouraging the development of a colony with native-born European immigrants or importing foreign migrants, the United States could do both. Shifts in Western Hemispheric territory were linked to European notions of the balance of power, though trade often figured as a more important metric, particularly for the British Empire.[12] In some measure, the relatively recent settlement and lower population density of some of the colonies and the distance from their national cores made changes in sovereignty more likely, particularly in the peripheral areas of the mainland Gulf Coast that European commerce did not prioritize in relation to the Caribbean. The importance of trade and security concerns created a large number of contested borderlands in North America, and in all of these regions individual ambitions as much as national efforts determined sovereignty.

Secondly, the United States succeeded in Louisiana by courting locals of European descent and in the short term appealing to as many groups as possible. In this way Louisiana conforms to the general pattern of territorial expansion. Historians of an earlier generation, such as Jack Eblen pointed out that this had less to do with a national governmental policy than with the mindset of the personnel who oversaw territorial governments: "The significance of the United States colonial system lies in its internal oligarchic character rather than in its legal structure and the mechanics of federal-territorial relations."[13] In Louisiana this oligarchical character appealed to local elites. While the Spanish administration also understood the need for local elites, the United States found itself in a much better position due to a third element: the federal structure and natural rights ideology advanced co-option because it promised opportunities for many, though by no means all, locals.

Florida like Louisiana went through multiple changes in sovereignty, and each nation in control attempted to reconcile locals to its rule. The necessity of populating borderlands and developing local economies often trumped the distrust that new governments had of subjects who might retain earlier loyalties. For instance when the British secured Florida in the aftermath of the Seven Years' War, they promised local inhabitants freedom of religion and recognition of their property rights in order to sustain the population base, though there proved to be few takers. The Spanish administration in the late eighteenth-century maintained some distrust of British subjects in Florida because of their religion and cultural differences, in addition to their propensity for smuggling. Despite this mistrust, the Spanish government turned to Anglo-Americans for immigration by issuing generous land grants to boost the population. In 1805, however, the Spanish closed East Florida to American immigration because of concerns over loyalty. Florida like Louisiana became economically and demographically linked to the United States well before its political takeover.[14] Thus, often imperial fears over local loyalty could be overcome by the need for greater economic development and defensive calculations that a larger population would allow them to retain control in the face of imperial competitors.

Imperial powers could accommodate foreign colonial populations because national identity remained highly fungible during the eighteenth and early nineteenth centuries. Citizenship and national loyalties could change, as Americans who had been born British subjects knew well. In Florida, planter and merchant Zephaniah Kingsley changed his citizenship from British to American to Danish to Spanish to facilitate his trading activities within the Caribbean, by allowing him to fly the flags of noncombatant nations.[15] Such shifts were indicative of good business practices and cynical judgments rather than true attachment. Indeed, Spanish efforts among not just the civilized tribes but also Anglo-Americans depended upon the fluidity of national loyalty. For instance, the Spanish encouraged settlers in Mississippi concerned over land titles to immigrate to Spanish Louisiana and Florida.[16]

U.S. officials also had more immediate precedents to draw upon from the U.S. experience in the Old Northwest, where it had also governed a French-speaking populace. Indeed, the first pieces of legislation that framed the territorial system dealt with territory with a large number of Francophones. The demographic challenges of the Northwest addressed not just the French speakers whom Congress distrusted but also local Anglo-Americans. Despite these assumptions, the reality of increasing Anglo-American settlement in the West influenced a more liberal approach to government, with less federal oversight and more local control.[17] Louisiana fits within this larger paradigm. Though complaints over Louisiana's extended territorial period persisted throughout its existence, this too was not unique, and Louisiana's territorial period was not excessively long compared to later territories.[18]

As Eric Hinderaker notes, in the Ohio valley the United States had multiple advantages over its European predecessors in the West, which attempted to control trade and land from imperial centers without an adequate administration or the support of local populations. Americans proved more capable in harnessing the abilities of individuals through a freer economic system and cheap land. In particular the American commitment not just to liberal and republican principles but linking full citizenship with race allowed it to appeal to European populations.[19] Local complaints in

Louisiana might have an ethnic character, but they differed little from the problems of locals across the continent when it came to U.S. territorial administration. Complaints from locals and their easy analogies of territorial government to the undemocratic British Empire continued throughout the nineteenth century in the territories; Louisiana's challenges had less to do with the Francophones than with the undemocratic nature of territorial government.[20]

Louisiana thus exists in a continuum with both earlier territories and later territories that had colonial governments that predated U.S. control. The colonial aspects of territorial rule in some ways made it easier for groups who had already undergone colonial rule to adjust. Laura Gómez argues that in New Mexico race relations could not help but be informed by the Spanish past. This allowed individuals within marginalized groups to attempt to improve their condition. Mexican American elites could gain socially by claiming whiteness and higher status, but this served to further divide them from even more marginalized groups such as Indians and African Americans. Understanding the need for Mexican American participation but also racial obstacles, New Mexicans like Lebaron Bradford Prince began to play on the Spanish past to argue for Mexican American whiteness. Pueblo Indians in contrast held no political rights but in some cases continued to hold their community land grants.[21] As in Louisiana, groups attempted to secure gains from the political changes brought about by territorial government. Arguments for a racial order driven by the federal government do not fully align with the reality on the ground as Anglo-Americans and Creoles crafted political partnerships. Race often is portrayed as driving the politics of nineteenth-century America, but often local politics drove how race was defined in ways that differed widely from the putative national narrative. This, too, proved to be an imperial strength given the nature of federalism.

Spain, which acquired Louisiana in 1763 and successfully governed it from 1769 to 1803, presented the greatest threat for U.S. officials given contiguous Spanish possessions to both the east and west of Louisiana. Spain had faced similar challenges over local loyalties and geopolitical competitors in North America. After the turnover of Louisiana at the end of the Seven Years' War, the Spanish government strove to build up the population through migration. Immigration debates within Louisiana for the Spanish as for the Americans centered on the need to bring in more immigrants given the doubtful loyalties of the current population, but like many policies it cut both ways. New immigrants might develop into new disloyal subjects if they did not come from Spain. Despite doubts over the loyalty of French speakers, the Spanish worried about a potential economic drain should French settlers choose to leave the area after the change in sovereignty, as exemplified by the comments of Intendant Martín Antonio de Navarro (1780–88), who warned of a potential exodus of French settlers after the Spanish arrival due to mercantilist economic policies. Navarro backed a policy of free trade and more open immigration that would include non-Spaniards.[22] Acadian migration into Spanish Louisiana in the 1760s and 1770s increased the French-speaking population.[23] Migrants from the United States proved more controversial. Governor Esteban Rodríguez Miró y Sabater (1785–91) hoped to build up an assimilated American population that would allow Spain to hold the territory. In 1787 and 1788 the royal government of Spain opened Louisiana and West Florida to American immigration, but the shift attracted few migrants, particularly among Protestants concerned about freedom of worship. In contrast, General Luis de Las Casas, the captain general in Havana, harbored serious doubts over U.S. migration into Spanish Louisiana.[24] Governor Francisco Luis Héctor, Baron de Carondelet (1791–97), a Burgundian, distrusted the French inhabitants, noting that in time he believed Louisiana would develop a population that could be of use in wars in the New World but not against the French.[25] Carondelet also worried about the potential for French revolutionaries on the frontier.[26] While Carondelet encouraged immigration, his successors proved more skeptical of American entrants and sought more loyal colonists.[27]

In its last decade of control, Spain did little to increase the population, at least with the kind of migrants who appeared loyal to Spain. The fear of American immigrants remained consistent with instructions to the intendant and governor Manuel Luis Gayoso de Lemos Amorín y Magallanes (1797–99) to not allow Americans to settle on the west bank of the river.[28] Lemos, in the later years of Spanish control did not trust in the loyalty of the French population of the territory in case of a war with France. Worried over Anglo-Americans between Baton Rouge and Illinois, Lemos advocated immigration from Spain, Germany, Holland, and Flanders to counterbal-

ance the Anglo and Francophone populations.[29] Policies of religious tolerance to attract settlers raised concerns about the quality of the immigrants,
as noted by Minister Joseph Antonio Caballero in a letter to Minister Antonio Coruel: "The tolerance of sectarians have brought a mob of adventurers to the colony who know not God or religion."[30] Increasingly Spanish
officials wanted policies to build up what they considered a more loyal and
Catholic population and looked to European migrants within the United
States.[31]

U.S. attitudes toward Spain in the early republic remained deeply ambivalent. On the one hand, U.S. leaders in Washington considered Spain to
be a declining power whose North American territories eventually would
fall into U.S. hands, yet at the same time officials along the American frontier with Spain in the West and on the Gulf Coast remained deeply wary of
Spanish settlements and military forces. Both the western boundary with
the Provincias Internas and the eastern boundary with West Florida remained in dispute. Spanish influence over Native American tribes on both
sides of the border troubled U.S. officials in Louisiana, as did the Spanish
practice of welcoming runaway slaves. Despite the long period of Spanish
governance, however, Louisiana in its population, language, and culture remained decidedly French.[32] Yet Spanish officials remained in the territory
with long-standing ties to locals. In addition, several men the United States
appointed to local offices retained connections to Spain.

Spain opposed the cession, and the Treaty of San Ildefonso in 1800 explicitly barred France from transferring the territory to the United States.
When the French chose to violate this provision so flagrantly, it represented
an embarrassing affront demonstrative of international appraisals of Spain's
weakness. The loss of face was not the worst of it. Not only did Spain lose
Louisiana and fail to gain the territory promised by Napoleon in Italy, it
now lacked a buffer between Mexico, the Floridas, and an expansionist U.S.
republic. Despite popular perceptions of Spanish weakness, in 1803 while
still in Natchez, W. C. C. Claiborne worried that Spain might contest the
cession militarily, though in a letter to Madison he noted the presence of
American supporters within the territory.[33] Considering these sympathiz-
ers, Claiborne speculated that he might be able to take New Orleans with
militia forces.[34] Regardless, Claiborne advocated a show of military force
upon the turnover to impress foreign observers of U.S. strength.[35]

Objections to the cession framed a series of disputes between the two nations. Other issues predated the transfer, such as arguments over compensation for privateering expeditions against the United States and compensation for losses due to the Spanish closure of New Orleans.[36] Spain maintained that Baton Rouge and West Florida were not included in the cession. The Jefferson administration remained suspicious of Spanish ambitions, and Madison informed Claiborne that Jefferson wished him to carefully monitor and report any Spanish movements or intelligence on Spanish intentions.[37] In letters to Spanish officials Claiborne insisted on U.S. rights to navigation of the Mississippi and rivers of West Florida and indicated that Spanish reinforcement of current positions might upset the delicate negotiations over territory.[38] The Spanish regularly impeded U.S. commerce, as Edmund Gaines reported from Fort Stoddert that Spanish authorities out of Mobile charged a duty of 12 percent on shipping out of Bayou St. John that Americans generally avoided, but in 1805 the Spanish commandant at Mobile seized a ship with a cargo valued at over $4,000 for failing to abide by these regulations.[39] Claiborne believed these issues might not be settled peacefully, as he noted to the senior officer of the U.S. Army, James Wilkinson.[40]

Despite Spanish anger at the French sale of Louisiana to the United States, Carlos Martínez de Irujo, the Spanish minister to the United States, and others accentuated the silver lining for Spain that the province had been a financial burden and would have proved difficult to defend.[41] The Spanish attempted to make the best of a bad situation by establishing a buffer between American and Spanish possessions. A fallback position sought to use the cession to get further recognition of Spanish Florida: "The military colony of the French in Louisiana would have been in reality a worse neighbor for us than the Americans. . . . In my humble opinion, if we have to lose Louisiana, the choice of a preference of that colony belonging to one nation or to the other is not worth the expense and trouble of war, provided that we conserve Floridas."[42] Even as they struggled to find a way to abrogate the cession, the Spanish recognized the popularity of expansion into Louisiana and Florida among both Federalists and Republicans.[43] Likewise the Spanish speculated about the presence of U.S. troops in New Orleans after the cession given the proximity to their own territories, and when Irujo inquired, Madison informed him that the large slave population necessitated the troop presence.[44] Such reassurances did little to ease Spanish fears in light of rumors that the United States planned to seize West Florida.[45] Alternatively, other Spanish officials argued for giving the Floridas to the United States in return for gains along the Mississippi. Juan Vicente Folch, the governor of West Florida, became quite concerned with the threat the United States posed to the Spanish empire: "The recovery of the right bank of the Mississippi is as indispensable to Spain for the security of its Mexican empire, as the acquisition of the Floridas is necessary to the peace, prosperity, relief, and profit of the United States."[46] Officials with a wider purview appeared less amenable to such a plan.

Spanish officials were right to be concerned, since many U.S. citizens coveted further Spanish possessions. In New Orleans, the Mexican Association advocated U.S. expansion into Spanish America. Several Mexican Association members met with Aaron Burr during his sojourn in New Orleans.[47] In 1817 an author styling himself an inhabitant of Louisiana argued for the legitimacy of French claims to Texas that then transferred to the United States with the purchase.[48] Governor Claiborne often entertained visions of Spanish weakness, even as he feared the loyalty of his own populace.[49] Other U.S. officials reflected this odd sensibility to simultaneous Spanish weakness and strength.

Similar to schizophrenic appraisals of Spanish strength, U.S. officials veered between warnings over the loyalty of "ancient Louisianians" and testimonials of their fidelity. General Wilkinson in 1804 sent President Jefferson characterizations of notable personages provided by Evan Jones and Peter La Bigarre, who lived just briefly in New Orleans.[50] The list indicated several men attached to the Spanish government and others formerly employed by the Spanish.[51] Several Louisianans actively praised the Spanish system, as when Pierre Derbigny, a French immigrant and friend of Pierre-Clément de Laussat, the French governor of Louisiana for a few weeks in 1803, wrote a pamphlet that criticized U.S. policy in contrast to Spain.[52] Claiborne reported to Madison that many inhabitants assumed Spain would reacquire the territory, which reduced the number of individuals willing to serve in offices under the new government.[53] Even so, Claiborne maintained that most Louisiana citizens believed they gained more than they lost by inclusion within the United States.[54] The first secretary of the territory, James Brown, saw this amiability as the result of the failures of the previous

Spanish government: "The strict and arbitrary government of Spain exerted upon the restless descendants of Frenchmen had broken their haughty spirits and accustomed them to implicit obedience."[55] During periods of external pressure, however, Claiborne issued warnings that Louisianans might side with Spain. Still, U.S. officials generally asserted that they secured the loyalty, or at a minimum the neutrality, of a large portion of the population. Several Spanish inhabitants of the region received posts and, given American fears over Indians, slaves, the Creole majority, and at times Anglo-American immigrants, former Spanish officials appeared relatively loyal in the eyes of U.S. officials.[56]

The presence of serving Spanish officers in the territory in the aftermath of the cession exacerbated the fears of U.S. officials.[57] In an 1804 letter to Jefferson, Claiborne noted that "the great mass of the Louisianians are an amiable people, and I believe well disposed to the U. States; But it is certainly true that Spain has left behind her some friends in Louisiana."[58] Claiborne explained to Madison that he believed most of the problems within the territory could be traced to partisans of Spain and France.[59] The Spanish personnel's presence contributed to an impression that Spanish sovereignty would be restored. In addition, such officers could turn personal feuds into diplomatic contretemps. When Manuel Salcedo, a Spanish captain, and Benjamin Morgan, a merchant originally from Pennsylvania, fell into a dispute, Claiborne needed to appoint arbitrators to settle the issue.[60]

Much of the suspicion over Spanish officers fell on Sebastian Nicolas de Bari Calvo de la Puerta, Marqués de Casa Calvo. Casa Calvo had earlier been the acting governor of Louisiana from 1799 to 1801 and then with the transfer to France returned as an advisor to governor Juan Manuel de Salcedo.[61] Casa Calvo served as the Spanish commissioner for the transfer to Spain, but he lingered after the transfer in order to establish the exact boundaries of the territory. In the minds of many Americans Casa Calvo went out of his way to sow discord, particularly among former Spanish officials and pensioners, whom he pressured not to serve the U.S. administration. In efforts to reach an accord with Casa Calvo, Claiborne received provocative replies, including comments published by the *Moniteur de la Louisiane,* which Claiborne passed on to Madison: "Every exertion has been and will be made to conciliate and perpetuate the affections of the Louisianians towards the Spanish Government, and those who may continue to profess attachment (now that their allegiance has ceased) may at all times find an asylum in his Majesty's dominions, and these are the 'convenient effects' which were alluded to. The President will see from the whole tenor of the Marquis's letter how great the probability is, that Louisiana will for some time be subjected more or less to foreign influence."[62] Casa Calvo requested an official guard of three men and a corporal, to which Claiborne acquiesced in the interests of diplomacy.[63] Nevertheless Claiborne needed Casa Calvo removed due to the impact he had on the local inhabitants: "The ancient citizens of Louisiana, will look up to him as a kind of chief; his counsel will be resorted to & this will serve to Keep alive among the inhabitants that attachment for their former Masters."[64] James Brown also worried over the high profile of Spanish officers. He wrote to Attorney General John Breckinridge, describing their use of uniforms and pageantry, which he believed impressed locals: "Ignorant of the true principles of government . . . they are caught by the glare of Spanish exterior, and suppose that it is ever the badge of power and superiority."[65] In contrast the civilian American government, and Claiborne in particular, in Brown's view, appeared unimpressive, thereby undermining U.S. sovereignty.

Casa Calvo believed that Louisianans wished to remain part of the Spanish empire: "They are clamoring for the Spanish government, and there would be very few of them who would not sacrifice half their interests to see the government reestablished."[66] Some Anglo-Americans kept ties to Spain; Casa Calvo made Stephen Minor and Thomas Power surveyors for the associate engineer for the Spanish in the boundary commission. The Pennsylvanian Minor had been an Indian agent for the Spanish, while the Englishman Power had served under Carondelet in missions to attach western American settlements to the United States.[67] Casa Calvo left New Orleans in late 1805, in his official capacity, and Claiborne granted him permission to go through Lafourche on his way to the Sabine, technically in order to allow him to hunt and gain greater knowledge of the geography.[68] Rather than engaging in his sporting or geographic interests in Lafourche, Casa Calvo created a stir by insinuating that the territory would soon revert to Spanish control. James Mather, the local county judge and a member of the Legislative Council, reported on the fears Casa Calvo instilled among local inhabitants that everything west of the Mississippi would return to Spain.[69] Others heard similar rumors, as Louis Brognier Declouet in New Orleans wrote to his uncle Pierre-Joseph Favrot in Spanish West Florida: "According to recent news, we must believe that the time of our reunion is not far off. Letters dispatched from Cadiz on October 20 assure us that the right bank of the Mississippi River decidedly remains in Spain's possession."[70] Whatever the pretenses for their presence Claiborne believed Spanish officials encouraged Spanish partisans among the population.[71] Reports that the Spanish might reconstruct a post opposite Natchitoches at Adais also raised alarm.[72] When Casa Calvo journeyed through Natchitoches, Claiborne instructed Edward Turner, the commandant at Natchitoches, to accompany him and to pass on any other information he learned.[73] Spanish officers needed to be accorded respect given the need for pacific relations, yet their behavior appeared designed to foment disloyalty.

Another Spanish official whose presence raised concerns was Juan Ventura Morales, who remained even as he exercised authority as intendant for West Florida.[74] In 1805 Claiborne warned James Madison that Morales with ample wealth secured several American friends in the territory, including one of Claiborne's rivals and former U.S. consul, Daniel Clark.[75] Morales sold land to citizens of Louisiana in Spanish West Florida in hopes of populating Spanish territory but also of weakening the population of Louisiana.[76] Claiborne vigorously opposed such transactions. When returning from Natchez at Concordia, Claiborne noted the hostile attitude of the Spanish.[77] When Claiborne worked to prohibit his activities, Morales complained over the disrespect shown to him, though he agreed to stop the land sales out of New Orleans but persisted in these transactions from Pensacola.[78] Despite Spanish efforts Claiborne in 1805 remained "impressed with an opinion that the Creoles of the Country are for the most part well disposed, and several influential natives of France who are here, seem fully to appreciate the merits of the American Government."[79] In 1806, the president finally ordered Spanish officers out of the territory.[80]

Local officials also regularly noted Spanish ambitions along Louisiana's western boundary with New Spain. Reports from John Sibley, the Indian agent, and Edward Turner at Natchitoches asserted that Spanish agents intrigued with both local inhabitants and Native Americans to undermine U.S. authority.[81] Sibley also served as a justice of the peace and collected depositions of witnesses who had encountered and become victims of Spanish soldiers on the U.S. side of the border. In October of 1805 multiple witnesses testified that they had been robbed by five Spanish soldiers on the road from Natchitoches to Opelousas: "One of the deponents, Madame Bodin, who speaks Spanish well, asked the one who appeared to be the commander of the party, what business he had to order them to stop, that they were all of them Americans and that was American ground; the commander of the Spanish party, replied, that he had a right to command there, and would do as pleased, and that he must have such a horse for the use of the King."[82] A day later in another deposition Sibley took down the testimony of Thomas Olivier of Natchitoches, who had been robbed by Spanish soldiers on his way back from the Caddo Nation, losing fifteen horses, over a hundred buckskins, three Spanish saddles, and two bearskins, altogether worth an estimated $754.50 belonging to himself and David Case.[83] Claiborne noted the absence of a large cavalry force within his territory, which could be of great use on the prairies of Attakapas and Opelousas.[84]

Natchitoches inhabitants continued to maintain commercial ties with the Spanish across the border.[85] The population of Natchitoches in 1803 was heavily Francophone and Creole, though some prominent Anglo families resided there as well.[86] After the cession, settlers from the Carolinas and Tennessee poured into areas of north Louisiana.[87] Several Spanish and French families left the territory altogether, which posed its own challenge for Spanish officials in Mexico suspicious of the loyalty of newcomers.[88] The Spanish rejected a plan to settle families along the Trinity River because of these security concerns.

Claiborne passed on information from local officials on the Texas and West Florida borders to the government in Washington on Spanish troop movements and dispositions. John Sibley in Natchitoches in 1805 noted an increase of 220 Spanish soldiers in Nacogdoches, writing that "considering the attachment to them of their militia, and the contrary towards us of our militia, they are stronger than we are counting numbers."[89] The potential connection between external forces and internal dissidents plagued U.S. planners' security concerns in Louisiana. U.S. officials found it easier to gain a reliable estimate of Spanish troops than to gauge the loyalty of their own populace and militia. In 1805, Claiborne wrote to Madison that he could trust in only a portion of his own militia forces.[90] Commandant Turner informed Claiborne: "The Spaniards and the bad affected, have been very busy in circulating reports, that the Americans are mere Hogs, that they do not live like Christians, and that they will keep the Planters constantly poor by the immense Taxes they will Levy &c &c there is not the least doubt that the officers in the Spanish Provinces from the Governor General down, are extremely inimical to the Americans, and that they make use of the meanest and most despicable means to sour the dispositions towards, and alienate the affections of the people of Louisiana."[91] James Brown similarly expressed his distrust of the population and the weakness of the militia: "There are more Spanish than American officers in the Country, that almost every respectable family has one or more of its members in Spanish pay or reaping the fruits of Spanish patronage, that the people are alarmed about their titles, that they are alarmed about their religion, that they are inflamed by the Marquis and his emissaries."[92] The polyglot populace of the territory amplified the external threat posed by Spain.

The crisis that raised the issues of the Spanish conventional threat and its resolution, which affirmed for many U.S. officials Creole loyalty (however tenuous) came in 1806. The exact boundaries of the Louisiana Purchase remained in dispute, with some U.S. officials asserting that the purchase extended to the Rio Grande or the Colorado River or the fallback position of the Sabine, while the Spanish maintained that the boundary was further to the east at the Hondo River. The Spanish settlements furthest east were at Nacogdoches, while the U.S. maintained its position at Natchitoches.[93] The region between Spain and the United States became a consistent source of problems exacerbated by individuals who journeyed into it to trade or to acquire land. By 1810 the region had become such a problem that the Americans and Spaniards briefly cooperated to remove squatters.[94] After Jefferson replaced Vice President Aaron Burr with George Clinton in the election of 1804 and Alexander Hamilton's death in their duel finished Burr's career in New York politics, Burr began to visit the West and the Mississippi valley, staying three weeks in New Orleans. Whatever his aim, whether a separatist plot or a filibustering expedition, a number of prominent citizens throughout the West and in Orleans met with him.

Burr approached several foreign governments with potential schemes. The British consul Anthony Merry reported that Burr informed him that the multiethnic population of Louisiana preferred British protection, but if it was not forthcoming he would appeal to France.[95] Months later Merry again reported that Burr believed separation could be achieved with little bloodshed given local unhappiness with the United States.[96] Claiborne fretted about rumors of British support for Burr, as did the Spanish.[97] Burr appealed to several potential patrons, and they all found doubts as to local loyalty credible. Louis Roux in his report to the French minister of foreign affairs, Duc de Cadore, in 1810 commented: "They are still fond of France, and they would fall in with a plan that would make them instrumental in reestablishing a colony of France or in making them independent."[98] Estimations of Louisianan disloyalty appeared credible well after the failure of Burr's expedition.

As Burr descended toward New Orleans with a small force, a Spanish force crossed the Sabine, potentially threatening Natchitoches and Rapides. When the Spanish force crossed the Sabine, Claiborne left New Orleans to organize the militia in Rapides.[99] Claiborne argued that the Spanish threat weakened the internal American position particularly when not met with proportional U.S. force to impress Louisianans.[100] Consequently, James Wilkinson led a U.S. army contingent to counter this Spanish force. Wilkinson had long been in contact with Burr, and the two had known one another since the failed Quebec expedition of the American Revolution. Wilkinson and his Spanish counterpart Simón de Herrera came to an agreement whereby the Americans agreed to stay north and east of the Arroyo Hondo and the Spanish south and west of the Sabine. This effectively created a neutral zone between the two powers that quickly became a safe haven for nonstate actors. Wilkinson then wrote to the president denouncing Burr. Wilkinson's reasons for this might have to do with his knowledge of Burr's expedition and its limitations, his assessment of the relative strength of the two forces, or the fact that he was a Spanish pensioner. The maneuvers of contesting armies along the Sabine in 1806 had made all too real the potential for armed conflict between Spain and the United States. The Spanish scare heightened fears of internal revolt, particularly since no one could ascertain Burr's ultimate goal.

During the crisis, U.S. officials harbored doubts about Spanish intentions to the east as well. Claiborne refused to allow Governor Juan Vicente Folch of Spanish Florida to travel through New Orleans on his way to Baton Rouge.[101] The governor also wrote to Cowles Mead, acting governor of the Mississippi Territory, to "keep a strict eye upon the Spaniards! Governor Folch is proceeding to Baton Rouge with four hundred men. His cooperation in repelling Burr and his associates is desirable but in the uncertain and menacing state of affairs between the United States & Spain, it is our duty to be vigilant."[102] U.S. authorities also detained an armed Spanish vessel at Plaquemines rather than letting it proceed to Baton Rouge. Folch responded by blocking U.S. citizens traveling through Mobile, hindering U.S. commerce.[103] These measures were precautionary, as contacts who previously served under Spain informed Claiborne that the Spanish believed Burr's intentions hostile. Claiborne also received information, however, from "a person attached to the Spanish service" that the Spanish minister to the United States, Carlos Martínez de Irujo, in the past gave Burr encouragement: "My informant gives it as his opinion, that had Burr appeared before Baton Rouge three weeks ago, the Fort could immediately have been surrendered to him; but that Irujo's last dispatches had given great alarm to the Spanish agents, & had put them upon their guard against the traitorous adventurer."[104] Claiborne's information about these meetings in fact was accurate; Burr had met with the Spanish minister, but given Irujo's inability (along with everyone else's) to discern his intentions, he chose not to cooperate.

U.S. officials retained doubts as to how the "ancient inhabitants" would react to either a Spanish invasion or Burr's supposed separatist plot. At first Governor Claiborne proved sanguine over a potential war with Spain, confident in a united populace and U.S. victory.[105] Yet as Claiborne relayed to James Madison that in the event of a conflict with Spain, local attorneys advised that: "Inhabitants of this Country who have not taken the Oath of allegiance (and they are by the bye much the greater number) could not under the existing laws be tried for Treason if they were to take arms against us in the event of a War between Spain and the United States."[106] A few months later Claiborne reversed himself, claiming that many Louisianans would prove loyal.[107] From the West Claiborne reported to Secretary of War Henry Dearborn that he trusted the Americans who immigrated to the area, but "The same degree of patriotism does not exist among the French part of our society, many of the ancient Louisianans are still attached to the Spanish Government, and others are so fully impressed with an opinion that the United States are unable to resist 'the mighty power of Spain,' that in the event of War, they would probably be disposed to take a neutral Stand, as the safest course."[108] At Natchitoches, however, these notions again were disabused, and Claiborne found Francophones eager to serve, as he noted to Colonel Cushing.[109] Claiborne stressed positive elements not just for self-interested reasons in order to secure a rosy assessment of his administration at the federal level but also in order to reduce ethnic tensions. In a letter to Judge Collins of Opelousas Claiborne excused the absence of support from the "ancient Lousianians" during the crisis: "They have been educated in a belief that the Spanish Monarchy was the most powerful on earth—and many of them are impressed with an opinion that the U.S. will fall an easy prey to the Spanish arms, hence arises their neutral stand as the surest means of safety to their persons and property."[110] Collins and other officials, though disappointed with the absence of enthusiasm from Francophone inhabitants, still needed to build support for the United States. Claiborne was a conciliator by temperament, and the best that could likely be hoped for in his view was inaction from such a populace.[111] At a minimum, the United States had earned Creole indifference.

With the border issue resolved Wilkinson and Claiborne acted in an extralegal manner to quash a potential insurrection in New Orleans, where the prime conspirators appeared to be Anglo-Americans. The potential invasion in 1806 came to nothing, and whatever Burr's project, it failed, in some measure due to Wilkinson's betrayal. On the limited evidence available, U.S. officials began to reevaluate Creole loyalty. Wilkinson's extralegal arrests and use of martial law during the crisis did not make him many friends among the majority of Louisianans. During the War of 1812, William Crawford wrote to Madison of the need to shift Wilkinson to duty away from New Orleans because of the public opposition to him.[112] Still the crisis ended successfully; Creole Louisianans did not appear willing to actively countenance a return to Spain or separatism under Burr.

Officials on both sides of the border needed to cooperate in the interest of order. While Spain from the view of leaders in Washington might appear a weak and fragile empire, political figures in Louisiana remained all too aware of their own weaknesses that necessitated a pacific border. In a letter to Edward D. Turner, Claiborne asserted that the shared border as a matter of course created tension and that Spanish officers acted to alienate Louisianans from the United States. Nevertheless, Claiborne maintained that the Spanish monarchy would be too prudent to actively pursue a war, which might then result in further U.S. conquests in Mexico.[113] Claiborne as an American on the periphery of the "empire of liberty" held a sophisticated understanding of the multiple centers that carried out Spanish imperial policy. Though at times confident of Spanish decline, and certainly an expansionist, Claiborne did not have the authority to start a war, nor did he wish to, given his own doubts about the loyalty of Louisiana's populace. In a letter to Colonel Hopkins, Claiborne instructed him that should he encounter Spanish officers at Natchitoches to inform them that the United States could be trusted to persist in its neutrality.[114] The governor instructed Edward Turner at Natchitoches: "In all your intercourse with the Spanish Authorities in your vicinity you will manifest a friendly disposition and I particularly request that you would restrain the American Citizens from passing into the adjacent Spanish provinces, with a design to take Horses."[115] U.S. officials strove to maintain good relations with the Spanish across the border, while continuing to expand U.S. influence. At the same time, they had to counter Spanish officials seeking to do exactly the same thing within Louisiana. Even as Spain descended into the civil violence of the Peninsular War, Claiborne continued to fret about a potential Spanish threat, writing to Dearborn in 1809: "I have had frequent intimations that the Spaniards (aided by the English) would attempt to repossess themselves of Louisiana, nor do I doubt, but that the Agents of Spain in the adjacent Provinces have been and are still intriguing with certain persons in this territory."[116] Still, as Spanish authority declined amid Spain's internal troubles, U.S. appraisals of Spanish strength in the New World shifted.

The political dynamics in West Florida proved to be the reverse of those in Louisiana. In West Florida, Spanish officials worried over the loyalty of a largely Anglo-American populace that might revolt, precipitating or coinciding with an external threat. Despite military successes in West Florida during the American Revolution, the region could not be easily governed by Spain given demands for the representative traditions that existed under the British and the United States. In light of its inability to stem the arrival of Anglo-Americans to West Florida, in 1787 the Spanish Crown officially authorized their entry and better regulated the process by requiring settlers to take loyalty oaths.[117] The Spanish governmental system of West Florida failed to impress a population versed in a political dialogue based on natural rights and representative assemblies, and there were frequent complaints over land titles and the fact that trials were held in Spanish. These problems mirrored those of Louisiana Francophone citizens unhappy with U.S. laws and attorneys.[118] Claiborne early on desired the conquest of Spanish territory to the east, and in 1804 wrote to Secretary of War William Eustis advocating the seizure of Pensacola and Mobile.[119]

The border between Spanish territory in West Florida and the United States in Louisiana gave control of a portion of the eastern bank of the Mississippi to Spain and the western bank to the United States, which allowed both nations to inconvenience one another's settlers and traders along the river. Federal officials worried that Baton Rouge could become a source for smuggling and piracy across Lake Pontchartrain or, in the event of hostilities, as a base for privateers.[120] Smuggling of both people and goods remained a persistent problem, which would have required greater Spanish-American cooperation to end it. Spanish officers often went through New Orleans to get to Baton Rouge, which required Claiborne to issue passports to allow their travel.[121] Both Claiborne and his Spanish counterparts regularly pushed to allow their own nationals greater access to the rivers and territory of the other side without passports, while refusing to grant the same.[122] In 1808 Claiborne obtained information from a citizen of Orleans who overheard a conversation between a free person of color and someone from Baton Rouge that the Spanish had designs on New Orleans. Even though Claiborne gave it little credence, he still forwarded it on to James Madison.[123] The presence of a foreign jurisdiction so close made both Louisiana and West Florida natural destinations for fugitives, but given Spanish-American tensions, Claiborne failed to secure an exchange agreement.[124]

Spanish officials' fears mounted as a series of upheavals took place within West Florida from 1804 to 1810, which the Spanish linked, rightly in some cases, to U.S. support across the border. Upon the cession of Louisiana to the United States, the Spanish put down a riot in Baton Rouge; the boundaries of the cession remained vague, and many Anglo citizens of West Florida had no love for Spain.[125] Spanish authorities expelled Reuben Kemper, along with his brothers Nathan and Samuel, after they launched a small insurrection in 1804 from U.S. territory in Mississippi against a local alcalde, Alexander Sterling. The Kempers originally came to Feliciana, dispatched by Senator John Smith to help develop New Valentia, though they also may have been agents of Daniel Clark and Edward Randolph of New Pinckneyville.[126] They reportedly killed a constable with a pistol and threatened the control of the commandant of Baton Rouge, Carlos de Grand Pré.[127] Sterling, with the aid of militia, had evicted the Kempers from John Smith's land after their business venture failed. The Kempers' initial goal appears to have been revenge and banditry, though their grander goal became the overthrow of Spanish authority. In truth, the Kempers failed to kill anyone, though they did threaten their former business partner, John Mills. The Kempers implied they obtained Claiborne's permission for their raids.[128] They had met with Benjamin Morgan, who at the time served as president of the New Orleans branch of the Bank of the United States.[129]

Sterling, a Scot, and Grand Pré, a Frenchman, both served as Spanish officials, which speaks to the liquidity of national allegiances in the period.[130] Grand Pré called on Claiborne to help keep order and refrain from encouraging rebellions. Claiborne informed Casa Calvo that the United States, and the commandant at Pointe Coupée, Julien Poydras, did not countenance the Kempers. Indeed, Claiborne's directions to local officials emphasized the importance of social order, and they attempted to prevent any such expeditions.[131] The Kempers based their operations out of Mississippi whose authorities were far less cautious. Claiborne instructed Poydras to utilize "all the means in your power to prevent Citizens of your District from aiding the Insurgents."[132] Poydras played an instrumental role in cooperating with the authorities in West Florida to frustrate the ambitions of freebooters.[133] Likewise William Wykoff of West Baton Rouge contacted leaders in West Florida and urged them to avoid foreign entanglements with the French or British.[134] Creole officials served as better instruments for suppressing such endeavors, and figures like Poydras and Wykoff had operated under Spanish government long enough that cooperating across the border with Spanish authority in West Florida proved less difficult.

For Claiborne the recent incident with West Florida demonstrated a need to operate with military forces without reference to the Secretary of War in the event of a crisis.[135] The need for federal troops along the border with the Spanish sometimes posed problems with the local populace, and Claiborne carefully instructed Colonel Thomas Freeman in 1805, as troops took up their positions at the fort at Pointe Coupée: "Manifest a respect for, and to cultivate a good understanding with the civil authorities, and that every caution be used on their parts to prevent the Soldiery from offering insult or injury to the Citizens."[136] The territory needed federal troops, but their presence also could potentially alienate local support for the U.S. government.

The Kempers escaped across the border into Mississippi after their 1804 raid. From there, they persisted in undertaking strikes into West Florida, and as a result Casa Calvo called on Claiborne to turn the Kempers and their accomplices over to Spanish authorities.[137] As Claiborne informed Madison in 1804, the Spanish governor in West Florida issued an amnesty except for Kemper and two others; the insurgency was never over thirty men, and those who escaped were in Pinckneyville, Mississippi.[138] Although there was no direct Louisiana government involvement, the Kemper revolt resulted in further Spanish complaints against Louisiana authorities. In Claiborne's view the Spanish amplified a small event in order to discredit the United States.[139] Madison took the Spanish complaints seriously enough to warn both Claiborne and the acting governor of Mississippi that aid to filibusters was unlawful.[140]

In 1805 a Spanish West Floridian party seized the Kempers on U.S. soil in Mississippi. U.S. authorities in turn captured the Spanish party, and Mississippi governor Robert Williams released the Kempers, an act that revealed the limits of U.S.-Spanish cooperation.[141] In the aftermath of these detentions of Spanish officers, U.S. relations with Grand Pré deteriorated to the point that John Graham, the secretary of the territory, warned Claiborne: "As you come by Baton Rouge, take care that Grand Pré does not keep you as a Hostage for their delivery."[142] Despite provocations on both sides, the peace held.

Claiborne kept aware of troop movements and fortifications within the Spanish territory between Pensacola and Baton Rouge, which he passed on to the governor of Mississippi, the secretary of war, and the secretary of state in case the movements were preparatory to a strike on the United States.[143] The governor also grew anxious over the possibility that there might already be Spanish soldiers in civilian clothing within the city.[144] Even as Claiborne informed his superiors about the state of Spanish garrisons and fortifications, Grand Pré continued to furnish reports of other plots in both Mississippi and Louisiana, requiring Claiborne to ease his distress.[145] Spanish fears were well based, as the United States began to interact with Spanish American territories in a significantly more aggressive manner with the advent of the Peninsular War in 1807. Relationships cultivated with Spanish officials, like Vicente Folch, the governor of Spanish Florida, paid dividends after 1807 as U.S. officials reevaluated the future of Spanish power. Claiborne speculated to James Madison that Jean-Victor Moreau and Folch wished to establish an independent Mexico.[146] When a Spanish revolution did occur against Joseph Bonaparte, Claiborne noted of Louisiana's population: "The Spaniards are greatly elated; the English and their Partisans view the event as most fortunate, and the French discover much chagrin. But the real Americans, and such of the ancient Louisianians whose feelings are American, seem only to wish, that the ultimate issue may prove favorable to the Interest of the United States."[147] In particular Claiborne hoped for an independent Mexico that might prove more susceptible to U.S. pressure. Unnamed Spanish officers sounded Claiborne out on what attitude the United States might take toward an independent Mexico, to which he responded: "I was unadvised of the sentiments of my Government, but had reason to believe that it would be a source of pleasure to the U. States to learn that the Spanish Provinces had determined not *politically* or *commercially* to resign themselves either to France or England."[148] Spain's decline further complicated the demographics of Louisiana. Political dislocations might lead to further immigration from Spanish territory, "which may retard the growth of the true American Principles."[149] The decline of the Spanish empire could create as many problems as opportunities.

Whatever the long-term benefits for the United States to the west, U.S. officials expected more immediate returns in West Florida. Spanish officers let it be known that there would be decided territorial benefits for the United States in the Floridas given their limited value to Spain.[150] Vicente Folch, the governor of Florida, conveyed the same message a month later when Claiborne dined with him while visiting Pointe Coupée and then crossing to Baton Rouge.[151] In the same meeting Claiborne noted his personal support for American independence movements but also his opposition to French or English domination of Spanish possessions.[152]

Grand Pré's replacement by Don Carlos de Hault de Lassus, a Frenchman in Spanish service, aggravated the situation in West Florida as he turned out to be a far less able governor as judged by his constituents and superiors. While Grand Pré irritated Claiborne in their intergovernmental relations, he managed to maintain control of his largely Anglo province.[153] Indeed, the inhabitants of West Florida expressed regret upon Grand Pré's recall. In 1808 Thomas Lilley of Baton Rouge recommended a convention of locals to address the colonists' grievances and received permission to proceed from Grand Pré, but once the convention got under way, it scheduled a second meeting before receiving official permission. Once these conventions began, it became difficult for Spanish authorities to bring the participants to heel. When another convention met over the course of 1810, it moved toward independence and contact with U.S. authorities in Mississippi and Orleans. Many of the leaders of the successful 1810 revolt had served as local officials in the Spanish administration in West Florida.[154] The 1810 revolt succeeded where previous attempts failed in large part because of the participation of elite figures. The West Florida Convention chose as its chairman Andrew Steele, clerks George Mather and Samuel Crocker, and a large number of Anglo-American representatives.[155] The West Florida Legislature elected Fulwar Skipwith the first executive of the West Florida Republic. Skipwith had been a U.S. diplomat in the French West Indies and France. He had married a French woman but was a recent arrival to the Baton Rouge area after giving up his consular post in 1808.[156] After attending a poor performance of Voltaire's *Le fanatisme, ou Mahomet le Prophète* with Skipwith, Architect Benjamin Latrobe described him as "almost a Frenchman."[157] Skipwith possessed national connections, the confidence of the Anglo settlers of West Florida, and the ability to communicate with the Creole inhabitants of Orleans.

Past experience taught Claiborne to be wary of West Florida insurgents. When the revolt of 1810 got under way, Claiborne hesitated to bring about direct U.S. involvement. In talks with Mississippi governor David Holmes, he learned that despite broad support for the United States in Baton Rouge the presence of unsavory adventurers from the United States in the West Florida Republic's army necessitated caution.[158] Once the Florida insurgents achieved de facto independence from Spain, Skipwith dispatched John H. Johnson as an emissary to Louisiana to delay any effort to attach West Florida to Louisiana until a commission could be sent to Washington.[159] Some individuals within the West Florida Convention desired independence, while others preferred to negotiate entry into the United States. These divisions within West Florida did not last long, as it quickly became apparent that the area would be annexed by the United States. President Madison authorized Claiborne and General Wade Hampton, the commanding general at New Orleans, in 1810 to cross the border with his forces to annex

West Florida to the United States. Pointe Coupée, whose officials six years before acted to prevent the actions of filibusters, served as the jumping-off point for moves into East Baton Rouge.[160] U.S. forces under Hampton upset many of the French- and Spanish-speaking inhabitants in Baton Rouge by appropriating public land, throwing people out of their homes, and using the Catholic cemetery to bury the Protestant dead.[161] Despite these missteps, no armed opposition to U.S. annexation emerged.[162]

Still, this did not stop complaints. Audley L. Osborne, whom Claiborne sent to West Florida to issue President Madison's proclamation annexing West Florida to the United States, informed Claiborne that many individuals within the area had no desire to be attached to Louisiana.[163] Nonetheless, after meeting with the Mississippi governor, Skipwith accepted U.S. governance.[164] Those members of the convention who flirted with the idea of independence or annexation on West Floridian terms quickly fell into line, but the manner in which it occurred upset some of the West Floridians: "Sir, there is a dissatisfied party, and if they should feel disposed to be troublesome there is a description of people in the District well suited to their purposes; I mean those adventurers of desperate character and fortunes, who always sicken and become restless under the rule of a good Government and just laws."[165] The most problematic group remained the individuals who had posed problems for Spain, individuals like the Kempers, bandits, and adventurers.

Claiborne did not fail to grasp the foreign policy implications of annexation. He justified annexation to the secretary of state: "In this quarter the act of taking possession is highly approved; and I pray God to incline Congress to support the measure with firmness."[166] The seizure of West Florida provided the Spanish, the West Floridians, and Congress with a fait accompli that none contested with much vigor. In a letter to Colonel Zebulon Pike, Claiborne wrote of the U.S. seizure of West Florida: "The taking possession of Florida, will give great displeasure to England and Spain; but whether they will be disposed on that account to hostilities entirely depends in my opinion upon the success of Bonaparte in Portugal and Spain."[167] U.S. observers remained aware of the connection between colonial weakness and difficulties in Europe. The addition of West Florida to Orleans made it easier for many Americans to back statehood for Louisiana given the addition of more Anglo-Americans.

Rapid change from one regime to another in West Florida presented a familiar problem for U.S. officials in Louisiana. While the West Florida population resembled that of the United States (far more so than the population of Louisiana), dissatisfied parties remained. West Florida included advocates for independence, Tories and British immigrants who opposed annexation to the United States, as well as a significant Creole and Spanish population. U.S. officials strove to avoid continued ill feeling between West Floridians within the annexed parishes. Claiborne instructed General Thomas to "check those little dissentions which have unfortunately arisen at Baton Rouge."[168] The Spanish under de Lassus had refused to appoint the Virginian Philemon Thomas to head the militia and Fulwar Skipwith to a court appointment despite the demands of the West Florida Convention.[169] Claiborne granted these individuals appointments.

The U.S. government also strove to protect its citizens from Spanish reprisals. When a West Floridian force under Reuben Kemper attempted to take Mobile, the Spanish captured ten men, including Major William H. Hargrave (who had fought in the American Revolution) and held them prisoner in Havana. Claiborne sought their release in order to avoid "that ill-will which the Citizens of Baton Rouge, and the Settlers on the Tombigbe now feel towards the Spanish authorities at Mobile and Pensacola; and which should those men be executed, I shall find great difficulty in controlling."[170] The prisoners from Mobile would spend five years imprisoned in Castle Moro.[171] The persistent presence of a small Spanish force at Mobile gave rise to anti-Spanish feeling within West Florida, as did the Spanish capture at Pensacola of another Anglo-American, Cyrus Sibley.[172] The Sibley incident increased calls for the release of U.S. prisoners from Spanish jails. Claiborne believed that any Spanish punishment of these prisoners would only continue to create "ill will" between the inhabitants of West Florida and the government of Spain.[173] The captain general at Havana disagreed with Claiborne's portrayal of the prisoners as innocents and kept them in custody.[174] While in much of the rest of Orleans U.S. officials worried that the local populace might wish to return to Spanish governance, in West Florida they had the opposite problem of cooling West Floridian anger.

Anglo-American ambitions for Spanish territory did not end with the annexation of West Florida. In 1815 Claiborne wrote to James Monroe from Iberville warning of potential filibustering expeditions coming from Louisiana into Mexico.[175] There also continued to be rumors of Spanish aggression, but most American observers took them far less seriously after 1815. By 1818 Andrew Jackson could confidently dismiss Louisianan worries of a Spanish operation: "Spain is at present too weak in the Texas, to effect any military projects against our territory from that quarter."[176] The West Florida example represented the first step in a series of increasing U.S. aggressions against Spanish (and after 1821 Mexican) possessions, some state-sponsored and others that took advantage of private initiatives.

France appeared well positioned to bring together the internal and external threats to U.S. control given the suspect loyalty of the Francophone population. Yet, unsurprisingly, given that France willingly sold the territory after the failure to reacquire Saint-Domingue, it posed the least threat. During its brief three-week tenure in control of Louisiana in 1803, French officials, like their American counterparts, worried over the presence of Spanish loyalists and the nature of government and civil society within the colony. Workman was not alone in pointing to corruption within Spanish Louisiana; a number of French observers came to the same analysis. Paul Alliot, who had been deported to France from New Orleans in 1803 for practicing medicine without a license, dedicated his *Historical and Political Reflections on Louisiana* to President Thomas Jefferson, writing positively of the change: "No longer shall be seen those arbitrary imprisonments and deportations which plunged good men whose talents were the only cause therefor into the deepest misery." Alliot, like American observers, blamed Spain not just for corruption but for retarding the economic development of the colony. Even so, Alliot believed not all the Creoles were of the same mind: "It is quite true that not nearly all the people beheld the arrival of the French among them with equanimity: and regarding them on account of their conduct in St. Domingo as the ruin of their country, would have preferred to be governed by the Americans. It is, nevertheless, unnecessary to conceal the fact that the royalist party of New Orleans would have preferred to have remained as they were, and to have continued to keep the governed under the most severe oppression."[177] Alliot blamed Spanish government and policies for every shortcoming within the colony: corruption, the slow population growth, disease, and economic and agricultural failures, which he contrasted with the economic development and security of the United States. To be sure Alliot was trying to curry favor with the new government of the territory, but his own experience had given him no reason to look to the Spanish system for justice.

C. C. Robin, a French traveler through Louisiana, observed corruption and incompetence in the Spanish administration, but without lauding the United States: "The local magistrates most of whom can hardly sign their names, decide matters at the lowest level which can then be appealed to the only tribunal in the city." Robin also noted that a number of Louisianans spoke of immigration to other Spanish territories due to their dissatisfaction with the American government.[178] François Marie Perrin du Lac concluded his volume of travels in the United States by pointing to the advantages of Louisiana and the importance of colonies for France even as he denigrated Spain and the United States: "Weak in Europe, and without force or consideration in America, neither knows how to make herself feared or respected. . . . In vain it is advanced that the Americans are not a warlike nation." In the long run du Lac believed the nations of the Western Hemisphere would be independent but that a French colony in Louisiana might slow the process.[179] The peripatetic James Pitot, a Frenchman from Normandy who settled in Saint-Domingue and then Philadelphia, where he became a U.S. citizen before coming to New Orleans in 1796, had similar criticisms.[180] Pitot differed from other French observers in that he had a vested interest in U.S. control. He received a city council seat under the U.S. before his election as mayor of New Orleans in 1804. Though he resigned in the summer of 1805, Claiborne appointed him to be the judge of the parish of Orleans in 1813, where he served until 1831.[181] Having lived in the colony under both the Spanish and the Americans, Pitot wrote that upon its cession to France, "The errors of the Spanish government in Louisiana are those that perpetuate the mediocrity of a country, but which individually do not bother its citizens. Such an administration restrains commerce, restricts population, and does not encourage agriculture; and, by this unchanging policy, as well as the mingling of Spanish families with French ones, it has hardened an indifference in the colony that scarcely suspects the possibility of a better existence. Finally, the administration is, in fact, often arbitrary and corrupt, but most of the inhabitants are, nevertheless, peaceful and perhaps content in their mediocrity." Even as he condemned the Spanish government, Pitot believed the population could not comprehend its failures. Consequently, the change in sovereignty would not meet with universal approbation. Pitot pointed to the isolation of the colony, the lack of community, and venality that hindered development. While he exempted Carondelet from this critique, he clearly viewed the Spanish government in a negative light. Pitot also acknowledged the commercial shortcomings that existed under the previous French government as well as monopolistic practices that benefited individuals rather than the colony as a whole. The organization of the government with an intendant and a governor also needlessly divided authority in his view, crippling administrative activity.[182] Throughout Pitot's account there is an indictment of Spanish policies but also recognition of the growing economic importance of the United States.

Attacks on Spanish jurisprudence, likewise, were not simply an American response. The French commissioner Pierre-Clément de Laussat noted to Duc Denis Decrès, the minister of marine and the colonies, "Let me tell you how justice is administered here: it is worse than in Turkey."[183] Laussat concurred with the judgement of many U.S. officials in noting Spanish efforts to destabilize American rule among Louisianans: "They viewed and referred to this cession with much bitterness. The Spaniards secretly encouraged them to do so out of spite for the preference which Louisiana has always shown for France, as well as by a national hatred incited by the plots and acts of some of their leaders. The tendencies and views of the Spaniards were, moreover, wonderfully assisted by the natural antipathy which the Louisianians entertained for the Americans."[184] Laussat realized, however, that American missteps aggravated the problems.

After the brief turnover in 1803, the French confronted the Spanish dilemma of needing a larger population to make the colony profitable and defensible, while preventing migration from the United States. Decrès in his instructions to the perceived next military leader of the colony wrote: "As to emigrants from the United States, they will demand more prudence, and must be permitted [to enter] because of the capital which they will pour into Louisiana, rather than with respect to a population which could end, perhaps, by becoming dangerous."[185] The presence of Spanish officials did not sit well with Laussat, particularly given Casa Calvo's earlier service in Saint-Domingue: "The War caused him to stay here for eighteen months, and he left the reputation of a violent man who hated the French."[186] Laussat also struggled with rumors that the United States would soon have control of New Orleans, which turned out to be true.[187] Once word reached Laussat, he noted the disappointment of the French-speaking population.[188] Laussat was chagrined by the new U.S. administration, which lost Francophone support in his view due to personnel changes that benefited native-born Americans, but also by too many governmental innovations introduced too quickly. Laussat characterized Claiborne: "Charming private qualities, has few means and great awkwardness, and is extremely below his place."[189] As for the Legislative Council, Laussat did not express high hopes: "Most of them [are] newcomers and the scum of the other states of the federation."[190] Even with this unhappiness, however, there were few alternatives for French speakers.

Commissioner Laussat and several locals remained upset by the sale of Louisiana to the United States. Just after the transfer Claiborne reported: "There were then two strong parties, in the Country, one Spanish, and the other French."[191] Bonapartists drew Claiborne's attention early on: "They feel mortified at the possession of the Province by the United States, and seem determined to sower the inhabitants as much as possible with the American Government."[192] U.S. officials noted locals who appeared to maintain too strong a connection to France.[193] The territorial attorney general and land registrar, John Gurley, informed the postmaster general about the strong attachment of several Louisianans, who proved dissatisfied with the failure of the United States to live up to the treaty obligations: "There are men who speak seriously of appealing to France & requesting the first Consul to give them aid."[194] When several citizens sent a memorial to Congress, Claiborne reported Bonaparists among the signers.[195] Jean-Noël Destréhan, who represented the memorialists in their mission to Congress, particularly was suspected as one too closely identified with Laussat.[196] French birth was not enough to warrant suspicion, however, as numerous Frenchmen achieved appointments to office.[197] Attitudes toward the U.S. government and time spent living within the United States served as credentials. Claiborne attempted to exercise discretion in evaluating loyalty, though some of his countrymen demonstrated an excess of zeal. Minor incidents could be blown out of proportion, as during an 1804 celebration of Bastille Day when the raising of a French flag caused a fracas with native-born Americans threatening to take it down. Claiborne convinced the Americans that such celebrations could be found among ethnic groups in the United States and Americans abroad on their own Independence Day and cautioned that it would take years for descendants of Frenchmen to lose their connection to France.[198] When U.S. observers detected French intrigues, they tended to either be minor affairs that failed to pan out, worries over French communities in border regions, or incidents that proved more important for complicating international relations with the British or Spanish than legitimate threats.[199] Despite the presence of malcontents who might desire a return to a French colonial empire, the international calculus prevented the possibility.

While U.S. officials perceived France as a great power, in contrast to their visions of a decrepit Spain, France did not pose a proximate threat, with no contiguous territory and a navy that after Trafalgar in 1805 could no longer project significant French naval might. The very fact that France sold the territory demonstrated to Creoles and other nations a choice to abandon North American mainland ambitions. Divisions within the Francophone population also barred it from speaking with one voice. French Louisianans were Creoles, Cajuns, and foreign French immigrants, some from France and others from the Caribbean. Francophones might be royalists, republicans, or Bonapartists. Even assuming France retained the capacity to pursue Louisiana, French-speaking Louisianans were not of one mind as to how it would be ruled.

One of the obvious demonstrations that the U.S. government did not perceive France as a particular threat was that it allowed French refugees to settle in Louisiana. The secretary of the territory, Thomas Boling Robertson, warned Secretary of State Robert Smith that the French exiles "will rivet upon us a decided and irresistible preponderance of French influence—and thus prevent us for many years to come from considering this in heart and in sentiment an American country."[200] Even so, the United States allowed for their settlement. Claiborne wrote to Smith that if he felt the newcomers to be a threat he would order their expulsion and that he regretted bringing in a larger foreign population, but humane practices demanded that he help.[201] French settlers, particularly those from the Caribbean, tended to support the territorial government. The hypocrisy of American ideology that so turns contemporary observers into knots was precisely what appeared so attractive to many newcomers. Refugees from Saint-Domingue admired the republican principles of the United States but also the legality of slavery and its connection to economic prosperity. The Creole community welcomed the Saint-Domingue refugees for the positive demographic impact they would make given their own resistance to some elements of Americanization. Yet the refugees had a consciousness of themselves as a separate group, one that could cross racial lines. The brain drain from Saint-Domingue benefited multiple cities in the eastern United States and Louisiana to an even greater degree.[202] Considering their recent experiences with the upheavals of Saint-Domingue, they had little appetite for radical revolutionary theories and proved attractive to an administration looking for loyal Francophones who could bridge the cultural gap.

Former British subjects did not raise the same sort of alarm within the territory as Spaniards and Frenchmen did. Whether it was James Mather or John Carr, American officials noted their British birth but then their attachment to the American government. An exception to this was Daniel Clark, who in a list to the president prepared by Wilkinson and La Bigarre, was characterized as "rather an Englishman at heart, that he is unpopular & too assuming here. [T]herefore it might be unwise to countenance at present his cunning & overbearing pretensions."[203] Even so, Clark proved the exception; in general Englishmen failed to register the same level of distrust, though Britain represented a far greater threat to U.S. ambitions than France or Spain in the New World after 1803.

The decline of Spanish power provided opportunities not just for the United States but for Britain, and U.S. political figures, especially Jeffersonian Republicans, remained deeply suspicious of British motivations. Indeed, this paranoia regarding foreign threats proved a consistent feature of U.S. foreign policy in the early republic. Claiborne felt that the United States needed to combat British intrigues in Spanish America and wrote to Paul Hamilton, the secretary of the navy, that U.S. interests would benefit from an independent Cuba but suffer from one dominated by Britain.[204] Filibusters could be the avant-garde of Britain as easily as the United States. In 1805 Claiborne received a letter from a resident in Spanish Baton Rouge who informed him that Reuben Kemper, Arthur Cobb Jr., and another man allegedly sailed to New Providence to gain British support to take West Florida.[205] Claiborne then informed Casa Calvo that he would endeavor to prevent another revolt.[206] Although Claiborne believed an attack unlikely, he instructed Colonel Thomas Freeman to strengthen the garrison at Fort St. John, as rumors persisted that a British vessel might appear on Lake

Pontchartrain.[207] While continuing to bar aid to West Florida's insurgents, he wrote Madison for instructions on what he could do should the British introduce forces.[208] Fear of British involvement with filibusters served as an incentive for cooperation with the Spanish but also as a spur to encourage U.S. backing for expeditions lest Britain gain influence. As diplomatic relations worsened between Britain and the United States over Jefferson's second term, territorial officials devoted increased attention to Gulf Coast defenses. By 1811 U.S. authorities tilted toward a warlike posture, as Claiborne noted when rumors persisted of British troops in the region.[209]

The British threat during the War of 1812, in combination with the large number of internal security threats, necessitated a series of defensive measures. Indeed, Claiborne recognized the shortcomings of the militia during the 1811 German Coast slave revolt and promised that if needed he would dispatch a force to protect the German Coast.[210] Despite the external threat that Britain represented, U.S. officials did not worry over internal white support; rather, they feared a British external threat might encourage a slave revolt. The British during the War of 1812 believed Francophone locals would not fight on behalf of the Americans. They likewise believed the Baratarians might aid them as well.[211] Thus, misappraisals of local loyalties were not unique to the Americans. Surprisingly, the population of West Florida proved particularly loyal to the United States during the War of 1812, providing a large number of volunteers, even though many had immigrated to the area as British subjects. West Florida's support for the war impressed Claiborne in contrast to the tepid response from many other parishes, and he praised the Baton Rouge militia in particular.[212] In part the enthusiasm for the war in West Florida can be explained by the anti-Creek nature of the war in Louisiana. Some Choctaw bands joined with the Red Stick Creeks, and as a result West Florida became exposed to Indian attacks.[213] Thus, ethnicity may have had less to do with the volunteer rates than exposure to native attacks.

Despite Louisiana's entry to the union as a state in 1812, U.S. authorities continued to doubt the commitment of many Louisianans to the union. During the War of 1812 many inhabitants resisted military service through claims of French birth, and the local French consul happily obliged. Claiborne wrote to Andrew Jackson in 1814 that he trusted the majority of his populace, Creole and native American, "But there are *others* much devoted to the Interest of Spain, and whose partiality for the English, is not less observable than their dislike to the American Government."[214] Jackson in turn warned Claiborne of foreign partisans in New Orleans, to tighten security, and to exercise care in making officer appointments.[215] Still, Claiborne's appraisals gave Andrew Jackson some confidence in local sentiment.[216] Upon his arrival Jackson assessed Louisiana loyalty in person. Jackson's aide de camp Thomas Butler warned the citizens of New Orleans: "The General with still greater astonishment, has heard that British emissaries have been permitted to propagate seditious reports amongst you, that the threatened invasion is with a view of restoring the country to Spain from a supposition that some of you would be willing to return to your ancient government—believe not such incredible tales—your government is at peace with Spain."[217] Jackson in his characteristic style appealed to hates rather than loves. In reading proclamations to the militia after Jackson reviewed them, the Creoles heard: "Descendants of Frenchmen! natives of France! they are English, the hereditary, the eternal enemies of your ancient country, the invaders of that you have adopted, who are your foes. Spaniards! remember the conduct of your allies at St. Sebastians, and recently at Pensacola, and rejoice that you have an opportunity of avenging the brutal injuries reflected by men who dishonor the human race."[218] Louisianans claiming French citizenship, however, frustrated Jackson more than British immigrants.

Even after the Battle of New Orleans, which modern interpretations portray as the unifying of ethnicities and races to defeat British invaders, divisions remained.[219] Jackson's declaration of martial law on December 16, 1814, appeared sensible during the invasion, but after the battle strict military measures appeared unnecessary.[220] Jackson failed to release volunteers, and many French speakers again approached the local French consul to certify them as French citizens and thereby remove federal requirements upon them. The German merchant Vincent Nolte criticized Jackson's behavior and Claiborne's weakness in acceding to it, pointing to the arrest of the French consul Toussard; Louis Louaillier, a state senator but a Frenchman by birth; and Judge Dominick Hall after issuing a writ of habeas corpus for Louaillier. Jackson persisted in keeping Louaillier in prison even after the charges were dismissed, although he later issued pardons.[221] Jackson then sidelined French subjects who he believed retarded the war effort. Adjutant

General Robert Butler issued an order from Jackson ordering all French subjects out of the theater to Baton Rouge or further upriver until the British
left or peace was declared.[222] These French subjects not only shirked military service but encouraged others to do the same. Talk of individual rights
proved all the more galling to Jackson when it came from non-native-born
citizens: "Aliens & strangers became the most violent advocates of constitutional Rights & native Americans were taught the value of their privileges by
those who formally disavowed any title to their enjoyment."[223] Jackson came
away with a far different sense of loyalty within the city than Claiborne, as
did Louisianan Alexandre Declouet, who privately charged members of the
legislature with "treasonable designs."[224]

Others lauded Jackson's approach. Philadelphia merchant Samuel Carswell wrote to Jackson: "I am sorry to find that you have not had it in your
power to drive out of Louisiana all the adherents to the British Government,
as well as those that were in arms against you, for a domestic enemy is much
more injurious to the Country than foreign."[225] Despite Carswell's concerns,
local citizens proved unwilling to embrace the British cause. Jackson felt
ill used by Claiborne after the fact given his political alliance with some of
Jackson's critics. He believed that Louisiana "with Claiborne . . . will always
be filled with faction—he will abandon principle, and attach himself to tories and Traitors, to raise his popularity regardless of truth or his countries
good."[226] Even so, those who dodged service formed a minority, while Louisianans of various stripes rallied at the Battle of New Orleans.

The behavior of the inhabitants of the territory demonstrated a great
deal of loyalty to the new union, but only with the victory did these appraisals emerge. In letters to Jefferson, Claiborne noted their "patriotic disposition."[227] Similarly, Jefferson's friend Elizabeth Trist wrote to him: "Doubts
had always been entertained of their stability and Attachment to our Government, but they have evinced as much patriotism and firmness as any of
the State have or could have done and a great deal more than her jealous
elder sisters have performed, they will now be convinced of the great advantage of that Country to us."[228] Jefferson concurred with these judgments as
he wrote to Henry Dearborn, pointing to the truths illustrated at the Battle
of New Orleans.[229] Even so, these proofs were more the results of the victory
at New Orleans than the immediate cause of that victory.

An implicit connection existed between doubts over internal loyalty and external threats. France could appeal to the internal population but had abandoned its North American mainland ambitions, whereas the British posed an external threat but failed in their appeal to the internal populace. Spain represented the greatest threat to U.S. control of Louisiana in most official estimations between 1803 and 1807. With good reason: Spain had governed the region for almost forty years and retained officers and officials familiar with its people. In addition, the Spanish empire retained holdings on both sides of the Louisiana Purchase in Texas and West Florida. The internal and external threats manifested in late 1806 and early 1807 as Spanish forces crossed the Sabine and Burr began his descent along the Mississippi. Once Creoles failed to rally to either the external or internal encroachments, evaluations of Creole loyalty shifted. The same year of 1807 saw the beginnings of the Peninsular War, which divided Spain and weakened Spanish power in the New World. As the external threat faded, so did fears of internal disloyalty. In addition, Spanish policies toward slaves and Native Americans ran counter to local elite prerogatives. American officials protected elite interests in meeting Spanish threats to the west while carefully posing their own to the Spanish in West Florida. As Spanish power declined, U.S. officials gained confidence in entrusting democracy to a Francophone populace just as military success at the Battle of New Orleans reassured U.S. officials of local loyalty.

2

Natural and Unnatural Frontiers

The appointment of Dr. John Sibley as Indian agent for the Territory of Orleans for the area west of the Mississippi proved a controversial choice. Sibley, selected by Secretary of War Henry Dearborn, had a less than honorable reputation; notoriety could be ascribed to many men in his line.[1] Having served in the Revolutionary War as a surgeon's mate, Sibley practiced as a physician in Massachusetts, where he started a family.[2] Before coming to Louisiana, he deserted his wife and moved to North Carolina and then to South Carolina, where he started a paper. At some point while he was in the South, his wife died and he remarried, but he then abandoned his new family to pursue opportunities in Louisiana, where he became a surgeon at the Natchitoches garrison.[3]

In spite of his personal failings, Sibley's professional record remained impressive. Sibley became an early correspondent and ally of Claiborne, frequently providing him with information on not just Indian affairs but the political disposition of Natchitoches. As a measure of his esteem for the doctor, Claiborne recommended him to the Legislative Council, describing him to Jefferson as "a Man of Science and a true Republican; I have understood that previous to his leaving the United States his Affairs were much embarrassed;—But during his residence at Natchitoches, he is said to have acquired some valuable landed property."[4] Sibley received the appointment from the president after three nominees refused to serve on the council.[5] Many of the most able territorial officials in Louisiana came to such a benighted location because they sought an escape from something else: in Workman's case, the limitations of being an Irishman in Britain; in Sibley's case it was marital difficulties. Rumors of infidelity and bigamy tarnished Sibley's reputation, and Claiborne to protect the doctor requested that the editor of the *Orleans Gazette* not print these scandalous stories.[6] By the time the rumors entered common circulation, Sibley had already secured his appointments. Claiborne defended Sibley's public character, while claiming that he lacked knowledge of his private life.[7] Ultimately, Jefferson chose to keep him in office, pointing particularly to Sibley's useful reports on the Native Americans of the area, and because the allegations "1. That he left his wife but it does not appear whether the separation was through the fault or the will of her or him. 2. That he attempted to marry again—this is a charge of weight, but no proof being adduced, it cannot weigh against the integrity of his character affirmed by others, and his unquestionable good sense and information."[8] Whatever his private weaknesses, Sibley gained support from local tribes for the United States and across the frontier in contested territory, while at the same time overseeing the Indian trade and assuaging tensions between incoming Native Americans and native-born American settlers with the Creole populace. Sibley prospered in Natchitoches. He shipped cotton from the Red River to New Orleans, set up a saltworks, and by 1810 had accumulated thirty slaves.[9] In addition, his role as Indian agent allowed him to sell merchandise to men dispatched into the West. The connection with Claiborne also benefited Sibley's mercantile efforts.[10]

Dearborn instructed Sibley to focus particularly on gaining trust from tribes that in the case of a war with Spain would be useful allies or dangerous enemies.[11] When U.S. army officer Amos Stoddard encountered problems among the Creek, Claiborne counseled him on gaining native support: "Act towards them with impartial justice; to protect all peaceable Indians from violence & wrong, and to exercise towards them every act of Kindness which your means will permit."[12] Sibley regularly issued optimistic reports as to U.S. prospects among the tribes. He noted after meeting a friendly Caddo chief that they would become useful allies on the frontier against other natives and might develop into good citizens with the appropriate guidance.[13] Far from being part of a vanguard sent to displace native tribes, as a federal official along a frontier with Spain Sibley strove to secure good relations with the tribes he dealt with in order to better secure the frontier. As the Spanish threat receded, however, and immigration and development proceeded apace, it became harder to justify the need for individuals committed to the policy administered by Sibley. After statehood in 1812, Louisiana politicians needed to court land-hungry voters rather than federal officials. Consequently, in 1815, after fifteen Louisiana legislators wrote to Madison requesting his replacement, Thomas Gales succeeded Sibley. Sibley later joined James Long's filibustering expedition into Mexico in 1819, where his knowledge and contacts came into use.[14]

U.S. territorial governors throughout the West exercised extensive control over Native American relations. Territorial government regularly touched upon native relations in keeping settlers off public lands, overseeing licenses for trade, commanding the local militia, and in the case of several governors, the military as well. Governors regularly served as superintendents of Indian affairs within their territory until 1834. Even so, Indian agents were not appointed by the governor but by the Department of War, which allowed them a level of independence. Who ultimately oversaw Indian policy in a territory often became a political football, all the more troublesome for territorial governors who needed to appeal to settlers. Indeed, the need to cultivate or provide protection for Native Americans posed political difficulties for territorial governors who faced opposition from white settlers who preferred a more bellicose policy of ethnic cleansing.[15] In some ways, the system proved so convoluted that at times it failed to function; those of a more cynical bent might view that as the point.[16] Local officials, as the individuals with power over Indian affairs on the scene, utilized their influence but often in a contradictory manner.

The need for individuals experienced in native relations was universal for all nations operating on American frontiers. After changes in sovereignty new powers often made use of the previous nation's agents. For instance, when the English took possession of New York in 1664, they turned to Dutch traders.[17] Frontiers as a matter of course allowed for greater freedoms in terms of attachment and identity. Adoption of elements of the material culture of both Native American and French societies allowed individuals to claim other identities, but in the Illinois country to a greater extent than in lower Louisiana, where racial identities proved harder to breach.[18] In the aftermath of the French and Indian War the British attempted to better regulate the trade in the Illinois country through the use of nationally appointed superintendents.[19] Russia in Alaska manipulated native elites, either through force, debts, or with a softer hand when foreign agents were present. Russians had a long experience in co-opting elites for use in their empire, particularly ethnic Germans, and in some ways cooperation with native elites in Alaska was a continuation of this process.[20]

The Spanish, French, American, and Russians in North America all engaged in distributing flags, uniforms, medals, and other symbols to native tribes.[21] Conversion to Christianity and intermarriage often proved far more effective for Europeans in co-opting natives than American commitments to impartiality. European powers demonstrated greater pragmatism in managing the Indian trade, unfettered by notions of natural rights or republicanism, but European paternalism exhibited its own hypocrisies. Stricter regulations at times could backfire by encouraging the trade to flow to competitors. After the French and Indian War the British feared Spanish and French commerce and influence over Indians in the Old Northwest, while the Russians fretted about Anglo-American traders' influence in Alaska.[22] Attempts to bar or control trade with natives regularly proved futile. Even though the Illinois and Miami initially benefited from the arrival of the French in the Illinois and Ohio country, when the French royal government attempted to bar the brandy trade and to control the trade through licenses or congés, the practice was regularly violated. Once the British replaced the French and required their traders to operate at only named posts, French traders captured a larger share of the trade, whereas British governmental restrictions and diplomatic requests to the Spanish to prevent French traders from operating failed to have much of an impact.[23] Likewise, American merchants' entry into the fur trade with the Alaskan Kolosh natives hurt the Russian trade because of superior American goods and prices.[24] Once the United States had possession of Alaska, it acted quickly in 1873 to bar the sale of liquor and breech-loading firearms to natives.[25] Efforts to regulate trade from the metropole were frustrated by disobedience from their own officials, foreign competition, and resistance on the part of both settlers and Native Americans. Gift giving could appear prohibitively expensive if the metropole did not perceive concrete gains, but failures to make gifts in line with Native Americans' expectations were a problem for multiple powers, whether the Spanish in Florida in the sixteenth century or the French in the Ohio country of the eighteenth century.[26]

Contests for loyalty in this frontier milieu were complicated further by the controversial matter of land sales between governments and tribes. By the time of the Louisiana Purchase, the cycle of land sales between tribes and imperial powers was well understood by natives. Problems arose over the ability to sell, with some chiefs claiming the right without possessing support for their actions. The U.S. government, like its British predecessor, took upon itself the sole privilege of negotiating land purchases, requiring the government to come to a treaty agreement with individual tribes.[27] Even so, speculators and squatters continued to exert pressure on Indian lands.

Territorial governors needed to keep white settlers and natives in line with U.S. law. This required an impartiality that both settlers and natives found unlikely.[28] Private sales of land by natives to settlers became a consistent problem for all U.S. territories. The federal government, despite the shortcomings detailed above, often could appear as a better ally for Native Americans than local settlers.[29] The native view, however, saw the U.S. government and military as a long-term ally of white settlement that disrupted the trade relationships established by Europeans.[30] In territories with extensive land grants that predated U.S. control as in Louisiana or California, pressure on native lands became much greater. Mexican Californian elites proved quite capable of cooperating with and integrating newcomers into a new leadership group.[31] This was not the case for Native Americans, as newcomers immigrated onto native lands and not the land grants already secured by Mexican citizens after the cessation of the missions. Incoming immigrants disrupted native communities, with some natives perceiving the settlers as threats, while others cooperated. In California after its seizure by the United States the government did not recognize private native land sales.[32] U.S. law remained in a state of flux when it came to Indian lands in the late eighteenth and early nineteenth century as conceptions of land ownership shifted to a conception of a right to occupancy.[33] While in theory the federal government needed to negotiate an end to occupancy from tribes, in practice states granted land rights to settlers. In terms of exploration and Native American affairs, the Louisiana Purchase enhanced federal power.[34]

Locals in many areas welcomed the entry of the United States as a defense against Native American raids and as an arbiter that might forestall them. Indian raids on ranchos facilitated American governance in California, where the United States proved more effective in preventing them than its Mexican predecessor had.[35] Territorial officials needed to tread the line between securing enough land to keep settlers happy without provoking a costly Indian war.[36] Texas, in contrast, after independence conducted a series of wars of conquest against the Comanche and Kiowa to completely remove native power from the region. The Native American experience in

Texas proved worse than in states that went through a territorial experience, with the federal government more interested in protecting natives than the nation of Texas.[37] California and the Pacific Northwest likewise failed to establish successful reservations before the Civil War.[38] Utah, as in so many ways, remained an exception, which, due to the federal/local divisions, lacked a consistent Indian policy.[39]

Native relations shifted rapidly with Spanish decline and the entry of American traders into the West. This proved particularly true in New Mexico, where prominent newcomers found it relatively easy to gain entrée to the social and economic elite. The white Anglo population in the West remained small as late as 1860, with a large percentage of that population in the military, which played a significant role in Indian relations.[40] Under both the Spanish and Mexican governments, New Mexico had a history of native rebellions from the Pueblo rebellions against the Spanish to the Chimayó Rebellion, which occurred in concert with the Texas Revolution. After New Mexico's conquest by the United States, another rebellion erupted that involved both Nuevamexicanos, generally individuals connected to the clerical and military establishment of New Mexico, and Pueblo Indians, who did not benefit from commercial connections but faced more pressure on their land rights.[41]

The Spanish in Louisiana encountered many of the same difficulties as the United States in their negotiations with natives. By 1763 many of the tribes near New Orleans had been reduced, moved, merged, or annihilated. Apalachees had settled near Rapides on the Red River and had been welcomed by the Spanish as a population that would serve to link Natchitoches with the rest of their territory. Later native groups would merge into the Pascagoula, Biloxi, and Taensa in the same area.[42] From the era of Spanish control to that of the United States the native population within Louisiana continued to decline and, with that, their political and diplomatic relevance.[43] Once Spain gained Louisiana, it encouraged tribes from British America to immigrate. As a result, groups of Choctaw and other bands migrated west. These migrations then caused conflict with the natives already present in the region.[44]

Spanish officials remained cognizant of the need for native allies given their weak position in Louisiana. Governor Manuel Gayoso de Lemos in 1792 wrote about the necessity of keeping these strong relations with the

natives in order to forestall Anglo-American efforts.[45] Baron de Carondelet in his report on the military condition in Louisiana likewise stated the
importance of native allies in case of war with Americans from Kentucky:
"By means of our allies, the Choctaw [Chactas], Chickasaw [Chicachas],
Creek [Criks], and Cherokee [Cheroquies] nations, who fearful of the usur-
pations of the Americans, will be disposed to make the most destructive war
on them whenever incited by presents and arms."[46] Even so, Spain did not
have a clear advantage over the United States in managing native relations.
While touring the western portions of the United States, James Pitot recalled: "I traveled at the same time among Indian tribes who, far from rising
up against the United States, were rather under the country's orders." Pitot
criticized the Spanish Indian trade, noting that it enriched military officers
and those with trading privileges rather than the province.[47] The French
traveler François Marie Perrin du Lac suggested that when it came to treatment of natives that trade should be cut off in the aftermath of a murder or
an attack until justice was done, a measure he believed the French enforced
more effectively than the Spanish, who failed to punish native murderers
in his view.[48]

With the brief turnover to France, Duc Denis Decrès in his instructions
to French officials noted the need for Indian alliances to counter western
Americans. Decrès assumed that France would inherit the native alliances
that Spain had garnered. Even so, Decrès insisted that France's support for
natives must contain a threshold so as not to antagonize the United States.[49]
Once in control of Louisiana, Laussat advocated appealing to the Creek and
Choctaw: "The only savages who, in the present circumstances are worth
the trouble of being won over. I would watch the Anglo-American of the
west in the midst of those savages."[50] The nation exercising sovereignty
needed to support its native allies, albeit not to such an extent that it might
create foreign policy problems. This mirrored the British problem with Native Americans in the Old Northwest. Local officials could not give enough
support to native proxies to trigger a major conflict without permission
from the metropole.

The purchase opened up a vast expanse that, despite Jeffersonian rhetoric on the potential of civilized natives as future citizens, provided areas
for relocation. Claiborne benefited from earlier experience with the same

problems, institutions, and policies, as territorial governor of Mississippi. Although the secretary of war was putatively in charge of Indian affairs, territorial governors, Indian agents, and local officials had a greater impact on policy on the ground.[51] In Louisiana the territorial government followed the general parameters of U.S. native policy as seen in the Old Northwest and Southwest. Trading houses facilitated future land purchases as indebtedness provided leverage for future concessions.[52]

As settlers immigrated, the potential for conflict over Indian lands grew, just as it did in Upper Louisiana.[53] In Louisiana, as on other frontiers, officials attributed Native American violence to outside agents.[54] Native American tribes could work imperial rivalries to their benefit. The need for trade and allies against geopolitical rivals necessitated peace and efforts toward justice. Once those needs no longer existed, U.S. policy would change, but during the early national period the approach utilized focused on stability in order to maintain useful relationships between the imperial power and the tribes.[55] Territorial governors did not view their role as simply one of expulsion or ethnic cleansing.[56]

U.S. policies of removal, however internally popular, contained foreign policy dangers that other nations could exploit. Casa Calvo readily perceived this: "The Indians all have a decided preference for our nation, from which we can derive advantages if we nurse with tenderness their hatred for the *Guachimangal* (American)."[57] Vicente Folch concurred:

> Spain ought secretly to promote the purposes of the United States that are directed to driving the powerful nations of the Creeks, Choctaws, Chickasaws, and Cherokees to the west of the Mississippi; for in that case the latter will bear with them a mortal hatred against the Americans for having compelled them to abandon their native country. In their new dwelling they may be able to be incorporated into one body, and since they are now accustomed to the use of firearms, and experienced in destructive warfare, they may be employed in, not only in checking the extension of the American settlements, but also, if necessary, in destroying every settlement located west of the Mississippi.[58]

Outside powers that did not exercise sovereignty possessed advantages when it came to cultivating native relationships, as they were unencumbered with pleasing local settlers or enforcing a comprehensive legal regime. For the occupying power, compromises were predicated on the need for internal stability in the face of external threats.

An ability to successfully manage native relations demonstrated for the local populace the benefits of their new nation. U.S. Indian policy in Louisiana proved to be bifurcated. On the one hand, officials attempted to reconcile several tribes in a state of decline like the Houma, Chitimacha, Avoyelles, Attakapas, and Opelousas, as they transitioned from independent political groups to postcolonial minorities. Louisiana also could provide a new home for peaceful groups of natives removed from the East such as the Biloxi, Choctaw, and Tunica. At the same time, the United States spread U.S. influence while countering the Spanish among tribes like the Caddo on the Red River and the Wichita, and Comanche further to the west. Territorial officials and U.S. Indian agents pursued these two policies; all the while, they remained conscious of the need to avoid violence lest an Indian war break out, leading to greater expenses and potential international ramifications. Such a conflict also might emerge from the Chickasaw or Choctaw in the Mississippi Territory.

At the time of the cession, policy makers in Washington had limited knowledge of the tribes of Louisiana. The scientist and naturalist William Dunbar estimated that Indians in the territory before the cession in 1803 "are few in number and harmless."[59] Daniel Clark prepared a brief breakdown of tribes in Louisiana just before the cession and noted that tribal emigrants along the St. Francis River near New Madrid occasionally attacked U.S. boats.[60] Clark explained to Madison that U.S. personnel would be essential to securing good relations with the western tribes beyond the Mississippi to counter Spanish ambitions.[61] Portrayals of Spanish influence among the natives mirrored the broader portrayals, focusing on fear of Spain as a security threat and a destabilizing power while at the same time anticipating Spanish weakness if countered by a consistent U.S. presence. Despite declining numbers, Louisiana Indians still journeyed to New Orleans, but local inhabitants no longer desired these journeys as much as in the past. Claiborne wrote to James Pitot, the mayor of New Orleans, complaining about the absence of an Indian interpreter but making sure that the mayor understood that he should inhibit Indian visits.[62] As the Indian trade declined in importance for New Orleans, the measures demanded for good relations increasingly came to be seen as hassles.

American Indian tribes by and large had withdrawn (with varying levels of willingness) from lands along the Mississippi in lower Louisiana. Native populations dwindled over the course of the eighteenth century due to European diseases as well as the effects of warfare.[63] Local officials served as intermediaries with Native Americans like the Houma Indians, who migrated to the Acadian Coast and Ascension Parish before moving further into the swamps of Terrebonne Parish later in the mid-nineteenth century. At the time of the American cession Claiborne described them to William Eustis as largely friendly but reduced to less than eighty individuals.[64] Other tribes like the Avoyelles and the Tunica, given their small numbers, began a process of merging. Along the Gulf Coast, one of the more warlike tribes from the French period, the Chitimacha of St. Mary's Parish, by the period of American control was isolated in the Atchafalaya River basin. Below New Orleans in St. Bernard Parish a Choctaw and Chitimacha presence remained, which concerned U.S. officials since the region controlled New Orleans's access to the sea. In 1805 the secretary of war wanted Sibley to pay particular attention to natives around the Bay of St. Bernard, to establish a trading post, and to meet with chiefs whom he might send to Washington.[65]

Northern and western Louisiana had a far stronger native presence. Ouachita had an Indian population that necessitated a military presence and demanded discretion on the part of local officials to keep order. At the time of the transfer to the United States, Lieutenant Joseph Bowmar wrote to Claiborne of some one hundred Choctaw near the parish.[66] The Choctaw nation resided largely in southwest Mississippi, but during the territorial period, bands like the Jena migrated west, a process that accelerated after the War of 1812. In the northwest around Natchitoches, the largest Louisiana tribe, the Caddo, resided along the Red River.[67] Coushatta migrants resided in southwest Orleans, as did groups of Biloxi.[68] The Caddo usually maintained good relations with the Biloxi and Coushatta, at times intermarrying into the tribes, but the Choctaw and Caddo were traditional enemies.[69] To the south of Natchitoches in Opelousas and Attakapas there resided Attakapas, Opelousas, Chitimachas, and Caddo peoples.[70] Attakapas and Opelousas Indians were greatly reduced by the time of the cession of

Orleans to the United States, and the Opelousas continued to decline over the territorial period.[71] The United States also faced a western frontier along the southern plains increasingly controlled by the Comanche. Indian commissioners who sought a stable frontier endeavored to maintain good diplomatic and market ties with the Comanche, which the Comanche reciprocated in order to bypass the Wichita and their control over the gun trade.[72] The United States attempted to keep tribes of Louisiana within its political and diplomatic orbit while maintaining trade and diplomacy with an expansionist Indian power to the west.

U.S. leaders hoped the Louisiana Purchase might provide a solution to the Indian problem of the eastern United States.[73] In setting up the government of Louisiana Congress authorized the president to make land exchanges with tribes east of the Mississippi to move them to the west, but with the understanding that they not enter negotiations with any foreign powers.[74] Proposals for such a policy came even before the purchase. Consul William Jarvis wrote to Madison from Lisbon in the spring of 1803 proposing, "If they could be persuaded to exchange lands in western Louisiana for those they hold in the U.S., 'the Sums we should save in extinguishing their title would reimburse part what we should be obliged to give to France.'"[75] The purchase did not expand the frontier for only white Americans. American Indians might find new opportunities in the West.[76] Secretary of the Indiana Territory John Gibson wrote to Madison speculating over the potential removal of the Delaware to Louisiana Purchase lands.[77] Likewise John Devereaux DeLacy, a merchant from the Bahamas, staunch opponent of the Spanish, and associate of the English adventurer and self-proclaimed Cherokee chief William Augustus Bowles informed Madison that while being held prisoner by natives under suspicion of being a Spanish agent he encouraged them to form a constitutional form of government and "then go and take possession of the Colony of Louisiana and enter into a close alliance offensive and defensive with the U.S. . . . And at some future Period Joining the Union I strongly recommended." Not all plans assumed an Indian declension; DeLacy conceived of natives as future citizens and pursued Madison's approval for an effort to settle the civilized tribes west of the Mississippi to act as a buffer between Spanish territory and the United States.[78] Some prominent U.S. leaders assumed that such transfers might better secure the West.[79] George King as judge of Opelousas received an appointment for Daniel Sutton to assure the Alabamas that Claiborne would obtain a land grant of up to three thousand acres in the area for their tribe.[80] Despite the grant many Alabamas immigrated further west between the Spanish and the United States. Claiborne wrote to John Sibley in 1806 that local tribes would receive land grants in line with what had been provided for the Alabamas.[81] Immigration into Louisiana of all groups—Native Americans, whites, and slaves—contributed to native decisions to migrate further west, often with Spanish encouragement.[82]

Territorial officials assumed tribal lands would be reduced over time, but in the short term operated under the premise that tribal claims would be respected. As the federal government surveyed the territory, a major concern was not to disturb Native Americans even as the president instructed Claiborne to assure the entry of surveyors onto native lands.[83] U.S. territorial officials strove to bar private land transfers. When commandant Henry Hopkins refused to allow such sales, Claiborne quickly approved.[84] Secretary of the Treasury Albert Gallatin confirmed this policy in subsequent instructions, and the Indian Intercourse Law further restricted private sales and forbade sales to any foreign power.[85] The secretary of war instructed Sibley to assure natives: "Their Great Father has a strong friendship for all his red children, and will always treat them as his children, as long as they shall behave well."[86] Land commissioners generally confirmed title in cases where the Spanish took land from natives, but longer-standing claims always appeared more aboveboard, as Judge Joshua Lewis pointed out: "Claims founded upon purchases made of the Indians without the concurrence of the Spanish Government, we reject as being unauthorized, except where the land has been settled we confirm them only as settlement rights."[87] Sales from Indians thus raised red flags, which Gallatin noted in his letters to land commissioner Gideon Fitz.[88] Pressure to engage in land seizures did not come primarily from the capital, except insofar as grants were desired for eastern tribes.

Federal officials did not pose the greatest threat to native land rights. Disputes with Louisianans, both newcomers and already established inhabitants, proved the greatest impediment to smooth U.S.-native relations. Locals pressed for greater restrictions on natives; for instance, U.S. agent to the Choctaw Silas Dinsmore requested that Lieutenant Bowmar stop the Indians from hunting in Ouachita, but Claiborne countermanded those instructions based on the disturbances it caused. Claiborne believed hunting should continue unimpeded in order to assure good relations with the Choctaw.[89] In turn, Claiborne requested further instructions from the president, since he did not exercise the powers of the superintendent of Indian affairs.[90] Sibley wrote to federal officials in order to secure land for Louisiana's Indians without recognized claims, as he felt this was the best way to avoid problems between the white inhabitants and the tribes: "In their present Situation they are a great nuisance to the white Inhabitants, & ungovernable—and Instead of improving in the Arts of Civilization are growing Worse."[91] American Indians' concerns that the United States might not recognize their tribal land rights resulted from the influx of Anglo-American immigrants. In 1807 a Choctaw, Captain Sam, approached Sibley with character testimonials from prominent citizens of Rapides requesting land to the west for fourteen adults in order to "not have them in the way of white people." Other natives approached Sibley with complaints that a Mr. Gillard claimed lands from sales, and Sibley promised to pass on their objections to the land commissioners.[92] Sibley's comments on the need for clear titles for Native American lands contributed to a general sense that he was too pro–Native American in the minds of some observers.[93]

Natchitoches served as a base for intelligence, extending U.S. influence into the West and managing relations with the western tribes. The United States Indian Factory as well as private Anglo-American and Creole traders exchanged blankets, firearms, and luxury items for bear and deerskins.[94] The United States wished to counter Spanish influence, but this is not to say that officials encouraged violent incidents. These parameters proved familiar to many U.S. officials, including Claiborne from his service as the governor of Mississippi when it bordered Spanish Louisiana.[95] Nor were U.S. officials' worries over foreign influence limited to Spain. Indian agent Colonel John McKee and Claiborne became concerned over Indian debts owed to a British trading house that might enable that trading house to accumulate lands along the Alabama or Tombigbee River.[96]

Given the distance from New Orleans, territorial officials placed a large degree of trust in officials in Natchitoches. Naturalist William Darby noted that it took thirty to forty days to get from New Orleans to Natchitoches.[97] After the U.S. cession Captain Edward Dumaresque Turner served as the first commandant for Natchitoches.[98] Turner held this post even as he remained an officer in the army. Turner distributed tobacco, powder, and lead to the local tribes, as well as U.S. flags, as a Caddo chief informed him: "It was customary to have the Flag of the Nation who claimed the Country in which they lived, and it was necessary the Spanish one should be superceded."[99] Sibley also frequently gave regimental coats, and in some cases native chiefs turned in Spanish flags, confirming for U.S. officials the success of their efforts. Even so, there was no way of telling whether the U.S. flags were regularly flown or what the natives told the Spanish in order to solicit gifts from them. Still, U.S. officials took heart from statements like that of the Hietan chief who laid a Spanish flag at Sibley's feet and requested an American one, insisting, "It was the same to them whether Spain was pleased or displeased and if I would give him one it should wave through all the Hietan Nation, and they would all die in defence of it before they would part with it."[100] It is no wonder Turner conveyed a sense of optimism in his bid to counter Spanish influence in the West: "The Cado's [sic] seem to have a Sovereign contempt for the Spaniards—and I am told it is the case with the Indians generally—If so, a little policy will secure their friendship."[101] On appointing Turner as commandant Claiborne highlighted the importance of gaining the loyalty of frontier settlements.[102] Sibley and U.S. officials remained wary of Spanish influence among the tribes. Indeed, Sibley had an agent among the natives desert to the Spanish.[103]

U.S. officials remained convinced that the Spanish might incite the Indians to rebel. In 1804 Claiborne warned Turner: "An Indian War would be peculiarly embarrassing to our Frontier Settlers, and would be attended with injury and expense. . . . How far the Spanish may encourage to hostilities, time will evince."[104] Claiborne gave Turner permission to distribute presents, and to prevent any abuse of the natives.[105] He warned Turner and other officials to be wary of the Spanish: "My impression is that Secretly they will offer the United States all the injury in their Power;—it may be Serviceable therefore to watch their movements, and penetrate into the Intrigues; I accordingly approve of your Sending a confidential person to the proposed conference on the Sabine."[106] Sibley reported back a positive result from these meetings with the natives, which Claiborne passed on to Secretary of War Dearborn.[107]

The Spanish succeeded in encouraging some emigration to provide a buffer to the United States, but U.S. policies proved just as important as Spanish entreaties, as when the American cession led to the removals of natives from around Rapides.[108] When a Coushatta native, Piamingo, encouraged natives near the Red River to move to the Sabine given recent flooding, Sibley believed this was part of broader machinations by the Spanish out of San Antonio to move multiple tribes into their area of control.[109] The United States did not seek the immediate removal of tribes from U.S. territory; to the contrary the United States wanted tribes in the West as clients.

Sibley in his rhetoric focused on commonalities between the United States and Native Americans that distinguished the two from the Spanish. In 1807 at a grand council that included delegations from the Hietans, Caddos, Tawakenoes, Nandacos, Nabedaches, Keychies, Inies, and Aiche, Sibley argued: "It is now so long since our Ancestors came from beyond the great Water that we have no remembrance of it, we ourselves are Natives of the same land that you are, in other words white Indians, we therefore should feel & live together like brothers & good neighbours."[110] Sibley here staked a claim for U.S. citizens as white Indians and Indians as native Americans. Far from being a racial exclusionist, Sibley rhetorically built cross-cultural bridges, though with the purpose of countering Spain.

Through gift giving and trade Sibley secured influence among the tribes near Natchitoches as well as those who regularly visited. Still, influence did not assure American interests prevailed. When a Choctaw chief, Chapanchaba, died, Sibley wished for Tuscatoga to be his replacement, but the tribe selected a closer family relation of the deceased, Tombolin. Sibley acceded to the choice: "Tuscatoga was my choice, who is not apt to get intoxicated & is a peaceable honest man; but I being unwilling to oppose them consented to their proposal, on conditions that Tuscatoga would act as second to him, which was agreed to." The appointment demonstrates U.S. influence among the Choctaw but also its limits; Americans could not select leaders but could offer guidance. Sibley recognized the new leadership in a ceremony, and the Choctaw agreed to send a delegation to the Caddo to reach an accord over a recent murder. The Choctaw leadership selection took a turn for the worse when the new leader Tombolin got drunk and threatened Sibley, whereupon Tombolin's uncles "told him in my presence if he ever insulted me again they would kill him, we however, concluded to depose him & took his Hat & Plum & Coat from him I gave him his Coat again by the request of Tuscatoga but kept his sword, which I afterwards gave to Tuscatoga who is now regarded as the first Chief on this side of the Mississippi."[111] Western tribes could retain political independence, and the presence of the Spanish allowed them to play the two imperial powers off one another. Nevertheless, there was no escape from the growth of U.S. influence among many tribes.

Despite U.S. influence, areas along the contested border remained dangerous. Just after the cession in 1804 natives killed three Americans around the Sabine.[112] Claiborne gave reports of Spanish intrigues among the tribes enough credence to complain to Casa Calvo, who dismissed the reports as rumors but promised to inquire.[113] Upon leaving his post as commandant, Turner reported that the Spanish attempted to poison relations between the tribes and the United States.[114] As Casa Calvo moved about the territory the following year, many assumed that he carried funds to purchase the loyalty of Native Americans.[115] Given these rumors, Claiborne advised Sibley to observe his movements.[116] Sheriff George T. Ross noted that when the marquis came to Natchitoches, the Native Americans arrived in large numbers despite it being the hunting season: "If he has so far forgot the feelings of humanity as to Tamper with Savages, with whom our Government is exerting every nerve to Humanize, that he deserves the execration of every feeling breast!"[117] Ross viewed the U.S. mission among the Indians as one of civilization and assimilation, whereas Spanish influence furthered barbarism. Claiborne likewise worried that to the east Governor Folch in Florida and Spanish officials at Mobile were "intriguing" with the Indians.[118] Claiborne found comfort in the fact that tribes generally chose to remain neutral.[119] As with his appraisals of Creole loyalty, Claiborne spun a neutral position as an American success.

Louisianans also feared Native Americans might ally themselves with free people of color or a slave rebellion. In 1806 Stephen, a free Negro, reported on hostile intentions of other free people of color and their connection to Native Americans, along with Spanish aid, centering again on Casa Calvo: "These people expect the Marquis to arrive shortly with three or four thousand troops, and that he is to bring one or two nations of Indians with him, or that they are to follow him."[120] Stephen's story likely had little basis in reality, but it touched upon all the perceived external and internal threats bound to gain the interest of territorial officials. When an actual crisis did occur with Spanish and American armies in close proximity along the Sabine, Native Americans did not take an active part despite early reports to the contrary.[121] Claiborne pointed to Sibley's efforts as a key reason for this.[122]

Given the amorphous border between U.S. Louisiana and Spanish Texas, both nations vied for native support, providing opportunities for groups like the Caddo who managed to maintain their independence, culture, and religion while stemming the population decline that had plagued the tribe over the course of the eighteenth century. Through their relationship and trade with the imperial competitors, the Caddo courted other tribes as allies and customers, whom they utilized in their competition with the Osage. Some of these newcomers, like the Choctaw, threatened Caddo preeminence, which prompted the United States to attempt to forge a peace between the two.[123] Caddo leadership believed the Americans might serve as a useful ally against the Osage and the Choctaw as well as a balance to the Spanish, whereas the Americans hoped the Caddo and their chief, Dehahuit, would influence other tribes while securing the border against the Spanish.[124] Sibley also passed on depositions from locals in Natchitoches that claimed to point to earlier French settlements among the Caddo to bolster American claims to the region.[125]

In addressing the Caddo, Claiborne stressed French-American continuity in opposition to the Spanish: "Brother! You know we got the country from the French, and that the Americans now claim all the land which the French formerly possessed. You are an older man, brother, than I am, and must know something of that matter." The Caddo chief in turn reciprocated in his wording: "My ancestors from Chief to Chief were always well pleased with the French. . . . If your nation has purchased what the French formerly possessed, you have purchased the country that we occupy, and we regard you in the same light as we did them."[126] That Claiborne connected U.S. governance to the French past with Native Americans was notable not just because of U.S. territorial claims but under the assumption that the French enjoyed better relations with the natives.

Federal law regulated the Indian trade in Louisiana as a territory, and federal funds went into maintaining relationships with the tribes.[127] U.S. officials were optimistic on their arrival in the territory about their ability to win friends. Governor Claiborne wrote in 1804 of the Caddo being pleased with the prospect of a trading house at Natchitoches to protect them from the sharp dealing of private traders.[128] U.S. goods remained in high demand and were frequently of superior quality to those of the Spanish. Though Republicans stressed reducing expenses, presents remained a necessity for maintaining beneficial relationships with Native Americans.[129] Under the Spanish, Baron de Bastrop, born in Dutch Guiana, claimed a monopoly for trade with the Native Americans along the Ouachita and wished to retain this privilege.[130] The territorial government refused to support him, and Jefferson made clear that Congress would not allow the existence of a monopoly in the Indian trade.[131] The removal of Spanish favorites from the Indian trade opened places for others, and Claiborne strove to limit licenses to Americans whom he considered competent men of good character. In theory, these licenses would be based on merit, rather than financial ties. Claiborne noted that he "granted my licenses Gratis (which was not formerly the case) to several respectable Citizens. Were all persons permitted indiscriminately to trade with the Indians, much Injustice would be done them, and the peace on the frontiers rendered very insecure."[132] Even when Indian agents conscientiously regulated the trade, however, unauthorized traders persisted. Claiborne instructed district commandants to forbid alcohol sales to Indians without permission.[133] In the northeast Captain Joseph Bowmar attempted to prevent unlicensed traders from traveling into Indian lands along the Ouachita River. Though Claiborne remained unsure of his own authority in this arena, he endorsed a policy of requiring traders to post bonds.[134]

This is not to say that political ties did not matter, but Claiborne wished the trade to no longer be simply an exchange of licenses for money. Political ties and military service helped to secure licenses. Allies of Claiborne like Benjamin Morgan and Jacob Bright received licenses.[135] Colonel Bartholomew Shaumberg obtained permission to operate trading houses at both Natchitoches and Ouachita.[136] Major Richard King also received a license to trade at Ouachita.[137] Administration figures found places for their clients within the territory. Jefferson's friend Philip Reibelt, appointed the U.S. factor at Natchitoches, went on to a more substantial post as a judge.[138] Even so, these Americans needed to operate within parameters that would influence and not alienate the tribes. In Reibelt's case, Claiborne reported: "He is under an impression that his Agency is to extend to the introduction of civilization among the Indians."[139] The president cautioned him that the Native Americans for whom he would be a factor "are entirely human-ized."[140] In order to interact peacefully with natives to the west and advance American power into the contested border zone, the U.S. government relied on a variety of individuals who knew or came to know the region far better than officials to the east.[141] The absence of control over these individuals and the presence of other imperial powers allowed natives to exercise con-siderable independence.[142]

Americans mounted a series of expeditions into the contested border region between Spain and the United States, some official, others less so. Even before the purchase, Spaniards worried about American traders and explorers in the Southwest. Philip Nolan, an Irish-American mustanger, entered Spanish Texas numerous times with passports in order to trade and acquire stock. In addition to his commercial activities he explored and mapped the territory, passing on information to Wilkinson. Despite earlier passports, Spanish officials became suspicious of his activities. In 1800 he set out on a fifth expedition with approximately two dozen men to acquire cattle, but the Spanish dispatched a force from Nacogdoches on March 21, 1801, which resulted in Nolan's death and the imprisonment of his men.[143] After the purchase the Jefferson administration authorized several explor-atory expeditions out of St. Louis into the Spanish West, the most famous being Zebulon Pike's 1806 journey that led to his arrest.

Sibley dispatched several expeditions to trade with the tribes of the Southwest. In 1806, he authorized John S. Lewis and William C. Alexan-der to trade with the southern tribes and issue invitations to a conference in 1807 at Natchitoches.[144] The following year Sibley dispatched Anthony Glass to trade with the Wichita and Comanche.[145] The expeditions extended beyond trade. Judge John C. Carr of Natchitoches informed Claiborne that Glass, with upwards of thirty men and maybe over a hundred, moved into the disputed area, ostensibly searching for a silver mine. Carr feared Glass had designs on Spanish territory and worried that Sibley's issuance of a U.S. flag lent an illegal expedition official authorization. Sibley had sanctioned the expedition.[146] Claiborne reported the incident to the president, since he felt Sibley had exceeded his authority and had a financial interest in the expedition.[147] Sibley in turn complained to Claiborne, taking offense at the governor's interference.[148]

The contested nature of the territory revealed itself at multiple points in Glass's dealings with natives. For instance, when Glass negotiated with a native unhappy with the price he offered for a horse, the native threatened to let the Spanish know of their presence: "A Woman replied you may go and inform them but if they come here to interrupt our trading with the American I myself will kill their Captain the other then said if that is your talk I don't go."[149] Beyond just negotiating tactics, Glass found some support for the United States among tribes. When visiting a band of Hietans, it appeared that the conference in 1807 paid dividends: "Some of those who are now with us were of the Party who visited Nackitosh last year and are highly pleased with the treatment they received from Doctor Sibley, the Indian Agent and say they intend to repeat their visit. They are very desirous of trading with us but say Nackitosh is too far off."[150] Discounting the praise for Sibley, which Glass might include to flatter his patron, Native Americans desired access to U.S. goods. When Glass heard rumors from the natives of a battle between Spaniards and Americans around Nacogdoches, he detected only indifference.[151] Even if not particularly sympathetic to the United States, Native Americans understood the value of an American presence in their dealings with the Spanish. Glass noted that "the Chief of the Lower Hietans who visited Nackitosh last fall has this day Joined Us and says that the Spaniards have treated him civil since he made that visit he is a great friend of the Americans." When threatened by natives who claimed to be sent by the Spanish from San Antonio to cut off Glass's head, a native defended him: "I farther tell you that this American is my friend and if you offer the least harm to him I will soon cut your head off." Even so, Glass cautioned the natives in the event of Spanish-American conflict to stay out of it.[152] Americans sought influence, but did not strive to attach natives to the American orbit overtly; often they publicly sought native neutrality. This was also the language most likely to elicit greater friendship rather than self-serving arguments for alliance. Glass's expedition then inspired subsequent traders. These trading expeditions to the west declined after 1810 with the onset of the Mexican Revolution under Father Hidalgo.

During Hidalgo's revolt his envoy to the United States, José Bernardo Maximiliano Gutiérrez de Lara, journeyed first to Natchitoches before continuing to Tennessee and then Washington. While officially the United States failed to support Hidalgo, the border remained porous, and volunteers and supplies often originated in Natchitoches. William Shaler, a former State Department consul in Havana, accompanied Gutiérrez to Natchitoches, and when Gutiérrez mounted his own expedition to Texas, Shaler contributed to the leadership of the movement, as did former U.S. Army officer Augustus William Magee. Sibley used his influence among the tribes to encourage Indian volunteers for the Gutiérrez expedition. Claiborne instructed Judge Carr to enforce the neutrality laws, just one day before the expedition left, which gave the United States plausible deniability.[153] Still, Claiborne wrote to the local militia commander Colonel Shaumberg to stop filibusters.[154]

The border zone between the United States and New Spain served as a refuge for criminal groups whose operations extended into the western portions of Louisiana. Natchitoches did a profitable trade with New Orleans and the Spanish by selling livestock and tobacco and with the Indians, exchanging trade goods.[155] U.S. traders generally exchanged manufactured goods (guns, ammunition, clothes, utensils, beads, and blankets) in return for deerskins, buffalo robes, horses, and bear oil.[156] The *Louisiana Courier* published reports from Natchitoches that bandits had begun to gather between the Arroyo-Hondo and the Sabine and to attack those on the road between Natchitoches and Nacogdoches and noted that the U.S. government had begun to respond.[157] Brigands who operated within the area did not discriminate; they happily attacked Americans, Spaniards, and natives. In 1812, according to the *Louisiana Gazette,* so many incidents occurred that "all commerce between this town and Nacogdoches has nearly stopped."[158] The same report noted that deserters from the U.S. military might join the brigands. Claiborne explained to Secretary of the Navy Paul Hamilton that "I shall take such measures as are in my power to disperse this Banditti;—A good Intelligence with our Spanish Neighbors is at all times desirable—But it is particularly so at this *eventful crisis.*"[159] Sibley also pointed out the dangers of bandit groups, in particular one led by James Elliot, an Anglo-American, who had earlier accused Louis Fontenot, a justice of the peace, legislator, and militia officer of Opelousas, of selling gunpowder to the Spanish.[160]

Consequently, Sibley dispatched a force to apprehend Elliot. Circumstances propelled official action: "Indians came in & told me they would go out & kill Elliot if I would not do something about it," whereupon Sibley seized Elliot and his compatriots, but they managed to escape: "Some government ought to exercise jurisdiction on this side the Sabine, we either ought to suffer the Spaniards to do it or do it ourselves."[161] Sibley did not state who these accomplices were, though they may have been members of the Anglo community, since Elliot earlier accused Creoles of being Spanish agents.

Areas where U.S. authority did not extend became centers for those dissatisfied with U.S. governance. Wilkinson felt that Spaniards abided by the agreement to stay on their side of the border far better than the Americans, though as a Spanish pensioner his analysis had a bias.[162] Sibley attempted to keep the peace on his side of the border, but he could not manage to hold on to Elliot and his group, and the proximity to the borderlands limited his actions. Given the dangers posed by bandits and filibusters, Claiborne urged the establishment of military posts after authorities uncovered a planned attack on Spanish Nacogdoches.[163] Claiborne worried over the threats to amicable relations with other powers but also the potential for dangers from nonstate actors to the United States.[164] As a result the territorial government requested passports in border regions from suspicious individuals and required local loyalty oaths. At times, Spanish vigilance required American intervention. When the Spanish arrested the officers and crew of the *Celestine* at Laguna over suspicions that they had hostile intentions, Claiborne worked to secure the release of U.S. citizens.[165] In a letter to Robert Smith Claiborne noted the large number of residents interested in bringing revolution to Mexico.[166] Controlling native American citizens proved as difficult as securing Creole loyalty.

Bandit attacks continued throughout the territorial period between the Hondo and the Sabine, with another incident in 1811, less than a year before Louisiana's statehood.[167] The presence of bandits posed such a menace that local judges requested military aid, and Natchitoches issued a memorial that the militia proved ineffective.[168] At other times Anglo-American bandits killed Spaniards, further complicating the border relationship.[169] In another incident after a gang of bandits robbed Mr. Lyon of Attakapas, they fled to Galveztown only to be pursued and eventually handed over by John Lafitte to Captain Madison of the U.S. schooner *Lynx*.[170] To actually arrest such individuals, however, required the cooperation of local Spanish authorities. Banditry reinforced for peoples of all ethnicities on the border the importance of U.S. protection. The growing Comanche presence likewise demonstrated the limits of both Spanish and American control, with incursions into New Spain endangering the cross-border cattle trade.[171]

Minor incidents held the potential to cascade into major conflicts, requiring territorial officials to take note of criminal cases that involved violence between whites and natives. Consequently, justice and the fair application of law often took a backseat to maintaining good relations. The general pattern for U.S. officials was to seek or give compensation for assaults, murder, or other misbehavior sometimes in concert with a judicial process and other times forgoing it. This pattern was not new for Claiborne, who used the same procedures as governor of Mississippi in dealing with the Choctaw.[172] Jefferson emphasized the need for farming and the Americanization of natives, and Claiborne remained hopeful for the prospects of the Choctaw to pursue such a course.[173] The priority in Indian relations for territorial officials, however, focused on the short term. When a Choctaw committed a murder in Mississippi, Claiborne made clear the role that local inhabitants in Natchez and the liquor trade played in the violence.[174] In Louisiana the tribes changed but the pattern remained the same.

The road from Opelousas to the west became dangerous for those who traveled it. In 1807 when Samuel Watson killed a Coushatta, Tom, the tribe protested to Sibley.[175] Not receiving a timely response, the Coushatta committed a murder in turn, "it being suggested to the Governor that this murder would not have happened if Watson had been apprehended & tried."[176] As Sibley wrote to Claiborne, "The Conchetta who Murdered the Young Man ONeal on the Road Leading from Opelousas to Nacogdoches has fled from the village on the Sabine where he lived to the Accokesaws. I have sent to the Chief of that village advising him to give him up. My Messenger has not returned. I do not expect he will be given up."[177] Claiborne recommended a conference at Natchitoches to pacify the natives. In the long term he hoped to codify arrangements to prevent misunderstandings through treaties that laid out clear procedures: "The Conchattas consider themselves a Separate Nation; they are not bound by Treaty to surrender a murderer."[178] The attitude toward these tribes differed from those east of the Mississippi, given the Spanish presence to the west. To prevent a conflict the governor recommended the distribution of presents, although the Choctaw offered their services to punish the Coushatta.[179] The federal government needed to act, however, as local settlers let it be known that they might attack the Coushatta, which could ignite a larger Indian war.[180] Yet Sibley doubted his ability to convince the Coushatta to turn over the murderer. If the federal government came down upon the tribes in too rough a manner, it might alienate them. The individual whom Sibley dispatched to investigate the death reported that the Coushatta planned to remove to Spanish territory and had sent emissaries to other tribes, the Appalachees and Pascagoulas, to join them in a war against the United States. Later in the year Sibley confirmed that the Appalachees received emissaries urging removal and advocating war.[181] The general federal solution was to spend to cover the deaths. Like all good compromises, it left everyone unhappy, but only mildly so. To be sure, the close relatives of the dead might resent the lack of justice, but everyone else benefited from the status quo.

The territorial government responded in a similar way, when the Alabamas killed two Americans navigating Louisiana waters. Courts convicted four Alabamas who took part in the murder. Claiborne's address to the Alabamas forthrightly defended the conviction: "The American custom is not to take head for head; but to punish all, whether one or more, who in cool blood, shall take the life of man." Rhetoric matters, and Claiborne no doubt believed in these principles in the abstract; in this case Claiborne's actions demonstrated quite a different approach. He pardoned the youngest offender, Shonepke, and the assailant who had the least to do with the crime, Shinpoke. He followed native practice in taking two heads for the two Americans lost. He then asserted: "Shinpoke and Shonepke are indebted for their pardon to the citizens of Opelousas, many of whom, as well those who are called French, as of those who are called Americans interceded in their favor."[182] The discussion of the French and American solidarity was politic, sending signals both to American Indians and the Louisiana populace that there were no internal divisions. Claiborne explained his reasoning to Henry Dearborn:

> The pardoning of the others, would be received by the Indians generally (in this vicinity) as evidence of the disposition of this Government, to be merciful and just towards them. There was another reason, which influenced my conduct; An Indian (belonging to a party of Chactaws who, have for some years past, been settled in the county of Opelousas) was some time ago, killed by an American of the name of Thomas, and

every effort to bring the offender to Justice having hereto failed of success, I was apprehensive, lest the execution of the four Alabama's might
awaken the vengeance of the Chactaws; The exercise of Mercy therefore
suggested itself, as a probable means of preventing the effusion of innocent Blood.[183]

If Claiborne exercised clemency, he anticipated others would as well. The
pardon achieved the desired result, with Claiborne reporting more amicable relations to Dearborn.[184] The United States could afford to be generous,
particularly when it advanced diplomatic efforts. Still, this did not sit well
with many locals, who believed in the system Claiborne so eloquently defended in generalities before he demolished it in the particulars.

Claiborne acted to reassure other tribes; he issued an address to the Attakapas making clear that whatever the behavior of the Alabamas, their
tribe had nothing to fear.[185] The difficulties with the Choctaw tribe represented a greater diplomatic threat. The Louisiana government could not be
seen to favor lesser tribes while failing to deliver justice to more important
ones. Claiborne reported the dissatisfaction of the Choctaw over the murder and that Sibley "apprehends the shedding of innocent Blood."[186] According to Sibley the Choctaw asserted that the American murderer, William
Thomas, paid witnesses not to testify and that Judge Collins failed to pursue
the case.[187] Claiborne issued an apology to the natives around Opelousas for
the murder: "Brothers! You know well the Inhabitants of Opelousas, & you
have long lived good neighbours with them; they have never injured you,
and are very sorry, for what has happened to one of your warriors."[188] The
chief of the Choctaw, Tom Boling, demanded that Thomas be brought to
justice for the murder.[189] Thomas ultimately delivered himself up to Judge
Collins, while Lieutenant Henry Hopkins made every effort to stop any
reprisals by offering money to the relatives of the murdered man.[190] The
trial for Thomas did occur, but there was not enough evidence to secure a
conviction.[191]

Two years later the Choctaw still demanded justice. Claiborne sent a
message to the Choctaw promising to deliver up Thomas when new testimony emerged, which resulted in Judge King ordering Thomas to be arrested again. Thomas by then had prudently left the area, and in order to
retain good relations, the governor ordered the distribution of blankets and

other goods to the deceased man's wife and children.[192] Claiborne addressed the Choctaw: "Mourn no longer for the death of your warrior, women may be permitted to shed tears for the dead; but men should only remember them. . . . I have requested one of my head men, Judge George King of Opelousas to give them some blankets and other goods to the value of sixty dollars:—but brothers do not mistake me;—this is not intended as pay for the blood—on the contrary, every effort will be made to have Thomas arrested, tried and punished according to the laws of this territory."[193] When justice proved less than sufficient, the government used money to ease the hurt, all the while denying doing so. Interest in impartial application of the law could be trumped by the need to avoid further violence. Local officials faced multiple pressures, from both white and native local inhabitants who desired justice for their own communities, but who appeared uninterested in securing it for others.

In contrast, officials avidly attempted to win the confidence of locals by pursuing justice with less important tribes. The commandant at Lafourche, Thomas Villanueva, oversaw a parish with frequent tensions between locals and Native Americans. Locals petitioned, complaining of too frequent inebriated native visits. Claiborne wrote to Villanueva to resolve the issues by setting a meeting with the governor where he would distribute gifts.[194] This proved to be a frequent tactic to discourage natives from coming into American communities. Problems persisted in Lafourche; in 1811 a local church was robbed, and the Choctaw suspects escaped.[195] Claiborne wrote to Father St. Pierre Manshac that the Choctaw agent would act to reduce the visits and that "I hope the Militia will soon be in a Situation, to enable them at least to prevent our Settlement from being plundered by Vagrant Indians."[196] U.S. officials found themselves in the impossible position of trying to keep the peace but also carrying out justice in a manner that increased regard from all sides.

It was not only American Indians who might engage in reprisals that required swift action by the United States. When a Native American attacked a Mr. Celestin in the Parish of St. Bernard, it resulted in the death of the native. Claiborne instructed Major Pierre Lacoste to get five comrades of the deceased to confer with the governor at New Orleans to stop the incident from snowballing into something greater.[197] The twin goals of keeping the peace locally while preventing Spanish influence were ever present. Claiborne's instructions to Judge Collins at Attakapas included an address to the Choctaw at Bayou Chico's village that if a warrior wounded by a white man died, then the white man would be punished, but he also quickly transitioned to the competition with Spain along the Sabine, requesting native neutrality.[198]

In the West Florida parishes, Indian threats united white settlers behind U.S. rule. The Spanish attempted to create a series of buffers between Spanish territory and the United States, and Choctaw territory could serve as one of those buffers between Louisiana and Spanish Florida.[199] In 1811 Claiborne responded to requests for arms and ammunition from the local militia and asked General Wade Hampton to place a military post near St. Helena due to local unease with Choctaw visits.[200] Claiborne's language illustrated U.S. officials' suspicions of the tribe. Even so, these disagreements stemmed less from the tribe than individual Choctaws quarreling with local citizens.

With the War of 1812 native and settler quarrels took on an added dimension as the British hoped to take advantage of these tensions. The Creek in particular could serve as a keen British ally given not just white settlement upon their lands but also the policy of assimilation pushed by Benjamin Hawkins.[201] The British during the War of 1812 believed they would garner support from the southern natives beyond just the Creek. An anonymous letter from Havana noted the native assets of the British under Colonel Edward Nicolls: "Promising all the tribes who will join him to reinstate them in all their lands taken from them by the United States, and to guarantee the same to them forever."[202] While Nicolls's efforts may have gained the British Indian adherents, they probably had quite the opposite effect on white settlers. Nicolls understood this as he proclaimed to Louisianans:

> The Indians have pledged themselves, in the most solemn manner, not to injure, in the slightest degree, the persons or properties of any but enemies; to their Spanish or English fathers, a flag over any door, whether Spanish, French, or British, will be a certain protection, nor dare any Indian put his foot on the threshold thereof, under penalty of death from his own countrymen; not even an enemy will an Indian put to death, except resisting in arms, and as for injuring helpless women and children, the red men, by their good conduct and treatment to them, will (if it be possible) make the Americans blush for their more inhuman conduct.[203]

Despite Nicolls's proclamation, the Americans made wide use of attacks by Native Americans and slaves freed by the British after the British offensive at Fort Bowyer.[204] Pierre-Joseph Favrot in Baton Rouge wrote to his son, Philogène Favrot, with the army in Nashville over the British promise that natives would not attack those with a British or Spanish flag: "Perhaps it is intended to calm people who are gullible or faint-hearted."[205] Nathaniel Herbert Claiborne served in Virginia's government during the war and unsurprisingly had high praise for his brother but also noted of Nicolls's behavior at Pensacola: "With the exception of a few negroes and Indians, no one was seduced by his proclamation."[206] The British use of natives gained some adherents but alienated others, which in Louisiana included many with relatively weak connections to their new nation.

U.S. officials attempted to counter British efforts by, at a minimum, encouraging natives to stay aloof from the Anglo-American conflict. Choctaw efforts on behalf of the British encouraged Anglo settlers in the West Florida parishes to volunteer in significantly higher percentages than the other parishes despite an often shared nativity with the British. Claiborne received numerous requests from citizens in the West Florida parishes for the U.S. government to provide greater security against the Choctaw.[207] Claiborne visited St. Tammany in 1813 in order to see to security measures, should the Choctaw join the Creek, which appeared likely.[208] Claiborne wrote to Thomas Flournoy, brigadier general of the 7th Military District, speculating that the Creek war might be (a distraction) incited by the British to draw forces away from New Orleans.[209] Claiborne reported increased Spanish influence over the Creek and Choctaw: "My impression has always been, that *he* [the enemy/British] would not force Spain to break with the United States, until it became his policy to attack Louisiana."[210] Claiborne sent entreaties to the Choctaw in an attempt to urge them toward peace. At the same time the British and the Shawnee leader, Tecumseh, in an attempt to create a pan-Indian alliance, encouraged the Choctaw toward war. In his message to the houses of the Louisiana legislature Claiborne presented a list of complaints against the British, a key one being inciting "ruthless savages" to attack Louisianans.[211] To U.S. native allies, however, Claiborne issued another message, warning them of the repercussions of intervention and cautioning them not to listen to Spaniards encouraging war.[212] The Choctaw sided with the United States during the conflict, though some bands fought alongside the Creek. Claiborne suggested that the U.S. military dispatch another fifteen to twenty men to the German Coast to better protect it from possible Choctaw attack.[213] Reporting to Thomas Jefferson on the beginning of hostilities with the Creek in the Mississippi Territory, Claiborne noted the Spanish practice of supplying them with arms through Pensacola.[214] Spanish influence decidedly benefited the British war effort. At the same time in the West the United States continued to cultivate the Caddo, who acknowledged Creek entreaties but stressed their commitment to peace.[215] Considering the Choctaw's importance, Claiborne asked for an additional Indian agent, preferably Colonel Simon Favre, to act as an ambassador.[216] Given recent attacks, Claiborne instructed Favre to gather intelligence from the Choctaws as to their numbers and dispositions as well as any information on their supplies from Spanish Florida and contact with the British, Tecumseh, and Tenskwatawa.[217] Unfortunately Favre ended up being arrested by the local Indian agent, Silas Dinsmore, for not having a passport from the superintendent of Indian affairs for the southern department. Outraged by the treatment of his emissary, Claiborne moved to secure an official appointment for Favre as an Indian agent.[218]

During the conflict Claiborne received a blank appointment for an Indian agent from the Secretary of War John Armstrong Jr., and he appointed Thomas Gales, who had served under Andrew Jackson.[219] James Monroe, serving as secretary of state and later simultaneously as secretary of war, had another figure in mind, creating difficulties for Gales in getting his expenditures covered. Claiborne inquired of Gales: "It is rumored here, that efforts are making to set on foot, in the vicinity of Natchitoches an other expedition against the Spanish Province Texas, and that the Caddoe and other Indians are likely to prove zealous auxilaries. . . . I must confess, I shall learn with regret, that any portion of our Citizens should engage in enterprises which the government of the United [States] as far as I know and believe / does not approve."[220] The government had more serious concerns in conducting the war without supporting another offensive operation, whether openly countenanced or not.

In the war's aftermath, an increasingly assertive United States placed added pressure on the Choctaw, despite their contributions in the war, to make further land cessions. As a result, tensions between the Choctaw and

settlers in West Florida increased. Local settlers' fears of the Choctaw before, during, and after the War of 1812 called for continued federal involvement to provide protection. Other groups like the Caddo in western Louisiana suffered as the period of great power competition in the West declined
with the beginning of the Mexican independence movement. The end of
the War of 1812 effectively brought about the demise of middle grounds,
which had heretofore afforded many tribes opportunities to thrive.

The Indian trade's importance in Louisiana declined over the territorial
period as settlement increased and native trade shifted to the west. By 1812
a series of figures pushed for basing Indian relations elsewhere. Major Amos
Stoddard, for instance, recommended moving the Indian trade away from
U.S. settlements given that troops often had to be used when inebriated natives upset local law and order.[221] Stoddard was not alone; Natchitoches's
judge P. D. Caileau Lafontaine in 1813 wrote to the secretary of war with a
petition from the police jury and a Catholic congregation requesting that
the U.S. Indian agency and factory be removed. This petition followed an
earlier land dispute over the placement of a U.S. fort and an Indian factory,
the latter located on land owned by the Catholic Church.[222] Indians and
bandit attacks made the area extremely dangerous, and men who styled
themselves Natchitoches merchants, largely Creoles, sent a memorial in
1812 to Governor Claiborne to step up patrols in the area.[223] Attacks and
the presence of immigrants and illegal traders in the region, who disrupted
older trade relationships and land arrangements, only encouraged further
Caddo and Spanish collaboration.[224] By 1816 Colonel John Jamison, the Indian agent, requested that the agency and Indian trade be relocated to a
position along the Sabine.[225] Claiborne noted to Secretary of War William
Crawford that given complaints of Natchitoches citizens the trading post
and agency should probably be moved further west to the frontier.[226] The
following year, in 1817 the factory shifted to the Sulphur River.[227]

U.S. relations with Native Americans helped establish U.S. authority in
Louisiana in the eyes of the Spanish and locals. The United States required
native clients in the West and native compliance in the East. Consequently,
U.S. officials strove to maintain good relations through gift giving, regulat-
ing commerce, barring private land sales, and the situational application of
U.S. law. When problems emerged, they generally originated from local in-

habitants, often newcomers interested in land, or misunderstandings over cross-cultural killings, rather than with U.S. officials. As Spanish strength upon the frontier declined and migration into the territory increased, pacific native relations mattered less. A democratic Louisiana government that empowered local white citizens discarded the imperial diplomatic priorities of federal officials.

3

Slaves and the Threat of Internal Revolt

Jean-Noël Destréhan forthrightly opposed the first form of U.S. territorial government in Louisiana. Destréhan's father, Jean Baptiste, had served as royal treasurer when Louisiana was a French colony, and his Louisiana-born son was educated in France. Destréhan received an appointment to the municipal council from the French prefect Pierre-Clément de Laussat. In an 1803 characterization of prominent New Orleans residents, Destréhan was described as "a native Frenchman in politics & affections, . . . one of the tools of M. Laussat & greatly mortified at the cession of Louisiana to the US wealthy. does not speak English."[1] In late 1804 Destréhan took a leading role in the remonstrance protesting the undemocratic territorial government, delivering the document to Washington with Pierre Derbigny and Pierre Sauve. The remonstrance advocated local elections for a legislature and a representative to Congress, but it also called for the continuation of the slave trade in Louisiana, which Destréhan as a sugar planter defended. The memorialists linked the two issues; as full members of the union, how could they be stopped from slave importations if the Constitution did not allow federal limitations on the trade until 1808? The remonstrance contributed to a congressional second look that resulted in a territorial House of Representatives, to which Destréhan secured election and served as speaker, but it proved less successful when it came to the slave trade.

Claiborne and Destréhan proved to be pragmatic in dealing with one another. Despite his earlier criticism, Destréhan secured an appointment to the Legislative Council from the governor, though he would resign in 1806, purportedly for reasons of ill health, as did his colleague Pierre Sauve, but actually because of their opposition to the undemocratic nature of the first territorial government.[2] Claiborne informed Madison at the time, "The services of an ancient Louisianian in the Legislature cannot with any certainty be calculated on. Few are disposed to make any sacrifice of private Interest for the public good."[3] The governor certainly did not believe the excuse of ill health: "He probably foresees, that the present grade of Government will not be popular."[4] Yet following his resignation Destréhan did not become an active critic, in contrast to many of Claiborne's Anglo opponents. When Destréhan was again nominated to the Legislative Council in 1810, Claiborne described him as "once a great advocate for a State authority, but . . . now . . . very friendly to the existing Government."[5] Destréhan represented the German Coast at the state constitutional convention and ran for the governorship in 1812 (though he came in third).[6] He secured election to the Senate of the United States, though he resigned before taking up his seat, choosing instead to serve in the state Senate.[7] Destréhan and many prominent Creoles who initially opposed the cession reconciled themselves to the change and secured patronage and high office. Destréhan's family intermarried with Anglo newcomers, contributing to the creation of a melded elite when his daughter Eleonore married Stephen Henderson, a prominent merchant and planter.[8]

The careful use of patronage and structural concessions won over Creoles like Destréhan despite the rejection of arguments for continuing the slave trade. The presence of a large slave majority served as a reminder of the benefits of a federal presence. After an 1811 slave revolt, Destréhan served as part of the tribunal that convicted its leader, Charles Deslondes, and sentenced him to death. In the aftermath of the insurrection Claiborne congratulated Destréhan on its suppression and commented, "It is just and I believe absolutely essential to our future safety that a proper and great example should be made of the guilty."[9] Despite his earlier defense of the slave trade and resentment at federal interference, as president of the Legislative Council, Destréhan expressed the sentiments of the body: "This, Sir, proves to us the imperious necessity of a prompt organization and discipline of the Militia. . . . We intend to express to the general Government our wish that one Regiment of Regular Troops be permanently stationed at New Orleans."[10] The United States won the loyalty of the local populace not just through concessions but by providing security.

Louisiana's large slave majority posed challenges for governance, but here too the United States had a long history in navigating this problem. In making comparisons on slavery, there are notable divisions when it comes to evaluating territories, the foremost being U.S. ideology before and after the Civil War. The U.S. territorial policy on slavery before the Civil War that limited slavery in the Old Northwest and northern regions of the Louisiana Purchase at times eroded elite support for U.S. control. By contrast, in the territory of Orleans and the rest of the South protections for slavery gained elite support.

Even in northern territories, influential locals often wanted slavery and the slave trade protected. In the Northwest Territory the issue came up immediately for the United States. Locals in Illinois, both French and American inhabitants, resented the proscription against slaveholding in the Ordinance of 1787, which contributed to out-migration to Spanish territory.[11] This was particularly the case with French speakers, who had additional problems with the shift to U.S. governance and proved far more committed to slavery than incoming Anglo-American migrants.[12] Franco-Americans in the upper half of the Louisiana Purchase similarly often supported slavery. U.S. slavery, with strictures on emancipations and the loss of other privileges, proved far more stringent than its European counterparts. For instance, when Upper Louisiana was briefly attached to Indiana, slaves quickly lost rights to testify, while their owners were freed from many of their paternalist obligations.[13]

There were notable cases where U.S. laws related to slavery weakened rather than strengthened local elites. The U.S. government's opposition to Indian slavery in New Mexico offers an interesting contrast to Louisiana, in that it not only undermined the local Mexican elite but fostered greater divisions between the Mexican and Indian communities.[14] The policy advanced U.S. interests at the expense of local elites, but it also benefited Native Americans. Louisiana in contrast protected slavery, which helped address elite concerns. Still, the territorial government's policy that barred the slave trade aggravated local elites.

The Spanish colonial experience often is depicted as far more open in terms of slave legislation. In the Gulf South native slave raiding from Carolina into Florida, encouraged by the British, decimated Spanish missions. In turn, the Spanish offered freedom to slaves who fled to their borders, a policy that persisted after the American Revolution for slaves fleeing the United States. The Spanish attempted at points to curb the practice in response to protests from English slave owners. For instance, Governor Torres y Ayala briefly began to pay English owners for runaway slaves, but the Spanish discontinued the payments, and the practice of welcoming runaways remained a persistent issue between the English and Spanish colonies along the Eastern Seaboard. In 1789 the Spanish proclaimed that black slaves who fled to Louisiana could find sanctuary. Two years later the Spanish promised to cease grants of sanctuary to slaves fleeing to their lines from the United States with the state of Georgia, but the agreement failed to be implemented, just as the United States took in Spanish deserters, and the Seminoles, unbound by the agreement in any case, persisted in taking in slaves.[15]

The Code Noir of France was never fully implemented within French Louisiana. Numerous restrictions and variances from the original French Code Noir occurred to limit the growth of the free black population, and the French restricted manumissions in 1724 when the Code Noir was reissued in Louisiana. The Spanish period, with increased manumissions, proved far more liberal, but these policies alienated members of the elite within the colony. The 1778 code of the Cabildo, though never enacted, represented the local elite's attempt to change Spanish practices and return to the greater strictures of the Code Noir.[16] In essence, the planter class within Louisiana opposed a more liberal slave policy pushed by the metropole. The same opposition led to the failure of a 1789 Codigo Negro drafted in Madrid from application in Louisiana.

Spain encountered pushback from planters in Louisiana convinced of the necessity of a stricter slave code and greater access to slaves. A widespread belief in the need for more slaves came from Americans, Creoles, and Frenchmen such as Paul Alliot: "A decree of the Spanish government, forbidding the inhabitants of Louisiana to bring in slaves since the beginning of the troubles in San Domingo, has entirely paralysed the progress of agriculture, the one single resource of abundance and riches."[17] The Spanish intendant Martín de Navarro likewise believed slaves to be necessary for economic growth.[18] Security concerns over slave importations remained consistent regardless of the sovereignty of Louisiana. With the turnover to France, Duc Denis Decrès in his instructions to the newly appointed captain-general of Louisiana, Claude Perrin Victor, charged that "trade in slaves shall be made only with Africa, and no slaves shall be received in Louisiana that come from the American colonies, as this is the only means of preserving Louisiana from the moral contagion that has infected those colonies."[19] Slaves coming from republican areas might pose a danger.

Nor did Spanish policy, however liberal, preclude resistance from the slaves. In 1795 the Spanish uncovered a major slave conspiracy in Pointe Coupée. As a result of the conspiracy, the Spanish barred further importation of slaves into the territory. Some observers retained doubts; C. C. Robin, a French traveler through the region, noted that regardless of the truth of the conspiracy, "one can see how gnawing is the anxiety, which far from diminishing with time, is growing, because the colored population is growing faster than that of the whites." Robin criticized local treatment of servants and slaves, which he contrasted with European treatment: "Habit and stupid ignorance of the Creole has fixed in them the idea that the Negro is only a property which they may dispose of at their pleasure like the meanest object." Robin in turn pointed to the failure to acknowledge the rights of blacks in Saint-Domingue as the cause for the rebellion, which provided a cautionary example for Louisiana.[20] Another French visitor, François Marie Perrin du Lac, while no abolitionist, urged better treatment of slaves given the experience in Saint-Domingue.[21] Perrin Du Lac argued for the treatment of slaves as one would treat animals in a humane manner, but he decidedly found fault with the current system.

Like the rest of the Gulf South and British, French, and Spanish Caribbean, Louisiana was a slave society. In 1810 slaves made up approximately 45 percent of the population of the territory. Claiborne, as a Virginian, Tennessean, and former governor of Mississippi, knew the challenges in governing a slave society, as were the presidents and (with the brief exception of Robert Smith) the secretaries of state to whom he reported. The shift in sovereignty to the United States altered the institution of slavery, but not in a manner that ran counter to the interests of planters. Slavery provided yet another link between local elites and the federal government. At the same time, however, slavery posed challenges for U.S. security. Debates over the continuation of the international slave trade created a potential wedge between U.S. officials and the local population. Ultimately, by creating a stricter slave regime and assuring local security, the United States consolidated elite support. Native-born Americans, in particular, argued for a stronger federal presence to counteract the slave population. The mayor of

New Orleans, John Watkins, in a letter to Territorial Secretary John Graham wrote of the dangers posed by the large slave population, free blacks, and foreign agents and the consequent need for regular units given the limitations of the militia: "I am not a friend to standing Armies in a free country but we are in a country of Slaves."[22] Even Jeffersonian Republicans recognized the need for a more capable militia and a regular military presence to retain control.

The territorial government took a number of steps to restrict the freedom of slaves. Claiborne instructed the commandants to forbid alcohol sales to slaves without their owners' permission, to establish militia patrols to make certain that slaves remained on their owner's property after 9:00 p.m., and to check passes.[23] Claiborne also checked up on local police practices regarding the conduct of slaves.[24] Despite these measures, New Orleans slave owners continued to complain over laxity in regulations and the sale of liquor.[25] Ad hoc measures needed to be reinforced with legislation.

The territorial legislature in 1806 passed the Black Code, which brought Louisiana's race relations more in line with the statutes of the rest of the American South. The code explicitly subordinated slaves and free people of color to the white population.[26] Some provisions had a paternalist slant that applied punishments to slave owners who failed to treat sick slaves, look after the elderly, grant Sundays off, or mistreated slaves. Other provisions penalized owners who weakened the institution. For instance, the code penalized owners who sold or gave liquor to slaves, neglected to report missing slaves, concealed runaway slaves, owned a slave who committed a capital crime within the United States, or kept a non-free overseer. Additional provisions required a certain number of whites on each plantation.[27] The code also mandated that slaves could not own, buy, or sell property without their owners' permission and barred slaves from testifying against whites, riding horses without permission, or carrying arms (except with permission for hunting and only on their owners' land). Provisions required permits if slaves left their masters' property and mandated death for slaves who committed murder or fomented insurrection. Acknowledging the connection between runaway slaves and Spain, the code required "fugitive slaves from adjoining Spanish territories to be delivered up."[28] This last provision proved difficult to enforce. The Black Code of 1806 crafted a system that restricted the behavior of slaves and required owners to abide by certain guidelines.

The 1806 code ended the Spanish practice of *coartación,* which allowed slaves to gradually purchase their own freedom, but it was not implemented from outside by Anglo-Americans. The code was a bottom-up document drafted with Creole authors within the territorial legislature who drew inspiration from the previous French and Spanish codes but also from U.S. law. The experience under Spain demonstrated that Creoles resented Spanish slave policies. The first full legal code for the American territory, the Digest of 1808, was the creation of Louis Moreau Lislet and James Brown, with Lislet as the primary author. Born in Saint-Domingue and educated in Paris, Lislet had served in Saint-Domingue's government before his migration to Louisiana.[29] As it did for so many Saint-Dominguan immigrants, the Haitian Revolution profoundly influenced his views.

By including slave law within the digest, local elites hoped to better protect slavery as an institution within Louisiana.[30] The slave code was another way in which Creoles could contrast the U.S. regime favorably with the Spanish. Still, Louisiana remained far looser in its restrictions on emancipations than other southern states, even as it became stricter over time.[31] Despite portrayals that view the increasingly biracial order being crafted as driven by American migrants and officials, white Francophones, both locals and newcomers, desired such a system.[32]

Some American leaders argued against the slave trade for reasons of morality. Isaac Briggs, the surveyor general of the Mississippi Territory, wrote to President Jefferson bemoaning slavery in Louisiana: "Is there no way of putting a stop to this crying, dangerous, national Sin? As I have ridden through some parts of this western world, and observed the numerous defiles and almost impenetrable recesses, I have reflected that these oppressed people are acquainted, far better than their oppressors, with almost every private path and every retreat—that they are already discontented and disposed to throw off their yoke, on the least prospect of success."[33] Moralists, however well intentioned, did not provide the prime motivation for officials in Louisiana, who tended to focus on public safety. Even Briggs, who felt slavery to be inherently evil, cast the issue as one of inevitable revolt. The slave trade might well be immoral, but in Briggs's and Claiborne's view, it was imprudent given the shaky nature of U.S. control in the region.

The United States attempted to limit importations given the looming end of the trade, but more importantly because of security concerns. Claiborne encountered similar worries as the territorial governor of Mississippi, where despite the efforts of legislators and officials, public safety concerns regularly came against the economic benefits of slavery.[34] Congress did not allow the international slave trade in the territories, but Louisiana's coast had a huge number of inlets, and planters avidly purchased merchandise, human and otherwise, brought in by smugglers.[35] As architect Benjamin Latrobe observed, "There is no country so favorably situated as to the facility of smuggling as Louisiana."[36] Latrobe noted that smuggling became so endemic that the Spanish approached the problem by forbidding the greasing of wheels, to more easily identify smugglers who picked up goods several miles away. The specter of rebellion shaped the debate on the slave trade. When the U.S. territorial government reappointed the previous Spanish commandant, Don Thomas de Villanueva Barroso, for the District of Valenzuela dans Lafourche he relayed disturbing news. In 1803, he reported to Dr. Watkins that a vessel that contained "twelve negroes said to have been brigands from the Island of St. Domingo. . . . Among other things they spoke of eating human flesh and in general, demonstrated great Savageness of Character, boasting of what they had been and done in the horrors of St. Domingo."[37] This potential introduction of black refugees (cannibals no less!) from Saint-Domingue into the interior of the country upriver alarmed U.S. officials and local inhabitants. Coastal parishes served as potential bayou gateways through which refugees, smugglers, and pirates traveled rather than braving Plaquemines and Fort St. Philip.

In the first days after the cession, Claiborne remained unsure of his authority to regulate the entry of slaves, but he moved beyond these doubts.[38] He wrote to the mayor of New Orleans: "As to the particular description of Negroes that shall or shall not be admitted into the Country, and the means of making the discrimination, it is a power devolving particularly upon myself nor can I transfer it to any other body."[39] Federal interference with the slave trade remained a consistent issue that focused the white populace's opposition to the federal government. New Jersey senator Jonathan Dayton wrote to Aaron Burr: "Dissatisfaction produced by our impolitic & ill judged regulations for the Government of that country, among which, that for prohibiting the introduction of slaves from Africa, is the most prominent, & to the Louisianians the most odious, because most injurious to their prosperity & interests."[40] Support for the slave trade represented one of the few topics that Anglo-Americans and Francophones agreed upon. Claiborne noted that he expected a memorial from the citizens of Louisiana on the subject.[41] James Madison wrote to Claiborne on the matter of whether a ship from Saint-Domingue with slaves should be allowed to enter, noting "the Political security of the place as it might be affected by the presence of such a body of strangers under such circumstances."[42] At first Claiborne attempted to regulate entry on a case-by-case basis, requiring the governor's permission before slaves or free people of color from the Caribbean could proceed.[43]

Claiborne explained to James Pitot, the mayor of New Orleans, that vessels would be stopped at Plaquemines and no slaves allowed entry to the city until after a committee from New Orleans visited and cleared them.[44] Government officials examined any vessel suspected of having foreign slaves on board and determined their origin.[45] Claiborne wrote to Colonel Freeman, the commanding officer of U.S. troops at New Orleans, about the problems of slave importations from the British Caribbean and Saint-Domingue: "I am particularly desirous to exclude those Slaves who (from late habits) are accustomed to blood and devastations, and whose Counsel and communication with our present black population may be pregnant with much future mischief."[46] Claiborne sent similar letters to the pilot at Balize and Captain Abimael Nicoll at the fort to conscientiously inspect vessels from foreign ports and to detain those with slaves on board.[47] Nor did this apply to slaves from Saint-Domingue alone, as Claiborne wrote to James Madison: "African Negroes are thought there not to be dangerous; but it ought to be recollected that those of St. Domingo were originally from Africa and that Slavery where ever it exist is a galling yoke."[48] For Claiborne the distinction between slaves with origins in Africa and those who experienced independence in Saint-Domingue proved false, given the harsh nature of the institution.

The governor warned of dangers not only from slaves coming into the territory but also those leaving. Claiborne sent instructions requiring vessels to be inspected downriver due to the dangers of slave importations but also of slaves fleeing Louisiana.[49] In the immediate aftermath of the cession, the number of runaway slaves increased. Claiborne took a moderate tack and issued a proclamation offering amnesty for slaves who returned but warned that they "shall not again experience the benefit of my interposition, but will be pursued, and may receive such punishment as their owner or owners, may under Law, choose to inflict."[50] Claiborne had the proclamation posted widely, going so far as to instruct his brother, the commandant in Concordia, on the specifics of placement.[51] In 1812 Claiborne received reports that a slave belonging to Major Lanusse of New Orleans fled on board a French privateer and instructed the officer at St. Philip to board the ship and retrieve him and if barred from doing so, to detain the vessel.[52]

Claiborne encountered opposition to the limits that Congress imposed on the slave trade. Dr. Watkins wrote to Claiborne on his impressions of the inhabitants: "No subject seems to be so interesting to the minds of the inhabitants of all that part of the Country, which I have visited as that of the importation of brute Negroes from Africa. This permission would go farther with them, and better reconcile them to the Government of the United States, than any other privilege."[53] Claiborne reported to Madison the general sentiment that the ban on the slave trade weakened Louisiana.[54] Both French and English speakers united in their hatred of what they perceived as U.S. coercion on the issue, which hampered Louisiana's economic development.[55] The fact that South Carolina could continue to import slaves aggravated them further, since many did not understand the difference between state and national prerogatives on the question before 1808.[56] Laussat likewise pointed to the American prohibition on slave imports as a misstep that alienated the local populace.[57] More paranoid thinkers saw the prohibition on slaves as a plot. Casa Calvo wrote: "It is not easy to adduce a reason for this conduct, unless it be to purposely weaken the colony, which was making great strides toward prosperity and wealth. The inhabitants are so angered that it is with difficulty that they will be able to be amalgamated with the rude citizens of the United States."[58] Benjamin Tupper, a Massachusetts man recently returned from France, proved particularly ardent in his defense of slave importations. Tupper, New Orleans mayor Étienne de Boré, Jean-Noël Destréhan, and others pressed Congress to renew the slave trade. Claiborne stressed to Madison that individuals like Tupper grasped the issue for their own gain but recognized that Congress created more opposition to American governance through the measure.[59] Despite the governor's private support for the ban, he believed it might be politic to permit the slave trade: "My opinion is that had the African trade been continued for a few years, no murmers against the Law of Congress would have been heard. It is certainly true (and I perceive it with great regret) that there is almost an Universal Sentiment in favour of this inhumane traffic, and the prohibition thereof is the great Source of discontent. On the subject of the Government the great body of the people have no opinion."[60] For the majority of inhabitants, opposition to the U.S. regime did not center on matters of philosophy or government but on economic and cultural touchstones, slavery the foremost. U.S. officials stressed the security perspective rather than engaging in the economic argument. Claiborne explained to Jefferson: "I have offered such Reasons against the African Trade, as I thought best calculated to reconcile the Inhabitants to its abolition, and frequently instanced the Horrors of St. Domingo, & reminded them of the cause of apprehension, of similar Horrors in this Province at some future Day: But the opinion of the Inhabitants remains the same."[61] The U.S. government failed to gain adherents from the planter class on this issue. Even so, leaving aside political expediency, Claiborne opposed the trade on principle and maintained that its continuation would create problems: "At some future period, this quarter of the Union must (I fear) experience in some degree, the Misfortunes of St. Domingo, and that period will be hastened if the people should be indulged by congress with a continuance of the African trade."[62] Slave rebellion remained a consistent fear exacerbated by the trade.

Memorials pressed grievances and called for immediate entry to statehood and respect of the French language, but the slave trade attracted Creole and Anglo support. In writing to Jefferson about candidates for the Legislative Council, Claiborne observed that Benjamin Morgan disapproved of the slave trade but most others wanted it to continue.[63] Though the governor acknowledged both the undemocratic nature of the territorial government and slavery as key issues in Derbigny's, Sauve's, and Destréhan's efforts, slavery was the more easily understood complaint.[64] Congress did not choose to allow the trade, despite the governor's estimation of it as the popular request, but it did alter the form of government. Congress paradoxically created a more democratic government even as it ignored the will of the free majority.

When Congress prohibited the trade, it created a rush to import slaves before the door closed.[65] Memorials and requests from Louisianans for exceptions from the slave trade legislation failed to persuade the administration. Madison denied a request from two locals, Winter and Harman, to allow a ship carrying slaves into the territory.[66] Contrary to the wishes of locals, the federal government retained the ban, and despite the ban an illegal slave trade continued as Claiborne noted to Jefferson.[67] Trade from Spanish territory also troubled U.S. officials. Claiborne proved powerless to prevent contraband slaves from entering from Spanish Baton Rouge, which received slaves from Pensacola and Mobile.[68] Claiborne informed Madison: "If Negroe Vessels are permitted to pass up to Baton Rouge, the law prohibiting the African Trade in the Territory will in effect be a nullity."[69] When Baton Rouge fell into U.S. hands, slaves continued to come in from Spanish-held Mobile.[70] Contraband slaves could enter in other ways as well; for instance, when a French privateer reached Louisiana and sold slaves seized from a Spanish vessel, the U.S. government attempted to reclaim the slaves. Secretary Robertson wrote: "It is difficult, indeed, almost impossible, to detect and punish frauds of this nature."[71] The government did not countenance slave smuggling, but it could not afford to pursue every transgression. A federal naval presence did as much as it could. Claiborne requested that Commodore Shaw follow any vessels suspected of containing slaves that he observed along the American coastline or into Mobile.[72] The governor also wrote to Paul Hamilton, the secretary of the navy, requesting that the navy disrupt slave importations into Spanish-held Mobile.[73]

Despite the ban, French refugees from the Caribbean brought slaves with them. As early as 1804 Claiborne wrote to James Madison that when French immigrants from Jamaica found asylum in Louisiana and brought domestic slaves, he detected no opposition from Louisianans.[74] Federal legislation aside, when humanitarian challenges to the policy emerged, territorial officials bent on the issue. Local citizens in Louisiana petitioned to allow entry of slaves in 1809 when a Frenchman tried to immigrate with thirty-six slaves.[75] Claiborne regularly issued orders to allow the entry of ships carrying refugees with slaves into the territory.[76] Claiborne sympathized with these émigrés, as he explained to Robert Smith.[77] The greater migration of Cuban refugees in 1809 did raise criticism. Whatever the governor's personal feelings, however, the issue remained under the purview of Congress. James Mather argued that if not brought into Louisiana these populations would arrive in other states.[78] Claiborne explained to John Graham that he allowed the slaves to continue in their masters' service as long as the owners posted a bond. Considering the expense of housing or imprisoning the slaves or sending them to another place, this was cost-effective;

even so, "These considerations, do not justify my conduct in the opinion of some of my Countrymen in New Orleans,—I am denounced by them as a Frenchman and am in the receipt of more Newspaper abuse than I ever before experienced."[79] Territorial help for Francophone refugees gave rise to more English-speaking criticism. In 1809 Claiborne wrote to Secretary of State Robert Smith explaining a letter he sent to U.S. consuls in an attempt to limit the influx of refugees from the Caribbean given Louisiana's limitations.[80] Despite efforts to increase security or to stem the numbers, the refugees increased the slave population. When the administration and Congress made provisions in 1809 to permit the entry of emigrants from Cuba and their slaves, Secretary of State Robert Smith wished to make it clear that future refugees would not be given the same consideration.[81]

The Black Code, a more active militia, and the presence of federal troops to protect against rebellions occasionally led to incidents that alienated locals; to assure good relations, territorial officials intervened on their behalf. Despite the harsh fact that violence buttressed the slave system, these methods could come up against the economic rationale for slavery. Slaveholders often wished their own slaves to be pardoned rather than lose their property in the name of maintaining public order. In 1805 John W. Gurley, Claiborne's attorney general, wrote to the governor after reviewing a judgment of a county court against seven slaves that belonged to James Roman;[82] a slave, Thelamque, who belonged to Alexis Miller; and Caudio, whose owner was Michel Cantrelle. Gurley believed the judgment should stand and recommended the sentence be executed.[83] Cantrelle, hoping to see the court's judgment overturned, wrote to Claiborne, who informed him that it was the decision of the court.[84] In order to keep good relations with local elites, Claiborne was not above hearing such requests, nor were local elites shy about making them, although in Cantrelle's case Claiborne did not grant clemency.

When authorities interfered with prominent locals, Claiborne could prove instrumental in securing planter property. For instance, Claiborne intervened for Pierre Bailly when three of his slaves on board *L'Espérance* were detained at the fort at Bayou St. John, writing to the officer to release them.[85] In a similar fashion, Claiborne reported to James Madison an incident involving three officers on a gunboat who intervened when a planter attempted to punish a young female slave: "Whose cries being heard by the officers and Crew of the Gun Boats, three of the young officers accompanied by a few Sailors entered the Citizens enclosure, and released perforce his slave;—The Planter is of respectable standing in this society, and many of his acquaintances feel equally indignant with himself, at this improper interference. . . . The Planters generally, think that the interference of the officers & crew may tend to produce insubordination among their slaves."[86] This is not to say that property rights always trumped federal priorities. Federal authorities frequently made use of slave labor regardless of local complaints.[87] For instance, during the War of 1812 authorities utilized private citizens' slaves to build defensive works around New Orleans.[88]

Overzealous naval personnel guarding against smuggling led to another incident. In 1808 Mr. Picou of the German Coast was making his way home in a pirogue with four slaves aboard when a U.S. gunboat fired after passengers failed to respond to a request to state their intentions. The navy then detained the passengers and questioned them. Informed of the incident, Claiborne wrote to Commodore Porter at New Orleans with a complaint from Judge St. Martin of St. Charles Parish of the German Coast, and advised: "It will be recollected, that many of the Pirogues or small Boats on the Mississippi are navigated by persons whose Language is French, and that if after being hailed & ordered to come to, they (for non compliance) be fired at and detained, it may often happen, as was the case with Picou, that peaceful and unoffending Citizens, may be unnecessarily alarmed and unjustly dealt with."[89] With a plantation that produced six thousand pounds of sugar in 1804, Picou was a figure of substance who had been fired upon for failing to understand English.[90] The federal solution to the slave trade might prove worse than the problem if it alienated planters.

External threats might also ally with the enslaved population. During the Burr conspiracy and Sabine crisis, General Wilkinson worried, "The Brigands provoked by the opposition, might resort to the dreadful expedient of exciting a revolt of the negroes."[91] The Spanish appeared to countenance illegal slave importations, runaways, and slave rebellion. The frontier created a tense atmosphere exacerbated by the large slave population of Natchitoches.[92] It remained unclear to U.S. officials whether the Spanish Crown condoned welcoming runaways or if it was a local prerogative at Nacogdoches. As early as 1804 Claiborne received reports from Commandant Turner at Natchitoches that Peter Samuel Davenport had seen an official Spanish decree that authorized the practice.[93] Claiborne speculated that the policy probably originated with a local Spanish officer: "May be a policy Suited to the views of the Chiefs of St. Domingo but I cannot readily believe that it would be resorted to by the King of Spain."[94] The governor ordered Turner to use the militia and regular troops to guard against runaways. In the meantime, Claiborne wrote to Casa Calvo about nine slaves, property of U.S. citizens reputed to have deserted along with several horses to Nacogdoches, and requested the recovery and return of the property and end to the practice.[95] Turner wrote of local anger: "I believe they would almost to a man willingly go to Nacogdoches and lay it in waste. In fact they have requested me in case the Negroes are not sent back to permit them to go, observing that if some thing is not immediately done, they will not have a Slave left in three months."[96] Claiborne alerted Turner that Casa Calvo would intervene and urged him to increase patrols.[97] After Casa Calvo's inquiries, it appeared that there was no existing official Spanish policy.[98] Claiborne believed both sides could provide safe haven for one another's runaways, which should necessitate cooperation.[99] Given the likelihood that rumors of Spanish practice would reach other parishes, Claiborne warned other district commandants to remain on guard.[100] Local officials like Turner believed the Spanish efforts were deliberate and that the Spanish gained more by the practice than they lost.[101] Casa Calvo's intercession worked to resolve the initial incident, and Antonio Cordero of Nacogdoches restored the slaves.[102] Upon their return, Sibley wrote to Claiborne:

> When your excellency's letter arrived advising their recommitment to prison after what had passed, it appeared to me you had been induced to do it from incorrect information relative to the character of the Negroes for since they have been restored to their owners there is not the slightest suggestion of their behaving amiss in either words or action, but the contrary, and it appeared to me after their having been punished so severely and discharged, without being charged with any new offense, their being apprehended and again put in jeopardy for the same offense was not only an infringement upon the Constitutional Principle of our Government but of common humanity that such a precedent might have an evil tendency, for a government untempered with mercy seldom fails to incite its unfortunate victims to acts of desperation, particularly while

their masters & I believe every inhabitant within five or six leagues of them were ready to testify that they had conducted since their release perfectly unexceptionable.

Captain Turner still felt the need to call a meeting of locals to get a sense if there was discomfort with the released slaves, and with the exception of a few malcontents the locals felt satisfied.[103] Still, news from Natchitoches spread to other areas, and slaves continued to escape to Spanish territory.[104]

Spanish territory persisted as a magnet for runaways. In 1807 Indian agent John Sibley reported: "The Spanish government have lately given New proofs of their unneighborly Conduct in encouraging Our Negroes to desert to Nacogdoches, & not only Protecting them on their Arrival, but Protecting them in the enjoyment of the fruits of their Thefts & Roberies from us."[105] Reiterating the obvious, Claiborne advised Governor Salcedo that any Spanish asylum policy, by injuring the material interests of Louisianans, endangered good relations between their two nations.[106] He also instructed Edward Turner to detach forces to Pointe Coupée to ensure its security.[107] Even Claiborne with his Republican dispositions wrote: "I never was an advocate for a Standing Army; I wish to God it could be dispensed with in this Territory;—But the present state of things will not justify a reduction. . . . The Civil Authorities are not sufficiently organized to preserve of themselves good order."[108] U.S. officials stressed to Spanish authorities, including Governor Herrera and Governor General Salcedo, that as long as the Spanish continued to countenance fugitive slaves, it endangered the relationship between the United States and Spain.[109] Herrera passed on U.S. concerns and reiterated denials, while Salcedo dismissed Claiborne's concerns, choosing instead to blame slave owners for giving credence to rumors[110]

Unconvinced, Claiborne wrote to Madison explaining the danger Spanish Texas posed to his territory.[111] Claiborne passed on to Madison the names of the slaves who fled to Texas from Louisiana and their valuation.[112] In the meantime Claiborne reminded parish judges of the need to better police slaves through patrols and the militia.[113] The large slave population removed all the benefits of interior lines, since in the event of a crisis shifting the military or militia to meet outside threats might encourage internal rebellions.[114] It proved difficult to even discuss the issue, lest it publicize the problem. As Claiborne wrote to Judge Carr, "I also feel unwilling to give publicity to occurrences, which policy requires, to be concealed from the Negro's in this Quarter."[115] In 1811, as the Spanish government faced the Hidalgo revolt, Claiborne reminded the governor of Texas of the bilateral agreement to deliver up slaves. Indeed, in 1811 two of Sibley's slaves escaped to Spanish Texas.[116] Spanish officials returned slaves when pressed repeatedly and disavowed the existence of any official Spanish policy, yet the practice demonstrated the limits of American control.

Inhabitants of Pointe Coupée regularly harbored fears of slave rebellion. In 1795 the Spanish uncovered a major slave conspiracy there, centered on Julien Poydras's plantation. The conspiracy proved to be multiracial in character, with a goal of abolishing slavery within Louisiana; fifty-seven slaves and three whites were convicted of plotting to revolt.[117] In 1804 Claiborne requested more forces from James Madison and additional boats in the area, given the dangers of slave revolt.[118] Henry Hopkins, the head of the militia in Pointe Coupée, made certain that should a slave revolt occur within the parish, neighboring militia commanders be alerted to provide aid.[119] Hopkins secured lines of communication to New Orleans, with biweekly status reports.[120] Citizens of Pointe Coupée sent a petition that contained 106 names, Francophone names for the most part but others as well, requesting a military force and a loan of arms, referencing the history of Saint-Domingue.[121] The same year citizens of New Orleans submitted a similar petition, and while Claiborne thought a revolt unlikely, he increased patrols and alerted the militia and federal troops.[122] Claiborne wrote to the president: "A general spirit of Insubordination which of late has been manifested, & the circumstances of several negro's having been found traveling by Night with Arms in their hands, the impression is general among the Inhabitants of the City that they are in eminent Danger."[123] Three years later, New Orleanians again petitioned over rumors of a slave plot.[124] The U.S. government could alleviate local fears by providing increased security in the form of federal troops, a harsher slave code, limits to the slave trade, and arms for the local militia.

When a revolt occurred upriver from New Orleans in the German Coast, it confirmed these fears but also the capacity of locals and the U.S. territorial government to meet the threat. The militia in theory provided domestic security in case of a slave revolt, but many observers worried it might prove insufficient. Lying north and west of New Orleans along the Mississippi River, the German Coast was named for the German immigrants who settled the parishes of St. Charles and St. John the Baptist, established small farms, grew crops for sale downriver, and raised cattle, largely for export to New Orleans.[125] Over the course of the 1790s sugar cultivation and the slave labor force it relied upon made tremendous headway in the area.[126] In 1807, Claiborne instructed General Wilkinson to distribute muskets and ammunition to the militia of the German Coast.[127]

In January of 1811, a slave revolt erupted in the German Coast.[128] Although initially alarming, militia and federal troops quickly suppressed the revolt, as Claiborne informed President Jefferson.[129] Claiborne's brief account to Jefferson, just two sentences in a longer letter, reflected the anticlimactic nature of the revolt. The revolt reinforced the common bonds between Anglo and Francophone planter elites and the necessity of their partnership with U.S. territorial authority as reflected in the territorial House of Representatives' response to Claiborne's address on the revolt: "The Blacks have been taught an important lesson—their weakness, and we have learned that our Security depends on the order and discipline of the Militia. We justly appreciate the conduct of the Military and Naval forces of the United States in this quarter, and of our Citizens cooperating with them, and emulating their generous example."[130] The cooperation of Louisiana's free population in putting down the revolt illustrated to federal officials solidarity among a common elite who supported the current social and political order, while the presence of federal forces demonstrated the indispensability of national aid to uphold the local order. Similarly, the revolt demonstrated cooperation among the slaves of the German Coast who came from multiple ethnic and linguistic groups. Regardless of their origins, slaves did not need a foreign revolutionary example or ideology to resist the evils of plantation slavery, but Anglo newcomers and Francophone locals regularly expressed fear of such an ideology.[131]

The German Coast revolt began on January 8, 1811, when slaves who belonged to Manuel Andry, a colonel in the militia and a former commandant for the area during the first phase of American control, seized control of his plantation. The primary leader of the revolt, Charles Deslondes, worked on Andry's plantation but was on loan from the widow of Jacques Deslondes, placing him in a position to maintain contact with slaves on two plantations.[132] Both the Deslondes and Andry families were part of the Franco-phone elite of the parish. The revolt killed Andry's son Gilbert in the initial fight and wounded the colonel. The slaves involved in the conspiracy at the Andry plantation gathered weapons, which may have been stockpiled by Andry as a militia leader. Deslondes's leadership of the revolt demonstrated a high level of military sophistication: he divided his forces into units and appointed officers. Despite this organization, in its conduct the revolt appeared more focused on vengeance than a concrete political program. Estimates of the number of participants in the rebellion differ widely from one hundred to five hundred.[133] Deslondes timed the revolt well, in that it coincided with the U.S. seizure of West Florida and the consequent reduction of the U.S. military presence at New Orleans.

Planters struggled in coming to terms with the scope of the revolt. The insurrection may have extended beyond St. Charles and St. John the Baptist Parishes.[134] Slaves who established maroon communities threatened planters who became convinced that these communities encouraged runaways and insurrections. Territorial officials and planters also worried over potential alliances between free people of color and slaves. After the attack on the Andry plantation, Deslondes's force gathered strength at each plantation, while killing the few planters it encountered, such as Jean-François Trépagnier, who died after refusing to flee his home. Some authorities traced Trépagnier's death to a slave, Gustave, who executed him for reneging on past promises of freedom.[135] Others testified that a slave of James Brown, Koock, killed Trépagnier, but Charles Perret, who raised the alarm among his fellow planters during the revolt, in his account attributed Trépagnier's death to Hans Wimprenn.[136] Despite initial success, the revolt faltered when the rebels paused at the plantation of Jacques Fortier.[137] This lapse provided local whites an opportunity to concentrate their own forces under Manuel Andry. The testimony of Jupiter, a slave of Manuel Andry, revealed the goals of the insurrection: "When asked why he had left the Andry plantation, he said he wanted to go to the city (New Orleans) to kill whites."[138] Nevertheless, officials often failed to probe motivations or plans.

U.S. officials responded quickly to end the revolt before it achieved further successes. On January 9, 1811, Governor Claiborne directed General Wade Hampton to secure the bayou bridge.[139] The same day he ordered Major Antonie St. Amand of the militia to send men to deal with brigands obstructing local roads.[140] In addition, Claiborne established a commandant of patrols and ordered parish judges along the Mississippi and militia colonels to maintain patrols night and day.[141] Claiborne dispatched two companies of militia from New Orleans, supplemented by sailors ordered out by Commodore John Shaw; meanwhile General Hampton dispatched federal troops under Major Homer Virgil from Baton Rouge to proceed downriver. In St. Charles Parish the federal forces in combination with locals from St. Charles easily put down the revolt on the morning of January 10, 1811, at Bernoudy's plantation.[142] Despite the relative ease with which the revolt was overcome, the presence of Hampton and Milton demonstrated U.S. power.[143] The U.S. response killed some sixty-six and captured around seventy-five slaves. For weeks afterward citizens of the German Coast attempted to track down those who fled.[144]

The aftermath of the revolt provided opportunities for U.S. officials to showcase the strength of the territorial regime. Local judges held trials in the wake of the insurrection's failure. In a context where differences between Spanish, French, and U.S. legal systems had proved contentious, elites cooperated across linguistic barriers to punish participants rapidly and brutally. Louisiana law required that judges establish tribunals made up of five property holders to try slaves charged with crimes and misdemeanors. A tribunal under Judge Achille Trouard in St. John the Baptist Parish questioned approximately seventy slaves and executed seven slaves, belonging to Creole (Trépagnier, Deslondes, and Pierre Bechnel) and Anglo-American planters (William Kenner and Stephen Henderson). Judge Pierre Bauchet Saint Martin, a Creole son of a New Orleans merchant who served as a syndic in the parish under the Spanish and later became the speaker in the state legislature, empaneled a tribunal of five local plantation owners in St. Charles Parish.[145] The slaves they interrogated belonged to members of both the Anglo community (like Brown, Henderson, and Kenner) and Creoles (such as Destréhan, Labranche, and Trépagnier). On January 15, the tribunal sentenced to death eighteen of the slaves, ordering the convicted decapitated and their heads "placed atop a pole on the spot where all can see the punishment meted out for such crimes, also as a terrible example to all who would disturb the public tranquility in the future."[146] The punishment served both a punitive and a deterrent function. Likewise Judge Moreau Lislet and a five-man tribunal tried slaves in New Orleans.

The revolt possibly encouraged further local resistance by slaves. Planters' paranoia and increased guard also might have raised a number of specious allegations. Almost a year after the initial revolt, on December 30, 1811, Simon and Juliet, slaves of Messrs. Drausin and Lucian Labranche, were accused of poisoning François St. Amant, Antoine Daprémont, Claudius Laloive, and Francis Debuey. A guilty verdict was not a foregone conclusion, however; Judge Moreau Lislet and the parish jury in the city court of New Orleans found Simon and Juliet innocent.[147] Officials continued to uncover plots; the following year of 1812, fraught for many reasons due to fears of a potential British invasion and Native American attacks, saw several rumors of slave insurrection.

After punishing insurrection participants, whites began to exercise clemency. Moderation signified confidence in the stability of the territorial order and fostered such a perception in local elites, slaves, and officials in Washington. On January 19, 1811, Claiborne wrote to Judge Pierre St. Martin of St. Charles Parish commending him for his role in suppressing the revolt. Claiborne then informed St. Martin that the tribunal in New Orleans condemned eight participants in the rebellion and recommended mercy for one slave.[148] The slave Claiborne referred to, Theodore, had been convicted the day before, but the jury and parish judge recommended that Claiborne commute his sentence.[149] Notably, Theodore provided information that aided the tribunal, but he also happened to be a slave of Judge Trouard of St. John the Baptist Parish. Claiborne pardoned Theodore from a death sentence on the condition that he receive thirty lashes and that he not leave his master's plantation for two years.[150] Claiborne attempted in the aftermath of the revolt, after the first trials, to sound a more conciliatory note. He wrote to Destréhan: "Justice, policy, our future safety required that the guilty should suffer; for the sake of humanity however it is greatly to be desired, that the list of the guilty may not be found still greater."[151] U.S. authority depended on assuring justice, but within limits. Claiborne made an argument pressing for moderation in the interest of humanity, essentially an idealistic and moral argument, but also practical in order to secure better relations with slave owners and slaves. At the direction of Anglo-American officials, local judges, Creoles like St. Martin and Achille Trouard of St. Charles, and French émigrés from Saint-Domingue like L. Moreau Lislet exercised moderation in sentencing after the initial trials. Judges trod more carefully for multiple reasons: to avoid convicting the innocent, to avoid the destruction of their neighbors' property, and to avoid ill feeling in the territory between federal authorities, local elites, and slaves. In late February of 1811, when Augustin, a captured slave of Etienne Trépagnier, testified that he only participated because Deslondes threatened him and that he fled at the first opportunity, Judge Saint Martin and the authorities ordered him returned to Trépagnier.[152]

Harsher punishments in the name of public order, however good they sounded in the abstract, could lead to significant property loss. Slaveholders often wished their own slaves to be pardoned rather than lose their property for the sake of maintaining public order, despite legislative compensation schemes. Claiborne intervened in the judicial process to protect the property of friends. For instance, he requested that Judge Lislet release a slave of Mr. Bernady, Telemachus, before he might be tried, since he supposedly took no part in the insurrection. Similarly, Claiborne passed on a request to Lislet that he attempt to achieve a pardon for a slave of Major Israel Trask, sentenced to death for his part in the conspiracy, pending the consent of the court and a majority of the jury.[153]

Local planters and territorial officials failed to recognize slavery as the cause of the revolt. Instead they traced the cause to outside forces, whether foreign governments or slaves of foreign origin. General Wade Hampton informed Claiborne: "The plan is unquestionably of *Spanish* Origin, & has had an extensive Combination. the *Chiefs* of the party that took the field are both taken, but there is Without a doubt *Others behind the Curtain Still More formidable.*"[154] Despite the absence of evidence, Hampton's suspicions appeared reasonable in the minds of many Americans. The West Florida rebellion of primarily Anglo settlers against Spanish control in Baton Rouge and surrounding parishes had just taken place. Yet Americans still did not hold Mobile and other territories in West Florida, and the slave insurrection distracted federal forces.

Saint-Domingue received the most criticism as a source of rebel contagion. Some traced the revolt to slaves introduced along with white immigration from Saint-Domingue and refugees expelled from Spanish Cuba. In the minds of planters, problems originated neither from Louisiana slaves nor because of any ill treatment but from radicalized or criminal slave populations from elsewhere. Pirates and smugglers regularly introduced slaves into Louisiana from multiple regions, including areas of the United States. U.S. officials recommended an expedition to suppress the Baratarian pirates both before and after the revolt. The year after the revolt, Claiborne wrote to General James Wilkinson that Thomas H. Williams, the collector of the port of New Orleans, requested federal help to combat Baratarian violations of revenue laws.[155] Despite the ongoing War of 1812, Claiborne continued to pass on such requests for military aid in order to stop pirates who seemed to operate on an "organized plan, for introducing Slaves and Merchandize into this State illegally."[156] Claiborne issued proclamations forbidding trade between the Baratarians and citizens of the state since the pirates preyed on foreign shipping at peace with the United States.[157] By stopping these exchanges, the territorial government hoped to end the illegal trade but also to demonstrate U.S. capacity to enforce law.

The slave insurrection contributed to white solidarity and gained adherents to federal control. Shortly after the revolt Claiborne wrote to Colonel John Ballinger, in command of U.S. troops at Baton Rouge, that the revolt could be interpreted as a positive event in that it helped to prepare the territory for future crises through a stronger militia. In the same letter, though, he attributed the revolt to the American South, urging the legislature "to interpose some check to that indiscriminate importation of Slaves from the southern States."[158] Complaints over slaves imported from the other states did not fade quickly. Baron de Sainte-Gême expressed the same worries over potential rebellions from problematic slaves sold into Louisiana from the United States.[159] Claiborne told the territorial legislature, "It is a fact of notoriety that negroes of Character the most desperate and conduct the most infamous.—Convicts pardoned on condition of transportation, the refuse of jails are frequently introduced into this Territory."[160] Thus Louisianans in their communication with one another perceived the revolt as a consequence of outsiders.

The revolt helped diminish some of the ethnic differences among the plantation elite. Both Anglo-American and Francophone plantations held slaves who participated in the revolt and endured significant property damage. Many well-established Creole planters lost property in the revolt, and these individuals held great economic and political influence. Manuel Andry, on whose plantation the insurrection began, was a colonel in the militia and justice of the peace in St. John the Baptist Parish and served in the territorial House of Representatives.[161] Another planter, Zenon Trudeau, was a Creole who had served in Spanish administrative positions and remained in Louisiana after the cession.[162] The Deslondes, Trépagniers, and Fortiers, who lost property in the revolt, belonged to families who had long resided in the parish.[163] Another Creole, Achille Trouard, served as a judge in St. John the Baptist Parish.[164] Many members of the Labranche family, which dated back to the original German immigrants to the parish, suffered losses. Alexandre Labranche served as a justice of the peace at the time of the revolt and later represented the German Coast at the state constitutional convention.[165] These individuals represented the economic, social, and political elite of the parishes, the very people whom the U.S. administration wanted to win over, as illustrated by their continued appointments to parish and militia positions.

Moreover, the revolt illustrated the existence of a common planter class, since the rebels did not distinguish between Anglo and Francophone plantations. Several recent Anglo-American arrivals and members of the planter elite with good political ties maintained plantations involved in the insurrection. Kenner and Henderson were partners in a mercantile firm and in several sugar plantations, though they both retained separate holdings. Kenner, an Episcopalian Virginian, came to Louisiana by way of Mississippi. He served on the Legislative Council and the board of directors of the New Orleans branch of the Bank of the United States; Henderson, who grew far wealthier than his partner, immigrated from Scotland and later married into the Destréhan family.[166] James Brown, whose slaves were involved in the insurrection, was another Virginian, who had held political office in Kentucky before becoming the secretary of the territory of Orleans and the U.S. attorney of the territory. He was instrumental in shaping the Louisiana Civil Code and would shortly serve in the state constitutional convention representing the German Coast, along with Alexandre Labranche and Jean N. Destréhan, and later secured election to the U.S. Senate.[167] Richard Butler, another Anglo settler, had been a captain in the U.S. Army and partnered with his brother-in-law Captain Samuel McCutcheon from Philadelphia.[168] Israel E. Trask was an American from Massachusetts who had come to Mississippi with his brothers and served in militia positions when Claiborne was governor of the territory before immigrating to Louisiana, where he received further patronage.[169] The revolt contributed to white racial solidarity for the future, as the specter of further slave insurrections reinforced planters' unease.[170] Regardless of language or lineage in the German Coast, all of these members of the developing elite faced the same threat from a slave insurgency.[171]

The slave revolt may have generated white Louisianan unity in the face of an immediate threat, but it had the potential to reveal divisions as locals searched for outside forces to blame. Foreign agents and outside forces received blame, while local notables escaped identification with one notable exception. Rumors circulated that Barthelemy Macarty refused supplies to the soldiers who put down the rebellion. It later became clear, however, that he had provided aid, and Macarty threatened those who leveled accusations to repeat them to his face at the risk of a duel.[172] The rumors did not stick, as Macarty continued to receive appointments and shortly received the nomination to be the first Louisiana secretary of state.[173] The fact that criticism of locals remained limited to Macarty, a planter with good ties to U.S. officials, reveals a growing degree of white unity within Louisiana. This unity cast a stark contrast to the last major slave conspiracy, in 1795 in Pointe Coupée.[174] The Pointe Coupée conspiracy involved slaves, free people of color, and whites. In contrast, the German Coast rebellion involved no whites or free people of color. The absence of any support from those groups may be due to the territorial regime's hardening of racial and status lines in Louisiana. In the aftermath of the Pointe Coupée conspiracy the Spanish governor, Francisco Luis Hector Baron de Carondelet, blamed the planters, and the planters in turn blamed Spanish policies.[175] In contrast, in the aftermath of the German Coast revolt planters and the territorial governor blamed outside sources.

The slave population followed a process parallel to that of whites in Louisiana in overcoming ethnic divisions. Slaves bridged language and cultural gaps far wider and more diverse than the Anglo-Creole divide of their owners. Of 217 slaves involved in the 1811 rebellion listed in Gwendolyn Midlo Hall's *Afro-Louisiana History and Genealogy, 1719–1820* database, only twenty-nine, or 13.4 percent, have a clear birthplace. Even so, that limited information indicates that slaves brought into Louisiana from across Africa and the Caribbean cooperated across ethnic lines of their own and those of the Louisiana Creole slave labor force. Those slaves with clear origins include 7.8 percent from Africa and 5.1 percent from Louisiana, with only one slave coming directly from the Caribbean. While no slave imported from the U.S. was identified as involved in the revolt, Claiborne and others believed that slaves from the United States participated. Participants from the Brown, Kenner and Henderson, Butler and McCutcheon, and Israel Trask plantations had Anglo names.[176] Likewise multiple Creole plantations involved in the revolt had slaves from the English-speaking world.[177] Albert Thrasher in his compilation of slave lists notes several slaves sold from the East Coast and South of the United States.[178] The same accounts of slave derivation produce one native slave of Saint-Domingue: Cupidon, who belonged to Adélard and the late Félicité Fortier.[179] The economic and political conditions within Louisiana broke down ethnic differences among both the free and enslaved populations.

This is not to say that the slave community reacted to the insurrection in a monolithic fashion. Several slaves, either because they believed the revolt would fail or due to moral concerns or personal loyalties, sided with the forces of control. In the months following the insurrection, the territorial legislature called for an inquiry into the conduct of slaves who chose not to rebel. Local officials found that slaves belonging to Etienne Trépagnier, Hermogène Labranche, Bernard Bernoudy, Adélard Fortier, Jacques Charbonnet, and Pierre Pain all aided local whites by warning them of the approach of insurrectionists. The heirs of La Meullion petitioned the judge of St. Charles, P. B. St. Martin, to emancipate a mulatto slave, Bazile, as "Bazile did alone fight the fire set to the main house of the plantation by the slaves of the recent uprising. Moreover, he, alone, prevented them from stealing many of the effects of the late Meullion."[180] Pierre, a slave driver, and François of Hermogène Labranche, warned their master of the revolt and aided the forces that ultimately put down the rebellion. Orestes, a slave of Jacques Charbonnet, took Charbonnet's elderly mother to safety, after which he secured his master's silverware.[181] In the aftermath of the insurrection territorial officials strove to reward individuals who stood with the planter class, with several slaves receiving freedom after petitions from their owners.

As a result of the revolt, the territorial government of Orleans worked to create a more stable regime, less susceptible to the internal threat that the slave insurrection represented. Changes that Claiborne recommended achieved fairly wide support. Creoles within the German Coast welcomed increased U.S. forces. Andry recommended, "I think a detachment of regular troops would be very useful for the tranquility of our coast, because I am obliged to order many detachments of militia to meet and destroy the remaining of those brigands."[182] The necessity for a regular military presence in Louisiana became a frequent refrain by whites of all backgrounds in the aftermath of the 1811 insurrection.

The militia encountered significant criticism in the aftermath of the rebellion. In fact, requests for U.S. regular military frequently came in tandem with complaints over the effectiveness of the militia. The territorial and subsequent state government proceeded to correct these security deficiencies by strengthening militia laws requiring regular musters and fines for failure to attend, as well as granting greater powers to officers to give orders and enforce them.[183] In the aftermath of the revolt the government continued slave patrols, lest the insurrection spread.[184] In December of 1811, Claiborne wrote to Major William McRae, the commander of regular troops at New Orleans; James Mather, the mayor of New Orleans; Manuel Andry; and Andry's successor as the local militia commander, Adélard Fortier on the need to be prepared given rumors of a potential slave insurrection on the German Coast that might coordinate with slaves in New Orleans.[185]

Military officers distributed arms and powder to local whites in case of another insurrection. Claiborne earlier endorsed such distributions and in the aftermath of the revolt in 1811 insisted that the military continue to provide arms in St. Charles.[186] Claiborne kept the secretary of war informed, making sure to note that while the militia did not require payment from the government, it would need federal funding for arms distribution.[187] On January 14, 1811, he wrote to Major St. Amand and Colonel Andry, congratulating citizens in putting down the revolt but noting that everyone should now be in favor of a stronger militia.[188] Jefferson likewise noted the weakness of Louisiana and the need for a U.S. troop presence given the growing tensions with Great Britain.[189] The legislature responded to Claiborne's requests, agreeing with much of his reasoning. The upper house, the Legislative Council, requested a regiment of regular troops to be stationed at New Orleans and the Orleans House of Representatives concurred in requests for a stronger militia.[190]

The territorial administration soon after the revolt felt relatively secure. On January 30, 1811, less than a month after the insurrection, Claiborne wrote to General Philemon Thomas that militia patrols could be left to local discretion.[191] In Claiborne's view, the government's handling of the revolt gave credit to local forces and his own efforts.[192] Claiborne did his best to assure that local citizens would be compensated for property loss, and the legislature granted $300 per slave to those whose slaves had been killed as a result of the insurrection.[193] In addition, Claiborne offered rewards for the capture of any other leaders of the rebellion.[194]

Changes within militia laws and the reliance on U.S. troops were not without some controversy. Writing under the name Cato in Dr. John Watkins's anti-administration paper, the *Orleans Gazette,* an author gave the traditional republican argument for dependence on militia rather than on regular troops and denigrated regulars as mercenaries. The more restrained but also opposition (and more Federalist) paper, the *Louisiana Gazette,* responded to the arguments and repudiated the use of the word *mercenary* in reference to regulars: "There is a harshness in the expression that is grating to an American ear. . . . Among those Volunteer Regulars, the epithet 'militia man' is held as degrading, and next to being called a coward, does a regular soldier hate being compared to a militia man. If the United States ever have to measure sword with a formidable foreign foe, they must depend on *Regular Troops.*"[195] The use of the phrase "grating to an American ear" lends credence to the notion that opposition to regular troops came from a Creole.

Others in the *Louisiana Gazette* criticized the liberal manner in which Claiborne distributed arms and ammunition during security scares without ever getting them back.[196] On another occasion the paper observed: "When the poor, deluded blacks committed the depredations in the coast last winter; when all was alarm; you excellency ordered the Arsenal to be thrown open and your Aides de Camp distributed 800 stand of arms to every man of every nationality that presented himself."[197] That the *Louisiana Gazette,* however critically, noted that the government distributed arms to people of every nationality was significant; nationality became less important than race on issues of public security within the territory from the perspective of U.S. officials. Others, however, continued to maintain ethnic/national biases, particularly the writer in the *Louisiana Gazette.*

Militia units within Louisiana often possessed either a heavily Creole or Anglo-American character. Even so, these militia units demonstrated a growing sense of a common Louisiana identity. For instance, on July 4, 1811, six months after the insurrection, a heavily Anglo-American regiment of the Columbian Infantry paraded before locals enjoying refreshments. After toasts praising the Revolution and U.S. institutions, on the eighth toast they raised their glasses to Claiborne and on the ninth to "the people of the Territory—to convince the world they are Americans."[198] Louisianans remained well aware that the outside world, including the other states, failed to perceive them as Americans. On December 20, 1811, the Columbian Infantry gathered to celebrate the anniversary of the cession. The *Louisiana Gazette* commented: "We are sorry that none of the Creole companies have showed themselves on this national day."[199] War with Britain advanced national unity, but the slave population created a far more immediate sense of unity for the free population, all the more terrifying because it was so quotidian. Two years later, in 1813, a more united Fourth of July celebration occurred, with militia companies attending a mass in French.[200] The war with Britain helped to consolidate Anglo-Americans and Creoles into an American Louisiana, where the Fourth of July celebration included a French mass. Threats, both internal and external, created an explicit sense of community, which reconciled Francophone planters and the U.S. territorial regime to one another.

Nor was the fear of slaves simply American paranoia, since the British utilized freed slaves in the Chesapeake during the War of 1812 and in 1814 in their invasion into the Gulf Coast.[201] The war also created opportunities for more slave imports, as noted by German merchant Vincent Nolte, who became a U.S. citizen in New Orleans during the war. He wrote of the Baratarian pirates: "[Barataria] was visited by the sugar planters, chiefly of French origin, who bought up the stolen slaves from 150 to 200 dollars per head, when they could not have procured as good stock in the city for less than 600 or 700 dollars." Nolte believed the illegal slave trade and the consequent shortage of specie contributed to bank runs in the city exacerbated by rumors spurred on by the competition between the Bank of Orleans and the Planters' Bank.[202] During the War of 1812 slaves from both American and Spanish planters fled to British lines to aid them in their war effort in return for freedom and the promise of land.[203] Arsène Latour, who served as a major and engineer for the United States, believed the British operation depended on slave insurrection: "The British were bent on the destruction of a country whose rivalship they feared in their colonial productions, and that the cabinet of St. James had determined to carry on a war of plunder and devastation against Louisiana." Latour reported on the circulation of a proclamation: "in French and Spanish, nearly in the following terms: 'Louisianians! remain quiet in your houses; *your slaves shall be preserved to you,* and your property respected. We make war only against Americans.' Signed by admiral Cochrane and major-general Keane." Latour remained convinced that while some slaves served to secure freedom, most were pressed into service.[204] While Latour misjudged slave motivations, he reflected white perceptions of British methods. British Lieutenant Colonel Edward Nicolls issued a proclamation appealing to the non-American populace: "Natives of Louisiana! On you the first call is made to assist in liberating from a faithless, imbecile government, your paternal soil: Spaniards, Frenchmen, Italians, and British, whether settled or residing for a time, in Louisiana, on you, also, I call to aid me in this just cause: the American usurpation in this country must be abolished, and the lawful owners of the soil put in possession."[205] The British practice of liberating slaves undercut efforts to recruit other groups within the territory who they believed could be detached from the American cause. Still, the large slave population impeded the war effort in Louisiana. As James Monroe noted in a letter to General Andrew Jackson, "The militia of Louisiana will be less efficient for general purposes, from the dread of domestic insurrections, so that on the militia of Tennessee your principal reliance must be."[206] U.S. officials played up the British policy of freeing slaves; W. C. C. Claiborne proclaimed: "If there be a citizen who believes that his rights and property will be respected by an invading foe, the weakness of his head should excite pity."[207] The practice of welcoming and recruiting slaves undercut the British appeal to whites within Louisiana.

After the British defeat at the Battle of New Orleans, Claiborne wrote to Andrew Jackson to see if he could aid in securing American slaves from his British counterpart.[208] Jackson found the entire prospect of asking the British for property venal and undignified: "Would it not be a degradation of that national character of which we boast, to condescend to solicit the restoration of stolen property from an enemy who avows plunder & burning to be legitimate modes of warfare? If the individual sufferers would disdain such humiliation, by how much stronger motives are those who represent the whole *majesty* of the state bound to shun it."[209] Louisianans had no such compunctions. Claiborne sent two Louisianans with a letter to British Major General John Lambert requesting the return of human property in line with the peace treaty between the two nations.[210] Despite the treaty, however, in the absence of Lambert, Major General John Power responded that while he tried to convince the slaves to return, "he did not feel himself authorized to resort to force, to oblige them to do so, as they threw themselves on his protection, which they were entitled to, having served with the British Army.[211] British cooperation in returning slaves to their American enemies proved little different from how they treated their own Spanish allies in Florida when such requests were made.[212]

The territorial government won the loyalty of the populace in a number of ways, but the large slave population provided a daily demonstration of the need for security. The territorial government provided that security by constructing a stricter slave regime, regulating and ending the slave trade, preventing fugitive slaves, and negotiating with foreign powers for their return. At times federal security concerns placed territorial officials at odds with the local majority, as in ending the slave trade. More importantly, in the nightmare scenario of an actual rebellion the federal government supplied military forces and arms. While the insurrection of 1811 demonstrated the cooperation of Louisiana slaves across ethnic lines, it also contributed to the formation of a more united white planter class within the German Coast. The revolt provided a clear example of the manner in which U.S. power could uphold social order in Louisiana and of the corrections needed for a more capable militia. Through their response to the revolt the Francophone and English-speaking planters came to grips with the reality that their economic and political interests aligned with one another and with the federal presence.

4

Free People of Color and the Limits of Collaboration

Like many Louisianans, Pierre (Pedro) Bailly welcomed the turnover to the United States; unlike many of those other Louisianans, Bailly was a free man of color. Bailly had served in the free black militia under the Spanish and held a syndic position on the Iberville Coast in 1796.[1] Despite these achievements Bailly was not a Spanish loyalist. Rumors of possible collusion among members of the free black militia in a planned slave insurrection at the plantation of Julien Poydras in 1795 ended further opportunities for Bailly under the Spanish regime. Even though an official inquiry cleared militia members of involvement, the rumors accrued greater credence in Bailly's case because he praised the French Revolution and publicly made statements advocating a French-backed insurrection and invasion of Louisiana. The Spanish government ruled against him in two civil cases that led to a less ideological though not less strident form of disgruntlement on Bailly's part. Bailly had encountered legal difficulties with Don Luis de Lalande Daprémont over the lending and recovery of money, hurting Bailly's reputation for solvency.[2] Given his statements of support for revolution, Bailly ran afoul of Governor Carondelet and was imprisoned in Havana from 1794 until the end of hostilities between France and Spain during the War of the First Coalition, whereupon he returned to Louisiana.[3] Given this treatment Bailly proved receptive to the incoming U.S. government.

The corporate nature of Spanish society limited resistance from free blacks. Privileges for free persons of color retarded the creation of a pan-black resistance, since the free black population saw themselves as stakeholders in the current system, though to a far lesser degree than others, and maintained familial and commercial ties to whites in Louisiana.[4] Thus Bailly had learned the limits of French revolutionary appeals to the free black population. Due to his recent treatment under the Spanish, he proved an early supporter of U.S. control. Whatever claims Spanish leaders or contemporary scholars might make of the Spanish regime's improved treatment of both slaves and free persons of color in law over its French predecessor, it failed to meet Bailly's standard.[5] Upon the transfer to French control, Spain gave members of the free black companies the opportunity to remain in Spanish service, but there were few takers.[6] Bailly and others hoped that the United States might remove racial strictures from free men with property. As a group these propertied free men of color constituted a category of elite who achieved civil and militia posts under the Spanish, but they hoped for more with the change in sovereignty. Bailly and other free men of color often did not object to slavery as such, but they desired greater levels of officeholding, equality under the law, and the right to vote. Consequently, Bailly and other free men of color, including his son also named Pierre Bailly, petitioned Claiborne early in 1804 offering their support and services to the U.S. regime and requested the continuation of the free black militia.[7] Free blacks in New Orleans, given the vocal opposition to the cession among white Creoles, believed they had an opportunity to get in on the ground floor of the new governing structure. At the same time, there was little to no downside in offering support in 1804 before the United States began to enact structural changes to Louisiana law and society, and opposition to the transfer did not appear as a likely path to greater equality. For Bailly, for a time at least, the supposition that the United States would improve the status of free people of color, rang true.

In 1805 Claiborne appointed a Pierre Bailly (Belly) as the commandant and then as the judge of Iberville parish. This could be the same man as the Pierre Bailly discussed above, but there are reasons to be cautious in coming to that conclusion. In 1810 there is a Pierre Belly listed in the census for Iberville, but also a P. Bailly listed in Orleans.[8] Kimberly Hanger's account of Pedro Bailly, the free person of color, covers him gaining his freedom from Josef Bailly in 1776, his marriage to a free pardo Naneta two years later, their five children, Bailly's purchase of his mother, his military service, and his taking part in the address to Claiborne, but not a judicial career.[9] Judy Riffel in her history of Iberville Parish traces Pierre Belly the judge's birth to Blaye France, using the name Belly rather than Bailly, as does the 1810 census for the individual located in Iberville. Riffel makes no mention of Belly being a free person of color but does mention that he emancipated his six daughters whom he had with his wife, a slave from Jamaica, Rose.[10] Thus, regardless of whether Pierre Bailly the commandant and judge of Iberville matches with the Pierre Bailly of the free persons of color militia, both had a clear interest in securing a future for free persons of color for their children.

Bailly replaced Francis Connell, who served as the first commandant for Iberville.[11] Connell proved ill-suited for the job and appeared to be over-zealous in his treatment of prisoners and personal enemies, exacerbating conflicts within the parish. A series of complaints and lawsuits emerged over charges that Connell abused prisoners.[12] Claiborne instructed Connell to release a citizen, John Baptiste Laurier, whom he had imprisoned, and to resolve any remaining issues by arbitration.[13] While in theory Connell's legal authority in the parish remained absolute as the commandant, Claiborne felt no compunction about intervening in local judicial rulings in Iberville. The controversy and local politics ultimately pressed Connell to the point that he left the parish, requiring Bailly to seize control of Connell's house in order to secure the records for Iberville.[14] Bailly replaced Connell as commandant and then became the first judge of Iberville in 1805 and served until 1807, when Nathan Meriam replaced him.[15] While Bailly's appointment serves as an example of territorial officials' flexibility, it proved just as contentious as Connell's.

A number of complaints emerged over Bailly's conduct, just as they did with his predecessor. In 1806, Claiborne received complaints from Eligius Fromentin, a recent American arrival who would later become a U.S. senator from Louisiana, blamed Judge Bailly for mistreating prisoners. Claiborne responded sympathetically, encouraging Fromentin to help bring individuals who committed abuses to justice. Claiborne wondered who was responsible, given that the sheriff oversaw prisoners, but in response to the complaint he attempted to gather more information.[16] Claiborne did not move against Bailly without further guidance from the territorial attorney general, John W. Gurley.[17] Still, the judge's actions concerned U.S. officials enough that rather than just request his resignation the governor considered legal action. Claiborne wrote to Gurley again over the summer concerning the affair: "Every person, who should abuse a public Trust, should be arraigned, and punished according to Law. I cannot too earnestly press you for an opinion as to the power of the executive to remove a County

Judge."[18] Judges retained four-year terms, and though the governor possessed the power to appoint judges, it was unclear whether he could remove them. While Claiborne requested a legal ruling from his attorney general giving him the power to remove Bailly, he also made his case with the legislature, securing legislation that judges could be prosecuted for misconduct.

Despite the complaints, Bailly remained in office for another two years, until the territory transitioned to parish judges. Many of the hopes of Bailly and the free people of color in New Orleans proved futile. The Black Code restricted the growth of the free black population, a population whose future Bailly helped to create. Despite recognition of the free black militia, the franchise remained closed to free blacks, with New Orleans elections restricted to free white men who had resided in the city for at least a year and met certain tax and property requirements.[19]

Though the territory of Orleans had a larger population of free persons of color than any other region within the United States, the phenomenon was far from unique in earlier North American colonies and even less so in the Caribbean. Dutch New Amsterdam possessed a significant population of slaves, many of whom gained half freedom and others eventually full freedom with all the legal status that entailed, which is not to suggest social equality.[20] By 1810 New York had a free black population of 2.6 percent, a full percentage larger than the slave population. Charleston, a city frequently compared with New Orleans in this regard, contained a significant free black population, and more than half of the free people of color within South Carolina resided in the urban environment of Charleston, yet in 1810 free blacks made up just 1.1 percent of South Carolina's population.[21]

Free blacks in slave societies persevered through careful interactions with the white leadership.[22] As in Louisiana, South Carolina's leadership became anxious about any immigrants from Saint-Domingue. In 1793 the governor of South Carolina, William Moultrie, mandated that all free persons of color from Saint-Domingue leave the state within ten days, and in 1809 many southern states likewise barred the same from entry.[23] Free people of color in Louisiana engaged in attempts to protect the rights already gained but also strove to improve their status, just as other free persons of color in the Gulf South. In some ways, these negotiations proved far easier in multiethnic and multinational monarchies that lacked the American creed's pretense for universal rights.[24]

The area that most resembled Louisiana in the multiple shifts in sovereignty as well as the multiracial and multilinguistic characteristics that offered opportunities for free people of color was Florida. After losing Florida to Britain at the end of the Seven Years' War in exchange for the return of Cuba, many Spaniards left rather than remain under foreign domination. The British struggled with the presence of free blacks in Florida after they gained control of the territory. The British administration began to enact and enforce stricter slave codes and curtailed freedoms for free people of color.[25] When Spain regained the colony after the American Revolution the free black population grew due to slaves being freed for their service to the British during the war and the persistence of runaways from the United States.[26] In order to repopulate the territory, with many British settlers choosing to leave, Spain turned to a headright system that allowed black settlers to take up land grants, and in 1796 new immigrants led by General Jorge Biassou arrived from Haiti.[27]

Spanish Florida had a long tradition of utilizing free black troops that dated to the late seventeenth century.[28] Legal rights and military service did not eliminate all social differences; Spanish officials and officers continued to expect deference.[29] Service in the militia and against the United States provided greater opportunities for land ownership by free blacks. Catholicism served as another way for free blacks to establish their cultural and religious bona fides within the greater Spanish community of Florida and beyond.[30] More important than just policy from on high, multiple white planters supported the Spanish system on the ground. One of the most prominent of these supporters was Zephaniah Kingsley Jr., the son of a loyalist, who had worked as a merchant and slave trader under the American, Danish, and Spanish flags and who had multiple common-law African wives. Kingsley advocated the promotion of a larger free black population in Florida. The use of the free black armed forces failed to raise concerns among the longer-standing residents regardless of their background in an English- or Spanish-speaking world, but as immigrants began to arrive from the United States by 1810, Spanish practices came under criticism.[31] Kingsley called for humane treatment of slaves and free blacks even as he defended slavery and a hierarchical society. At the same time he proved an eloquent proponent of a more liberal slave system as had been practiced by himself in Spanish East Florida with emancipations, the free exercise of

Catholicism, and a task labor system with extra payments for extra work.[32] Free people of color formed the key middling status group in a slave society, and planters within East Florida favored the Spanish approach toward easier manumissions.[33] Free black service during the Patriot War served as another way to demonstrate loyalty to white residents.[34] Free blacks fought for a royalist government regardless of the natural-rights language of the Americans, and in general blacks within the Caribbean during revolutionary periods became highly transactional in siding with forces that served their interests regardless of ideology.[35] The multiracial system that emerged in Florida was neither uniform nor imposed immediately; rather, it evolved over the next two decades, much as it did in Louisiana. Kingsley was not alone; a number of other prominent planters in Florida had African wives, and this encouraged many of them to support a free black population. This more fluid situation developed in Florida as a result of the corporate nature of Spanish society and connections between whites and blacks but also because of the political realities of Florida, in which Spanish authority depended upon the military prowess of black and Indian allies.[36]

Florida resembled Louisiana in that the cession treaties stipulated a legal requirement on the part of the United States to respect the status of free subjects regardless of race. Even so, in Florida a large number of free blacks chose to migrate to Cuba rather than stay under the incoming regime.[37] Other free persons of color remained dissatisfied with the social and political life of Spanish America and looked to inclusion within United States with some optimism. In Florida, the persistence of elements from the Spanish system, such as blood ties to white families, military service, property ownership, and systems of manumission, provided opportunities for free people of color. Not all of these elements disappeared immediately under U.S. control; constraints on the free black community emerged over time. Consequently, some free persons of color could identify positive elements within the new order implemented by the United States at its inception and into the 1820s, even as they hoped to retain elements of Spanish culture in race relations.[38]

Under the U.S. government in Florida, Kingsley served on the Legislative Council and opposed measures that flew in the face of his own practices, such as barring interracial marriage, preventing manumissions, and enacting racial poll taxes. Kingsley vigorously outlined his defense of both slavery and the free people of color in *A Treatise on the Patriarchal, or Co-operative System of Society*. He firmly believed that free people of color would side with the white free population but that slaves had something to aspire to within a slave system with manumissions. His argument failed to persuade the Anglo immigrants who came to dominate Florida, and as the legal system became less cooperative Kingsley planned for those members of his family who would be hurt by this legislation by accumulating property for emigration to Haiti.[39] In Florida as in Louisiana, locals, including free people of color, quickly seized on republican language in defending their natural rights. The population became more circumscribed as legislators over the course of the 1830s acted to restrict the rights of free people of color. In contrast to Spain, the United States during the Second Seminole War failed to make effective use of black officers or black militia units.[40] In Florida, with whom Louisiana might be best compared in the first federal census applied to the territory in 1830, free people of color made up just over 2 percent of the population.

In Louisiana the Spanish strove to build loyalty among multiple groups, including free people of color. The free black population saw its greatest growth during the Spanish period for a series of reasons, but also for reasons of political and economic policy, since Spain sought to bring in many settlers, whether as immigrants, slaves, or runaways, in order to counterbalance their geopolitical competitors. Under the Spanish the growing free black population and economic factors allowed for the creation of a kind of group consciousness.[41] As in other Spanish territories under the Bourbons, free persons of color received rights to form militia units, and Governor Carondelet in 1791 created two companies of free pardos and one company of morenos.[42] These militia regiments formed divisions within the free black community in terms of group identification and pedigree. Free blacks also served in militia units in Opelousas and Natchitoches alongside whites. The interests of free people of color and those of slaves did not align.[43] Nor as a class were free people of color opposed to slavery. The Frenchman Perrin du Lac in his journey through the region thought free people of color treated slaves far more harshly than did white slave owners.[44] After the transfer back to France most members of the free black militia maintained strong attachments to Spain.[45]

Free persons of color became increasingly conscious of themselves as a separate group as part of the United States. As did slaves, free people of color after the American cession increasingly found their liberties limited, bringing Louisiana more in line with other states.[46] Particularly in the aftermath of the War of 1812, American immigration greatly reduced the percentage of the free black population in New Orleans.[47] Free people of color attempted to secure higher status under the Americans by cleaving to their Catholic background that connected them to the Spanish period.[48] In the territorial and early statehood period, however, free persons of color in Louisiana, unlike in territorial Florida, had a potential military role that allowed them to continue to claim greater status as equal citizens. The address from General Andrew Jackson read to the units of Free Men of Colour by his aides pointed to these commonalities: "I knew that you loved the land of your nativity, and that, like ourselves, you had to defend all that is most dear to man—but you surpass my hopes."[49] The War of 1812 that ended the immediate security threats to the United States and closed a period of diplomacy in the early republic that entangled the nation with Europe made the country far more secure, but it weakened the ability of groups like free blacks in Louisiana to impress on local and national leadership the need for their support.

The United States contained populations of free people of color, but there were essential differences: outside southern urban entrepots like Charleston the free black population remained miniscule, whereas in 1810 in Louisiana free blacks accounted for almost 10 percent of the population as a whole and in 1820 over 6 percent.[50] The largest concentration of free people of color was in New Orleans, but free persons of color also resided in other areas such as Natchitoches, though in these other areas they often lacked a clear sense of community, as they remained economically tied to whites and in many cases were manumitted rather than born free.[51] Many of Louisiana's free blacks looked forward to the change in sovereignty to the United States, and with good reason. Several free black subjects of Spanish Louisiana were influenced by the American and French revolutions and familiar with Enlightenment thought dealing with natural rights and contract theory, and the Spanish monarchy, regardless of how generous it might be in granting privileges to free people of color in Louisiana, was loathe to recognize natural rights or to promote equality, even rhetorically.

Consequently, free people of color looked to the cession with some optimism. The racial dynamics of Louisiana in 1803 were not the racial dynamics of Louisiana in 1860 or 1960, nor were those dynamics the same for both slaves and free blacks when it came to interacting with federal authorities. More importantly as a territory under federal control there was a legitimate opportunity in Louisiana to create a society in which free blacks in law, if not in social practice, would be treated as equal citizens. This decidedly did not happen, but at the same time, the racial order that eventually emerged was not imposed solely from outside, as it often is portrayed by historians of both the West and the South. As opportunities opened up for whites to participate in a republican form of government, they closed for free people of color. Louisiana's white population appeared far more averse to expanding the freedoms of the free black population than federal officials. Indeed, given native-born American distrust of the local Creole population, particularly during the first few years of U.S. control, federal officials proved sympathetic to the requests of the free people of color, and when they dismissed their concerns, it was in the name of greater concord within the territory, not a concerted effort to enforce a national racial order. The sort of democratic governance that gradually came into existence within Louisiana became far more detrimental to the hopes of free people of color than federal authorities who exercised territorial power.

At the time of the transfer many Americans did not know what to make of Louisiana's heterogeneous population. U.S. officials and observers had reservations about the loyalty of white Creoles, and they encountered an organized group of free people of color who welcomed the shift in sovereignty. No clear policy existed as to how this population should be treated, whether they were full citizens, or what rights they were due.[52] Writing to Chandler Price in 1803, Benjamin Morgan, a Pennsylvanian who established his mercantile firm under the Spanish and served in the territorial legislature, questioned the status of the free black population: "Upon what footing will the free quadroon mulatto & black people stand; will they be entitled to the rights of citizens or not. They are a numerous class in this city say 1/3 or 1/4 of the population many very respectable & under this government enjoy their rights in common with other subjects—It is worth the consideration of government they may be made good citizens or formidable abettors of the black people say slaves if they should ever be troublesome."[53] For Morgan citizenship and rights for the free black population were not only questions of legality or justice but prudential questions. As he pointed out, if free people of color failed to achieve equal status it might increase the potential for slave rebellion.

Given U.S. officials' distrust of the Francophone population, free persons of color seemed to some figures at the beginning of their tenure in Orleans as more trustworthy. James Wilkinson wrote in 1803:

> The Jealousies of the People of Colour & the Whites seem to be increasing, & if I may judge from what I see & hear, the former are most to be relied by us for they have universally mounted the Eagle in their Hats & avow their attachment to the United States—while the latter still demonstrate their love for the Mother Country and do not conceal the fond Hope, that some incident of the depending War, may return them to Her Bosom—I speak generally—The People of Colour are all armed, and it is my Opinion a single envious artful bold incendiary, by rousing their fears & exciting their Hopes, might produce those Horrible Scenes of Bloodshed & rapine, which have been so frequently noticed in St. Domingo.[54]

Alliance with the free black population made practical sense to some, since they welcomed U.S. sovereignty. Wilkinson assumed they would prove more loyal than the Creole white majority and at the same time feared that if scorned they might ally with the slave populace.

Like Morgan and Wilkinson, Claiborne worried how free people of color might react at the turnover to the United States, but initially he came to a different conclusion: "It is not impossible, but these people may be disposed to be riotous, and the organizing and Arming the white Inhabitants, (which the American Commissioner might immediately do), would not only discourage any disorderly spirit, but give entire safety to the Province."[55] Morgan, Wilkinson, and Claiborne recognized the need to take the free black population into consideration, but Claiborne assumed that trust would be better placed in whites.

While American observers weighed the sentiments of the free black population, several prominent free people of color believed that since U.S. rhetoric acknowledged natural rights as endemic to all humanity regardless of color, they could achieve in law the same rights as white citizens. They might then enjoy freedoms, privileges, and opportunities barred to them under the Spanish. Consequently, free black leaders reached out to U.S. officials with professions of loyalty but also requests. Even as they hoped that greater rights might come, free men of color quickly moved to ensure that they retain privileges secured under the Spanish.

The continuance of Spanish institutions like the two militia companies of free men of color became points of central contention. Claiborne conveyed to Madison problems with the territorial militia and the need for loyal and experienced officers: "To re-commission them might be considered as an outrage on the feelings of a part of the Union; and as opposed to those principles of policy which the safety of the southern states has necessarily established. On the other hand, not to re-commission them would disgust them, and might be productive of future mischief. To disband them would be to raise an armed enemy in the very heart of the Country, and to disarm them would savour too strongly of that desperate system of government which seldom succeeds."[56] Claiborne tilted toward maintaining the free black militia, but requested further instructions. Unlike the regular militia, whom Claiborne complained of in the same letter, the free men of color eagerly wished to serve. In 1804 free men of color who served the Spanish as a volunteer militia corps issued an address to Claiborne: "We therefore feel a lively Joy that the Sovereignty of the Country is at length united with that of the American Republic. We are duly sensible that our personal and political freedom is thereby assured to us for ever, and we are also impressed with the fullest confidence in the Justice and Liberality of the Government towards every Class of Citizens."[57] The petition made grand claims in taking U.S. principles at face value, but at the same time, the address made one clear request: for the government to allow free black volunteers to continue in service.

Despite Claiborne's initial instincts, he did not prove a hard-liner on racial matters, for the same reasons as identified by Morgan and Wilkinson. The U.S. administration was short on friends, and here was a group that celebrated the change in sovereignty. In his reply to the address, Claiborne assured the free people of color that "their liberty, property and religion were safe, and that their confidence in the justice and liberality of the American Government would increase, as they became acquainted with its principles, and the wisdom and virtue with which it was administered."[58] In the meantime, as to the militia, he awaited guidance from Jefferson. The administration may have been short on friends, but still, too close a connection with free people of color might alienate some of the few friends it did have. Consequently, Claiborne proceeded in his characteristically cautious manner.

While the existence of free black militia troubled some Americans, federal authorities considered the issue and allowed the institution to persist. Nevertheless, the force raised the ire of local whites, the population whose loyalty the territorial government strove to cultivate. The militia served as an institutional vehicle for free black advancement and community as well as an establishment that linked the territorial government with the free people of color. Claiborne observed of the racial divisions,

> There is great dislike between the white Natives of Louisiana, and the free men of colour, the cause of which, I do not know that I could assign with accuracy, but the fact is unquestionable, and from this and other considerations, the Battalion I speak of, should engage much of the attention of the Governor, and be managed with delicacy and caution, I believe that some of the Old Inhabitants of Louisiana would much rather have seen this corps disbanded & neglected but the more reflecting part of Society seem impressed with opinion that Under existing circumstances the policy observed is most wise.[59]

The U.S. government authorized Claiborne to continue the free black militia, justifying it on grounds of prudence and security. Even so, the government used the militia within clear limits. While the battalion wished to have men of its own race as officers, Claiborne met with its leaders and secured the men's acquiescence in appointing Michel Fortier and Lewis Kerr, white men.[60] These meetings became standard practice for Claiborne with the free black community, and generally his views prevailed. Claiborne also instructed Major Fortier not to enlist any further recruits for the time being nor any ever from outside the city and its suburbs.[61] Thus the force remained small and localized.

The racial politics were such, however, that as Claiborne won support from one group, he alienated others, providing an opening for opponents to attack him. These attacks came from both Creoles and Anglo-Americans. A Louisianan, most likely Pierre Derbigny, in the *Orleans Gazette* criticized the recognition of the free black militia, as did Daniel Clark, who charged Claiborne with preferring the free black militia to their white counterpart.[62] Claiborne countered Clark directly, asking if he were insinuating "that the

Militia of this Territory had been neglected," noting that "they were totally unorganized; they had seen a black Corps preferred to them and a Standard publicly given it, whilst their own repeated offers and wishes to be employed in their Country's service has been rejected."[63] Claiborne defended his actions as to delays in organization of the militia to Madison, while noting that authorization of the free black militia came at the instruction of the Secretary of War.[64] To dismiss the free black militia would invite trouble, which the governor strove to avoid, though rarely successfully. Clark designed his criticism to appeal to multiple audiences, portraying Claiborne as lapse in administration eyes, while also courting local constituencies by adopting their criticism of free black units. In order to shore up his profile, Claiborne addressed the impugning of his private character by challenging Clark to a duel after he refused to retract charges of disorganization within the militia. Although he was injured in the exchange, the duel strengthened Claiborne's reputation. Despite Claiborne's recognition of the free black militia under his temporary government, in October of 1804 the territorial legislature also needed to recognize the militia, and it failed to do so. That failure to some minds endangered the territory. James Brown noted "that the free people of color have lost their consequence by being stripped of Arms and are anxious to regain it; in short that with the most dangerous materials amongst us we possess hardly sufficient strength to ensure internal tranquility should foreign intrigue give motion to the disaffected."[65] With the many worries that faced the United States in Louisiana in 1806, given the Sabine crisis, the Burr conspiracy, and anxieties over Creole loyalty, it made little sense to upset yet another constituency. After multiple meetings with free black leaders and experience in dealing with their community, Claiborne, though by no means an advocate of equality, at least felt confident in the loyalty of free blacks.

Given the legislative impasse, Claiborne was at a loss as to how to proceed. The militia continued to be of importance within the free black community, but without official sanction its continued existence proved controversial. Claiborne explained to Madison: "Their reorganization, during the late temporary government, was not liked by the ancient Louisianians, nor were there wanting Americans who, with a view to my injury, reprobated the proceeding . . . So much was said upon the subject, that the late Legislative Council thought it prudent to take no notice of the Mulatto Corps in the General Militia Law;—this neglect has soured them considerably with the American Government, and it is questionable how far they would, in the hour of danger, prove faithful to the American Standard."[66] Failure to officially sanction the units decreased support for the territorial government among free blacks. Even so, Claiborne believed that the best men among the free people of color would come around, particularly those who owned property.[67] The two constituencies could not be balanced in a traditional sense, as one lacked the vote and any voices in either the Legislative Council or the territorial House of Representatives. When the legislature did eventually recognize the units again, Claiborne utilized the same organization with white officers in command.[68]

The demands of the free black community proved worrisome to some Anglo-Americans and locals uncomfortable with petitions from the black community. In 1804 Claiborne wrote to James Pitot expressing regret for the recent activity of free people of color, which were "of a nature to create anxiety," and upset the white populace.[69] Free people of color did not engage in requests to upset the white community but to reaffirm privileges and to claim their rights as U.S. citizens. Yet any time free blacks brought forth demands or critiques of U.S. administration, even when they mirrored the demands of the white community, racial discord ensued. As the white community came to protest the policies of the territorial government, focusing generally on the lack of representation, failure to recognize the French language within the legal system, and restrictions upon the slave trade, the black community threatened to do the same (though the last issue was decidedly not a priority for their community). As the free black community grew disappointed with the newly instituted government, its members hoped to express these complaints in a biracial manner. The white community did not reciprocate free black desires. When free people of color attempted to present demands and complaints in a public forum, the territorial governor went out of his way to ensure that they would be sidelined. Claiborne wrote to James Madison:

> The free people of Colour have manifested some dissatisfaction at not receiving an invitation to the meeting of citizens who adopted the memorial to congress. A piece addressed to the free men of Colour and signed by an influential character among them inviting a meeting in order that

they might consult together as to their rights, and the propriety on their part of drafting a memorial to Congress, was handed to a printer for publication, who very prudently declined it, and for which I have sincerely thanked him. It is believed that the Free people of Colour are well attached to the present Government and that it will only be necessary to have recourse to advice, to induce them to decline a general assemblage or publicly manifesting any disquietude;—but if other means should be necessary, I shall use them.[70]

Claiborne took a softer approach, but it became quite clear that if push came to shove he would counter free black protests. When the free black community organized to bring forward the issue, rather than meet the issue publicly, which would only serve to upset the white community, Claiborne strove to quiet the demands of the group more reliant on the good graces of the territorial administration (the weaker or more loyal group, depending on one's view). After meeting with leaders of the free people of color, Claiborne secured their agreement not to press the issue.[71] These private meetings helped stave off discord, since much of Louisiana's white population opposed public black meetings. The territorial government could muffle free black complaints; in essence, they were the only game in town, because white opponents of the regime did not seek or want free black support. In the long run, racial animosity between Louisiana's blacks and whites proved more instrumental in shaping the status of free blacks than federal policy.

The white Creole population wanted the U.S. administration to adapt to local conditions for their interests, but they opposed black Louisianans expressing the same sentiment. Indeed, a regular complaint of the white community centered on the inability or unwillingness of the territorial government to restrict the political voice of free blacks. After the free black community's attempt to hold a public meeting and publish a pamphlet to advertise it, the local white population desired an official reprimand of the individual responsible, but once again Claiborne exercised moderation. He chose not to pursue any more inquiries regarding the author, lest it aggravate racial discord, which as usual he saw through the lens of the example of Saint-Domingue.[72] Foremost, Claiborne wished to prevent a racial breach within the free population. Claiborne proceeded in the same cautious and nonconfrontational manner when whites levied demands for restrictions on free persons of color, acting under the impression that stricter measures might push the free black population to side with slaves rather than free men. Claiborne's references to Haiti were telling, but they also may have been the interpretation most persuasive to local whites, in that it articulated the need to avoid splits within the free population. In these meetings Claiborne stressed the importance of status. The U.S. government reached out to free people of color, assuring them of future openness. Indeed, the fact that territorial officials would meet with free black leaders could be taken as a sign of respect. In return, the free black community could usually be convinced to present discontent privately.

Federal officials used white discontent to quiet the free people of color, but they also became adept at making the argument that the white Creole community should in turn silence their discontent lest they endanger the social order. These arguments often proved far less successful with whites, given the persistent complaints over the conduct of territorial government. The fact that the free black community wished to join in the memorial actually dissuaded whites from greater action on this score.[73] Nevertheless, the free black community never represented the existential outside threat that the Spanish, Native Americans, or the slave population did, which could better bind the Creole populace to the United States, for the simple reason that free blacks desired recognition of their current privileges and greater inclusion. Unlike those other groups, free blacks could claim a role in the body politic as free men with claims to citizenship. In part, this was a matter of numbers; when whites perceived free blacks as a threat, it was generally as a threat folded into the greater danger of slave rebellion, but the other reason why it proved more difficult to view free blacks as a threat was because they early and regularly evinced support for the federal government. Federal officials failed to fulfill the hopes of the free black community, but at the same time they did not treat the free people of color as an explicit danger except in the context of their siding with slaves; representations of the free black community as a threat more regularly arose from local white inhabitants.

Greater democracy failed to benefit a free black population excluded from the vote. The territorial legislature, once established, restricted the rights of free people of color. The Black Code instituted in 1806 restricted not just the freedom of slaves but of all people of color. These restrictions emerged through a legislative process in which local Creoles as well as more recent Francophone and Anglo-American arrivals took part. Rather than treating all free men as equal citizens, the code made it quite explicit that race trumped status: "Free People of Colour ought never to insult or strike white people, nor presume to conceive themselves equal to white; but on the contrary that they ought to yield to them in every occasion, and never speak or answer to them but with respect, under the penalty of imprisonment according to the nature of the offence." The legislature also restricted emancipations by requiring that slaves be over thirty years of age and free of any major disciplinary infractions, except in extraordinary circumstances such as saving the life of a master or member of his family. Once a citizen chose to grant emancipation, the county judge would then issue a notice for anyone with objections to bring them forward. The legislature also obligated the owner to have responsibility for the emancipated slave should ill health or other circumstances prevent the former slave from providing for him- or herself, thereby extending supervision of freed slaves.[74]

The code also placed free blacks in a lesser position to whites over the large underclass of slaves. While the code forbade slaves from testifying against whites, it still allowed slaves and Indians to testify against free people of color, though free blacks retained a right to trial by jury.[75] When a bill came up in 1812 that offered freedom to slaves if they came forward to testify when their masters committed crimes, Claiborne opposed it on the grounds that it might encourage claims against innocent men.[76] Notably in 1816 the legislature reversed course and barred testimony from slaves against free people of color except in cases dealing with insurrection. Free people of color could carry arms, but they needed a certificate from a local justice of the peace that established their free status. The code added regulations to the slaves of free blacks that did not apply to the slaves of whites. For instance, free people of color could not allow their slaves to sell goods except in New Orleans, and their slaves could not carry baskets upon their heads.[77] In stipulation after stipulation the Black Code reinforced the connection between slavery and race. For instance, if free people of color chose to leave the state, they had to go before the mayor of New Orleans or a local parish judge to prove their status. Even so, greater strictures that emerged in the 1830s would make the Black Code of 1806 appear lenient.

Acknowledging the status of free blacks proved easy in part because restricting emancipations assured that the free black population would re-main limited in the future. It was one thing for the territorial government to discourage emancipations while carefully refusing to allow greater privi-leges for free blacks, but incidents outside U.S. borders created refugees that challenged territorial attempts to prevent the growth of the free black com-munity. Claiborne in the long term hoped the federal government would restrict immigration, particularly free black immigration, lest it introduce the dangers that whites ascribed to Saint-Domingue.[78] When French refu-gees who earlier fled the violence of Saint-Domingue were pushed out of Cuba, many immigrated to Louisiana.

As refugees poured in from the West Indies, U.S. officials desired to limit the immigration of free blacks. Claiborne wrote to William Savage, the com-mercial agent of the United States at Jamaica, to stem the flow of refugees, particularly free people of color: "We have at this time a much greater pro-portion of that kind of population than comports with our interest."[79] Clai-borne at first attempted to block entry, as he wrote to Julien Poydras: "The vessels having negro's on board are not permitted to entry."[80] Despite white fears, however, free black refugees were not likely to be adherents of revo-lutionary doctrines. In reporting the different classes of exiles from Cuba, James Mather observed: "A few characters among the free People of Colour have been represented to me as dangerous for the peace of this Territory; . . . in every other Territory but this, the most part of them would not, I think, be viewed under the same light if due attention should be paid to the effects of the difference of language, and if it should be considered that these very men possess property, and have useful trades to live upon."[81] De-spite Mather's arguments that as property holders, free blacks would oppose revolution, Claiborne responded to Mather using the same language that he utilized in writing to Savage to discourage immigration.[82]

Federal officials discouraged immigration at the source, through diplo-matic officers, but the local government also acted to punish those who un-lawfully entered the territory. The territorial legislature in 1806 demanded that free people of color immigrating from Hispaniola provide written proof of their status, or they would be treated as fugitive slaves and "employed at the public works, until they shall prove their freedom, or be claimed by their owner by virtue of good titles." In 1807 the legislature went further, passing legislation that barred further free black migration into the territory, with a twenty-dollar-per-week fine for violators.[83] If an individual failed to pay the fine, he or she could be jailed and sold into slavery.

The great worry of territorial officials remained that free people of color might come to identify with slaves rather than with fellow free men. The generalization that race trumped class for whites contained an element of truth, but the racial and class hierarchy of territorial Louisiana proved more complicated for free people of color. Free blacks continued to retain rights, privileges, and institutions. At the same time, the territorial government strove to eliminate bridges between the free and enslaved black populations. Fraternization between free people of color and slaves threatened slaveholders. Claiborne relayed to the mayor of New Orleans rumors that free people of color and slaves mingled in cabarets and taverns owned by members of the free colored community, which disturbed the white populace.[84] The Black Code subordinated free people of color to white citizens, yet free blacks retained personal and economic rights if not political ones. In part, this could be seen as a buy-in for free blacks to the social and political order of Louisiana. To be sure, however, territorial officials often saw this quite differently than the local white community.

Free people of color frequently chose to cooperate with white authorities despite the Black Code. This illustrated a commitment to the current economic and governing structure, whatever their specific social and political complaints. In 1805 a slave, Celestin, alerted the authorities that he had uncovered an insurrection plot under the leadership of a white, who called himself Le Grand. Le Grand was a former French soldier who fought with Charles Victoire Emmanuel Leclerc's force in Haiti before deserting and finding his way to Louisiana.[85] In order to draw Le Grand out, Watkins advised using Celestin to introduce him to free persons of color who could then report back to U.S. authorities. The use of free blacks and Celestin to entrap Le Grand speaks to a degree of trust between authorities and free people of color. John Watkins, at the time the mayor of New Orleans, noted these security fears given Louisiana's proximity to the West Indies and the precedent of Saint-Domingue, while also pointing to potential problems within the militia given the presence of "free people of colour whom we must necessarily always consider in a country where slavery exists to the extent it does here as political enemies."[86] The plot convinced Watkins that the territory needed more regular troops, since he could not rely on the local population.

Certainly, there were free people of color who were less than sympathetic to the United States. At the same time, however, there was rarely a shortage of informants when there appeared to be cooperation between slaves and free people of color. In 1806 Stephen, a free black, reported to Governor Claiborne of the existence of a plot involving free people of color and Spanish partisans who would rise up and proceed to massacre whites once the Spanish under Casa Calvo returned.[87] Despite Stephen's testimony, Claiborne noted that "I do not credit it in whole; I have however no doubt, but that the free people of colour have been tampered with, and that some of them are devoted to the Spanish interest."[88] Given these worries, Claiborne increased patrols and supplied the militia with ammunition from the federal government.[89] Apprehension over these plots would often be discounted. Thus, in 1806 Claiborne could write to the secretary of war that despite these worries, he believed the estimations of free black disloyalty were exaggerated.[90] Though contentious, a working relationship between federal authorities and free blacks emerged.

The German Coast slave revolt in 1811 demonstrated the complicated nature of Louisiana's racial regime, as free blacks constituted part of the territory's militia forces. The incident served to promote the potential for free black loyalty in the eyes of the legislature. Free people of color did not side with slaves; freedom and class proved more salient than race in their support for the territorial regime. The free people of color's militia offered their services to Claiborne, and one company placed under the command of Peter F. Dubourg, the son of a prominent New Orleans merchant, guarded New Orleans.[91] The government thus entrusted free blacks with defense in a crisis, albeit within limits. Once the government suppressed the revolt, on January 14, 1811, Claiborne instructed Dubourg to discharge the company with his thanks.[92] In siding with the local government, the free black militia followed a larger tradition of military service dating back not only to French rule but to a tradition of combating runaway slaves and rebels under the Spanish during the 1784 Cimarron War.[93] Claiborne commended the free people of color to the territorial legislature for their support during the insurrection.[94] Even so, U.S. officials neither kept the force in the field for long nor allowed it to march toward the insurgents. That the militia volunteered speaks to the persistence of a more fluid racial regime as a legacy of the French and (to a greater extent) Spanish colonial experience within Louisiana that did not equate race with slavery.[95] In 1811 counterrevolutionaries in Louisiana came from both the white and free black populations. During the revolt, the ability to coalesce around status (free or enslaved) triumphed not just over ethnicity and language but also race.

While the German Coast insurrection demonstrated a level of free black loyalty, federal officials remained far more interested in a black military force than the local populace, in part because U.S. officials viewed Louisiana's current defense as deficient. A year before the War of 1812, Jefferson wrote: "Orleans will fall for want of a force within itself capable of defending it."[96] Shortly before the War of 1812 Claiborne advocated for recruitment of free blacks into federal service.[97] The governor felt far more interested in the continuance of such a force than did a legislature elected from the white majority Creole populace. In 1812 General James Wilkinson requested that the free men of color's corps be put under his command.[98] Claiborne wrote to Andrew Jackson in 1814 on a meeting with officers from the free people of color's battalion: "These men sir, for the most part sustain good characters; many of them have extensive connections and much property to defend, and all seem attached to Arms. The mode of Acting towards them at the Present Crisis is an Enquiry of Importance; If we give them not our Confidence, the Enemy will be encouraged to entrigue & to corrupt them."[99] While recommending the use of the free black militia, Claiborne warned that failure to do so might attach them to the other side. Along with the use of the force, the governor suggested raising another corps of three to four hundred with six-month enlistments. The legislature in 1812 authorized the governor to increase the size of the force and provided him with authority to make appointments, though it set forth guidelines: specifying that there be a white commanding officer, that it be raised from among those who paid a state tax, and that it not exceed four companies, each not to exceed sixty-four men, and that these men all own or be the sons of owners of property worth at least three hundred dollars. In 1815 the legislature authorized a smaller force, no more than eighty men for the parish of Natchitoches, though in this case the minimum property requirement was $150.[100]

While free people of color welcomed the opportunity for military service, many of their white fellow citizens remained unenthusiastic. As Elizabeth Trist, who lived with her son, Hore Browse Trist, the collector of the port, in New Orleans before returning to Virginia in 1808, wrote to Thomas Jefferson in 1814 criticizing Frenchmen who proved unwilling to serve against the British.[101] The interest of free people of color in military service was in stark contrast to others who claimed French citizenship through the local consul.[102]

Jackson mustered an enlarged free black force into federal service in which the ranking free black officer, Vincent Populus, served as a second major, though he reported to a white officer, Major Lacoste.[103] Claiborne cautioned Jackson that he trusted these troops, but that many others did not: "They think, that in putting arms into the hands of men of Colour, we only add to the force of the Enemy, and that nothing short of placing them in every respect upon a footing with white citizens (which our constitution forbids) could conciliate their affections." Unfortunately, the greater the contribution these units made, the greater the threat they represented to white planter hegemony once the war ended. Claiborne noted that two unnamed prominent citizens approved of a free black regiment, but only under the condition that the members of the regiment not return to Louisiana when the war concluded.[104] Despite these warnings, Jackson, with Claiborne's support, created another free black battalion commanded by Captain Joseph Savary, a black Saint-Dominguan. Like Populus, Savary was made a staff officer as a second major and attained his appointment directly from Jackson.[105] Problems associated with the free black forces had less to do with the abilities of the free men of color than with the tensions they raised among the racially divided population, as Claiborne wrote to Jackson that he felt that the force would acquit itself well but that the opposition from whites exacerbated tensions.[106] Despite their poor opinions of one another, both Jackson and Claiborne agreed free men of color could make a valuable contribution to the war effort.[107] Others agreed, as three men approached Claiborne to raise companies from the free men of color, despite local opposition.[108] In the aftermath of the War of 1812 the legislature passed a joint resolution offering their gratitude to the free black units.

Prominent leaders within the free black population welcomed the changeover to U.S. sovereignty. Yet the territorial government strove to secure the loyalty of the Creole populace, which made federal interactions with the free black population highly ambivalent. Consequently, territorial officials pursued a series of different strategies to garner loyalty from the heterogeneous populace. Federal leaders recognized leaders within the free black community and reaffirmed some of their traditional privileges. Free black leaders would be invited to meetings with Claiborne and the free black militia remained in place. At the same time, however, Claiborne's administration regularly played the free black and white communities off of one another in an attempt to quiet opposition by charging one side or the other with creating openings that might upset the political, economic, and social order that rested on slavery. The administration acceded to a series of legislative steps, like the Black Code of 1806 that subordinated free people of color to whites. Yet in the Black Code as in much of the opposition to the free black militia, the most strident advocates for race trumping status came not from U.S. officials but the local white population. The shift toward a more democratic order of free citizens, within which free people of color were a distinct minority, served to curtail opportunities for free blacks rather than expand them. All slaves emancipated after statehood in 1812 had to register; freedmen needed to carry proof of their freedom, and black testimony would no longer be accepted against whites.[109] The legislation impacted free people of color who saw consistent declines as a percentage of the population over the next decades. The Spanish monarchical world of corporate privileges proved far freer in addressing the needs of free blacks than did the United States, as it began to institute its egalitarian republican system. Indeed, as Louisiana turned more democratic, with institutions like a territorial legislature, it became increasingly less free for free people of color. Despite the strictures of the Black Code of 1806 and the many shortcomings for free people of color during the early national period, greater strictures were still to come. It would not be until 1830 that the state legislature barred the immigration of free people of color into the state and required that those who had entered Louisiana since 1825 leave in two months' time. A militia bill in 1834 ended the existence of the battalion of free men of color. The same year the legislature required that owners post a $1,000 bond that any emancipated slave would leave the state in one month's time. The hopes of individuals like Bailly, with their trust in the rhetoric and principles of the American and French revolutions, were dashed on the reality of the new democratic structure erected in Louisiana.

5

Imperial Compromises

Michel Cantrelle of the Acadian Coast personified the colonial elite whose support the territorial government so desperately sought. He served as a commandant under the Spanish, in a Louisiana infantry regiment during the American Revolution that captured Baton Rouge and Mobile, and in the militia. Before his appointment as commandant, his brother-in-law Nicholas Verret held the position, having succeeded Michel's father Jacques Cantrelle.[1] From the settlement of St. James until the Spanish acquisition of Louisiana, Cantrelle's father and his two sons-in-law Verret and Judice controlled the greatest amount of land in the parish, with a large swath along the east bank of the river, as well as property in New Orleans.[2] Cantrelle owned a sugar mill and a lumber mill, that lesser planters could make use of, and in 1809 the Cantrelle family provided the land to erect the Church of St. Michael in St. James.[3] Cantrelle's military experience, his family's tradition of leadership along the coast, and his own economic status secured him a prominent place in the leadership of his region of Louisiana.

In a letter to Jefferson in 1804 General Wilkinson described Cantrelle as "a man universally revered but [who] understands the French and Spanish languages only."[4] He agreed to serve as the commandant and then first county judge for Acadia, which comprised the parishes of Ascension and St. James. Jefferson included Cantrelle's name on a list of five for Claiborne to pick three for the Legislative Council.[5] Despite the confidence U.S. officials placed in him, Cantrelle remained wary. Though the government printed official acts in both English and French, knowledge of English remained essential, since the major legal texts were in English.[6] Claiborne informed Jefferson that despite being a good judge Cantrelle "is very uneasy, lest his proceedings may be marked with some illegality, and the Lawyers may bring him into difficulties; *this fear* extends generally to all the Civil officers, and occasions frequent resignations."[7] Cantrelle turned down the proffered seat on the Legislative Council but still his service as a local appointee demonstrated a level of support for the territorial government.

As a judge Cantrelle scrupulously observed the letter of the law. In 1806 after his son-in-law Anselm Roman was found guilty by a jury for assault and battery, Cantrelle sentenced him to a month in prison and a $500 fine. U.S. officials hailed the case as demonstrating the superiority of the U.S. legal system. As Claiborne informed Jefferson: "It has shown them that Justice is distributed with an impartial hand; It was indeed a novel spectacle to a people, who were lately Spanish subjects, to hear a Judge pronouncing a sentence against the husband of his Daughter."[8] The case raised Cantrelle's profile with the U.S. government in New Orleans and within his parish, though probably not with his son-in-law and one would hope not with his daughter.

The incident with Cantrelle's son-in-law illuminates a number of elements with the governmental transition. Rather than deciding guilt, a task left to a jury under U.S. law, Cantrelle meted out an appropriate punishment. The sentencing perhaps helped him appear impartial in the eyes of people within the parish but more importantly those of U.S. officials observing local officials. Yet the changing nature of Louisiana law and society proved more apparent than real. Shortly after the conviction Claiborne pardoned Anselm Roman.[9] For all the talk about the impartiality of justice, Roman remained the son-in-law of the judge of the parish, an important and trusted U.S. ally. In contrast to the conviction, Claiborne did not laud the pardon in his letters to the president. Territorial government proved to be business as usual, with U.S. officials protecting elite prerogatives. It was not impartiality, honesty, or justice that so pleased U.S. officials in New Orleans but rather the putative acceptance of U.S. law and Cantrelle's scrupulous regard for its forms.

The unwillingness of some former officeholders to follow Cantrelle into U.S. service stemmed in part from problems over technical knowledge of U.S. law and rumors of a Spanish return but also from disappointment with the new method of doing things and concern that old privileges might not be respected. The territorial government established its authority through individuals like Cantrelle, but only because local officials came to understand that federal officials would meet their obligations. Thus U.S. officials continued to respect the privileges of local notables who administered their government, which in certain cases, mandated overturning rulings made in line with U.S. jurisprudence. This hypocrisy was the compliment that necessity paid to ideals. Everyone involved benefited in cases like these: Cantrelle, in the minds of U.S. officials, became trustworthy and a man of integrity, while U.S. officials, in the minds of local elites, garnered much the same reputation.

The implementation of U.S. law and governmental systems in Louisiana as in other areas of the American West did not occur de novo. Often U.S. colonization replaced an earlier Spanish, French, British, or Mexican system (in several cases more than one of these). Attorneys and military officers played essential roles in bringing about new U.S. political and legal systems and establishing stability, but they did not do so in a vacuum. Military officers exercised a key role in assuring loyalty in Louisiana just as they did in the Ohio valley, where a large number of loyalist inhabitants needed to be counteracted with a military presence in order to build nationalist sentiment.[10]

Legal changes after shifts in sovereignty proved more controversial than changes in governmental forms because they had a more immediate impact on individuals' pocketbooks. Americans implemented a written legal code pushed forward in part by incoming judges and attorneys. In addition, federal spending and patronage served in Louisiana as they would elsewhere to win adherents to the federal government.[11] Even so, many imperial powers found it necessary to abide by earlier modes of legal thought in the short term. Britain in the aftermath of the Seven Years' War failed to provide guidance on a legal system for Illinois, and as a result French legal practices persisted under English officers.[12] Both the British and Spanish governments needed to compromise legal methods in order to retain the loyalty of French settlers, as the British learned to their chagrin when settlers abandoned the region for Spanish territory to the west.[13] Americans in their territories likewise depended on earlier legal systems. Governor Meriwether Lewis, the second governor of the Louisiana Territory (Upper Louisiana), had to adapt the law to fit local French practices, thereby creating a mixed legal system rather than forcing locals to adapt to American law.[14]

Similar shifts in law occurred in the territories taken during the Mexican

War, which posed difficulties for Anglo-Americans as well as the descendants of Spaniards and Mexicans. Mormons in Utah represented a far more unified opposition group to U.S. administration as a persecuted religious community. The church remained deeply involved in the development of the region's economy in the 1850s so that it became hard to distinguish private from church capital, and this created further opposition to the church from nonmembers.[15] The United States had to reconstruct Utah's economic and legal system after it gained the territory. Utah offers an interesting contrast with Louisiana in its long territorial period and its failure to reach compromises on legal codes, despite being more ethnically and linguistically similar to the United States. Only with Mormon elites establishing clearer connections to the Republican Party did their prospects for statehood improve. Early in the territory's existence the territorial assembly attempted end runs around U.S. courts by expanding the purview of local probate courts and creating a slew of local officials rather than depending on federal appointees. Given complaints from non-Mormons and more recent arrivals the federal government dispatched new officials with a military show of force. In Utah non-Mormons ("Gentiles") gravitated toward the Liberal Party, which had the backing of federal officials, while Mormons created the People's Party.[16] Given these divisions, but also the disjunction between Utah and the rest of the country, Congress attempted to bring Utah into line by punishing the Mormon practice of polygamy through a series of pieces of legislation.[17] The U.S. ended the Mormon-dominated court system through the Poland Law, which returned the probate courts to their proper sphere and eliminated several local positions. The Supreme Court ruled that Congress could legislate for the territories, and while it could not touch upon religious beliefs it could prosecute actions. The federal response eventually led to territorial legislation, with an 1888 law that prohibited polygamy. In addition, an 1885 Idaho test oath law that disenfranchised Mormons worried the Mormon population within Utah. The federal legislation had an effect, and only with the Church of Latter Day Saints' shift on polygamy did statehood become a possibility.[18] Louisianans, in contrast, despite greater linguistic divides found it easier to find a place within the U.S. system.

Legal transformations could also precede changes in sovereignty, as in the case of Hawaii. Hawaiian chiefs embraced Anglo-American legal forms in order to secure recognition of their sovereignty from foreign powers but also from internal foreign-born critics. Hawaii resembled Asian nations that modernized along western lines in order to avoid colonization and to render invalid arguments of the "mission to civilize." Even while under Hawaiian sovereignty, foreigners figured prominently among the personnel selected to man the new legal system, and their importance grew with the inauguration of private property. The American acquisition of Hawaii appears far more colonial than earlier acquisitions given its overseas status and the legal shifts that preceded sovereignty. Even so, American interactions with natives in Hawaii differed from other powers, since they were premised on assimilation and inclusion through the creation of a uniform legal system, albeit one that weakened chiefly government and native land ownership.[19] Equal justice served to convince locals that a change in sovereignty did not entail domination. As Jack Eblen notes of government during the district stage of territorial government, "When justice was egalitarian, it was a function of expediency rather than of democracy."[20] Equality before the law often came about because it was good politics more than because it was inherently good.

Another consistent challenge nations encountered after a change in sovereignty concerned land disputes. The presence of a population with recognized land rights, though considerably larger in Louisiana, was not novel in the American West. U.S. administrators regularly struggled with pioneers (squatters) who preceded federal surveys.[21] Louisiana, like Illinois, Florida, and the territories taken from Mexico, contained a significant population of landowners who possessed prior claims. At the onset of the American Revolution Kentucky and western lands in the Ohio country experienced land disputes that Virginia and the Continental Congress needed to resolve. The divisions became so contentious that ultimately the military removed squatters.[22] In Illinois contested land claims created fissures between earlier and later inhabitants with many French speakers angered by a 1790 requirement from Arthur St. Clair, the governor of the Northwest Territory, that they prove the validity of their claims, resulting in French families selling to speculators before moving west to Spanish territory.[23] The federal government could appear as a more honest broker in contrast to land-hungry Anglo-Americans who immigrated from the East. This was the case with the French population in Vincennes when it came to both land claims and attempts to regulate the Indian trade.[24] After the British takeover of Florida in the aftermath of the French and Indian War land titles were called into question despite promises to respect previous arrangements. When the United States acquired Florida in 1821, authorities needed to determine the validity of land grants, with similar problems over squatters and securing Indian lands.[25]

In Upper Louisiana land rights were of great importance for locals especially in the context of a new legal code. The land disputes created significant tensions between earlier inhabitants, who received land grants from the Spanish, and later inhabitants with designs on the first group's claims.[26] Unsurprisingly Upper Louisiana encountered difficulties with land titles from Spanish grants, in many cases forged or backdated to establish a better claim. Amos Stoddard, the commandant of the military district of Upper Louisiana, strove to secure local attachment through compromise, particularly on land titles. Despite federal requirements to invalidate claims made between the Treaty of San Ildefonso in 1800 and the purchase treaty and stipulations that claimants occupy and improve the land, most titles would be confirmed to secure local loyalties. Local Creole merchants secured land grants readily, particularly those with connections to Governor Wilkinson of the territory of Louisiana to the north of the Territory of Orleans.[27] In Mississippi a large number of land grants went to individuals with government connections and military officers in the waning days of the Spanish administration, which proved difficult for incoming administrators to sort out. During his tenure as territorial governor of Mississippi, Claiborne backed a program to give titles to residents of multiple years and those who had improved the land, which Congress ultimately confirmed.[28] Claiborne's experience in Mississippi proved useful when it came to these land issues. Indeed, for all the problems of Louisianan land claims, they paled next to those of Mississippi.[29]

Legal and land title changes had to be conducted in a manner to reconcile locals to the United States. Participation in a U.S. legal system that recognized and reassured locals as to their land titles helped to advance the assimilation of foreign-born settlers or, in the case of Utah, Anglo-American settlers. The United States enacted a series of structural changes for Louisiana's society that disrupted local communities and provoked significant opposition to the changeover to U.S. sovereignty. Locals interacted with the federal government from the U.S. postal system to the Bank of the United States in many ways (until 1811), but interaction with these institutions did not result in significant opposition. Rather, the most serious criticism focused on the U.S. system of law, with its use of jury trials and questions over the legitimacy of land titles.

The territorial regime bore the brunt of criticism for the political structure erected after the transfer, but the federal government quickly moved to grant greater representation. Indeed, the local Creole community quickly utilized the language of citizens who wanted to operate within a democratic republic. An anonymous writer calling himself a native in 1804 published a harsh critique of the introduction of U.S. institutions, jurisprudence, and the English language without preparing the locals for participation and entry into public political life.[30] Opposition to the form of government, however, never turned violent, and federal officials for their part did not engage in legal reprisals against their critics. American observers often criticized this soft approach, but Claiborne deemed it the most sensible course. In a letter to Madison he noted the criticism of his administration from Edward Livingston and Daniel Clark: "This clemency or rather *conciliatory justice*, men who are tyrants in principle have called a want of energy: but experience has proved, that, it was a wise policy, for the effects have been, a continuance of good order, and in increase of union in the public sentiment."[31] Criticism of the government as tyrannical would not be overcome by acting in a more vigorous manner.

A conciliatory policy aided by demonstrations of U.S. authority through institutions and services slowly attached local leaders. The territorial government created several institutions within the territory that failed to give rise to serious opposition, in some cases acting contrary to policy out of Washington. Claiborne, after petitions from local citizens, on his own initiative decided to charter the Bank of Louisiana for the development of the province, noting that "I feel some inquietude in sanctioning the Bank establishment, but I am pressed on the occasion by the application of the People, and under existing circumstances, it seems to me my duty required that every thing in my power should be done to conciliate general confidence."[32] Claiborne believed the bank would develop Louisiana's commerce and agriculture, but as he explained to Madison, the prime motive centered on securing more popular support for the new American government.[33] Claiborne hoped to demonstrate Republican and federal concern for the wishes of local residents.

Political leaders in Washington did not see the bank the same way. Treasury Secretary Albert Gallatin found Claiborne's conduct inexcusable, as the Bank of the United States wished to establish a branch in New Orleans.[34] As a Jeffersonian, Claiborne was not a banking enthusiast, but his calculus remained largely political, as he explained to Gallatin: "By opening a new door to pecuniary Speculation, I was able to divert for the moment, the most influential part of the Mercantile interest from within the Pale of Political discontent."[35] Directorships in the bank went to elite figures, several of them New Orleans city council members, thereby winning good will.[36] When making recommendations for appointees, Benjamin Morgan, on the board of the Bank of Louisiana and later president of the New Orleans branch of the Bank of the United States and the Bank of Orleans, wrote: "We have a mixed population of almost all nations & it will require men of integrity & talents to overcome the prejudices of these people & reconcile them to the government of free men."[37] Claiborne recognized his mistake in administration eyes but asserted that repeal would lead to more acrimony.[38] Claiborne hoped that the bank would simply disappear due to a lack of subscribers, freeing him from criticism in Washington.[39] The president believed the charter needed to be suspended, as Congress provided for a branch of the Bank of the United States, and consequently no other charters could be authorized.[40] Territorial government birthed a series of ironies, with Jeffersonians like Claiborne chartering banks and Republicans at the national level defending the prerogatives of the Bank of the United States.

For local political reasons Claiborne did not want to suspend the charter.[41] The subscription problem did not pose quite the obstacle the governor imagined, as Anglo-American investors, several of them his critics like Livingston, Jones, and Clark, bought stock.[42] Thus, despite, and in some quarters because of, the central government's dictates there continued to be support for the bank. As Claiborne wrote to the secretary of state, "My own doubts as to the Validity of the *Charter* are known, as is *also* the opinion of Some of the Officers of Government, that *it* was in itself a Nullity: But many Citizens seem nevertheless determined to adventure."[43] Ultimately, the bank sold enough stock and proved both popular and successful even with the doubts over its charter.[44] James Brown, a frequent Claiborne critic, likewise supported the creation of a bank.[45] Not only did the bank persevere, but in Claiborne's speech to the legislature in 1811 he spoke of sentiment for more banks, which led to the incorporation of the Bank of Orleans and the Planters' Bank.[46] The banks became valuable institutions in providing credit and securing deposits but also demonstrated the advantages of the territorial government. The Bank of Louisiana was not a huge financial success, but it served a valuable political purpose.[47] During the War of 1812 the absence of ready money and competition between the boards of the banks created a run, as recounted by Vincent Nolte, who served on a five-man commission to examine the solvency of the financial institutions.[48] Territorial government worked to create institutions popular within Louisiana, especially for Louisiana's elites, and, in the case of banks, implemented despite opposition from Washington.

U.S. officials also strove to improve sanitation conditions, which they believed had been ignored by the Spanish. Infrastructure and disease control ranked high among complaints of James Pitot, who ascribed these failures to Spanish negligence. It was not naturally unhealthy in his view, but only the concentration of population in New Orleans that posed the problem. Pitot noted that "an active government, benevolent and enlightened, would have soon eliminated it; and surveys, landfills, and, of course, drainage, would generally provide in healthfulness of the area compensation for what other colonial countries freely provide under similar conditions."[49] New Orleans suffered its first major yellow fever epidemic under the Spanish in 1796, but from that point on smaller outbreaks occurred almost every summer and early fall. Incoming Americans and Europeans from outside the Caribbean were most likely to contract the illness. The disease proved disruptive to public health and order, but all the more so for U.S. officials attempting to establish a new territorial government.

The unhealthiness of the climate in Louisiana represented a perennial source of complaint. Before the Louisiana Purchase, U.S. consuls in the city used federal funds to pay for medical care for infected American sailors, and Claiborne wanted this practice to continue.[50] New Orleans Charity Hospital had been found insufficient to meet the needs of American seamen, with the federal government paying seventy-five cents a day for each patient admitted; consequently U.S. consul Daniel Clark recommended, and Secretary of the Treasury Albert Gallatin considered, the establishment of a federal hospital for American seamen.[51] In his letter to Jefferson Clark included remarks from Dr. William Barnwell, who noted the shortcomings of both local conditions and doctors.[52] Despite these recommendations for a federal maritime hospital, throughout the territorial period Charity Hospital continued to treat American sailors.

In 1804 and 1811 New Orleans suffered from major yellow fever outbreaks. At the beginning of 1804 Claiborne wrote to President Jefferson speculating that the summer would bring worse conditions for new arrivals.[53] During the summer of 1804, yellow fever significantly impeded the administration and establishment of government in the territory. Claiborne informed Madison in July of 1804 that he needed to reduce hours and hire additional clerks, as his staff and private secretary had fallen ill.[54] Three weeks later, the collector of the port, Hore Browse Trist, reported to Madison that Claiborne could not leave his bed due to his contracting a fever.[55] A month later Claiborne's private secretary, Joseph Briggs, wrote to Madison about the governor and Mrs. Claiborne's ill health as well as the health of Mr. Trist but noted: "The City is generally free from disease. There have been it is true a number of Deaths but they were principally confined to Americans."[56] Briggs's optimism proved misplaced; both he and Trist would be dead from the fever less than a month later, along with many recent arrivals such as John Gelston of New York and Benjamin West of Philadelphia.[57] As the fever began to dissipate by September, Claiborne reported five to eight deaths a day and observed that U.S. troops dispatched into the countryside fared better than in the city.[58]

The ill health of troops could weaken the U.S. image in the minds of the local populace, an important perception at the outset of the transfer. In January of 1804 Wilkinson wrote to Secretary of War Henry Dearborn of sickness among his troops and the consequent failure to impress locals: "Every hour evinces more & more the necessity of a strong Garrison here, with a Military executive Magistrate for the Government of this province— our puny force has become a subject for ridicule, and the old women begin to exclaim 'quel triste governement.'"[59] The potential for internal problems from locals required a U.S. presence at New Orleans and in southern Louisiana that consistently endangered the lives of U.S. troops during the summer and fall.

Sickness in New Orleans diminished the American capability of meeting an outside threat elsewhere in the northern and western frontiers of Louisiana that bordered Spanish Texas. In 1804 as Edward Turner, the commandant at Natchitoches, warned of a potential Spanish attack, Claiborne denied him requested reinforcements because of the already reduced capacity of U.S. troops at New Orleans due to fever.[60] The Spanish presence in West Florida, concerns over local discontent, and potential slave revolts necessitated the presence of forces within the city, but urban areas concentrated the health risks of communicable diseases.

By September of 1804 many American had left the city.[61] The disease debilitated the U.S. presence and exacerbated local fears of a slave rebellion. In order to contain the threat, Claiborne increased patrols, alerted both the militia and the army, and made plans to distribute muskets to free white citizens within the city.[62] While the rebellion never emerged, the fever took a toll, particularly on the governor's family with the death of his wife, Elizabeth, daughter Cornelia, and his brother-in-law. Claiborne wrote to Madison: "My misfortunes have been uncommonly great; to lose on the same Day my whole family was indeed a heavy affliction—But my God willed it, and I must submit with fortitude and resignation."[63] The fever significantly impeded the establishment of American law and governance, with many officials delaying entry until the weather cooled.[64] James Brown slowed his entry into the city, as did Legislative Council member William Wykoff.[65] Governor Claiborne allowed for these delays, even as he regretted the absence of two territorial judges.[66] The delays helped forge better ties between incoming American migrants and locals outside the city, since many gentlemen willingly housed incoming U.S. officials until the fever abated.[67] Claiborne estimated in October of 1804 that over a third of the Americans who arrived in the last year had died.[68] The fever increased expenses for the governor both for medical care and hiring additional clerks.[69] Poor health is a perennial justification for resignation, but it had added credence within Louisiana.[70]

After their first experience with yellow fever, U.S. officials enacted formal and informal changes. In order to formulate and implement preventive measures Mayor James Pitot suggested and Claiborne created a five-man board of health for New Orleans.[71] Death rates among new arrivals without local connections became so prevalent that Claiborne changed the estate laws in response to the frequent embezzlements that occurred, appointing an officer to take charge of the estates of those deceased intestate in New Orleans who resided less than two years within the city.[72] In addition, Claiborne expressed a renewed interest in Jefferson's checkerboard pattern for the city, which proposed open spaces or parks between residential zones.[73] Regardless of the governor's interest, the city government undertook limited sanitation efforts, such as filling in some of the ditches around New Orleans, but they never adopted Jefferson's schema for city planning.[74]

Informally recent arrivals left for the country during summer months in years after 1804, and officials strove to place U.S. troops in healthier sites, with varying results. The following year, the new territory secretary John Graham noted on his arrival: "I was told by the Physicians that it would be extremely imprudent in me to remain in Town, coming here as I did, at this advanced season of the year, from a Northern climate."[75] Despite this knowledge and precautions American officials continued to contract the illness, with Judge Prevost becoming ill that year.[76] Claiborne made it a regular practice to journey outside the city every year after 1804 during the summer partially for reasons of health, though he also needed to visit the parishes to observe local conditions and appointees.[77] Claiborne's second wife, Clarisse Duralde, came from Attakapas and Opelousas, which he visited on one of these trips. By 1811 Claiborne wrote of both purposes, health and visiting the interior, and he advised newcomers to avoid the city during the summer.[78]

Despite efforts at prevention every year from summer to fall cases of the fever occurred, and New Orleans required a contingent of troops regardless of disease. In 1805 Claiborne called for reinforcements, noting to Madison that "I never was an Advocate for a Standing Army; I wish to God it could be dispensed with in this Territory;—But the present state of things will not justify a reduction. Our troops here are few in number,—greatly reduced by sickness."[79] In 1806 Claiborne reported that 60 of the 280 men, including officers, within the city were sick.[80]

When tensions rose with Britain in 1809 the government dispatched more troops to New Orleans, raising their numbers to around two thousand, but introducing more forces from outside the region increased chances for infection and the spread of the disease. Given the pattern already observed by U.S. officials and the fact that one-fourth of the force had taken ill, Secretary of War William Eustis directed General Wilkinson to remove the majority of troops from New Orleans during the summer and autumn to either Fort Adams or Natchez, while leaving a garrison of the old troops in New Orleans.[81] Wilkinson felt that troops needed to be near New Orleans in case of a threat but wanted them to stay out of the city proper. He also required naval transports to get his men to Fort Adams, since they could not march through Spanish West Florida. Consequently, he left 150 men in the city, while he took the rest to a site at Terre aux Bœufs, which he believed to be healthier.[82] Finding a healthy location could prove difficult, as Claiborne acknowledged, but he concurred in thinking the area well situated for guarding New Orleans.[83] Others, such as Alfred Thruston, the surgeon of the Seventh Infantry, believed the site was as healthy as could be found around New Orleans.[84]

The site, some four leagues below the city, turned out to be anything but healthy. The presence of mosquitos proved a constant irritant. At the time of the move south in June somewhere between a fourth and a third of the troops were sick, and they then had to dig drainage ditches, clear the land, and construct a hospital and camp. Troops contracted scurvy, dysentery, and fevers and bilious illnesses that resembled yellow fever. The situation worsened due to shortages of medicine and provisions. By July a number of officers signed a petition requesting that Wilkinson move the army.[85] The same month Claiborne optimistically reported to Secretary of State Robert Smith dismissing rumors of widespread sickness: "You may be assured, they are greatly exaggerated.—This climate is, in truth, unfavorable to strangers, and it could not have been expected, that the troops would have been exempt from the diseases common to the Country.—The number of deaths have been considerable, and the sick List is not unusually numerous."[86] The effects of the fevers had become a commonplace occurrence over five years to many Americans, but the death rate among Wilkinson's force proved inordinately high.

Wilkinson received Eustis's orders on June 19, but two months later the force remained at Terre aux Bœufs, despite a second order from Eustis that provided for the naval transport.[87] It would not be until September 1 that the troops made serious preparations for the journey to Fort Adams, which occurred between the seventh and eighteenth of that month.[88] A year later Eustis acknowledged that by the time Wilkinson received definitive instructions it came too late, as the sickness had already spread, and the navy suffered as well, hampering transportation, but the secretary could not understand the shortages of medical supplies and provisions.[89]

Ultimately, 764 troops died and another 166 deserted.[90] The House of Representatives committee that inquired into the case identified multiple causes: the newness of the levies, the climate, the selection of the camp, Wilkinson's failure to follow orders, problems with supplying the troops, the strenuous work the soldiers undertook to create a camp, the absence of mosquito nets, and shortcomings in sanitation and proper medical facilities.[91] Given the high death toll Wade Hampton replaced Wilkinson, and a general court-martial considered charges of neglect of duty in 1811, but Wilkinson was found not guilty. Deposed officers in the House committee investigation varied on whether the troops should have remained near New Orleans given local conditions and the military utility of the position.[92] Wilkinson's second in command at the time, Colonel Alexander Parker, however, detected no threats from local citizens.[93] Changing estimations of local sentiment allowed for a less significant military presence within the city. Parker also believed higher ground around Washington, Mississippi, made more sense from a military point of view than the camp below New Orleans. Dr. Alexander Macauley in his deposition testified that he believed Terre aux Bœufs to be healthier than New Orleans, but also that "many of those who are enlisted are of debauched habits, and weakened constitutions, and that such constitutions are little able to resist the violent attacks of the diseases on the Lower Mississippi, where the most robust habits so frequently sink."[94] Many doctors of the time attributed deaths from fever to moral shortcomings.

Despite efforts at both avoidance and better medical practices in 1811, there was another major outbreak of yellow fever. Mayor James Mather reported 210 deaths from the Protestant and Catholic churches as well as Charity Hospital and noted that a French physician downplayed any current contagion: "That these fevers become dangerous in Certain individuals from their mode of living, the fears which they entertain of the Malignancy of the disease, then from the mode of Curing the same which is attempted by Strong and irritating medicines."[95] For September the death toll was 262.[96] Claiborne reported to Madison on the higher mortality rate of new arrivals, and Mather suggested that Congress should assist the hospital, as so many of the patients were recent American arrivals or discharged soldiers and sailors.[97]

Once the fever season passed, well-meaning reformers emerged with their recommendations. With the death of his second wife, Clarisse, from yellow fever in 1809 Claiborne once again turned to Jefferson's ideas on city planning: "I have no doubt, but your opinions as to the precautions necessary, to prevent the prevalence of *Yellow Fever* in New-Orleans will have great weight with the Legislature, nor is there any thing I more desire, than to see all such precautions immediately resorted to. That dreadful *Malady* has made a great inroad upon my happiness—My beloved Companion fell its victim."[98] Jefferson's plans made eminent sense, given what most individuals observed about yellow fever, but they would have been prohibitively expensive. While the plan would have put more space between the infected, it also may have created more space conducive to mosquitos. In contesting Edward Livingston's claim in the batture case, petitioning citizens asserted: "Disease generally generates on the water side where this is much matter for putrefecation and if a considerable space is not left between the buildings and the water's edge (as is now the case) for the free circulation of air New Orleans will probably be often visited by that dreadful scourge The Yellow fever."[99] Locals used arguments over putrefaction to far better effect in stopping construction that they did not approve of than in tearing down established sites, or supporting new construction. During the 1811 outbreak Claiborne cautioned Secretary of the Navy Paul Hamilton that new arrivals tended to fall victims of yellow fever.[100] The naval forces at New Orleans that year suffered enough losses to necessitate their removal to the Bay St. Louis.[101] In light of these losses, in recommending two young men as second lieutenants for the Marine Corps, Claiborne requested they be stationed at New Orleans since as locals they were acclimated.[102] In November of 1811 the physicians and surgeons of New Orleans petitioned Congress for a change in burial practices and hospital placement.[103] These arguments, based as was Jefferson's on a belief in vapors from the sick, however well-meaning would prove too expensive to implement.

The postal service also demonstrated the federal government's utility to local citizens. Yet it became a herculean effort to erect and sustain the enterprise, particularly in finding and retaining quality personnel. Mail service proved unreliable due to the geographic and weather conditions in frontier regions but also due to violence. Isaac Briggs noted before the cession that between Mississippi and Louisiana, "The mail has, in some measure, become an uncertain channel of communication between these Southwestern Territories and the general Government."[104] As Claiborne possessed greater awareness of local conditions, Postmaster General Gideon Granger often solicited advice on appointments and routes, and in at least one case simply included blank commissions for Claiborne to disperse as he saw fit.[105] In typical fashion, at one point the blanks failed to arrive.[106] Mail delays, interruptions, and outright incompetence in the post office proved constant sources of complaint.[107] In 1806 New Orleans merchants petitioned for better mail service, which they relied on as commercial intercourse with the United States grew.[108] In response the postmaster general apologized, promised more regular service, and acknowledged mistakes in past personnel decisions.[109]

U.S. officials attempted other reforms. For instance, officials regularly commented on a public-school system, but action remained limited. Spanish funding for education generally fell short of even the limited expectations of Americans of the early nineteenth century. Both Claiborne and Clark noted that the Spanish Crown funded just one school, and that for elite pupils.[110] In 1805 John Watkins urged Claiborne to turn the public school building, currently inhabited by Colonel Freeman, back to educational purposes.[111] John Watkins, the mayor of New Orleans, similarly argued for the importance of the nation's youth and the need to educate them in principles of self-government.[112] American observers criticized Spanish educational efforts, which they tended to connect with locals' fidelity to the worst elements of monarchism and Catholicism: "I fear that if education be left entirely to the patronage of the inhabitants, it will continue to be neglected."[113] In 1805 the Legislative Council provided legislation for a University of Orleans, to be funded by proceeds from a lottery. The legislation remained unimplemented, and while territorial officials encouraged parishes to establish schools, they failed to provide funding.[114] There would be repeated pleas for aid for public education from the federal government from the territorial House of Representatives, the Legislative Council, and the regents of the University of Orleans.[115] Despite these efforts education proved to be a better rhetorical weapon to attack Spanish government and local inhabitants than a real U.S. priority.

In banking, postal service, health and sanitation, and education, the territorial government attempted to meet local needs, however haphazardly. In other cases, however, U.S. policy brought about opposition. Trade restrictions, such as Jefferson's embargo in 1807, retarded Louisiana's economic development and gave rise to numerous complaints.[116] Theoretically these embargoes should have triggered greater opposition, but Louisianans' perennial talent for smuggling made federal policy in this realm less damaging.[117]

The shift to the U.S. system of common law and juries represented a significant break from the previous system of justice. The Spanish system invested judicial authority in local commandants, with an appeals process that ended with the governor-general. Before Congress established courts, citizens pressed the governor to exercise judicial functions, and at times he acceded.[118] Governor Claiborne assumed that local inhabitants welcomed a change to a society in which the judiciary would represent a separate impartial branch.[119] The first courts created by the governor met with opposition due to unfamiliarity with the jury system and U.S. law. A persistent problem became finding appointees with knowledge of U.S. law, as Claiborne noted: "Ignorant of Law, and unaccustomed to it's forms, these Gentlemen may have been often betrayed into little Irregularities, and sometimes perplexed, by jarring Sentiments of Right or by Indecision."[120] While English was necessary for the theory and application of law, judges needed fluency in Spanish and French to communicate with plaintiffs, defendants, witnesses, and juries, as James Brown noted shortly after his arrival in Louisiana.[121] The assumption of U.S. officials that the jury system mirrored the political change from rule by the few to the governance of fellow citizens failed to garner wide respect: "Some of the oldest and most respectable Inhabitants of this Territory are of opinion, that in Civil Cases the Trial by Jury, will at first be unpopular, and I have heard this reason assigned, 'That Men who have long appealed for Justice to great Personages, whom they looked up to as wise and learned, cannot at first, without reluctance, submit to the decrees of Men, no better than themselves.' . . . In criminal cases on the contrary, the Trial by Jury (it is thought) will be extremely acceptable."[122] Criminal trials had higher stakes, so juries might assuage fears of abuse of power (local elites of course felt they could be trusted to rule against the guilty). In civil cases, however, juries added to the expense and trouble of trials, placing a burden on local citizens. Daniel Clark judged the local populace incapable of serving on juries and asserted that "Americans ought for some time to be the only Jurors with now & then the admission of a Creole by way of explaining to him the nature of the subject."[123] The lack of familiarity with the system, the added expense of jury trials, and the foreign nature of many of the appointees upset local sensibilities. As a result, U.S. officials searched for positive signs. Claiborne took the long view that over time jury trials would gain acceptance.[124] The judicial system erected by the Americans raised a series of concerns, but because U.S. officials worried over the competence of local judges, they added another irritation by turning to a large number of Anglo-American judges.

In 1804 Congress organized the territory of Orleans and established a three-judge Superior Court, while lesser courts and justices were left to the discretion of the territorial legislature. Criminal cases, but not civil cases, would be jury trials and the territory's inhabitants accorded the protection of habeas corpus; white men who had lived for a year within the territory qualified as jurors.[125] Despite the new courts, the U.S. legal system displeased locals. As Claiborne acknowledged to the president after a visit to Acadia: "Wherever I go, I find the Judicial System of the Territory objected to; during the last week a County Court was holden in this vicinity; It was attended (for the first time) by two Lawyers, and their presence excited among the people much uneasiness;—they are considered as the harbingers of many vexatious Law-suits & seem really to be much feared by the old Inhabitants."[126] The unfamiliarity of locals with the new judicial system meant that Louisiana quickly became a magnet for U.S. attorneys, with whom locals lacked a substantive connection.

In 1806 Claiborne stayed at the German Coast home of Judge Achille Trouard. He believed the Parisian-born judge to be an advocate of American law and wrote to President Jefferson: "He, alike with his guests, professed to be admirers of the principles of our Government, but were of opinion that the American Judiciary was not adapted to the present state of the Territory; they thought the Trial by Jury, was not desirable, and complained most heavily of the conduct of the Lawyers." Trouard, though not a Creole, had married into the local populace and gauged local resistance to the U.S. system to be substantial. Judges like Trouard and Cantrelle supported the territorial administration; they were U.S. appointees, yet they remained cognizant of the failures of the U.S. legal system in the parishes. What was immediately clear to local officials gradually became clear to federal officials, that the U.S. system of jurisprudence was not widely accepted by the local populace. In the same letter to Jefferson, Claiborne made sure to note the presence and success of two Anglo-American sugar planters in Louisiana, Richard Butler from the Mississippi Territory and James Brown from Kentucky.[127] U.S. officials hoped newly arrived Anglo-Americans would help to change the character of the country. Ultimately the Americans conceded to local demands with the Civil Law Digest of 1808, which supplanted the common law system. Claiborne in a letter to William Wykoff Jr. of West Baton Rouge wrote that while he wished Louisiana brought into line with American law and that native-born Americans would resent the change, "Educated in the belief of the *excellencies* of the civil law, the Louisianans have hitherto been unwilling to part with them, and while we feel ourselves to the force of habit and prejudice, we should not be surprised at the attachment which the old inhabitants manifest for many of their former customs and local institutions."[128] This concession on the civil law speaks to American practicality and both the limits and strengths of American imperialism.

Disputes raised by U.S. land policy proved familiar to Claiborne, as he had encountered these issues as the territorial governor of Mississippi.[129] In Mississippi dates on land grants often could not be trusted given the collusion between Spanish officials and local inhabitants before the period of American control.[130] Indeed, the men who benefited from such corruption often freely admitted it, and Claiborne did not wish to pursue a legislative solution due to fear of political fallout. Instead he and others endorsed a judicial solution by creating a Court of Chancery.[131] Struggles with speculators in Natchez reached a point where Claiborne feared violence, even his own assassination.[132] Louisiana's new government encountered the same problem of a Spanish government that had been lavish in land grants in the waning days of its sovereignty.[133]

While still in Natchez Claiborne received reports of the misconduct of Louisiana officials in making specious land claims.[134] He inquired of then U.S. consul at New Orleans, Daniel Clark, over how land sales in Louisiana operated and what powers the commandants had in the matter.[135] Clark confirmed the presence of a land office in New Orleans but noted that it engaged primarily in selling West Florida lands and that commandants could grant land but only with the government's approval.[136] After Clark's response Claiborne wrote that he received reports that a local commandant, Captain Joseph Vidal, engaged in granting lands and permission for surveys despite the absence of any authority.[137] Several Spanish officials and speculators who saw the writing on the wall with the transfer to France and then the United States made grants to themselves, their families and friends, while the Spanish policy of selling land in West Florida became particularly contentious.[138]

The U.S. Congress in the initial legislation that set up the territorial government declared null and void any land sales made by the Spanish government between the Treaty of San Ildefonso, which transferred the territory to France, and the purchase treaty. Congress, however, made exceptions for settlers and their families who inhabited lands granted during this period, though only up to a square mile with lesser amounts for dependents. It also authorized the military to remove squatters.[139] Congress validated land claims if made in the period prior to October 1, 1800, but only for adult individuals whose name was on the title; the individual needed to have lived on and improved the land, and thus only one tract, not multiple, could be legitimized.[140]

In the absence of clear title, commissioners decided cases. In order to assess these land claims the federal government set up two land districts for the territory of Orleans.[141] The land commissioners appointed then reported their findings to Congress. The Treasury Department appointed John Gurley as the land commissioner and split the territory into eastern and western districts, with New Orleans and the parishes along the Mississippi and Lafourche as the eastern district and the parishes along the Red and Ouachita Rivers and Attakapas and Opelousas as the western district.[142] Federal legislation had the added benefit of allowing territorial officials to dodge tough decisions that might alienate locals. As Claiborne became aware of the coming legislation, he advised Henry Hopkins, the commandant of Attakapas and Opelousas, not to have the surveyor oversee a contested tract of land.[143] Claiborne welcomed federal legislation on land grants, which he hoped would proceed quickly, while also noting that the situation currently benefited speculators.[144]

The Spanish system of granting land titles never was enforced particularly strenuously. Pierre Louis Berquin-Duvallon in his survey of Louisiana before the purchase wrote: "But perhaps not one quarter of the lands granted in Louisiana are held by complete titles; and of the remainder a considerable part depends upon a written permission of a commandant. Not a small portion is held by occupancy, with a single verbal permission of the officer just mentioned."[145] Major Amos Stoddard, who served as the French commandant for Upper Louisiana and continued in the position for the U.S. in 1804 at the time of the transfer, reported that the Spanish made a number of large land grants after officials learned of the territory's transfer to France and explained that many individuals possessed claims that had yet to be recorded. Stoddard noted many such claims in the frontier regions of Attakapas, Opelousas, and Ouachita.[146] The legislation, however well intentioned, could not be implemented in the territory in a strict fashion without alienating landholders; U.S. officials quickly recognized this, resulting in many exceptions to the law.

In late 1805 Claiborne journeyed to Attakapas and Opelousas to deal with factional divisions that the local judge failed to ease and with complaints over the new land policy. Claiborne instructed Hopkins to inform local inhabitants: "The honest claimant of lands has nothing to fear by the act of Congress, requiring an exhibition of their Titles, but on the contrary, that their claims will be liberally confirmed according to the equity of their situation and not to rigorous law."[147] By placing decisions in the hands of federal land commissioners who reported ultimately to the Treasury Department and Congress, the territorial government could for the most part remove itself from the process. Claiborne believed his visit to the area helped assuage worries over land rights and other issues.[148] His efforts made headway, but there was still reason for complaint in Attakapas over American lawyers and the judicial system that might lead to out-migration to Spanish territory, as Claiborne informed Jefferson.[149] Due to internal divisions, Attakapas contained dissidents, but land and legal changes brought about by the United States caused still greater local dissatisfaction.

Immigrants who arrived to speculate in western lands posed a difficulty for the U.S. territorial government. Claiborne sympathized with older Francophone inhabitants, writing to Secretary of State Madison that "among the Emigrants to this Territory there is a description of people which I consider the greatest pests than (that) can afflict any honest society. They are those avaricious Speculators who go about with a little ready Cash to seek whom they may devour. Some of these hungry Parasites have, I am told fattened on the labors of these ancient Louisianans who have and are about to emigrate to the Trinity."[150] Claiborne, though not explicitly, likely referred here to Casa Calvo and Edward Murphy; Murphy was a Natchitoches local who served as an agent for Spain.[151] The Anglo-American immigration served to push some Creole citizens out of the western portions of Louisiana as older inhabitants considered immigration after choosing to sell to new arrivals.

The influx of attorneys and speculators did nothing to win adherents to the American territorial regime. Indeed, despite coming from the United States they actively calumniated the territorial government.[152] U.S. attorneys came in for a lot of blame, as newcomers who understood the new legal system better than locals and who prospered in buying land.[153] The widely traveled German commercial agent Vincent Nolte, who first arrived in New Orleans in 1806 and then returned just before the War of 1812, wrote of a clear declension in morals and society that he ascribed to American politics, but also attorneys: "The lawyers who came thither from the northern states, and whose interest it was to stir up litigation to keep themselves from starving, had, by a certain acquaintance with the technicalities of American jurisprudence, and by a spirit of low cunning and adroitness which they introduced and even managed to communicate to some of the old inhabitants, been the real cause of this moral retrogression."[154] The speculators' arrival, in combination with lawyers, exacerbated unease over the new rule set.

The local population resented the congressional land requirements. In an 1805 memorial the territorial House of Representatives complained about many issues, but land claims featured prominently. Unsurprisingly, the legislators wanted titles upheld regardless of habitation or improvement. They also opposed stipulations that land grants after 1800 not be legitimated. After explaining the Spanish practice in Louisiana that grants, once given, were rarely taken back by the Crown even when obligations went unfulfilled, the legislators asserted that it would be grossly unfair for Congress to deny citizens title on the basis ex post facto rules.[155] James Brown quickly picked up on the local anger. He reported to Madison: "The enemies of the Government are already actively engaged in disseminating the alarming idea, that the titles are to be discussed and scrutinized with the utmost rigor, and that few will bear the severe test to which the Commissioners and the Land law will subject them; whilst some of the well meaning, but weak friends, of the Administration, are so indiscreet as to exult at the prospect of the wealth which the United States will derive from the defects to be detected in the Titles of the Ancient Inhabitants."[156] Brown did not believe the Spanish made that many controversial grants, excepting only West Florida grants and two in Ouachita to Barton de Bastrop and Daniel Clark.[157] Brown saw the land commissioners as a source of discord, and it became yet another arrow in his quill to undermine Claiborne privately to cabinet members and publicly to rile up local opposition.

Given the discontent, territorial officials proved adept at bending and in some cases ignoring the finer points of congressional land policy. As Claiborne wrote to President Jefferson, he did not want the law strictly enforced lest it alienate the local population: "Assurances which will be given by the Officers of Government, that no injustice will be done them, but on the contrary, that their rights will be liberally confirmed, according to the equity of their cases, and not to rigorous Law, will serve to appease anxiety and to ensure general confidence."[158] Claiborne used the same phrasing when communicating to John Gurley, that claims not be based on "rigorous law."[159]

Locals hoped that greater leeway might be granted, particularly for preemption rights for owners along the Mississippi for backlands that local inhabitants took cypress from, but that the Spanish failed to include in titles because such lands frequently were swamps of little use to anyone but the landholder. If these lands failed to be secured by locals they might be purchased by speculators and then resold. By giving preemption rights the U.S. government could gain a reputation for fair dealing among locals that would attach them to their new nation.[160] Common local practice mandated changes in federal land policy.[161]

Levi Lincoln, the attorney general, maintained that land without a legitimate title belonged to the U.S. government, with the burden on the private claimant.[162] Even so, U.S. officials chose to focus on the worst perpetrators of land fraud. Within Ouachita the Baron de Bastrop received two large land grants from the Spanish, one in 1796 for twelve square leagues along the Ouachita River on the condition that Bastrop bring in five hundred families.[163] Claiborne noted that despite failing to bring in the number of families promised, Bastrop and others continued to insist on the grant's validity.[164] In 1804 the Superior Court of the territory ruled against Bastrop's claim and ordered his property seized.[165] By this point, however, Bastrop had sold the land to other parties, much of it to Moorhouse, Lynch, and Livingston, all prominent citizens, through a land agent, Allan B. Magruder. Either because of doubts as to the original grant, the fact that Magruder later was dismissed, or because some of the buyers were political opponents, Claiborne ordered a further investigation of the legality of the Bastrop grants. He feared Daniel Clark might take these claims to Congress.[166] Claiborne wanted it well known that Lynch, Livingston, and Moorhouse had purchased rights to a fraudulent grant, to discourage other purchasers but also to discredit political rivals.[167] Concordia in northern Louisiana proved another troublesome spot for fraudulent claims. Claiborne in his correspondence to Madison focused on grants made after the cession to the United States by Captain Vidal of Concordia. Despite not acting to overturn every illegitimate claim, Claiborne still found himself criticized by speculators.[168] The most flagrant cases tended to get the most attention, even though many lesser holdings also were legally specious.

Federal officials in Washington understood the need to confirm smaller holdings. Secretary of the Treasury Gallatin focused particularly on claims made after 1800.[169] The political dimension of the problem did not escape him; Gallatin wanted most of the grants confirmed. He asserted that Congress clearly did not want to focus on land claims previous to 1800, and in other cases it would act on the commissioners' recommendations, since claims dated after that needed to be filed with the registrar and if title could not be confirmed, local inhabitants would have recourse to the courts. Gallatin wanted Gurley to understand that land seizures needed to be rare, while those that fell on newcomers who arrived after 1800 would be less contentious.

The national government proved responsive to complaints from Louisianans. When Senator Thomas Worthington requested input from Gallatin on a House bill dealing with land acts in Louisiana and Orleans, Gallatin found many of the measures reasonable, including allowing the commissioners' judgments to be final for smaller claims, and went on to recommend that landowners be given concessions for untillable swamp lands next to their claims. Other provisions, however, Gallatin found problematic. He pointed particularly to wording that Spanish and French claims if valid would be approved, disregarding the earlier legislation over timing and settlement. He then laid out what he perceived as the clear difference in Spanish and U.S. land policy: "The fact is that that Government had no fixed principle but favoritism. Land was often taken away if not settled and given to greater favorites; and very often the condition was not enforced."[170] Of course there were speculators, but Gallatin's approach in theory bene-fited the yeoman farmer. When Congress passed clauses that allowed claims to be decided upon Spanish laws and usage, Gallatin recommended that instructions should be given for the attorney general to examine the va-lidity of land claims. In a letter to the president, Gallatin noted that if the land commissioners began to operate soon, it would lessen local discontent fomented by uncertainty.[171] Gallatin then wrote to Gurley, John Thomp-son, and other commissioners, noting the positive aspects of the bill that would allow them to settle on most claims but also that "every doubtful case should receive the most serious investigation before it is confirmed."[172] The strict legal requirements could be used to appropriate a great deal of property, but Gallatin as the figure in control of this process in Washington, Gurley the official on the ground, and Claiborne the local territorial leader, wanted small landholders to retain their property.

Land commissioner John W. Gurley grasped the political dimension; he published and then republished the act.[173] He sought Claiborne's advice on implementing the measure and made clear that he understood that "indeed there can be no doubt that this law is regarded by the enemies of ye Gov-ernment as a powerful engine by which to excite discontent in this Terri-tory. Already it is represented as intended to rob the people of their rights to destroy the equitable titles which exist in the Country and finally to be-come instrument of the most vexatious oppression."[174] In order to combat these sentiments Gurley proposed that he journey into the counties to re-assure the local populace about the law. A number of applicants sought po-sitions as land commissioners, but John Thompson, an appointed registrar of the land office, communicated problems over both appointments and retention to Gallatin.[175] Many federal appointments tended to go to Anglo-Americans, which afforded the individuals appointed with an entrée into local politics. James Brown similarly noted the problem of retaining a sur-veyor from the land office, Benjamin Porter.[176] Porter became the attorney for Opelousas and went on to be a representative in the state legislature.[177] Allan B. Magruder, who acted as agent for the Bastrop sale, originally of

Kentucky, was appointed in 1805 to the same surveyor position.[178] Philip Grymes, Judge Joshua Lewis, and Secretary Thomas Robertson complained to Gallatin on the time-consuming difficulties of serving as commissioners, with one claim at times taking several days.[179] In 1806 John Thompson resigned to return to Kentucky. He noted ill health and private business that necessitated his resignation. Though he felt his own conduct corrected many misapprehensions, he observed "the Inhabitants of this Part of the Country much prejudiced against the Character of the Americans, and disaffected to the Government of the United States."[180] Thompson discerned anti-American sentiment, but as a land commissioner his unpopularity may have had as much to do with his conscientiously doing his job as his national origin, since others in the same line tended to do well economically or politically. Thompson, despite his intentions, did not leave. He secured an appointment to the Superior Court, where he served until his suicide in 1810. Though there were difficulties in retention, there was always a pool of further potential appointees; a number of patronage seekers attempted to secure the positions Magruder and Porter had held.[181]

The land office appointed several local leaders as deputy registrars, reassuring the local population that the process was not simply a land grab. In recommending Trouard and Cantrelle to Gallatin, Gurley wrote: "I can only say that they have exercised the office of the Judges in their respective Counties under the American Government, that they are antient inhabitants and highly respected in their districts." In the same letter Gurley wrote that he hoped to avoid appointing a deputy within the German Coast because of its proximity to New Orleans but the locals desired one.[182] Gurley went out of his way to coordinate his approach with the lone commissioner of the Opelousas board at the time, Colonel John Thompson.[183] Locals desired to have property assessed by one of their neighbors, whom they knew and could be counted upon to give them greater leeway on an assessment.

Perhaps because of these local appointments and the offices that outsiders at times then moved onto, the Department of the Treasury found several of the commissioners, particularly within the western district, lapse in following federal instructions. Gallatin in his letter to the Boards of Commissioners in 1811 clearly indicated his disapproval: "You have adopted some rules not sufficiently strict, & calculated to confirm many unfounded claims."[184] Gallatin wrote to three of the commissioners stressing that settlement was the sine qua non for attaining title and that titles be limited to less than 960 arpents. Given their failures, Gallatin restricted decisions made by the commissioners: "Being informed that not only the construction which you have assumed opens a door to numerous frauds, but that it is altogether different from that adopted in the other districts, & that it has created in one of them a considerable uneasiness & dissatisfaction at the proceedings of their own board, the President of the United States requests that you will on receipt of this letter immediately suspend any decisions in favor of claimants under order of survey or requêtes not accompanied by settlement."[185] Judge Joshua Lewis and Secretary Robertson of the eastern district in contrast proceeded in a much more pleasing fashion.[186] After someone in New Orleans published Gallatin's 1811 letter scolding the Opelousas board in the *Orleans Gazette*, Gideon Fitz of Opelousas defended the practices of the board to Jefferson, explaining that if claims were in doubt many locals would have sold to American speculators, creating opposition to the government.[187]

Some locals failed to register their titles because they assumed the federal government implemented the entire process to steal land. Others believed that an eventual Spanish return would preclude any need to establish title.[188] The transition to a new legal system combined with the difficulty of registering land became a source of passive resistance in some cases.[189] Land claims within Louisiana, particularly in frontier regions, remained in a state of flux as Anglo-American speculators bought up land, and the presence of a new system of law accelerated sales.[190] Small landholders, particularly Acadians, lost out in this process.[191] In his instructions to land commissioners of the eastern district of the Territory of Orleans, Gallatin clarified that in the absence of clear land titles the United States recognized land claims in three cases: "1, order of survey—2nd permission to settle—3rd Possession for ten consecutive years prior to the 20th December 1803." If the land was surveyed prior to 1800, there was no limit on how much land could be validated, but if only settled prior to 1803 tracts were limited to 640 acres, with additional acreage for wives and children, and if settled ten years prior to 1803, to two thousand acres.[192] Individuals without clear title could lose land, with older titles retaining greater validity.

Without local land commissioners, appointees from the United States could find it almost impossible to gain trust. Controversies over land persisted even as the territorial period came to a close. In 1811 despite all of the controversy, publication of the land regulations in both French and English, and six years of the process, citizens of the western district petitioned that their lands failed to be registered because "they are Ignorant natives of the Country, and Unacquainted with the views of the Government, and Consequently, were frequently advised by the Enemies of that Government, not to make an Entry of their Claims, as their Titles would be lost; That, others of your petitioners, were discouraged from Enregistering their Claims, under the defects of the first Land Laws."[193] Land commissioners concurred in these judgments, as Eligius Fromentin and Allan B. Magruder claimed that some citizens failed to achieve registration because of their remoteness from population centers, ignorance, and fear.[194] Still others lacked documentation or claimed they remained in Spanish territory. Territorial officials regularly advocated for more time and exceptions for landholders who failed to prove their titles. As Louisiana prepared to enter the union, Claiborne recommended further measures to aid those with land claims who through either ignorance, negligence, or mistaken views, failed to come forward. Thus, once again officials operating at the local level urged greater leniency for Louisianans.[195] The federal government could afford in Claiborne's view to spend more time and money in order to ensure that more citizens retained titles. In 1812 when serving as land commissioner, William Garrard led a U.S. delegation to Attakapas to assuage locals' suspicions of U.S. motives and to settle questions of title. Garrard's duties as a land commissioner for the western district proved especially difficult: "My situation was highly delicate and responsible; in a strange Country in the midst of a People already too suspicious of the American character and of the views of the Government towards them rendered thus odious and unpopular by wretches disaffected to it."[196] Local suspicions persisted despite all the efforts made to explain the process.

The territorial government regularly exercised leniency in other areas as well. Road maintenance and levee construction constituted constant concerns in Plaquemines, given its location and the danger of flooding. The local police jury took bids for any levee work that proprietors failed to undertake themselves.[197] Roads concerned officials in all parishes within the territory, but especially in Plaquemines, as it required lines of communication with the capital if a foreign ship appeared.[198] The jury and parish judge of Plaquemines fined local property owners for failing to keep roads in good repair, but complaints became so widespread that Claiborne offered pardons for those fined because of recent flooding from the Mississippi.[199] The following year the inhabitants of Plaquemines still failed to keep their roads in good condition, resulting in fines and further pardons, though the local police jury felt that the pardons were not applicable.[200] Repeated cases of citizens appealing to the governor for financial relief from judges and police juries demonstrate the manner in which territorial officials built support for the U.S. government when local officials failed to do so.

No sooner had issues over land title begun to fade in Louisiana than they reemerged with the acquisition of West Florida. John Ballinger wrote to the secretary of state complaining over further Spanish titles in West Florida, particularly the large grant of intendant Morales, but noted too the generous policy of Governor de Grand Pré in selling smaller plots. Ballinger regretted the failure to take the territory sooner, which necessitated a continuation of the looser land policy: "A liberal policy towards actual settlers, would in a degree mitigate the evil. A donation of a small quantity of land to every actual settler who has not heretofore obtained a Legal grant from the Spanish Government, would materially lessen the difficulties incident to land affairs."[201] The same position had become commonplace practice for U.S. officials by this time.

Several leaders in West Florida feared attachment to the United States unless the government would be willing to sanction land sales made by the Spanish.[202] Claiborne requested that he be allowed to look into the local inhabitants before the federal government made judgments.[203] Morales sold enough land to make it politically unfeasible for the U.S. to institute in West Florida requirements that failed to authenticate sales after 1800 or 1803, in Claiborne's opinion.[204] Land confiscation, though time tested against Native Americans, could not be exercised against white settlers in Louisiana or West Florida except within strict limits.

The United States instituted a number of new policies and institutions within Louisiana, and some of these proved widely unpopular with the local population. In these cases, U.S. officials regularly acted as local advocates seeking change from the federal government. Educational efforts by territorial leaders garnered limited results, but these measures did not engender significant opposition, nor did the U.S. postal service or banks when erected in the region. At the heart of local criticism lay the new legal structure and land policy of the United States. In both these areas U.S. officials met local complaints by altering the legal structure and in the case of land policy by interpreting or ignoring it on a case-by-case basis. This same ability to meet local needs while occasionally bending or ignoring federal mandates represented a key element in winning loyalty to the United States, and it occurred through the intercession of figures at multiple levels of government. By appointing men who knew how to bend but not flagrantly break U.S. law to meet local needs, the territorial government successfully integrated Louisiana into the federal union.

6

Co-option and Collaboration

Like many Americans in Louisiana, James Brown retained serious doubts as to the loyalty of Creoles and their capacity to exercise the prerogatives of U.S. citizenship. Brown came from Virginia by way of Kentucky, where he served as secretary of state. His brother John was a U.S. senator from Kentucky until 1804, and his wife's sister was married to Henry Clay, which ensured Brown's continued influence in the capital. President Jefferson appointed Brown to the position of secretary of the territory and as a judge of the territorial Supreme Court, though he resigned the first post and refused the second due to the office's limited compensation. In 1805 while serving as the U.S. attorney of the territory, Brown wrote to John Breckinridge, who had recently resigned his office as a U.S. senator to become Jefferson's attorney general, over his concerns about the upcoming territorial legislature election: "I anticipate the election of Representatives not one of whom can speak the English language, and most of whom ardently pant for the fraternal embrace of the French Empire. God grant that I may be mistaken." Brown's assessment of the election to the first territorial legislature proved correct, as he declared in a footnote: "Destrehan & André [sic] are elected— My Predictions are so far verified."[1] Manuel Andry served as the first commandant of St. John the Baptist Parish, and Jean-Noël Destréhan was an early critic of the first form of territorial government.[2] Legislative figures as a matter of course tended to better represent the demographics of the electorate than appointees. Thus it came as no surprise when the German Coast elected to the territorial and then the state legislatures men like Jean-Noël Destréhan, Alexander Labranche, and Louis Labranche.[3] These individuals possessed long-standing roots in the parish and were large sugar producers with substantial holdings.[4] Brown as a newcomer initially failed to garner local support from the Francophone populace, and his rocky relationship with Claiborne soon barred him from gubernatorial support (though not federal patronage). Brown attacked Claiborne's approach to appointments and governance in a letter to Henry Clay in 1810:

> For the feeble authority who is nominally American here is so true to the Republican maxim of a Government by a Majority that he submits to it where foreigners compose that majority and were the majority act in opposition to the most sacred principles of good policy and of the Constitution. Indeed such is his rigid adherence to the maxim that he did not fail to yield his whole civil authority to the majority composed of Wilkinson's Army and adherents, and I am firmly persuaded that should a minion of Bonaparte's arrive to morrow at the head of an army he would advise submission upon the principle of the inviolability of the Majority.

Brown's solution to better protect the territory was to turn to Americans, first by including West Florida in the territory and enacting a generous land policy to encourage American immigration.[5]

Brown's criticism of Claiborne, however self-interested, reflected others' appraisals of the governor's weaknesses, and the Jefferson administration on multiple occasions considered potential replacements.[6] Jefferson and Madison understood Brown to be a political opponent of Claiborne, but his criticism carried added weight due to his prominent political connections.[7] The peripatetic merchant Vincent Nolte who first went to New Orleans in 1806 contrasted Claiborne with Laussat: "of fine personal appearance, but in all other respects, a coarse, rude man, and at the same time, very sharp, and *knowing*, as most Americans are."[8] Despite the criticism from multiple sources, Jefferson supported Claiborne, writing to Madison that while private criticism might be informative, taking that information to the public was another thing altogether.[9] Should someone like Brown have been appointed, it might have led to more Anglo appointees and perhaps greater Francophone alienation. As things stood, Claiborne pursued a middle course, appointing locals and Francophones in the parishes along the Mississippi in south Louisiana while turning to larger numbers of native-born Americans in western and northern parishes.

Brown's assumptions about the limits of electoral possibilities for Americans proved untrue. He made inroads with the local population of the German Coast, some of whom shared his dim view of the governor. Shortly after moving to the territory he and his nephew purchased a plantation in the German Coast, and in 1811 he won election to the territorial legislature from the region. In addition, after Louisiana's admittance as a state in 1812, Brown's connections made him a natural choice for election to the U.S. Senate. Brown thus could gain support from the populace of the German Coast and territorial representatives. His election demonstrated English speakers' political adaptability even in predominantly Francophone regions.

Changes in sovereignty necessitated significant alterations in policy, law, and governing institutions, but personnel implemented these changes. This required sensitivity on the part of appointees from the incoming government but also the appointment of local figures familiar with community needs. The experience of French speakers in Louisiana resembled that of numerous peoples in North America who faced transfers of power. Problems of pluralism regularly confronted governments after changes in sovereignty. Generally during transitions the incoming power strove not to make changes so drastic as to incite resistance.

After the change in sovereignty from Dutch New Amsterdam to English New York, English officials governed a diverse population with a large number of prominent Dutch subjects. English grants of property rights and religious freedom allowed for continued Dutch participation and the continuation of Dutch officials in some prominent cases.[10] Even after the Dutch reconquest of the territory in 1673 and its return to England in 1674, the English persisted in these practices. Economic cooperation both legal and otherwise also grew between the English and Dutch merchants in the colony through their use of contacts in both the West Indies and the Netherlands.[11] The Church of England, through the Society for the Propagation of the Gospel, likewise promoted Anglicization. Wealthier colonists of Dutch descent began a gradual process of Anglicization in terms of language, intermarriage, and inheritance practices that benefited their families. Others of lower social status failed to do so, leading to greater ethnic resentment on their part, which contributed to Leisler's Rebellion during the Glorious Revolution.[12] Indeed, some Dutch subjects immigrated out of New York to Pennsylvania and other middle colonies.[13] Over time Dutch prominence in politics faded, along with their commercial dominance in the 1680s, such that by the early eighteenth century much of New York society was Anglicized.[14]

In other areas, the British found it harder to achieve Anglicization. In

Illinois after the British takeover of the Old Northwest, the French popu-
lation wished to have a functioning civil government rather than rule by
British military commanders, and the replacement of French courts with
English ones created discontent and some out-migration.[15] Ultimately the
British bent to local demands by placing the area under the control of Quebec with superintendents and judges dispatched to the communities of the
Old Northwest, but the American Revolution made the legislation, however
well meaning, irrelevant. When George Rogers Clark seized control of the
Illinois country during the American Revolution, he appointed locals in the
militia and authorized judicial elections. Many French inhabitants proved
avid supporters and aided Clark but quickly changed sides with the requisite oaths of loyalty on their recapture by the British and then back again
to the Americans. After the Revolution John Todd as the county lieutenant
of Illinois appointed by Virginia established courts and regularly appointed
French and Anglo-American locals to key positions Despite the efforts of
individuals like Todd, however, French and English speakers often fell out
with one another in the Illinois country, which led to further French immigration to Spanish territory.[16] Upper Louisiana underwent similar shifts in
sovereignty, with the Spanish in control of the area in the aftermath of the
Seven Years' War. Under the Spanish a lieutenant governor in St. Louis depended on French appointees for local offices and the maintenance of trade
with Native Americans.[17]

Changes in sovereignty and identity could also be facilitated by economic
ties, as was the case in Texas and New Mexico well before their incorporation into the United States.[18] Many Tejanos and Nuevamexicanos desired
a more porous border to enhance trade.[19] Indeed, the inclusion of Louisiana in the union helped advance the American economic frontier further
west as so many of the merchants trading with Texas and New Mexico were
Frenchmen from New Orleans or St. Louis.[20] Commerce thus split communities while building bridges to other ethnicities and potentially different
identities. Ethnic or national identities mattered, but they could be trans-
formed through ideas and economic interests. When the American conquest came to New Mexico, prominent individuals quickly adapted to the
economic integration with the United States but also federalist political
impulses.[21] Identity is not primordial, but neither is it created by print cap-
italism alone. For many border residents, the United States offered signif-

icant ideological and material incentives; border residents readily grasped these incentives as they understood their own interests better than distant politicians. Identity had a plasticity, as Americans in the early national era knew, given their own revolutionary experience.

Individuals who manned governmental posts in the territory sought expedient compromises that arose more as prudential than ideological judgments. A number of U.S. appointees' earlier experiences in territorial governments provided them with an education in gaining local support. Territorial governors as outsiders found themselves in a tenuous position with no full party backing; consequently most strove to work with local elites. Appointments could raise controversy when governors upset local leaders by appointing too many outsiders.[22] Claiborne appointed Creoles, but he also utilized outsiders. Native-born Americans from the East with the appropriate professional, experiential, or political credentials regularly received appointments, and in the West of Orleans multiple army officers who took part in the occupation chose to stay and received patronage. Congress passed the Orleans Act of 1804 and then an Organic Act in 1805, which created a legislature that redressed early inhabitants' opposition to the first stage of government, but this was not unique in that it resembled the regular second state of government for territories. Military rule was not unique to Louisiana, lasting in multiple areas for years, as in California and New Mexico. When Congress organized a territorial government for Florida, it had the same type of government as Orleans, with an appointed council and governor. Orleans was unique in the lack of a delegate in the first stage of government, however, as other unicameral territorial governments all received one.[23]

The failure of the U.S. Congress to grant full political rights and quick admittance to statehood proved a constant complaint regardless of the demographic makeup of territories. In the early republic, admittance proceeded quickly, considering Jeffersonian Republican dominance in the West and control of the national government for over two decades after 1801. Locals' concerns over colonial governance due to the absence of representation in Congress and violations of their natural and constitutional rights would be a constant refrain for future territories throughout the West.[24] In Upper Louisiana the demographics did not allow Francophones to dominate territorial legislatures, particularly when it became attached to Indiana. Inhabitants appealed to Congress, arguing for the return of their original jurisdiction, French-speaking officials, protections for slavery, and the fulfillment of treaty obligations by placing them on a quick route to statehood.[25] Congress in 1805 partially acknowledged these complaints by separating Upper Louisiana from Indiana. Despite the desires of their constituents, many territorial governors argued for a slower approach to statehood. Claiborne's early resistance to immediate statehood was far from unique. In his study of territorial government, Jack Eblen places at the two polls William Blount in advocating for statehood in Tennessee and Arthur St. Clair in Ohio for opposing it, with other governors on a spectrum between the two.[26] The territorial period became longer over time, with the average shifting from thirteen to thirty years. Orleans's experience resembled that of many other U.S. territories with European populations present before territorial government. Louisiana gave legitimacy to local control relatively early, with Congress and the military dominating only the period from 1803 to 1804 before it began to empower locals.[27] In contrast in Florida the legislature disenfranchised Spanish Americans, regarding them as noncitizens. Indeed, the powers given to the Orleans legislature would not be given to all other territories until 1815.[28]

In contrast to the early nineteenth century, the party dynamics in Washington figured prominently for territorial admittance in the latter half of the nineteenth century. Republicans as the majority party had less interest in the admittance of New Mexico or Utah, whose People's Party might add to Democratic support in the Senate. The first civil government of the state of Deseret in its personnel essentially replicated the church leadership. Indeed, church control proved so prevalent that four federal territorial appointees left to complain of Mormon dominance.[29] Territorial arrangements based on patronage and co-option proved constant well into the twentieth century in Hawaii.[30]

Patronage practices within Louisiana that depended on collaboration proved relatively successful. In areas where such practices failed to be exercised, the process became far more contentious. For instance, in New Mexico the absence of local appointees and participants in the first territorial government combined with problems in the management of relations with the Pueblo led to a planned coup by Mexican Americans. Forestalled by the new government, the coup in turn triggered a full-scale rebellion by Pueblos with support from Mexican Americans in 1847 that resulted in the death of territorial governor, Charles Bent, and then military rule of the area until 1850.[31] In the aftermath of the 1847 Taos Revolt Americans understood more than ever the need for elite buy-in to the new government and proceeded to court elite Mexican American figures. Despite clear social distinctions between whites and Mexican Americans, political and legal equality provided for a modus vivendi in New Mexico as did the majority Mexican American territorial legislature that allowed for a local voice in politics. In New Mexico complaints over the long territorial period frequently would be ascribed to the racial animus of whites against the large population of Mexican Americans and Indians.[32] Elites served as willing participants within these territorial governments for individual, family, and class gains. Utah, with a population made up of native-born Americans, in 1857 also engaged in a revolt.[33]

Co-option and collaboration boasted successes elsewhere. Territorial officials needed to court local inhabitants if they desired a future in state politics.[34] The demographics and culture of the territory necessitated Claiborne's alliances, and his decisions proved politically astute, as demonstrated by his election as governor in 1812. This contrasts with William Clark, the territorial governor of Missouri, whose alliances with Creole merchant elites in St. Louis and support for the land rights of Native Americans alienated the majority, resulting in his loss in the governor's race.[35]

Personnel decisions in the territories posed perennial problems. The general pattern from Arthur St. Clair, the first governor of the Northwest Territory, onward demonstrated a large amount of delegation to local officials.[36] Nathaniel Herbert Claiborne, brother of the governor, noted that "Mr. Claiborne was resolved, and uniformly acted up to the resolution, that the greater part of the offices should be filled by natives of the country. To treat the people as a conquered province was in his view odious. By attaching the natives to him, the prejudices in favor of the ancient regimen [sic] were subverted, and the most necessary innovations were effected."[37] This use of locals in key positions was not a new innovation in Louisiana.

When turning to outsiders the United States utilized Francophones for many positions. There were a large number of prominent Saint-Domingue expatriates in prominent positions: Jean-François Canonge, translator and judge of the Criminal Court of New Orleans; Paul Lanusse, member of the

Cabildo and a judge under the Spanish who then became an officer in the Bank of Louisiana and an American justice and a captain in the militia; Augustin Dominique Tureaud, judge of St. James Parish; Thomas Patrice Dubourg, judge in Plaquemines Parish and brother of the archbishop Louis-Guillaume Dubourg; Gallien de Préval, a city judge in New Orleans; Jean-François Canonge on the criminal court and then the Louisiana Upper Court of Appeal; Jean-Baptiste Donatien Augustin, a district judge; and Pierre Dormenon, parish judge of Pointe Coupée.[38] Similarly a number of Saint-Domingue émigrés held prominent militia appointments.[39] Other prominent political figures had Saint-Domingue connections, such as Edward Livingston, who married the widow Moreau, who had come to Louisiana by way of Jamaica with her brother Auguste Davezac, who was an interpreter in the courts and later served in the Legislative Assembly.[40] The presence of Saint-Domingue refugees and their connections to the United States predated the cession to Louisiana with significant immigration and trade between the two during the 1790s, particularly in Philadelphia. Saint-Dominguans threaded the needle of American republicanism, avoiding both royalism and the evils of revolution. New Orleans, with its French language and culture, proved an attractive destination for those fleeing Saint-Domingue.[41] Charges of revolutionary fervor among this group had little basis. Moreau Lislet had studied law in Paris and become a practicing attorney before returning to Saint-Domingue, where he quickly became a government prosecutor. His time in Philadelphia and Havana gave him the requisite knowledge of Spanish and English to advance quickly in New Orleans. In 1807 he replaced James Workman as the judge of the parish of Orleans and was offered a position on the Superior Court, which he declined for financial reasons. He remained, however, on the parish court through 1812, when he asked not to be reappointed. James Pitot replaced him in 1813, though Workman continued to act as attorney for the city of New Orleans.[42] Even so, the immigration of Saint-Dominguans complicated Louisiana's prospects for statehood, likely causing a further delay.[43]

In addition to finding locals willing and able to serve, the U.S. government needed to evaluate its own native-born citizens who offered their services. In the Mississippi Territory, the Adams administration struggled in filtering out those who wanted to profit either politically or financially from appointments.[44] The same dilemma recurred in Louisiana, where office seekers poured forth.[45] Appointees from the United States generally had solid Republican credentials, but others also secured appointments. John B. Prevost, Aaron Burr's stepson and a recorder of New York City, received an appointment as a judge on the Superior Court, given the need for his stepfather's good will during the impeachment trial of Justice Samuel Chase.[46] Burr also influenced the appointment of Rufus Eastin as a judge in the territory of Louisiana, as well as Dr. Joseph Brown as secretary of that territory.[47] Writing during the brief period of French control, Daniel Clark noted to Madison that "Laussat wishes to know which Americans are Federalist and which Republican, 'a thing which I believe it would be a difficult matter for most of us to determine with respect to ourselves, as party Spirit evaporates in foreign Countries.'"[48] After the transfer Louisiana ceased to be foreign territory, yet the foreign nature of much of the population would go a long way to eliminate many (though by no means all) of the partisan divisions between American appointees. Partisan differences often meant less in the territory, and it served as a convenient dumping ground for discontented Republicans and occasionally Federalists. Thus Abraham Redwood Ellery, who originally came down the Mississippi in order to chart the river for Alexander Hamilton, could serve as a recorder in the territorial Supreme Court under judges like Prevost.[49]

Occasionally conflicts over patronage occurred. The president of Princeton's son, John W. Smith, assumed a position as a clerk of the Supreme Court, but as his father reported to Madison, Claiborne believed the office was his to disburse, leading to Smith's dismissal.[50] Claiborne no doubt felt on firm footing with the Virginians of the party in this dispute. Within the territory, however, Claiborne found himself operating at cross-purposes in attempting to secure locals to positions while also disbursing appointments to incoming Americans. There was no way to please everyone; locals could establish legitimacy of the new government among the original inhabitants, and Anglo-Americans with connections to federal authorities in Washington proved more capable in securing appointments than Americans already on the ground. Consequently, aspiring local Anglo-American office seekers without federal ties became deeply disappointed with the government. Still, parishes in the northern and western portions of the state tended to receive Anglo-American appointees rather than locals. In these regions smaller Creole communities obviated the need for the appointment practices that officials utilized to the south and east.

Generalizations as to Francophones versus English speakers or outsider versus locals fail to recognize the various gradations present in Louisiana. Many Americans could claim local status through long residence in the area before the cession or intermarriage; for instance George King came from Virginia by way of Kentucky and immigrated to Louisiana in the 1790s and secured positions under the Spanish. Other immigrants arrived in the United States from the French-speaking Atlantic before coming to Louisiana. They were decidedly not local, but their entrée could be eased due to their language and pedigree. There were Britons who possessed the requisite knowledge of English or political ties but lacked a clear American identity on their arrival. Appointees at the local level often had multiple national attachments.

In many regions, Anglo appointees represented the rule rather than the exception. Even where local appointees dominated like the German Coast, native-born Americans could secure election from their neighbors. In order to do so, however, Americans needed to form alliances with Francophone Louisianans. The *Louisiana Courier* in 1810 characterized Daniel Clark's efforts to court Creoles: "Clark, who cajoles and splendidly entertains on his plantation at Houmas some Creoles, whom he had endeavored but a few days before to ruin, neutralizing at the same time their influence by that of another party whom he commands and equally deceives at once, for the purpose of securing the triumph of his true cause."[51] Regardless of the attacks on Clark's character, the remarks illustrate that Claiborne's administration, as well as the opposition to it, were multiethnic. Clark's enmity toward Claiborne proved virulent and long-standing. Claiborne wrote in 1811: "Mr Clark, it is believed, designs to leave the Territory, and I pray Heaven, he may be followed by some 'other Choice Spirits.'"[52] These were understandable sentiments given that four years earlier Claiborne received a bullet in a duel with Clark.[53] Brown and Clark were not alone; other Anglo-Americans secured election as representatives from even heavily Francophone regions. James Mather, an English immigrant who became a large sugar planter and owner in a mercantile house with George Morgan represented Acadia in the House.[54] Many of these Anglo-Americans found the prevalence of local appointees galling in the first years after the cession. These attitudes would die hard. In 1812 William Garrard, who earlier served as a U.S. land commissioner, noted: "As to the Creoles of Louisiana they are ignorant of the characters of our most distinguished Men and of course of our Government and its policy."[55] These complaints often came from Anglo-Americans who secured offices but remained frustrated by a perceived absence of progress and assimilation. What Brown, Clark, and Garrard failed to appreciate was that U.S. administration functioned due to the selection of the right instruments within the parishes.

U.S. administrators struggled in selecting individuals who could retain local support while enacting the legal and political changes necessitated by the transfer. Still, a number of local leaders welcomed the transfer. Letters from Daniel Clark, while a U.S. consul, demonstrate the contrast in sentiment between the cession from Spain to France and then from France to the United States. In 1802 he reported: "All the People of Property were indignant at it. Many intimations were given me of the general wish that the U.S. should get Possession of the Province."[56] Clark included a memorial from locals expressing these sentiments. A year later after news of the U.S. purchase, Clark again pointed to support from prominent inhabitants: "The news of the Cession gives general satisfaction to the Planters & Spaniards (even in Office) and is disliked by a few of the merchants and lower Classes of the Towns People only."[57] Tensions between Spanish officials and the French prefect further eased the American entry. The better sort, as Clark conceived of them, approved of the cession.[58]

While some officials who had served the previous Spanish government welcomed the turnover, others who had prepared for a French turnover remained wary. Daniel Clark recommended to Madison that Claiborne be instructed to dismiss partisans of France.[59] Yet even those with French sympathies felt betrayed by the French government's sale.[60] In stark contrast to Clark's voluble (and unsolicited) advice, Thomas Jefferson issued more concise guidance:

> Instructions to Claiborne to suppress useless officers
> to remove any existing officers
> to appoint others.[61]

As with so much of Jefferson's republican simplicity, these instructions proved exceedingly difficult in practice. The first instruction falls in line with Jefferson's general republican principles and fiscal beliefs, but the second point demonstrates distrust for men attached to the previous government. As to the third point, Jefferson left the selection of officeholders largely to the governor's discretion, and it quickly became evident that prominent local supporters would be needed to secure confidence in the new government. Proximity mattered; locals trusted their neighbors more than outsiders. Indeed, Jefferson's own republican political theory was founded on this understanding. Claiborne frequently struggled in filling positions, as local officials rarely were well compensated.[62] Still, in a number of parishes local appointees proved common. Often the native-born American population vocally expressed their discontent. Claiborne wrote to Madison in 1804 that he saw a circular letter from Mathew Lyon that attempted to persuade westerners toward disaffection from the United States, but he noted: "If the natives of the United States should not excite discontents, the Louisianians will become well pleased with the temporary Government."[63] Claiborne bemoaned betrayals by native-born Americans and remained convinced that greater democracy would have to wait for the future.

> It seems to me impossible, that a Man of reflection, can suppose the people of Louisiana at this time, prepared for a complete Representative System, But there is no accounting for change of opinion, with respect to the Government of this Territory; I remember for the first two or three months, after our taking possession, my colleague General Wilkinson was impressed with an Opinion, that a strong military Government would alone suit Louisiana, and *that no one but a Military Character should be the Governor;* But a few Weeks previous to the General's departure, his sentiments were quite changed.[64]

These turnarounds may have been a result of a reappraisal of the facts on the ground, but they also proved politically convenient for recent American arrivals seeking inroads among Francophone elites. Anti-Louisianan attitudes died slowly, but territorial officials understood the indispensability of local support. In Washington contact with Louisianans helped dispel earlier prejudices. For instance, when Federalist senator William Plumer met the memorialists Pierre Derbigny, Pierre Sauve, and Jean-Noël Destréhan, he wrote: "I was much gratified with their company—they have little of French flippery about them—They resemble New England men more than Virginians."[65] While a decided compliment from Plumer, Jefferson and Claiborne would not have taken the New England comparison as praise. Territorial politics during the early national period was highly personal, often as a contest of ins and outs or court and country. Politics in territorial Mississippi under Claiborne had also lacked an ideological division, with familial connections proving more important and frequent turnover among appointees.[66]

In the absence of a democratically elected government, the most important practice taken by the territorial government to secure local support was the co-option of local elites. Often this occurred as a result of federal officials compromising or contravening U.S. policy. Just as important, however, was local cooperation in the governing structure. Often this caused controversy among more recent Anglo-American immigrants who expected appointments to flow their way. In an odd manner, this actually furthered Louisiana's inclusion within the union. An unintended consequence of Claiborne's appointment practice was that both Anglo-American and Francophone malcontents cooperated in criticism of the territorial government. Both the ins and the outs formed interethnic alliances that forestalled the development of a politics based on language, religion, or ethnicity.

After the transfer of sovereignty, the United States established its authority on the local level outside of New Orleans through the appointment of commandants for existing communities, who served until their replacement by judges ten months later. The commandants exercised police and judicial functions within their area. Claiborne selected them based on their social position in their communities and their attitude toward the United States, except in parishes along frontiers with Spanish territory, where he frequently turned to U.S. military officers. Many of the men appointed had held analogous offices under the Spanish government, denoting continuity. Early in 1804 Claiborne dispatched Dr. John Watkins with instructions for choosing commandants: "Talents will be a great recommendation, but integrity and attachment to the Government of the United States you must consider indispensable requisites."[67] Watkins, a Virginian who lived in the Illinois country before coming to Spanish Louisiana, received an appointment to the New Orleans city council under the brief French tenure of Pierre-Clément de Laussat and later served as mayor of New Orleans.[68] Claiborne through Watkins reappointed many former commandants who had served the Spanish government: Antonie St. Amand in St. Charles, Manuel Andry in St. John the Baptist, Michel Cantrelle in St. James, Villanueva of Valenzuela Dans Lafourche; all continued in the U.S. service.

Others refused: in Lafourche Rafael Croquer, in Iberville Francis Rivas. In West Baton Rouge an American was appointed, and in Galveztown the new civil commandant, Alexander Morie, a Scot who lived in the area for two decades replaced Thomas Estevan, a Spanish officer.[69] Local Francophone loyalties proved fluid, informed in part by their experience under Spanish governance.[70]

Individuals with a strong French connection invited suspicion. In an 1810 letter to Madison, Claiborne gave brief descriptions of the ten nominees from the House of Representatives to the Legislative Council and wrote of Jean Blanque, an ally of Laussat, that "Mr. Blanque is much disliked by most of the native Americans residing in & near New Orleans; His attachments are supposed to be wholly foreign, & they consider him a dangerous man. Mr. Blanque has, *I am persuaded strong partialities for his native Country, France:* But I should be wanting in Candour, were I not to add, that his conduct has not (in my opinion) been such, as to justify the fears & the prejudices." Of the nominees, five were natives of Louisiana and five foreigners. Claiborne argued: "It might not be proper wholly to exclude the foreigners from the Council; but that it would be politic to give the natives a decided preference."[71] Unsurprisingly, Blanque was not among those selected. On the council as elsewhere, however, the U.S. government strove for balance, with five Francophone nominees and five native-born Americans. The upper echelons of government in the council reveal a decided effort to maintain this balance, but lower-level appointments proved less suitable for obvious ethnic balancing.

Despite some prominent appointments, local French speakers charged Claiborne with favoring native-born Americans. One such "Native" argued that Claiborne relied too extensively on Americans, particularly when it came to militia appointments: "Though the population of native Americans was scarcely in the proportion of one to a dozen throughout Louisiana, the government commenced by choosing, among the two kinds of citizens, an equal number of subjects to fill the public employments. I have even reason to think that the Louisianians were considered very happy to be admitted to offices in that proportion. As to lucrative places, they were almost all distributed between the creatures of government, newly transplanted among us, and especially given to native Americans in preference to other citizens."[72] For all Claiborne's efforts he opened the U.S. government up to the charge of favoring native Americans, but even the "Native" realized that a fifty-fifty split appeared acceptable to many. Legal historian Mark F. Fernandez counts only four local appointees on the civil list in 1809 to judgeships: Peter B. St. Martin in St. Charles, Charles de Latour in Plaquemines, Michel Cantrelle in St. James, and Charles Fagot in St. Bernard.[73] What proves so interesting is less the number of those appointees than the heavily Creole parishes from which they came. Those same parishes continued to receive large numbers of local appointees. Anglo dominance proved more prevalent at the highest echelon of the judiciary in the Superior Court of the territory and then the Supreme Court of the state.[74] The question of who counted as a local was also an issue. At the time of the transfer many men appointed to office, though not born in the territory, had lived there for decades. Claiborne defended his wide appointive practices in terms of nationality but also explained: "My object has been to avail the Public of the services of deserving and well informed Citizens, and as there are many Native Americans of this description residing in Louisiana, it ought not to be a matter of surprise, that some of them should have received Offices."[75] Anglo-American appointments also made immense sense since judges needed to be familiar with U.S. law.

In the Acadian and German Coasts local appointees and recent French immigrants proved prevalent. As county and then parish judge of St. James, Cantrelle strove to retain stability while overseeing the change to different modes of law and government, as did his successor in 1812 as the parish judge, Augustin D. Tureaud, who served until 1826.[76] Tureaud, though an exile from Saint-Domingue, was through marriage allied with the Bringier family, who maintained substantial holdings in the parish and positions within the militia.[77]

In Ascension Parish (Lafourche des Chetimachas), Joseph Landry served briefly as commandant and then as justice of the peace, since the former Spanish commandant of the heavily Canary Islander region, Lieutenant Rafael Croquer, moved to Spanish West Florida.[78] Landry was an Acadian who spent time in Maryland before moving to Louisiana in the 1760s. He had been active in the Spanish militia and served the Spanish as an interim commandant.[79] In 1807 Claiborne appointed Edward Turner to the parish judgeship. Turner was an army officer from Massachusetts who had earlier served in Natchitoches.[80] Shortly after the appointment Turner established a business venture, a large sugar plantation, with Daniel Clark.[81] Turner served but three years in the position before he succumbed to yellow fever and Philip Cartier D'Outremer succeeded him, serving until 1826. After his replacement by Turner, Joseph Landry served in both the territorial and state legislatures. In 1806 he resigned his seat as a representative from Acadia in the territorial legislature and when elected to the state assembly he repeated his action, resigning on Claiborne's election as governor.[82] Genezi Roussin, also of Acadia, followed Landry in resigning his seat in the General Assembly in 1812 as did P. B. St. Martin and T. E. Arnauld of the German Coast.[83]

The two commandants of the German Coast, Antonie St. Amand and Manuel Andry, served the new government as they did the old.[84] Andry refused a further appointment, at which point the county judge became Achille Trouard, a French immigrant who had married into a Creole family and lived in Louisiana for decades prior to the cession.[85] Trouard continued until 1813 as the parish judge of St. John the Baptist.[86] Local ties did not always assure a smooth career. In 1805 when the earlier commandants of the German Coast refused to turn over public documents in their possession, Claiborne wrote to Trouard, promising to instruct Andry and St. Amand to turn over the papers but also sending them commissions for justices of the peace that would be distributed based on their recommendations.[87] This use of patronage helped to build broader support within the parishes. Claiborne continued to back Trouard while he established authority in his parish and commended his behavior in not pressing the issue over the documents.[88] A local, Terense Leblanc de Villanueva, succeeded Trouard and served into the 1820s.[89]

In St. Charles Parish the judgeship had a far higher circulation rate. A Louisianan born in New Orleans, Pierre Bauchet St. Martin, succeeded Trouard when the territorial government created parish judges in 1807. Andre Latour, another local, succeeded him in 1811; François Bazile succeeded Latour in 1813 and was replaced by Claude Dejan in 1816. Latour's replacement by Bazile resulted in a petition from over seventy citizens (most of them with French surnames) of St. Charles requesting that Latour retain his post.[90] Latour's response to this petition also illustrated his perception of injustice: "I may be of some use to you, if not as a magistrate at least as a private citizen. In a country like this where every thing is cabal and intrigue, this last title is the only one which an honored man may boast of and enjoy."[91] Latour had been sidelined, and his supporters quickly embraced the political language of the United States.

Upriver, to the north of the German and Acadian Coasts were the counties of Iberville and further north Pointe Coupée, which included its eponymous parish and the parish of West Baton Rouge. The English-speaking populace in Pointe Coupée, rather than representing a boon for U.S. governance in Louisiana, required constant intervention on the part of U.S. administrators in disputes between two factions. U.S. territorial governance proved more difficult when it had to accommodate both older colonial elites and more recent Anglo-American inhabitants. Although Pointe Coupée grew to become a comparatively wealthy and prosperous parish, many in New Orleans considered it provincial. As Claiborne observed to Jefferson, "In the settlement of Pointe Coupée where the Society is esteemed wealthy and polished, that not a third of the free Inhabitants can write their names and among the illiterate, are *those,* whose annual income exceeds $6000: my informant adds, that Mental Ignorance pervades the other parts of the Province in an equal, and he believes in a greater degree."[92] The central figure in Pointe Coupée was Julien Poydras, whom Evan Jones characterized as "in conduct and sentiment a Republican,—of immense fortune—of education and travel—He speaks the three languages of the Province and is fond of politics."[93] Originally from Nantes, Poydras lived in Saint-Domingue and arrived in Louisiana around 1768, where he prospered in commerce and as a planter.[94] Poydras served as the first commandant of Pointe Coupée and was succeeded in late 1804 by Alexandre Leblanc, a local Louisianan, with Simon Croizet exercising the prerogatives of the post in Leblanc's absence.[95] The powers of commandants remained wide, yet Claiborne made clear that any controversial cases should be passed on to him.[96] Poydras then received a judicial appointment, became the president of the Bank of Louisiana, and in 1806 held a seat on the Legislative Council.[97] The Legislative Council position came at an embarrassing time, when several critics of Claiborne refused proffered seats. Poydras wrote that if he excused himself, "I should not act the part of a Patriot.—A beginning must be made; we must be initiated in the sacred Duties of Freeman and the Practices of Liberty."[98] Poydras's language evoked exactly the sentiments U.S. officials wanted to hear, and Claiborne quoted it extensively in a letter to Madison. Poydras became an important ally of the governor and the president of the last Legislative Council.[99] In the major court case of the territorial period, Poydras brought suit against Edward Livingston, who claimed ownership of a batture (the land between a river and levees) in New Orleans and began to dig a canal across it. Poydras and others argued that the land belonged to the public, not an individual.[100] Ultimately, after landowners with land across from the batture achieved legal ownership, they petitioned the governor to be given land that they had taken from the river through levees as well.[101] Poydras defended his own and the community's interests, but it put him at odds with Livingston, one of the most prominent Anglo-American critics of Claiborne. Poydras also served as a member of the Louisiana constitutional convention at Claiborne's urging.[102] Despite or because of Poydras's cooperation Pointe Coupée failed to achieve an internal political consensus.

Poydras's successors proved to be men of lesser stature, and a vocal opposition party gave political contests within Pointe Coupée a more contentious cast than parishes downriver. Poydras's successor as judge in 1806, Pierre Dormenon, was a French émigré who resided in Maryland before migrating to Louisiana. After Dormenon the judgeship went to an Anglo-American from Kentucky, Richard Cocke, and then to Robert MacShane, originally from Pennsylvania. Upon Judge MacShane's death Claiborne appointed John H. Ludeling, another Frenchman, to the office of judge in the county, and he served until 1818.[103] Pointe Coupée's judges lacked Poydras's large holdings, but many local officials engaged in commercial and financial ventures with Poydras.[104] Ludeling's tenure became contentious as he failed to act in an objective fashion. Despite complaints over his conduct, Claiborne informed Ludeling that he did not care to find a replacement for him, in part to discourage him from running for the legislature.[105] Though he chose to keep Ludeling in his post, Claiborne intervened within the parish on behalf of Francis Duplessis over a dispute with Judge Ludeling's brother-in-law, recommending that he attempt to bring about a rapprochement before turning to the legal process. In the same letter Claiborne brought up Paul Lanusse, who had similar issues with the judge over a monetary matter. Claiborne stressed that Ludeling should act impartially but also make sure that no further problems emerged in a parish that he hoped would remain peaceful.[106]

Pointe Coupée's factions did not divide along strictly ethnic divisions. Several Anglo-American citizens of Pointe Coupée opposed the governor, and at the same time, some Creoles criticized Poydras's conduct as a judge. When an auctioneer, Alexander Plauché, criticized Poydras, Claiborne expressed his sympathies for Poydras, promising to consult the attorney general, and then informed Plauché as to the limits of his office.[107] Despite both Anglo-American and Francophone criticism of Poydras, Claiborne portrayed the anti-Poydras faction as ethnic: "the Society of Point Coupee, is still divided into parties" and he regretted "that there should be so much Jealousy between the American and French population. Or to speak more properly between the modern and the ancient Louisianans."[108] Anglo-American immigrants expressed dissatisfaction with high-level parish appointments going to Claiborne's "ancient inhabitants." One needs to be careful in analyzing the phrase "ancient inhabitants" as synonymous with Creoles, as Claiborne used the same phrase in Mississippi to refer to long-term residents regardless of national origin.[109] Shortly after problems began within the parish, one of Claiborne's most important militia appointees, Colonel Henry Hopkins, moved to Pointe Coupée and purchased a cotton plantation.[110]

One of the main complaints of Anglo-Americans such as Charles Morgan centered on the ethnicity of Claiborne's appointees, particularly the sheriff, James Petronny, appointed in 1808 to the 3rd Superior Court district. Claiborne responded to Morgan's concerns, explaining: "The circumstances of his not being born 'an American,' is not considered an objection to him: I certainly feel for my Countrymen, the native Citizens of the U. States, a sincere and ardent attachment, nor is it possible for me, in any situation, or under any circumstance to be unjust toward them. But in my official Character, I can acknowledge no other distinction, between the Inhabitants of this Territory, who by birth or the Treaty of Session, are entitled to the rights of Citizenship, than personal merit." Claiborne's actions reveal an appointment practice based on co-opting French-speaking elites, but in Pointe Coupée, Anglo-Americans expected appointments to go to individuals from the United States. Even as Claiborne reaffirmed his faith in the appointment of Petronny, he gave Morgan advice on a better tack to bring about the sheriff's removal by bringing specific charges forward with proof.[111] Claiborne in his typical conciliatory manner portrayed himself as a friend to Morgan, even as Petronny's appointment stood.

Another conflict in Pointe Coupée that required the intervention of the governor occurred over the use of public buildings. At Pointe Coupée, a small fort and its buildings came under the stewardship of Julien Poydras as commandant, then that of the U.S. Army, and then of the local judge, Pierre Dormenon. Local officials supervised the use of public or government property within the parish for the army.[112] Dormenon in 1808 discovered that Charles Morgan, Dr. William Goforth, and Ebenezer Cooley occupied the buildings despite the fact that none of them possessed authorization to take occupation from territorial officials. Claiborne directed the authorities to retake the facilities; Cooley, Goforth, and Morgan objected.[113] The governor clearly preferred that government officials (in this case a Francophone judge) control the fort rather than private Anglo-American political critics. Cooley and Morgan in an effort to retain possession reported the matter to General James Wilkinson and Secretary of War Henry Dearborn. Morgan wrote to the secretary of war, stating that the fort had been given into his care by Wilkinson and that "our governor has thought proper to Issue an order to one of his petty Judges to take it and apply it to the use of the District, this order I have Refused to Comply with—so far as delivering the property to the Civil department, tho as the Judge tells me he is Civil & Military."[114] The issue then became a turf war within the federal government with Dearborn claiming that Claiborne, as a civil authority, exceeded his proper sphere. The secretary of war instructed Morgan not to surrender it, forcing Claiborne to justify his course of action to the administration in Washington. Claiborne argued that regardless of who charged them with the facility, Cooley and Morgan retained no military authority themselves, and he maintained that the buildings should be given over to his care unless or until they transferred back to military use.[115]

The issue raised by custody of the fort became not just a civil/military conflict, but a local/territorial conflict over control of the facility, despite the fact that locals had their authority from the Department of War. Several members of the parish of Pointe Coupée wanted those buildings under local control, at the urging of Morgan, Cooley, and their allies. They put forth a proposal to buy the buildings for public purposes, which forced Claiborne to explain the local divisions to the secretary of war to give him some sense of the issues in the territory:

> At Point Coupee there are two parties—the one headed by Julian Poydras President of the Legislative Council, and Mr. Dormenon the Parish Judge, who have with them more than two thirds of the People; the other party is headed by a Colonel of Militia, to whom Morgan, a Mr. Cooley and the *other Americans there 5 or 6* in number have attached themselves.—The Colonel of Militia calculated (I believe) on being appointed the Parish Judge, and Cooley lately lost his election to the assembly—I do not know the particular cause of Morgan's displeasure—But his conduct as relates to the public' [sic] Building proceeds from party Spirit.[116]

Claiborne's perspective on the conflict as a party split between Creoles, whom the U.S. government appointed, and disgruntled Anglo-Americans helped to justify his conduct, as territorial politics did not necessitate reaching out to Anglo-American newcomers, particularly those who attempted to evade his authority. The two-thirds number that Claiborne approximated appears optimistic, considering that individuals from the other faction achieved election to the territorial legislature from Pointe Coupée. The ethnic dimension of the split was more apparent than real; it was just as much a split between insiders and outsiders. Anglo-Americans who complained thought they would attract a U.S. audience willing to listen to their grievances at the federal level.

These political disputes spilled over to a conflict in Pointe Coupée regarding control of the local church in 1808 and 1809. With the cession to the United States, for the first time in Louisiana the Catholic Church lost its place of primacy as the only recognized religion, though in practice other faiths had been given leeway under both the French and Spanish. Church personnel turnover proved to be as significant a problem as governmental personnel with the transition to U.S. sovereignty.[117] The Louisiana Catholic Church came under the purview of the center of U.S. Catholicism in Baltimore and a largely Irish-American hierarchy. The jurisdictional disputes of Catholicism mirrored those in other areas. Upon the U.S. securing Illinois, a similar situation occurred with the Baltimore Prefect Apostolic Carroll appointing a vicar general whom local priests failed to recognize.[118] In Louisiana Patrick Walsh, an Irish-born and Spanish-educated vicar general, began to direct the Spanish and French priests of Louisiana. Walsh quickly fell out with the pastor of St. Louis, Capuchin priest Antonio de Sedella, who believed Walsh's appointment to be illegitimate, since he became vicar general on the death of his predecessor and had yet to be appointed in his own right. Sedella possessed an almost congenital problem with authority regardless of nationality, as he disputed with Spanish authorities in the past and would oppose Walsh's successor, Jean Olivier, and then a consecrated bishop, Valentin Dubourg. The more politic Catholics in Louisiana, including the Ursuline nuns, tended to side with Walsh, recognizing the shift in sovereignty.[119] Governmental support for Walsh, however unofficial it might have been, when it came to church appointments in the disputes with Sedella demonstrated another manner in which U.S. territorial officials acted not as impartial federal authorities but as individuals operating in an imperial capacity to secure preferred individuals and groups influence.

In Pointe Coupée a local priest, most likely Father de l' Epinasse, fell out with Judge Dormenon over the use of the church, though both men were Francophones.[120] The disagreement arose over who would have the key to (and therefore control of) the parish church and resulted in repeated complaints about the conduct of the parish judge. Claiborne acknowledged the impropriety of governmental involvement in such disputes in his letter to the judge and justices of the peace, but he authorized them to step in if the peace was breached.[121] Dormenon in Claiborne's estimation was "supported by Mr. Poydras and a majority of the Planters of the Parish," while the parish priest was "patronized by a few respectable Creole families, and some native Americans who have recently emigrated to the Territory." Thus the conflict became another touchstone for the factional divisions within the parish. The citizens of the parish split, but with control of the sheriff and the judge, Poydras's group could easily bring charges against the other faction.[122] The disturbances became so great that Claiborne needed to visit the parish.[123]

Both parties made every effort to establish a legal argument for their actions.[124] The Poydras faction sent a petition to Claiborne proclaiming that they wished to act in a strictly legal fashion, despite the wishes of the other faction.[125] One party wanted the priest removed, something Claiborne did not have the power to do, while the other faction wanted the judge removed, which would result in a victory for the Morgan faction over Poydras's group.

Although Claiborne lacked the power to remove a priest directly, he exercised the necessary influence to bring it about with the highest Catholic authority in New Orleans, the vicar general, which he acknowledged to Poydras.[126] Claiborne supported Poydras's faction, a group that tried to secure the moral and legal high ground with U.S. authorities in the matter, although a private church building technically lay beyond the authority of a local judge. Judge Dormenon continued to receive the support of the territorial government and secured election to legislative office.

Though members of Poydras's faction often secured election, members of the opposition also achieved victories. Ebenezer Cooley, an American from the opposition faction, and Simon Croizet represented Pointe Coupée at the first territorial legislature, though Croizet later resigned, requiring a new election in 1806.[127] In 1809 Pointe Coupée elected Arnaud Beauvais and Eugene D'Orsiere to represent its interest at the territorial legislature.[128] Claiborne held Beauvais in high esteem: "a Cotton Planter . . . a young man of great Integrity, & I believe much esteemed in his Country;—he speaks French and English."[129] Pierre Dormenon represented Pointe Coupée in the first state House of Representatives.[130] Ill feeling between the two factions in Pointe Coupée persisted, however, and a number of citizens urged that the election be overturned because of irregularities. The complaints alleged that underage voters, voters from the parish of Feliciana, voters who had not paid the state tax, and voters who had no taxable property were allowed to cast ballots; in addition, the polling places were moved and the election judges refused to fix their seals to the election box.[131] Subsequently, in the second legislature, Beauvais, one of Dormenon's opponents in the previous election, represented Pointe Coupée.[132]

St. Bernard and Plaquemines maintained the two smallest white populations in the territory in both 1810 and 1820. Frequent storms, hurricanes, and the dangers of flooding posed challenges to inhabitants, and deforestation exacerbated the effects of these phenomena, providing a serious disincentive for settlement. The largest settlement south of New Orleans was Terre aux Bœufs in St. Bernard Parish. The area had remained sparsely populated with isolated plantations until 1778, when Bernardo de Gálvez settled the area with Canary Islanders.[133] Further south was the settlement of Balize within Plaquemines Parish, located on the mouth of the Mississippi. The land surveyor and geographer William Darby wrote of Plaquemines:

"No towns have yet been built in this parish, or from the proximity to New Orleans, will any, in all probability, rise, possessing any considerable population."[134] St. Bernard, as an extension of New Orleans and a less prosperous region of Louisiana, lacked the independent leadership class found in other parishes. Sugar cultivation continued to expand during the first decades of U.S. control in St. Bernard. Claiborne appointed a former Spanish official, Antoine Mendez, as the first civil commandant of Terre aux Bœufs in St. Bernard Parish and then later as the judge of the parish. As in other areas, newly appointed judges enforced U.S. law, though when it could cost them or their friends' money or property, they appealed to Claiborne to subvert it. For example, Mendez wrote to Claiborne about a convicted slave, Ben, whom he wished to see freed from prison. Claiborne asked his attorney general whether this was appropriate, since he had no doubts as to the guilt of the accused.[135] Mendez's appointment proved unpopular within some quarters of the parish: "Mendez altho' a catholic, is said to be of Jewish extraction, and on this account (and for reasons unknown to me) is by no means a favourite with his neighbors, who manifested a disquietude at his appointment, and a few were imprudent enough to talk of not recognizing him as their Commandant."[136] Claiborne met with several of the local leaders, and despite the fact that he found Mendez largely above reproach replaced him as the civil commandant with James Carrick, a Scot active in business and member of the city council of New Orleans.[137] This decision came about in large measure as Claiborne did not wish for the United States to be associated with unpopular government at the local level. Even so, Mendez continued to receive lower-level appointments as a justice of the peace.[138]

After the U.S. cession, St. Bernard Parish faced domestic discord, due in large part to a local priest. This was the second of at least three internecine Catholic Church struggles that arose in concert with the dispute between the church hierarchy and Sedella in New Orleans. A priest appointed by the new church authorities, Jean Marie Rochanson, proved unacceptable to the older priests' adherents. The former priest had the support of Sedella in New Orleans.[139] Having learned of the problem, Claiborne instructed the commandant of his authority to act in response to any threat to public order.[140] The dispute resulted in violence between the two priests: "A priest who had been superseded by the Vicar General, had assaulted his Successor at the door of the Church, and expressed a wish to submit his case to the people. The Commandant added that the dismissed Priest excited disorder in the District and he apprehended a serious riot in the Church would ensue."[141] The manner in which the priest in St. Bernard chose to argue with the choice, by an appeal to the people rather than to the church hierarchy, reveals the adoption of new methods within Louisiana.

Soon thereafter Charles Fagot de la Garciniere, a native Louisianan who earlier served as sheriff in St. Bernard, became the judge of the parish.[142] Fagot had articles of impeachment introduced against him in the House of Representatives for a host of charges, including abuse of power and incompetence. For instance, he was accused of seizing the estate of Peter Dragon in favor of Martin Duplessis, William Beaumont, and M. Cornen and allowing his clerk of court to levy fees against Augustin Dupre and J. D. Saucier. Other alleged misconduct included fining Augustin Dupre for failing to give the sheriff the tax rolls and trying a slave of Colonel Shaumberg in a remote location without a defense and allowing his clerk of court to testify.[143] The House backed the petitioners and impeached Fagot.[144] Mendez then served in the interim until Claiborne appointed an Anglo-American, David Harper, as his replacement.[145] By 1815 another Francophone, Pierre Allard, served as the parish judge of St. Bernard.[146] St. Bernard as a majority Creole parish with strong connections to New Orleans frequently garnered Creole judicial appointments.

Below St. Bernard lies Plaquemines, where the Mississippi River enters the Gulf of Mexico. At the time of the U.S. cession the town of Balize held the customhouse as well as Fort St. Philip, which guarded the entry to New Orleans. In his overview of the territory before the U.S. administration took control, John Pintard wrote of the poor condition of the fort and the area around it.[147] Similarly, when architect Benjamin Latrobe arrived in New Orleans early in 1819, he came by sea, thoroughly unimpressed with Plaquemines.[148] As a point of strategic importance Claiborne at first turned the parish over to an army officer. Captain Henry M. Muhlenberg, descendant of a prominent Pennsylvania family, served as the first commandant.[149] His father, Major General Peter Muhlenberg, served in the American Revolution and was elected to the U.S. House of Representatives and then the U.S. Senate; his uncle, Frederick Augustus Conrad Muhlenberg, was the first Speaker of the House. Unfortunately, Captain Henry Muhlenberg lacked the strict morality of this prestigious Lutheran heritage. General Wilkinson believed him incapable of overseeing his duties: "Poor Mughlenburgh is devoted to drink, with good dispositions but feeble Intellect."[150] He would later be arrested for leaving his post. After Muhlenberg, Claiborne turned to Louisianans. Charles de Latour, a native-born Louisianan, served as the first parish judge in 1807 and continued in that post throughout the territorial period.[151] Despite coming from the region, Latour engaged in disputes with other authorities. In order to gain greater knowledge of the problems in the parish Claiborne sent George W. Morgan, the sheriff of the 1st Supreme Court District, to secure the parish records. One day later Claiborne instructed Morgan, a justice of the peace, and other citizens to deliver the seal of office and records to a justice, effectively entrusting him with the judicial authority. Claiborne continued to wonder about the specifics of Latour's problem, writing to Morgan: "I will thank you to inform yourself of the nature of the contest which has arisen between Judge Latour & Mr. Shaw a Justice of the Peace & of the causes of so much division among the Citizens & Civil Magistrates of Plaquemine."[152] Arnould-Louis de la Loubere Dubourg succeeded Latour and then in 1815 Gilbert Leonard became the judge of Plaquemines, a post he would hold for the next three decades.[153] As someone more familiar with the locality he proved more acceptable; in Plaquemines as in many southeastern parishes locals more easily secured positions.

One of the members of Orleans's county delegation to the state legislature with an interest in the downriver parishes was James Carrick.[154] The parish's first representative to the state House of Representatives was Godefroi Olivier. Voting irregularities barred Olivier from an active legislative career. Rather than a locked box for ballots, voters placed votes in a tin box or sugar dish, which allowed votes to be removed from the box by commissioners to check against the voter list, along with the denial of some citizens' suffrage, "on the ground of their being colored people, when nothing appeared to the commissioners to support such a charge." Fellow Creoles put forward the complaints, and the legislature ruled that white citizens had been disenfranchised falsely on the basis of race. The House's rulings invalidated Olivier's election, though after a motion by Stephen Hopkins of the Acadian Coast, the House gave Olivier time to meet the charges. Ultimately Olivier resigned, citing ill health.[155] Magloire Guichard replaced

Olivier in the second session and retained his seat through the third session.[156] At the third legislature Felix Forestall from Plaquemines served as part of the Orleans delegation.[157]

In several cases Anglo-American appointees presided over parishes throughout the territorial and early statehood period. Before the turnover to the United States, West Baton Rouge was administered from East Baton Rouge, so no resident commandant existed for U.S. officials to entrust with the office. In 1804 Dr. John Watkins appointed William Wykoff Sr. as a civil commandant, deeming him "remarkable for his attachment to the Government."[158] In addition to being a prominent planter, Wykoff, like most of the commandants, could speak French.[159] Though not a native French speaker, he knew the language and had settled in Louisiana before the American cession. In 1809 Claiborne recommended him as a potential candidate to fill a Legislative Council seat, calling him "a very honest man—is held in high estimation by his neighbors," whose command of English, Spanish, and French also distinguished him from others.[160] His son, William Wykoff Jr., served from 1807 to 1819 as the parish judge.[161] This is not to suggest that the administration ignored Creoles in West Baton Rouge, only that they did not attain the office of judge. James Wilkinson noted that a likely U.S. ally in Baton Rouge was Armand Duplantier: "aid de Camp to the Marquis de la Fayette towards the close of our Revolution, holds with the principles of those times,—His fortune and influence are very extensive—of good understanding, and speaks the three languages of the Province."[162] Still, in West Baton Rouge the governor entrusted the higher leadership positions to the Wykoffs.

In Rapides, appointing outsiders instead of local elites resulted in the creation of factions, with Anglo-Americans with ties to local Francophones at the heart of the opposition. Initially the U.S. government appointed William Miller, the son-in-law of the former commandant, Edmond Meullion, as the new commandant.[163] The Meullions were prominent landholders within the parish.[164] Miller, a Pennsylvanian, came to the area with his partner Alexander Fulton to engage in the Indian trade.[165] Miller served as the first judge of the parish, and after his tenure Thomas Dawson, previously of Mississippi, briefly took up the post in 1807.[166] Governor Claiborne then appointed his cousin, Richard Claiborne.[167] The governor rarely disclosed the family connection and occasionally denied it, most likely because he did not wish to be seen engaging in an act of nepotism for a member of his family who succumbed to chronic financial difficulties.[168] Richard Claiborne had served in the Virginia House of Delegates and held the rank of major in the Continental Army during the American Revolution as a quartermaster; in Louisiana he served as Claiborne's secretary and then as a clerk of court before his judgeship.

Once in Rapides, the new judge failed to reach an accord with the local population. Richard Claiborne wrote to former secretary of the territory John Graham about the party within Rapides that opposed him:

> In this party was a man bearing the name of Alexander Fulton . . . and if report be true belonged to the "whiskey Insurrection." . . . This fellow and another of the party by the name of Levi Wells . . . forwarded a memorial to the Territorial legislature to get me dismissed from office, but in this they failed and I was continued—these adversaries then took a stronger ground by having recourse to the Laws. . . . I was indited and trid before the Superior Court, and was honorably acquitted—not a single fact appeared against me.[169]

Fulton, Miller's partner, also from Pennsylvania, allegedly participated in the Whiskey Rebellion, which for Richard Claiborne proved reason enough to oppose him, since Richard favored the Federalist Party.[170] Fulton founded the city of Alexandria and along with Miller set up a store on the Red River in Rapides Parish before marrying Henrietta Wells. He also held a number of posts in Rapides, including coroner and postmaster. Levi Wells, Fulton's father-in-law, served in the territorial legislature, the state constitutional convention, and then in 1812 the state House of Representatives. Wells had moved from Opelousas to Rapides, where he received large land grants under the Spanish that he retained under the United States.[171] Colonel Fulton represented Rapides in the territorial legislature, illustrating the popularity of many members of the opposition to Richard Claiborne. Still another Richard Claiborne opponent, Hatch Dent, secured election to the state Senate in 1812. Dent came from Maryland, where he had practiced law. He migrated to Louisiana, where he became a planter, attorney, and clerk of court, justice of the peace, and later sheriff for the fourth superior district.[172] Like Miller, Dent married into the Meullion family.[173]

The nature of political conflict within Rapides did not arise out of local divisions, but due to the outside appointment and external political differences. The disagreement between Americans took on an ethnic dimension, through Miller's in-laws, but the contretemps would be more accurately framed as a conflict between an appointed outsider at odds with fellow Anglo-Americans with local connections. The party division continued to resonate in Rapides when Fulton and Wells leveled accusations that Claiborne as the judge charged with the collection of taxes defaulted on over a thousand dollars. A grand jury indicted him for extortion and malfeasance in office, though ultimately he was not convicted. After his term Richard Claiborne moved on to New Orleans and then to Alabama.[174] Dent resigned his civil and militia offices on June 1, 1809, after Claiborne escaped conviction. The local sheriff, R. Sackett, may have been responsible for the missing funds.[175]

Governor Claiborne attempted to defend his cousin and appointee, while simultaneously searching for an alternate office to remove him from the scene. His cousin's politics, however, remained an obstacle. In filling a position in Concordia he wrote: "I am unwilling to send to Concordia an Officer, who in any manner would interfere in the Elections, of the M. Territory and particularly one who would do so, in order to advance the cause of federalism; nor will I commission Major Claiborne if there should be just grounds to suppose, that he would pursue such a course."[176] He ended up offering the judgeship to David Lattimore.[177] Claiborne professed confidence in Richard's ethics if not his judgement: "I trust and verily believe, that the presentments, against you 'for extortion and oppression [no end of quote] in 'office' are without foundation; But pending such accusations, (exhibited as they have been by a Grand Jury) were you to be named Judge of another Parish, your Enemies might attribute such nomination to an unwillingness on your part to meet the charges, and a disposition on mine, to arrest further investigation."[178] To give his cousin an appointment elsewhere would subject both of them to further criticism. Ultimately Claiborne kept his post as judge of Rapides until his term expired.[179] William S. Johnson (son of a district judge) succeeded Claiborne and then Thomas C. Scott, who had served as a clerk of court.[180] Josiah Stoddard Johnston of Alexandria served as the judge from 1813 to 1821 before his election to Congress. Still, Claiborne did not turn to his cousin's prominent critics.

Until the cession, Avoyelles had been administered from Natchitoches or Pointe Coupée. When Claiborne received complaints that Francophone appointees, two syndics, Joseph Trelon and Robert Mayeaux, had exercised favoritism, Claiborne called on Edmond Meullion to investigate with full authority to retain or dismiss them and appoint others.[181] Meullion was a royalist doctor from Normandy who left France at the onset of the French Revolution. Meullion and the governor apparently felt that the complaints did not justify removal of appointees, although Claiborne instructed him: "State to them the necessity of punctuality and the most prompt and impartial execution of justice."[182] While U.S. officials carefully managed investigations of Creole appointees, Avoyelles included a number of Anglo-American outsiders in key appointed posts. In 1807 the first judgeship of the new parish of Avoyelles went to Philip Reibelt, who achieved his position principally due to his connection to Thomas Jefferson.[183] Indeed, Reibelt earlier garnered a factor appointment at Natchitoches and reported on the political situation as part of General Wilkinson's unofficial staff. Claiborne wrote that "Mr. Reibelt is certainly a very learned man, and as far as I know a very honest one;—But he is ill calculated to fill an office under a Republican Government."[184] When Claiborne appointed Reibelt, he did so knowing that Reibelt's circumstances would not be those of a great planter in Avoyelles.[185] Reibelt's position in some ways made him far more an administration man than local appointees, though he proved unsuited for the job. Thomas F. Oliver, originally from Massachusetts, replaced Reibelt in 1808.[186] When Oliver resigned, Claiborne proposed appointing Kenneth McCrummins as judge of Avoyelles, though if McCrummins accepted, he only briefly retained the post.[187] Claiborne shortly thereafter turned to a Francophone and native Louisianan, Alexander Plauché, who served from 1813 to 1816.[188] Plauché actively engaged in land speculation with Julien Poydras.[189]

Even further west, with the exception of Natchitoches, Claiborne appointed Anglo-Americans to judgeships. Travel and communication occurred across a complicated and large system of bayous that attached Attakapas and Opelousas through the Atchafalaya River basin to Bayou Lafourche and Bayou Plaquemines to the east and the Gulf of Mexico. The distance from New Orleans made it imperative to place loyal and capable men in appointments, but the problem was not strictly geographic; it was also demographic. Daniel Clark in 1803 wrote to James Madison explaining the challenges in these isolated western regions that remained uninformed of the advantages of American governance: "These are the only Places where the Prefects Emissaries had met with any success in persuading the lower Classes of the People that they would be benefited by the arrival of the French among them."[190] Evan Jones, U.S. consul at New Orleans before the transfer, described the population and the difficulties of governance for the United States in the western settlements of Opelousas, Attakapas, and Natchitoches: "Few men, if any, capable of exercising advantageously, the small portion of authority which the constitution and laws of the U.S. put into the hands of the ordinary magistrates."[191] A key difference for these western regions when compared to the east would be the impact of Anglo immigration on local demographics. Over time this immigration allowed the U.S. government a long-term solution to Jones's concerns. In general Claiborne's appointments in the western parishes reveal a habit of turning to Anglo-Americans, usually recent arrivals, in larger numbers than in the east.

H. M. Brackenridge, who came to the lower Mississippi in 1810 and remained over two years, described Attakapas as "destined to become one of the riches districts of Louisiana."[192] William Darby also noted the fecundity of the region.[193] Under the Spanish a significant number of immigrants to the region came from the United States, first as British loyalists fleeing the aftermath of the American Revolution and then as Americans seeking land.[194] The counties also contained a large proportion of Acadians.[195] While Opelousas and Attakapas contained large slave populations, they were not majority slave parishes.[196] Attakapas and Opelousas produced cotton, but their prairies proved ideally suited for raising cattle, as reflected in the tax lists and brand books of the parishes.

The area's location next to substantial Native American populations and Spanish territory encouraged Claiborne to appoint military officers to civilian positions in the region. For the first commandant of Attakapas and Opelousas, Claiborne appointed Lieutenant Henry Hopkins, an army officer from Maryland. In contrast to his critique of American personnel elsewhere, French traveler C. C. Robin praised Hopkins: "He was sober, gentle, honest, and well brought up, and by diligent application, soon reached the point where he no longer needed an interpreter." On the whole, though, Robin viewed the new government in a negative light given the large number of American appointees, which he believed ultimately would be counterproductive to U.S. control.[197] Claiborne explained to Madison that he could not divide the parish by favoring one party over another; an outsider thus provided an ideal choice, and petitions from Attakapas citizens regarding Hopkins's conduct confirmed this judgment.[198] In 1805 Captain John Bowyer, another American army officer, took over Hopkins's duties as the commandant of Opelousas. Despite their common profession, the two men failed to get along.[199] Their disagreements in part could be traced to conflicting personalities, but Hopkins also opposed Bowyer's practice of recognizing the legality of land sales from local tribes to private U.S. citizens. Claiborne sympathized with Hopkins and instructed him not to approve any further conveyances by Native Americans.[200] The disagreements persisted, with Claiborne mediating as best he could.[201]

Hopkins replaced a member of the local elite as the commandant of Attakapas and Opelousas, Louis-Charles Deblanc, a Creole born in Natchitoches, though Deblanc continued in office as a civil commandant.[202] When Hopkins arrested two citizens just after the cession in 1804, he called on Claiborne for advice. Hopkins failed to note their crime, so Claiborne instructed him to send them to New Orleans if they committed murder and to otherwise exercise mercy at the onset of U.S. rule.[203] The territorial government desired law and order, but did not want to engender resistance, and as a result commandants needed to tread softly.[204] Upon Hopkins's appointment Claiborne informed him that the area was divided into two parties and instructed him to treat both equally, something Deblanc failed to do. Deblanc welcomed U.S. governance in his letters to Claiborne, and his persistence in other offices proved politic given his popularity among segments of the local populace.[205]

In Attakapas internal divisions predated the Louisiana Purchase, centering on a murder accusation to which three governments reacted in quite different ways. In 1774 the commandant in the Attakapas was Alexandre Etienne Declouet, who initiated the factional division by prosecuting and jailing some locals for killing cattle. Land boundaries also began to be established under Declouet, which led to a series of feuds over property.[206] In 1795 the Spanish appointed Louis-Charles Deblanc as commandant, generating opposition from Declouet's sons, who felt the position should have gone to middle son Alexandre Declouet as captain of the local militia.[207] Alexandre Declouet proved popular in Attakapas according to C. C.

Robin, among "Acadians who were entirely devoted to him, not so much because he was the commander of the militia, but because of his simple, affectionate manner." The Declouets also had the support of the local parish priest Father Miguel Bernard Barière. Robin described Deblanc as a former French soldier from Paris: "His royalist inclinations naturally inclined him to the party of nobles. . . . He was incapable of the dark sentiments of hate, and still less was he able to retain them over long periods of time. But light-minded and weak, he was, without wishing it, susceptible to becoming an instrument of evil. How often are such men more dangerous than wicked people!"[208] Deblanc should have had few troubles with the Declouets, but the division was more about position than ideology, as Louis St. Julien noted: "This individual had long been linked with the Declouet family. At first, we saw great intimacy between these two families, but soon these warm relations cooled and quarrels followed."[209] St. Julien immigrated to Louisiana from Bordeaux and married into an Acadian family in Attakapas and became drawn into the Deblanc faction.[210] With the imminent turnover to France, Deblanc cultivated recent French immigrants.

When Deblanc ordered a census of Attakapas, he addressed the order to M. Sorel, whom Robin describes as "rich miser," but the execution of the census would be carried out by St. Julien, which created opposition from the Declouet faction, who believed any census not undertaken by Deblanc should fall to Alexander Declouet. Robin's account makes it appear that Deblanc did not have the authority from the Spanish to conduct such a census but instead took his instructions from the incoming French prefect Pierre-Clément Laussat. While St. Julien had contact with Laussat, multiple commandants received orders from the Spanish to conduct censuses in 1803.[211] Even so, Deblanc may have thought by appointing St. Julien he could ingratiate himself with the incoming government. When Laussat arrived, "M. Deblanc hastened to have himself introduced to M. Laussat, who welcomed him, the more so, because he wanted from this commander important information on the western regions of Louisiana and its boundaries." The controversy centered not on the census but on the official conducting it, and when faced with opposition, according to C. C. Robin, "Saint Julien in the course of this debate assumed the pose of a French patriot, and his statements rang with cries of liberty. The gist of his remarks was that everything connected with the Spanish regime should be abolished."[212] St. Julien's verbiage drew the attention of the Spanish authorities.[213] When Governor Manuel Salcedo and the Marqués de Casa Calvo learned of the troubles in Attakapas, they replaced Deblanc with a Basque appointee, Martin Duralde (a future father-in-law of Claiborne), and mandated that Deblanc remain in New Orleans.

Shortly thereafter, on June 17, 1803, an attack occurred on St. Julien in his home at night, resulting in the shooting of his wife. St. Julien's account was that his back was to the door when he heard a noise and saw a man with a gun. He struggled with the weapon; it went off, hitting his wife in the back. When he chased the assailant, two other men, whom he identified as members of the Declouet faction, beat him. His opponents charged him with committing the murder himself. As Robin noted, "The Party of St. Julien profited from this to heap opprobrium on the Desclouettes [sic] family." St. Julien failed to appear before Duralde despite multiple requests after his wife's murder.[214] When finally interviewed, St. Julien was sent to New Orleans for imprisonment.[215] Robin, as a French outsider journeying in American Louisiana, had a unique perspective, but his own inclinations color his narrative, and he ultimately believed the accusations leveled against St. Julien after speaking with the elder Declouet. Robin believed the motive for the murder was an extramarital affair between St. Julien's wife and a hired hand, Auboin.[216]

With the shift to French governance on November 30, 1803, the incoming French commissioner and prefect Pierre-Clément de Laussat released St. Julien just three days later. Laussat saw St. Julien as a French victim of Spanish injustice. In his account, Laussat described St. Julien as "a worthy and estimable planter," "Leblanc" (Deblanc) as "a military man of the greatest honor, a descendent of the St-Denis who founded Natchitoches," and Duralde as "a creature of the government secretary, a great demonstrator of exclusive and blind zeal for Spain, and to prove it, a declared persecutor of everyone in his district who avows himself to be French."[217] The French proclamation freeing St. Julien stated: "The origins of this affair lies in the attachment of Sieur Saint Julien to France, his country and that this fact notoriously had the effect of rendering him suspect and was regarded as criminal although the least discreet of his words could, under the circumstances in which the colony found itself hardly have been called imprudent."[218] The

Spanish according to Robin had been so damaged in the eyes of the public that it behooved Laussat to release the prisoner.[219]

Laussat endorsed one party within the parish with the release and Deblanc's reappointment as the commandant; in addition, Laussat removed Father Barière from the church he had served since 1795 and replaced him with Father Etienne Bernard Alexander Viel.[220] Robin reported that Barière had heard a confession from St. Julien's wife after her shooting and mandated a penance of silence as to the identity of her assailants. St. Julien's account confirms Barière's involvement, noting that he "apostrophized me as the author of offensive songs, which, he well knew, had not come from me. At the time I had a more violent dispute with him regarding certain liberties he had permitted himself with my wife." According to St. Julien's account, as his wife lingered for seven days before dying, the couple thought it best not to name the assailants for fear of reprisals, with Barière's encouragement.[221] Despite being removed from the church by Laussat, Barière continued to say mass.[222] The split thus turned religious, with St. Julien's advocates supporting the incoming priest Father Viel and his opponents supporting Barière.

The controversy surrounding St. Julien had an inherent national dimension with a Spanish government jailing him and a French government freeing him, disparaging Spanish justice in the process. The United States initially distrusted both factions due to their connections to monarchical Spain and Bonapartist France. Saint Julien noted of the more conservative faction, "At that time they were decidedly monarchists, and they made me, as well as the majority of the post, pass as determined republicans. Everything has changed on the surface, already they are all Americans, and I know that they will not represent the post as opposed to the actual government and often which if we put to the test, any other change we will see them turn against the authority which exists."[223] The situation in Attakapas required the incoming commandant Hopkins to navigate local politics defined in national terms.

Three key issues faced Hopkins and the territorial government. The issue of the murder and whether St. Julien should be tried, how to resolve the split within the local church, and how to heal the divisions in the political community. Deblanc supported St. Julien's release, but a number of

Attakapas inhabitants wanted a trial under the newly established legal system. Claiborne issued directions to Hopkins to act impartially. Depositions would need to be taken from St. Julien's opponents and defenders.[224] Claiborne reaffirmed this position to Madison: "St. Julien has many friends, and the general Sentiment is greatly in his favour: his accusers however have great Wealth, and Stand high in the confidence of the Spanish Government."[225] Citizens connected to the Spanish government, such as the Declouet family, wanted another trial. Declouet and a Mr. Pedesclaux, who were removed from office by Laussat during the affair, appealed to President Jefferson. Secretary of State James Madison instructed Claiborne to inform Declouet that the issue remained a judicial one and that any loss Pedesclaux felt his removal incurred should be addressed to the legislature.[226] Hopkins maintained St. Julien's accusers had connections to the previous Spanish government.[227] This was not American paranoia. Louis Declouet, the younger son of the former commandant, penned a memorial to the Spanish government during the War of 1812 that proposed a Spanish invasion of Louisiana with one force of cavalry entering from New Spain, while two other prongs would enter Lake Pontchartrain and the Mississippi River. Declouet listed over three dozen citizens, some of them Anglo-Americans, friendly to the Spanish cause, a number of whom had received offices from the American government as commandants, judges, and members of the Legislative Council as well as militia positions.[228] The Declouet memorial demonstrates the fungible nature of national loyalties in a region that had undergone so many changes in sovereignty. Casa Calvo also intervened, writing to Claiborne that Laussat miscarried justice by freeing St. Julien and issuing his insulting proclamation.[229] Spanish entreaties likely proved counter to their interest given U.S. suspicions over Spanish machinations and Claiborne's specifically about Casa Calvo. U.S. officials in New Orleans desired a reputation for impartiality to hold the respect of all factions, and Washington officials wished to keep the process as locally centered as possible. Jefferson wrote to Madison noting that St. Julien could be prosecuted under U.S. authority but that "the local judge must decide I. whether crimes committed against the nation of Louisiana under it's former organization, can be punished under it's present one? and 2. whether St. Julien is guilty?"[230] Claiborne permitted St. Julien's return to Attakapas but ordered him to appear when called upon by authorities.[231] Ultimately

St. Julien appeared before Hopkins to be deposed, but Declouet and other accusers failed to appear, resulting in his continued freedom.[232] Neither Hopkins nor Claiborne pressed for another trial.[233]

The political division within the locality divided the local Catholic congregation, as both Father Viel and Father Barière, backed by supporters, claimed to be the parish priest.[234] Madison issued instructions on the church controversy in Attakapas: "The dispute between the two Priests at Attakapas may be considered 1st. as a litigation of private rights. 2nd. in relation to a breach of the peace. In the first view it falls under the judicial cognizance, like other controversies between individuals. In the 2d. it requires penal or preventive measures, as in other cases for a breach of the peace. These are the ideas of the President, but they are not meant as dictates to the judicial discretion."[235] It did not matter to officials in Washington who controlled the church, but they did not wish to be seen interfering in religious disputes. The violence that did ensue forced Hopkins to close the church temporarily in the name of public safety. Vicar General Patrick Walsh settled the issue by confirming Barière in the post, which territorial officials preferred, rather than have the government directly alienate one of the priests and his partisans.[236] Still, Claiborne instructed Hopkins to take back the key if violence recurred, cautioning that "this step must not be taken, unless it should be absolutely necessary to the preservation of peace and good order."[237] Barière's continuation as priest allowed the Declouet faction a victory in light of the failure to prosecute St. Julien.

Jefferson regretted Hopkins's intervention: "I think it was an error in our officer to shut the doors of the church, & in the Governor to refer it to the Roman Catholic head. The priests must settle their differences in their own way, provided they commit no breach of the peace. If they break the peace they should be arrested. On our principles all church-discipline is voluntary; and never to be enforced by the public authority; but on the contrary to be punished when it extends to acts of force."[238] Events on the ground, however, outpaced the president's instructions, which benefited Father Barière. C. C. Robin in contrast approved of the decision to close the church, since it likely prevented violence.[239] The territorial government's relationship with the Catholic Church's leadership became important in other church disputes. Two days after Jefferson's letter was written, Claiborne requested a commission from Secretary of War Henry Dearborn for Walsh's brother in the U.S. Army, which helped cement the connection between the Catholic and territorial leadership of the territory.[240]

Hopkins's decision to preserve public order while allowing Catholic officials to handle internecine disputes remained in keeping with the general tenor of the U.S. approach. Hopkins received Claiborne's approbation, and the governor requested an extension from Wilkinson when Hopkins's commanding officer, Colonel Freeman, moved to reassign him.[241] When the army did reassign Hopkins to Detroit, Claiborne informed Hopkins that he would secure an appointment for him should he resign.[242] Hopkins accepted and took command of the territorial militia. While previous regimes operated by viewing St. Julien through a revolutionary or counterrevolutionary lens, the U.S. administration successfully triangulated by keeping as aloof from the process as possible. Given the fluid loyalties in the region the territorial government needed to not aggravate elites who feared the French Revolutionary radicalism to which the United States offered a moderate counterpart but also to retain the support of the popular faction.

When Hopkins moved on to his new appointment, Edward C. Nichols replaced him in Attakapas as the judge.[243] Nichols was born in England but educated in France by Jesuits at the College of St. Omer. He then settled in Maryland after leaving his religious education and migrated to New Orleans after the cession.[244] Nichols as an Anglo fluent in the local language advanced quickly and came highly recommended. When Nichols chose to move to Louisiana, he informed Madison, mentioning his friendship and trust in James Monroe's patronage. Nichols also had served as a clerk under Albert Gallatin at the Treasury Department.[245] Despite his friends in high places, Claiborne failed to be fully satisfied with Nichols as a clerk of court in New Orleans.[246] In Attakapas Nichols again disappointed. As Claiborne pointed out to Madison, "The gentlemen whom . . . I appointed to Offices within Atachapas, have not profited by Mr. Hopkin's good example;—on the contrary they have neither commanded, for themselves, or for the Law, the public respect; and such is (at this time) the state of things."[247] Nichols proved unpopular with the citizens of Attakapas. James Brown in his report to the secretary of the treasury wrote: "The County of Attacapas, where the extortions, resistance of law, and oppressive acts of the County Judge Edward Nichols *are said* to have rendered the presence of the Executive necessary in order to tranquilize the public mind. The conduct of Mr. Nichols has excited much clamor; and were you to credit one half the rumors respecting him, you would believe that the barbarities and extortions of Verres in Sicily were outdone by this dilapedator of the Attacapas."[248] In June of 1805 Louis Brognier Declouet wrote to his uncle Pierre-Joseph Favrot in Spanish West Florida: "Attakapas, an infernal country. Truly I do not understand why my family wants to live in a place inhabited by such contemptible people."[249] The factional split again erupted when the Declouet family won a land dispute and the sheriff carried out the order to remove the other proprietor; locals stopped him with force, bound him, and took him to Nichols. According to Robin, Judge Nichols, "fearing the same treatment of his honorable shoulders, welcomed these noble knights courteously and found no illegal action." Given this attack on a sheriff, the dispute over St. Julien, and the church affair, Claiborne journeyed to Attakapas in December of 1805. Robin, though initially quite critical of Claiborne, noted: "His manner was peaceful, his face and even his voice displayed his good intentions. If he expressed himself badly in French, he made up for it by his genial manners. His stay in Louisiana had caused him to lose the stiffness of the Americans without losing that noble simplicity so distinctive of officials of popular governments." Claiborne met and visited with members of both parties. Robin believed the real purpose of the United States was to make both parties dependent given the value of Attakapas and its proximity to Spanish territory: "It was, then, politically expedient not to alienate the inhabitants of this district from the American government; to attempt to secure the support of both parties but to allow them both to exist in order to encourage their rivalry in soliciting the help of the American government." The governor dismissed the sheriff while keeping Nichols in office, which Robin attributed to Nichols's character: "Wily, adroit, and knowing the district, he was useful to the government in observing what went on. This view of things required the sacrifice of the spotless lamb and the retention of the goat, loaded with iniquities."[250] This was a cynical analysis but retained an element of truth in that the U.S. wished to retain support from multiple factions.

Robin as a Frenchman in the early nineteenth century came by his cynicism honestly, but the cynical take was shortsighted. Claiborne during his visit stayed with Martin Duralde, whom the Spanish appointed after Deblanc's removal. The governor did not visit Nichols, however, and in a letter likely from Nichols, he received a long diatribe that insisted:

> First I will not be immolated to gratify party spirit.—My reputation will not be the mangled sacrifice by which, a measure of popularity may accrue to any man! I have made sacrifices enough through my ardent attachment and zeal for your Excellency's person and welfare.—be pleased to recollect my petition to the legislature and the subsequent additional sacrifices of my interest at your Excellency's desire in my compromise with Major Trask. I say nothing of the injury I have received in the loss of the good will to say no more of a certain highly respected family in town; through my endeavors to promote your happiness and poorly indeed very poorly have I been requited. . . . Your Excellency could not procure proper characters to fill the different departments and this office it to[o] is well known was not lucrative, if there were any obligation on either side, your Excellency and my Government *owe it to me* for my acceptance.

The letter went on to note that it was appropriate for the governor to visit Deblanc and Declouet to ease community tensions but that by failing to visit the author first he had been insulted and abandoned in the eyes of his constituents:

> In all countries the countenance of the chief is deemed necessary, and polite; in this country, where the chiefs have been usually looked up to, as demigods that countenance from you; was absolutely necessary *though not by me expected on my own personal acct. solely.* By this neglect you have held me up to the public eye, as a man unworthy of your protection, or rather the protection of his government and below its consideration and you have fixed me as an object of derision and scorn, *as far as your neglect and inattention toward me, will go.*

The letter then asserted that Claiborne had publicly insulted him in these meetings with locals: "You there said 'you had sent to their country a *young gentleman* in whom you had placed your whole confidence who had executed his duty faithfully and satisfactorily' [most likely Hopkins] and there your Excellency said nothing but the truth though perhaps *not well timed.*— that he had been recalled you had sent on an old man and in him you had *been deceived.*—that you had sent for a sheriff strongly recommended and in him you had been deceived." The author then contended that Hopkins told him that he had far fewer difficulties and the use of soldiers to back his decision, whereas the author had to introduce American law and government into a wilderness alone.[251] If the letter was from Nichols, he was infuriated with Claiborne. Far from backing the judge, as was Robin's take, Claiborne had abandoned him, and he was soon replaced.

Nichols's successor, Judge James White, was an Anglo-American from Philadelphia who served in North Carolina's State Assembly and as a delegate to the Continental Congress. After the Revolution he served as a superintendent of Indian affairs for the southern district, where he became familiar with Spanish officials, and moved to Louisiana around 1799. Like Nichols, he too attended the College of St. Omer in France. White possessed all of Nichols's qualifications plus greater experience in dealing with Native Americans and the Spanish. After White's death in 1809, Claiborne turned to yet another Anglo-American, Seth Lewis of Massachusetts, who served as the chief justice of Mississippi when Claiborne was Mississippi's governor; Lewis served as judge until 1813, when he became a district court judge.[252] Attakapas commandants and judges were all Anglo-American newcomers to the area rather than local grandees. When Attakapas split into St. Martin and St. Mary Parishes the trend continued.[253]

Claiborne asked for Lewis's recommendation for the position of judge of St. Mary, and shortly thereafter Henry Johnson received his appointment.[254] Johnson came from Virginia and arrived in the territory around 1809. He served as a clerk to the Second Superior Court before his appointment.[255] Johnson held the post until 1813 and went on to election to the U.S. Senate in 1819 and the governorship in 1824.[256] When Martin Duralde and Major Charles Olivier became potential Senate candidates in 1812, Claiborne relied on Johnson to get one or the other to drop out.[257] Members of the Francophone community of St. Mary criticized Claiborne for these Anglo appointments, as he noted: "It had been asserted, that I had in the most positive & solemn manner promised the appointment of sheriff to a Creole Gentleman, & the very next day nominated G. W. Morgan."[258] Despite the criticism, the trend continued, as John Wilkinson succeeded Henry Johnson as judge in St. Mary.[259]

In St. Martin Creoles discerned the same dominance of outsiders. Ransom Eastin, originally of Virginia, took the place of Seth Lewis in 1813 when he moved onto the circuit court.[260] Judge Eastin was replaced in 1815 by Attakapas's first Francophone judge, Paul L. Briant, who held the post until 1845, when his son succeeded him.[261] Briant was an immigrant from Saint-Domingue who had served in the French army and then immigrated to Jamaica and New Orleans. He operated as a merchant in St. Martin Parish, practiced law, and then attained the position of sheriff.[262]

In the legislature, in contrast, Attakapas's Francophones regularly secured office. The first representatives elected from Attakapas to the territorial legislature were Joseph Sorrel and Martin Duralde.[263] Other elected representatives initially came from the Francophone elite of the parish rather than Anglo-American newcomers. For instance, Joseph Sorrel arrived in the area before the transfer to Spain as a member of the French army and established a "vacherie" to ship cattle to New Orleans. By 1812 Anglo-Americans secured election to the Louisiana legislature from Attakapas. Among their number were Colonel Joshua Baker, who served in the Revolutionary War and the Kentucky constitutional convention, and David Rees, a Revolutionary War veteran from Pennsylvania. Nathaniel Kemper, elected to the state Senate, had actively advocated rebellion within Spanish Florida.[264]

Appointments within Opelousas went to Anglo-Americans exclusively. The Opelousas post commandant after Henry Hopkins in 1805, Captain John Bowyer, had his own problems with some of the locals, particularly a prominent landholder, Robert Rogers, who was charged with assaulting the captain.[265] When Bowyer was involved in a court-martial, Claiborne briefly appointed Theophilus Collins as the commandant of Opelousas in his stead.[266] Collins, from the United States, lived in the territory before the U.S. cession and served as a judge until 1807. Anglo-American judges from the parish of St. Landry included John Thompson (1807–12) and George King (1812–42), both of Virginia.[267] King immigrated to Louisiana by way of Kentucky. He served on diplomatic missions to New Orleans and in 1794 fought alongside General Anthony Wayne in the Ohio country before moving to New Orleans around 1795. King served as the clerk for Opelousas County and a major in the eighth militia regiment before becoming the local judge.[268] He failed to be particularly conscientious in his tax collecting duties, and the state House of Representatives recommended his removal from office in 1818 due to his negligence.[269] The incident was all the more odd, since Judge King earlier removed a Kentuckian, Cornelius Voorhies, as a tax collector for holding on to public money too long without turning it over to Colonel William Wykoff as instructed by the territorial treasurer.[270]

Wykoff was one of the most prominent Opelousas citizens. Claiborne described Wykoff and Collins as: "Native Americans, Men of clear property, sense and Integrity;—of their political sentiments I have no knowledge."[271] William Darby in his examination of the prairies of Opelousas wrote: "It may be presumed that Mr. Wikoff is at this time the greatest pastoral farmer in the United States."[272] Wykoff was one of the first people to be recommended to the U.S. government when Wilkinson provided characterizations of locals to the president: "Wikoff of the Appalousas an American is reputed, the man of first fortune and influence there (for in Louisiana they are inseparable) and it is certain he was among the most early settlers, but He is ignorant."[273] Despite Wilkinson's estimation of his ignorance, Claiborne recommended both Wykoff and Collins to the president for appointment to the Legislative Council, and the president selected Wykoff.[274] Representatives from Opelousas demonstrated greater heterogeneity. The most long-standing legislator for the period from Opelousas was Garrigues Flaujac, who represented Opelousas in the state Senate.[275] Flaujac had served as a French infantry officer and resided in Saint-Domingue before immigrating to Opelousas and marrying into the Fontenot family. In 1812, he became a brigadier general in the Louisiana militia.[276]

In Iberville, American appointees tended to be the rule. The United States replaced the commandant of Iberville, Francis Rivas, as he deliberately chose not to serve the incoming government, but according to Dr. Watkins, "begged me to assure you that the American Government might calculate upon his cordial support." Despite Watkins's recommendation of Nicholas Rousseau, Claiborne appointed the individual whom Rivas recommended, Francis Connell, originally of South Carolina, though as discussed in chapter 4, Connell's tenure and that of his successor, Pierre Bailly, became contentious.[277] Claiborne in his appointment letter made clear that "the office of Commandant should be to some person better qualified and in whom greater confidence can be placed than in Francis Connell."[278] After 1806 Claiborne took a greater interest in Iberville, and to set things right appointed Judge Nathaniel Meriam, originally of Massachusetts, who served until 1813.[279] After Meriam's appointment, Claiborne specified a series of officials for appointment to the lesser offices within the parish, the sort of decisions often left to the discretion of the local judge.[280] These directions might indicate less trust in the judge but also may be due to Claiborne's familiarity with the parish.[281] In addition to his judicial duties, Meriam represented Iberville in the state Senate.[282] When Meriam resigned in 1812, Claiborne urged him to continue to serve until a suitable replacement could be found and asked Meriam for recommendations.[283] Ultimately, Claiborne selected John Dutton of Pointe Coupée.[284] Dutton came from the planter class and served in his position into the 1840s.[285]

Concordia and Ouachita in northeast Louisiana had small slave populations and larger Anglo-American populations than regions to the south.[286] In Concordia a local Spanish grandee, Joseph Vidal, served as commandant from 1802 to 1805, straddling the Spanish and U.S. periods of control.[287] Vidal's successors tended to come from the United States. Ferdinand Claiborne, the governor's brother, served as the civil and military commandant until Governor Claiborne turned the civil commandant position to L. Wooldridge.[288] James Williams of Mississippi became the first judge of Concordia County in 1805 and the following year Samuel Sidney Mahon replaced him.[289] Mahon was a large landholder, captain in the ninth militia regiment, and served in the territorial House of Representatives.[290] In 1807 Colonel James Ross, an American from Pennsylvania, became judge and would serve until 1808.[291] Ross's son George served as the sheriff of New Orleans until his purported involvement in the Burr conspiracy. The same year James's daughter, Catherine, married Richard Claiborne. While George was not pleased by the connection, his father benefited from the union.[292] Claiborne next offered the post of judge of Concordia to Dr. David Lattimore, originally of Virginia, who hesitantly accepted because he intended to leave the territory shortly thereafter.[293] In 1809 Benjamin Tennell, an American from North Carolina, assumed the post.[294] In 1811 James Dunlap became the parish judge of Concordia until 1813, when John Perkins succeeded him.[295] Dunlap was the son of Presbyterian minister and president of Jefferson College Reverend James Dunlap, though he was lately of Natchez, Mississippi.[296] Perkins was born in Maryland and immigrated to Mississippi Territory before coming to Concordia, where he accumulated large holdings. This series of judges for Concordia illustrates a high degree of turnover but also the dominance of Anglo-American outsiders. Elected representatives likewise included a large number of Anglo-Americans. James Dunlap and David B. Morgan secured election to the state constitutional convention. Morgan, a recent immigrant from Massachusetts, arrived in 1803 and became the surveyor general for Louisiana and Mississippi while he served in the militia.[297] Older inhabitants still retained influence too, as demonstrated by Joseph Vidal's election in 1811 to the territorial legislature.[298]

Ouachita Parish likewise received Anglo appointees, and when Francophones secured office they were not from the locality. In Ouachita Robin noted the first commandant as the Frenchman Filiol and his successor Cotard, a Spaniard. Robin described the new American commandant of Ouachita, Lt. Bowmar: "His education and abilities were very limited, and yet he was dispatched to this distant post, and provided with extensive powers of the Spanish commandants to govern the heads of families of whom some were venerable grey-beards, including veterans of military service. I was much surprise at this choice, having previously had an impression that the United States Government was more prudent than this." The predicament of finding competent and well-respected parish officials who could also fulfill the needs of the metropole linked the Spanish and American periods, as Robin observed that under the Spanish commandants in the interior knew only French. Robin maintained a negative opinion of American appointees over the older local commandants of the Spanish: "These American commandants: young, ignorant, drunkards; not knowing a word of French, or having the least notion of the customs of the people they were governing; often had resident in their districts, venerable heads of families who were former French and Spanish military officers. The haughtiest conqueror never treated the vanquished with less consideration. I saw the commandant in Ouachita dispensing justice in his fort, amidst the cacophony of fiddles and thick fumes of tafia. He reversed in the evening, judgments in the morning."[299] Claiborne appointed C. L. P. Danemours as a judge in 1805 in Ouachita. Danemours had been a French consul in Baltimore under the royalist government.[300] As a French speaker he could gain some measure of Creole trust, but as a recent immigrant, a royalist, and an individual who had resided in the United States, territorial officials believed he could be trusted. Danemours's time as judge proved short, however; in 1806 James McLaughlin of Virginia succeeded him.[301] The following year Henry Bry became the judge of Ouachita.[302] Claiborne noted his respectability and facility with both French and English.[303] Bry was born in Geneva and after immigrating received a position in the U.S. Land Office.[304] The yearly turnover came to an end in 1809 with the appointment of Thomas C. Lewis, originally from Kentucky.[305] In 1813 New Englander Oliver J. Morgan took up the post of judge, which he held into the 1820s.[306] Ouachita representatives tended to be Anglo-Americans, with Bry, who served as a state senator, a notable exception.

In Lafourche locals at first garnered the highest local office but then gave way to Anglo-American officials. Lafourche contained large areas of bayou that branched out of the Mississippi. The region closest to the river along the north and west became Assumption Parish, while the area to the south and east that touched the Gulf of Mexico was referred to as the Interior of Lafourche and later simply Lafourche Parish. Geographer William Darby described the interior as largely unfit for agriculture, though Darby and H. M. Brackenridge both noted that the regions next to the river allowed for successful sugar cultivation.[307] Despite this, Lafourche and Assumption contained small slave populations.[308]

Rafael Croquer served as a Spanish officer in Lafourche before the U.S. cession. Like several other former Spanish officials, Croquer refused to serve the United States, so instead Dr. Watkins turned to Joseph Landry as the civil commandant of the upper part of Lafourche or Lafourche de Chatimachur. Watkins described Landry as an Acadian of long residence in Louisiana: "Speaks the English and French Languages, professes strong attachment to the Government of the United States, and possesses the unlimited confidence and affections of all the inhabitants of the District in which he lives." The former Spanish commandant for the District of Valenzuela dans La Fourche, Thomas de Villanueva, a Canary Islander, accepted the U.S. appointment.[309] Both Villanueva and Landry proved cooperative in fulfilling instructions from United States officials, but when the shift from commandants to county judges came, Claiborne selected Anglo-Americans; James Mather, a British immigrant, merchant and Legislative Council member, became the judge of Lafourche County.[310] In the letter informing Landry to turn over his papers, Claiborne noted that Mather held two new commissions for him.[311] Judgeships within Lafourche changed quickly, however, as just a year later Bela Hubbard, originally of Connecticut, replaced Mather.[312] In 1807 when the county split into two parishes, Hubbard became judge of Assumption and William Henry the judge of Lafourche.[313] Henry was replaced in 1808 by another American, William Goforth.[314] Goforth, a doctor, came originally from Connecticut, though he had spent time in Ohio.[315] In 1813 François B. Courvoisier succeeded Hubbard as the judge for Assumption.[316] The appointments illustrate a tendency on Claiborne's part to turn to Anglo-Americans in Lafourche.

In contrast, voters in Lafourche regularly elected Creoles as their representatives. Nicholas Verret and Henry S. Thibodeaux represented the county at the first territorial legislature.[317] Thibodeaux was an orphaned French Canadian who had been raised by General Philip Schuyler and educated in Scotland before coming to Louisiana in 1790.[318] In 1807 Joseph Brown served as a representative from Lafourche, replacing Verret, and upon his death Claiborne called for a new election.[319] When Joseph Hebert, a local Acadian, secured election to the territorial House of Representatives, the House resolved not to accept his election because of voting irregularities.[320] In 1809 Thibodeaux served alongside Pierre Aucoin of Assumption in the territorial legislature.[321]

Natchitoches contained a prominent Creole community. The Spanish had encountered problems in governing Natchitoches due to strong French attachments, and under the United States the first commandants and judges came from the United States.[322] On appointing army officer Edward Turner, originally of Massachusetts, as commandant of Natchitoches, Claiborne wrote: "The Friendly disposition of the more remote and frontier Settlements, is particularly desirable."[323] In 1805 Turner wrote to Claiborne of a small opposition: "At present every thing is tranquil here, and in fact I flatter myself that except by a few people of wealth who are here, there never has been any demonstration shown, but these gentlemen I believe sincerely wish the American Government to the Devil."[324] The Indian agent in Natchitoches, John Sibley, likewise detected opposition to the United States owing to the necessity for a district Superior Court in Natchitoches, doubts over land claims, and the circulation of the opposition *New York Herald* in the district: "There is certainly considerable distance between American versus French Republicans, the latter are so much taken with whatever is fashionable in France of St. Domingo, that if John Adams was a candidate for emperor & his election was advocated by the *New York Herald* he would [hold] a pretty respectable Poll in Louisiana; but Thomas Jefferson would stand but little chance."[325] Sibley went on to explain his signing of the memorial to Congress for local political interests, not over any opposition to the governor. Opposition to the U.S. territorial government given the prominence of the *New York Herald* in Sibley's estimation could not just be centered on Francophones. Turner focused on the Creole element, writing in 1805 that Claiborne should appoint Lieutenant Bludworth to act when he had to leave for a court-martial because of disorder in Natchitoches that he traced to Prudhomme:

> Mr. Prudhomme's party I suspect are secretly working to injure the government. They have lately had a meeting glossed with the pretense that it was to devise means to induce the Cure to continue with them who on Easter Sunday gave out to the astonishment of his congregation that he was about to leave the parish, but who I believe in truth, had no such ideas and was only scheming to get the people together—at the meeting I am informed he kept the ostensible in sight, but deviated much in substance after reading an exordium which accused the people of being led away by the *Americans,* they professed to discountenance all persons settling within this district, but true Romans.

Thus Turner believed Spanish encouragement played a role in Prudhomme's faction's opposition.[326] Despite these assessments, Claiborne on several occasions observed the loyalty of the Natchitoches population. In a letter to Colonel Cushing in 1806 he noted his surprise at the level of support from the local population after visiting the area, and again in a letter to Secretary of War Henry Dearborn a month later he wrote of Natchitoches: "Every American residing there, with whom I conversed, agreed in opinion, that the French part of the society was generally disaffected. But I trust, we shall all be disappointed; of one thing, I am convinced, that the Louisianans who are not for us, will remain neutral."[327] Less than a stellar endorsement to be sure, but it illustrates a growing confidence. Yet locals still did not receive appointments. In 1805 Claiborne appointed a recent Anglo-American arrival, John Alexander, as the first judge of the county of Natchitoches.[328] Claiborne wrote to Alexander specifying that he should appoint lower officials with his blank commissions but noted that the coroner and treasurer and two justices should be "ancient Louisianans" and two of the justices Anglo-Americans.[329] This was intended as an attempt to balance ethnic divisions in lower-level positions. When Alexander left the position Claiborne turned to a former commandant, making Edward Turner judge of the parish.[330] Turner served for a year, until 1807, whereupon he shifted to Ascension Parish. Then another outsider, John C. Carr, became the judge of the parish.[331] Carr came from England via Kentucky and quickly became a large slaveholder.[332] He proved unwilling or unable to prevent filibusters and may have resigned in order to join an expedition in 1812.[333] When Carr left his position, Claiborne nominated the first Creole to a judicial position in Natchitoches, Evariste Lauve, originally of New Orleans.[334] Lauve served but briefly and was replaced by P. D. Gailleau Lafontaine, who served from 1813 to 1819. As in other parishes, the men elected to the legislature from Natchitoches included a greater number of Creoles from the planter class. For instance, J. Prudhomme's father had been a prominent local planter and physician who had been active in the militia.[335] The parishes that emerged from Natchitoches likewise had judicial officials from outside. In Catahoula the first parish judge, serving from 1809 to 1810, was an American, Benjamin Tennell.[336] Tennell's son-in-law Robert Hall succeeded him and served until 1813. Hall in turn was replaced in 1814 by Sam Lightner, who held the post into the 1820s.

The Anglo population of West Florida outnumbered Creoles by a substantial margin. Though the West Florida parishes never became part of the larger sugar plantation culture of the parishes of southern and eastern Louisiana, cotton and slavery made inroads, and the planter class came to dominate political offices.[337] The West Florida rebellion left a series of political fissures, but the demography allowed Claiborne to have his cake and eat it too by empowering local elites and Anglo-Americans simultaneously. In making appointments in West Florida, Claiborne wrote to Secretary of State Robert Smith about the division between supporters of the West Florida rebellion and their critics: " It is wished that I also should participate in those prejudices, and act under their influence in appointing to office; but such a conduct does not comport with my disposition to be just to all parties."[338] Individuals involved in the West Florida rebellion achieved appointments, but the territorial government did not entrust one faction with all appointments. Feliciana and East Baton Rouge remained firm advocates for attachment to Orleans, in contrast to St. Helena and St. Tammany.[339] A number of citizens sent memorials to Congress urging that they not be separated from the territory of Orleans; petitioners also appealed to Congress to relieve the debt they had acquired from West Florida's movement for independence.[340] Rumors of the future of the West Florida parishes further weakened Louisiana's authority in the region, as Claiborne observed of Feliciana when rumors emerged that they might not continue as part of Orleans: "It occasions many good Citizens to believe that their political destiny is yet uncertain; and the base and designing are incessant in their attempts to promote discontent."[341] Claiborne reported that a group of citizens in Feliciana raised the Florida flag (the lone star flag, a white star on a blue background) though General Hampton had it taken down, as the governor wrote to General Thomas: "But the rearing of the Florida flag and the reluctance with which it was taken down, may by some be construed as evidence of ill-will toward the American Government. For myself I feel assured that the great majority of the people of Feliciana are real Americans."[342] Claiborne's reference to these people as real Americans is telling. "Real Americans" may refer to native-born Americans, but the individuals who raised the West Florida flag were decidedly not adherents of the Spanish system, with many of them likely native-born Americans. "Real Americans" for Claiborne in this case were individuals who did not take part in opposition.

Officials selected in West Florida by and large came from within the parishes; many of the appointees were first-generation immigrants who arrived before the U.S. takeover. Claiborne turned down numerous outside requests for patronage. He wrote to Biddle Wilkinson informing him and his friend Mr. Andrews that they would not receive offices in Feliciana: "I have deemed it an Act of Justice to the Inhabitants to give them in all cases the preference."[343] These patronage practices offer a sharp contrast to other areas of Louisiana. Claiborne informed Robert Smith of his general policy for judicial appointments for West Florida in describing George Mather and Andrew Steele: "My appointments to office will for the most part be taken from the old inhabitants of the District. . . . Each of these Gentlemen have acquired the confidence of this Society and are capable honest men, and well affected to the American government."[344] Both of these men took part in the West Florida Convention; Mather received a judicial appointment from Claiborne, and Steele received a commission to replace Mather in Baton Rouge shortly thereafter in 1811.[345] Steele oversaw a contentious parish; in 1813 the local sheriff, James Neilson Sr., was accused of head-ing a party that invaded a man's home and killed two men.[346] Claiborne on January 24, 1811, appointed William D. Nicholas as the judge of East Baton Rouge Parish.[347] In 1815 Charles Tossier became the parish judge.[348] Claiborne also offered justice appointments to men such as Fulwar Skipwith, the former executive of the brief West Florida Republic and the son-in-law of Nathaniel Greene.[349] Skipwith had refused an earlier appointment as a justice, but the offer illustrates Claiborne's commitment to appoint supporters of the West Florida rebellion.

In Feliciana, Claiborne appointed John Rhea as judge.[350] Rhea, originally from Pennsylvania, served as an alcalde from 1802 to 1810, represented Feliciana at the West Florida Convention, and eventually became its president.[351] Claiborne described Rhea to James Monroe as committed to the American government.[352] Rhea quickly grew tired of the post, yet Claiborne urged him to stay on given the high level of support among his constituents but if he insisted on resignation to make recommendations as to his successor.[353] To replace Rhea, Claiborne inquired about Henry Hosford Gurley, James Bradford, and Captain Griffith. Gurley, originally from Connecticut, served as a justice of the peace but in Claiborne's estimation was too young to receive the appointment.[354] Bradford, originally from Virginia, had owned the *Orleans Gazette* and printed for the Orleans government but lost this contract over criticism of Claiborne's handling of the Burr conspiracy.[355] After Bradford's arrest by James Wilkinson during the crisis, he grew increasingly critical of the government, at which point he moved to St. Francisville, established the *Time Piece,* and published documents for the West Florida Convention.[356] The governor remained no more fond of Bradford's editorials at the *Time Piece* than those of the *Orleans Gazette:* "The Editor possesses Genius, But neither Judgment nor discretion."[357] When the governor floated Bradford's name, it was more likely to gain a reputation for evenhandedness than for serious consideration. Claiborne justified his decision as if Bradford and Gurley canceled one another out: "When the people of a parish seem divided in their wishes as to the nomination of a parish Judge, I deem it expedient to select some worthy & capable Character, in whose favour, neither party had taken an active Interest."[358] Consequently, Claiborne appointed Thomas Butler from Pennsylvania. Butler had been involved in the Burr expedition and after its failure worked as an attorney in Mississippi before moving to Feliciana in 1811. Butler declined, whereupon

Claiborne turned to John P. Hampton of Mississippi.[359] Claiborne explained to Rhea that despite his lack of familiarity with Hampton, "Gentlemen in whom I confide, represent him, 'as a young Man of accomplished education—possessing' 'a fund of legal information—of exemplary morals, and 'the purest integrity.'"[360] Hampton quickly resigned and returned to Mississippi, and Bradford continued to seek the appointment.[361] Instead Claiborne appointed John Hunter Johnson, whose father had been an alcalde. Johnson founded the city of St. Francisville, participated in the Florida rebellion, and served as the sheriff for the circuit court of Baton Rouge as well as on the Feliciana police jury for four years and later as a state senator from Feliciana.[362]

St. Helena and St. Tammany in contrast to East Baton Rouge and Feliciana were less developed frontier regions, and consequently the selection of officers proved more difficult. The governor wrote to Robert Smith of potential judicial appointees in St. Helena and St. Tammany: "There is in that quarter a great scarcity of talent, and the number of virtuous men too (I fear) is not as great as I would wish."[363] Claiborne made Audley L. Osborne, his emissary to West Florida during the rebellion, the first judge of St. Helena.[364] Judge John J. Salisbury succeeded Osborne and served until his death in 1822.[365] Claiborne in an address to the Louisiana legislature said: "Within the parishes of Feliciana, Baton Rouge, St. Helena & St. Tammany (which have recently been annexed to Louisiana) the Civil Authority has become so weakened & relaxed, that the laws have lost much of their influence, & in the parish of St. Tammany particularly are scarcely felt."[366] Many inhabitants of St. Tammany, as the parish farthest east, wanted to be part of Mississippi, but their petitions fell on deaf ears in Washington.[367]

Elected representatives from West Florida reflected an Anglo-American dominance. Llewellyn Griffith, originally from Virginia, represented Feliciana at the West Florida Convention and served as the parish judge from 1813 to 1814, was active in the militia at the Battle of New Orleans, and later worked as a postmaster. Philemon Thomas was a Virginian who fought in the American Revolution, the Kentucky militia, and then immigrated into Spanish Florida. He served in the West Florida Republic's Senate and became a brigadier general in the West Florida Republic Army.[368] Philip Hicky was a state senator who owned several plantations within the parish and had served in the Spanish militia as well as in the West Florida rebellion.[369] Fulwar Skipwith represented East Baton Rouge at the first session of the second legislature and was elected president of the Senate, but upon his resignation at the second session George Waggaman represented East Baton Rouge, and he continued on to the third legislature.[370] Waggaman arrived in New Orleans in 1810 from Maryland and served as a district attorney and then a circuit court judge.[371] Henry Gurley became East Baton Rouge's senator for the fourth legislature.[372] Feliciana's elected representatives similarly illustrate an Anglo dominance. Robert McCausland, elected to the first state House of Representatives, was an Irishman who served under General Anthony Wayne in the U.S. Army. He came to Feliciana in 1795, became a planter, and participated in the rebellion as a major in the army of West Florida. James Ficklin, a representative in 1815, was a merchant who came from Philadelphia and began a business with John Horton. Robert Young was the son of a Revolutionary War hero who arrived in Feliciana in 1796, and served as a major in the West Florida rebellion.[373] John H. Johnson, the local judge, represented Feliciana until his resignation along with Skipwith before the second session, whereupon John Wharton Collins served. Elected representatives from St. Helena and St. Tammany demonstrated the same Anglo-American dominance with the election of John Wharton Collins, who came from a Tory family that made its way to New Orleans and then into St. Tammany.[374] Jesse R. Jones of St. Tammany won an election for the state Senate against Collins's ally James C. Bushnell.[375]

U.S. officials struggled to please Anglo-Americans and more recent immigrants while still managing to effectively govern Louisiana. Claiborne wrote to Secretary of State Robert Smith in 1809 explaining his approach to appointments: "I must fill a portion of the offices of honor and profit with those whose native language is french; But this policy is much censured by some of my fellow Citizens, and made a cause of opposition to my administration."[376] That the governor referred to Anglo-American immigrants as "fellow Citizens" was telling. Much like his opponents who accused him of favoritism toward the Creoles, Claiborne thought of them on some level as foreign. Claiborne provided Smith with a list of his appointees to demonstrate the fairness of his appointive practices. Despite his longevity in office, Claiborne could be remarkably thin-skinned about criticism, particularly when it reached federal authorities. Claiborne's assertion was largely correct: Anglo-Americans received a larger number of the more prestigious judicial appointments. Even so, Creoles and Francophone officials proved prevalent in the parishes, particularly in southeastern Louisiana.

When Governor Claiborne pursued the governorship in 1812, the election involved an apparent ethnic dimension. Two anti-Claiborne editorials, under the pen names Phocion and Philo Phocion, argued explicitly for a Creole governor.[377] Still others took a different line, as when another editorial, also anti-Claiborne, from "An American" began: "Let every American (for I know not the distinction between a Creole and an American) lay his hand on his heart, and ask, Is such a man fit to govern us? No."[378] Opposition to Claiborne included Anglo-American opponents such as Edward Livingston and John Watkins, while Claiborne pointed to French-speaking supporters such as Poydras and used letters from federal authorities like Gallatin to enhance his candidacy.[379] The election demonstrated the persistence of interethnic alliances past the period of territorial control. Once Claiborne became an elected official, patronage practices shifted at the federal level. Madison wrote to William Jones concerning the appointment of revenue officers in 1813 and noted, "There may be a resource in the sending a blank Commission to Govr. Claiborne; but considering the local divisions, and the sentiments of the Members of Congs. from that State it might not issue agreeably."[380] Democratic politics increased the reliance on ethnicity by factions. In 1819 Isaac Lewis Baker wrote to Jackson over the future of the state: "I long to see the day when we can claim & enjoy complete ascendancy over the French—who tho: in general an excellent well disposed people are too much under the influence of certain corrupt chieftains—who would do more honour to a gibbet than to the best and most responsible posts in the government."[381]

The appointment practices of the territorial government attempted to secure local support, empowering local elites within established Creole communities where consensus was possible, but turning to Anglo-Americans in areas with internal factional rivalries and in the western portions of the state, where the Spanish and native threat appeared imminent. The fact that both English and French speakers believed the other community benefited from Claiborne's appointments suggests an evenhanded approach. The opposition to Claiborne mirrored the supporters he garnered in making interethnic alliances, thereby propagating a system that revolved around personalities and insider versus outsider interests rather than rallying around religion, language, or heritage. The politics of Jacksonian Louisiana relied on those identities in order to secure votes to a far greater extent.

Conclusion

The Louisiana Purchase transferred a vast territory containing a large European colonial population who were guaranteed the rights of U.S. citizens. Changes in sovereignty from one nation to another had become commonplace for European colonies in the Western Hemisphere, but this was the first time the United States acquired such a large European colony with multiple layers of ethnic tensions, which proved far more difficult to govern than smaller French communities in the Old Northwest. Consequently, the territorial administration became a trial-and-error process. Unlike earlier colonial cessions between monarchical empires, Louisiana's transfer to U.S. sovereignty merged a republic with a population with little experience with republican government. The United States dealt with these complications by instituting an extended territorial period, which lasted from 1803 until statehood in 1812, and by utilizing the same methods European powers adopted in dealing with foreign populations. Worries over the Spanish threat from the East and West, the internal and external Native American tribes, and the large slave population facilitated U.S. control as local elites came to recognize how the federal government could counter security threats. Fear plays a foundational role in the creation of community. As Paul A. Rahe writes, "When Machiavelli advocates a frequent recurrence to first principles, he does not have in mind the kind of political restoration that is rooted in a return to the particular understanding of justice and the transcendent good that originally animated a given regime; he means a salutary return to the primeval terror and the oppressive awareness of solitude that drove Machiavellian man into civil society in the first place and remains thereafter the foundation of the only loyalty and friendship and the only sense of common purpose he will ever know."[1] The Creole population was not in a position to go it alone, and federal officials adeptly reached out to multiple groups in the first years of territorial government who appeared willing to support it. Yet it was not simply fear of internal and external threats that secured local loyalty. U.S. officials deliberately garnered support both by pursuing institutions and policies that appealed to local constituencies and by ignoring or subverting federal policies that alienated the same constituencies. The place of free persons of color proved contentious, with U.S. officials often acting as allies in confirming institutions like the militia of free people of color, but as confidence in local Francophone loyalty grew, opportunities for free persons of color diminished. Territorial officials became quite facile in responding to local complaints and turning to Creole elites to provide local leadership in key regions.

The government varied its appointment practices by geographic region. In heavily Creole areas of southeastern Louisiana, U.S. officials strove to ensure that Francophone inhabitants achieved representation at all levels of government and that the United States addressed Creole and Anglo-American security concerns involving large slave populations. Upriver at Pointe Coupée and Iberville, U.S. officials felt more comfortable in turning to more Anglo-American appointees. In some parishes, this appointment practice went relatively smoothly and created a political system in which both Creoles and Anglo-Americans held elected and appointed positions. In Pointe Coupée, however, the appointment of outsiders to key positions resulted in local opposition. This opposition stemmed primarily not from the Creoles but from Anglo-American immigrants who had formed their own connections to the Creole community and expected a U.S. administration to appoint them to local offices.

To the southwest in Attakapas and Opelousas, U.S. officials and appointees also faced problems from Anglo-American immigration into the territory, which increased land speculation and complicated titles, while also potentially inciting violence from Native Americans. Many of the same issues affected Natchitoches, Rapides, Ouachita, and Concordia, as U.S. appointees strove to address security concerns from the Spanish, Native Americans, and slaves. Anglo-American settlers, speculators, Indian traders, and bandits disrupted older relationships and aggravated earlier inhabitants. U.S. officials frequently balanced the concerns of older Creole populations with those of incoming Anglo-American immigrants, but in general in the West the territorial government turned to Anglo-American appointees. The West Florida parishes by contrast represented an alternate system of U.S. governance, with participation in the West Florida rebellion serving as a confirmation of loyalty to the United States and in some cases as a qualification for appointment after annexation. Localities differed in the issues that mattered most to them, and the United States treated them accordingly, while taking into account its own agenda based on a given parish's geographic position and demography. U.S. appointment practices worked best in cases that either acknowledged the leadership of stable local elites or relied on outsiders who accommodated local issues while overcoming internal divisions.

The assumption of many Anglo-Americans upon the transfer of Louisiana to the United States was that the foreign nature of the Creole population made it incompatible with U.S. republican government. In 1804 John W. Gurley, a member of the Legislative Council of the territory of Orleans wrote:

> They may love liberty and those who think may be pleased with ye idea of a free Constitution. But they know not yet in what these consist, and if they are now left to form a Government for themselves I believe no man could ever conjecture what would be either its principle or its form. Accustomed to rule as well as to obey the French Inhabitants of this Country are at ye same time servile & proud and jealous of power whenever it does not appear in the common form in which they have been accustomed to respect it.[2]

Gurley's remarks reflected the view of many U.S. leaders, both Federalists and Republicans, in Washington and in New Orleans, that the Francophone majority was not ready for full republican government and that this same majority would resist changes to administrative processes and personnel, especially when changes reduced their role in government or required them to negotiate dramatically new procedures. In fact, the Creole population adeptly learned the new language of republican politics and adopted its procedures, but personnel mattered more than policy. Territorial officials in turn became instrumental in subverting those policies that Creoles found most troublesome and regularly co-opted local elites. Given the emergence of ethnic political competition in Louisiana during the Jacksonian period, historians have tended to trace Anglo-American and Creole competition to the territorial period, with good reason given the levels of mistrust between the different populations. Yet the politics of the territorial period did not regress or progress to competition between ethnic groups, in large part because of the system of patronage adopted. The election of 1816 in some ways inaugurated a new era of ethnic politics. A piece in *L'Ami des Lois* criticized a handbill from "A Louisianian" that backed the gubernatorial candidacy of Creole Jacques Villeré: "Denouncing the native Americans by the sneering appellation of a 'new population'—as alien from the true interests of the state—as enemies to our laws, usages and institutions—and, kindly apprising us, that we are now in the very crisis of our fate—that if we totally exclude them from public confidence in this election, we shall forthwith be free—and that otherwise we must sink into the degradation of 'colonists.'"[3] Despite this theme of ethnic discord, in the territorial period, because of the absence of fully democratic politics, ethnicity failed to be an organizing principle for political struggle. U.S. administrators co-opted enough local elites to frame politics as ins versus outs, with the outs building their own interethnic coalitions to cooperate in opposition.

While the transition to U.S. law and government disturbed the Creole population by challenging land titles and older legal practices, by and large the Francophone population grew attached to the new government because of its ability to combat external and internal threats and its facility in meeting their complaints legally and extralegally. A decade after the creation of the territory, U.S. observers possessed a far different impression of the Creole inhabitants of Louisiana than that put forth by figures like Gurley. In 1816 geographer William Darby wrote of the Creole population in Louisiana:

> The character of the Creole of Louisiana may be drawn in few words. Endowed with quick perception . . . if found ignorant, it is not the ignorance of stupidity, but arising from an education under circumstances unfavorable to improvement. Open, liberal, and humane, where he is found inhospitable, it is the fruit of a deception he dreads. . . . Mild in his deportment to others, he shrinks from contention. . . . Sober and temperate in his pleasures. . . . If the Creole of Louisiana feel but little of a military spirit, this apathy proceeds not from timidity; his ardent mind, light ath-

letic frame of body, active, indefatigable, and docile, would render him well qualified to perform military duty, should this part of his character ever be called into action. The peal of national glory was never rung in his youthful ear. One generation has arisen since Spain held his country and noble was the germ that retained its fructifying power, under the blighting influence of that government. Louisiana has escaped the galling and torpid yoke; its inhabitants will share the genius and freedom of the empire in which they are incorporated.

Darby pointed to Creole virtues and effectively excused what others thought of as Creole vices. More importantly, he believed Creoles would have a place in and advance under an American empire, which effectively removed the governmental causes for Creole weaknesses. The French-speaking population of Louisiana was not congenitally unfit for republican government; instead Darby blamed the Spanish government for its failures on that score. Indeed, Darby attributed what problems emerged after the cession to the character of many of the first Anglo-American immigrants to the area:

> Many men of candid minds, classical education, and useful professional endowments, have removed and settled in Louisiana; but some without education or moral principle, prejudiced against the people as a nation whom they came to abuse and reside amongst. Too ignorant to acquire the language of the country, or to appreciate the qualities of the people, this class of men have engendered most of the hatred existing between the two nations that inhabit Louisiana. The evil of national animosity will gradually subside, as a more numerous and orderly race of people become the improvers of public lands.[4]

For Darby Anglo-American settlers, not Creoles, caused many of the problems within the territory. Though often unrecognized by officials in Washington, the interactions between local officials and their parishes demonstrated that it was often Anglo-Americans who created difficulties for U.S. administration. Anglo-Americans believed in Creole cultural inferiority but assumed that culture would be altered by U.S. government and society.

Three years after Darby's impression, architect Benjamin Latrobe on his brief visit to New Orleans wrote his observations of the city: "There are, in fact, three societies here—first the French, second the American, and third the mixed. The French side is not exactly what it was at the change of the government, and the American is not strictly what is in the Atlantic cities." Latrobe's impressions revealed that the city itself had become more like the United States in some of its cultural traits, changes that mattered for both Anglo-Americans and French inhabitants. He went on to note,

> Americans are pouring in daily, not in families, but in large bodies. In a few years, therefore, this will be an American town. What is good and bad in the French manners and opinions must give way, and the American notions of right and wrong, of convenience and inconvenience, will take their place. When this period arrives, it will be folly to say that they are better or worse than they now are. They will be changed, but they will be changed into that which is more agreeable to the new population than what now exists. But a man who fancies that he has seen the world on more sides than one cannot help wishing that a mean, an average character of society may grow out of the intermixture of the French and American manners.[5]

Latrobe, like any good architect, took the long view. While noting that New Orleans would change to bring itself more into line with U.S. sensibilities, he hoped that it would bring about something new, without casting the changes as inherently positive or negative. This observation proved true of the rest of Louisiana in that while changing to meet the requirements of U.S. administration, local elites required that U.S. officials meet their needs and those of their communities. Latrobe and Darby were intellectuals, not U.S. policy makers or implementers, but both observed that the project under way with the annexation of Louisiana was not one of blatant Americanization or resultant ethnic division.

U.S. officials accommodated Creole populations in many ways, and these practices shared traits with other changes of sovereignty of colonial populations in the Western Hemisphere. The process in Louisiana functioned relatively smoothly for at least two reasons. First, as Latrobe observed, there was a massive Anglo-American immigration, which posed any number of problems for colonial U.S. administrators and for the native Creole population in the short term, but that gave U.S. leaders confidence that demographic trend lines headed in the right direction. Second, the Creole population had citizenship rights and could make its own claims to U.S. identity.

This is not to say that U.S. governance overwhelmingly bent to the Creole population. A clear power dynamic existed within U.S. governance in Louisiana that demanded significant changes for Louisianans. The immigration of various groups under the United States helped to both facilitate and hinder U.S. governance. Francophone immigrants into Louisiana over the territorial period posed few problems. As a group, they sought accommodation and made fewer claims on the territorial government, as they lacked a sense of entitlement found among both Anglo-Americans and Creoles. Many of them arrived with capital, both cultural and actual, that allowed them to advance. In practice the United States adopted various strategies to gain local loyalty in Louisiana, and yet there was always an endpoint in mind. With statehood in 1812 Louisiana entered as an equal member of the union, and the state government was selected through an internal democratic process, though assuredly one based on planter hegemony rather than being imposed on the people of Louisiana externally.

The first wave of United States expansion across the North American continent, as it dealt with foreign populations in the Old Northwest and Louisiana and later Florida, Texas, New Mexico, Arizona, and California (as well as not-so-foreign in Utah) shared traits with other expansionist powers and with later extracontinental U.S. imperialism. U.S. claims to superiority along republican, religious, and racialist lines evolved over the course of the nineteenth century. In some ways, this earlier era of U.S. expansion offered greater access for foreign populations in that it allowed Creole populations entrée to U.S. citizenship. This access to citizenship was not based strictly on geography but on an acceptance of U.S. republican government and political principles, though race played a large part. In certain ways and for certain peoples this first phase of U.S. expansion, from the foundations of the republic through the Mexican War, was classically liberal in its approach and allowed greater access to U.S. citizenship and identity (within real limits) than U.S. imperialism over the latter half of the nineteenth century and into the twentieth. Despite arguments for universal values, later U.S. expansion employed a far more restricted idea as to what constituted the U.S. nation in geographic terms and U.S. citizenship in racial and cultural terms. In Louisiana U.S. officials offered and local elites embraced U.S. citizenship. At the same time U.S. governance functioned along collaborative and colonial lines. The methodology of U.S. expansion in Louisiana resembled earlier colonial enterprises in many ways, but the marriage of such a methodology to liberal republican ideals in the early national era points to marked differences between U.S. and European colonial efforts and to important distinctions within the trajectory of the United States' development as a democratic nation and an imperial power. A more democratic United States did not become less imperial, but it became exclusionary in ways that came to hinder imperial ambitions.

Notes

ASPMA   *American State Papers: Military Affairs.* 38 vols. Washington, DC: Gales and Seaton, 1832.

DLB   Conrad, Glenn R., ed. *A Dictionary of Louisiana Biography.* 2 vols. New Orleans: Louisiana Historical Association, 1988.

IA   *Interim Appointment: W. C. C. Claiborne Letter Book, 1804–1805.* Edited by Jared William Bradley. Baton Rouge: Louisiana State University Press, 2002.

JHR   *Journal of the House of Representatives of the State of Louisiana.* New Orleans: Thierry, Baird & Wagner, Peter K. Wagner, J. C. de St. Romes, 1812–20.

JS   *Journal of the Senate of the State of Louisiana.* New Orleans: Thierry, Baird & Wagner, Peter K. Wagner, J. C. de St. Romes, 1812–20.

LB   *Official Letter Books of W.C.C. Claiborne, 1801–1816.* 6 vols., edited by Dunbar Rowland. Jackson: Mississippi State Department of Archives and History, 1917.

LUR   Robertson, James Alexander, ed. *Louisiana under the Rule of Spain, France, and the United States, 1785–1807: Social, Economic, and Political Conditions of the Territory Represented in the Louisiana Purchase.* 2 vols. Freeport, NY: Books for Libraries, 1969.

PAJ   *The Papers of Andrew Jackson.* 10 vols. to date. Edited by Harold D. Moser et al. Knoxville: University of Tennessee Press, 1980–.

PJM:PS   *Papers of James Madison: Presidential Series.* 7 vols. to date. Edited by Robert A. Rutland et al. Charlottesville: University Press of Virginia, 1986–.

PJM:SSS   *Papers of James Madison: Secretary of State Series.* 9 vols. to date. Edited by Robert J. Brugger et al. Charlottesville: University Press of Virginia, 1986–.

PTJ:RS   *Papers of Thomas Jefferson: Retirement Series.* Edited by J. J. Looney et al. 8 vols. to date. Princeton, NJ: Princeton University Press, 2004–.

TP   *Territorial Papers of the United States*. Vol. 9, *The Territory of Orleans, 1803–*
          1812, edited by Clarence Edwin Carter. Washington, DC: Government
          Printing Office, 1940.

Introduction

1. William Plumer, 20 October 1803, *William Plumer's Memorandum of Proceedings in the United States Senate, 1803–1807*, ed. Everett Somerville Brown (New York: Macmillan, 1923), 7.

2. Peter S. Onuf, "Empire for Liberty," in *Negotiated Empires: Centers and Peripheries in the Americas, 1500–1820*, ed. Christine Daniels and Michael V. Kennedy (New York: Routledge, 2002), 302.

3. For the difficulties posed by the purchase, see Roy F. Nicholas, "Challenge and Stimulus to American Democracy," *Louisiana Historical Quarterly* 38, no. 2 (April 1995): 1–25.

4. William Charles Cole Claiborne to Robert Smith, 18 May 1809, *LB*, 4:361.

5. Paul F. LaChance, "The 1809 Immigration of Saint-Domingue Refugees to New Orleans: Reception, Integration and Impact," in *A Refuge for All Ages: Immigration in Louisiana History*, edited by Carl A. Brasseaux, Louisiana Purchase Bicentennial Series in Louisiana History, vol. 10 (Lafayette: Center for Louisiana Studies, University of Southwestern Louisiana, 1996), 10:277.

6. *Aggregate Amount of Persons Within the United States in the Year 1810* (Washington, DC: Census Office, 1811).

7. *Census for 1820* (Washington: Gales & Seaton, 1821).

8. Jane Burbank and Frederick Cooper, *Empires in World History: Power and the Politics of Difference* (Princeton, NJ: Princeton University Press, 2010), 8.

9. Charles S. Maier, *Among Empires: American Ascendency and Its Predecessors* (Cambridge, MA: Harvard University Press, 2006), 29–30.

10. Joseph G. Tregle Jr., *Louisiana in the Age of Jackson: A Clash of Cultures and Personalities* (Baton Rouge: Louisiana State University Press, 1999), 23. See also Tregle, "Louisiana in the Age of Jackson: A Study in Ego-Politics" (PhD diss., University of Pennsylvania, 1954); Perry H. Howard, *Political Tendencies in Louisiana*, rev. ed. (Baton Rouge: Louisiana State University Press, 1971), 27.

11. John M. Sacher, *A Perfect War of Politics: Parties, Politicians, and Democracy in Louisiana, 1824–1861* (Baton Rouge: Louisiana State University Press, 2003); see also Michael F. Holt's work on the second party system, *The Rise and Fall of the American Whig Party: Jacksonian Politics and the Onset of the Civil War* (New York: Oxford University Press, 1999).

12. Carl A. Brasseaux, *The Founding of New Acadia: The Beginnings of Acadian Life in Louisiana, 1765–1803* (Baton Rouge: Louisiana State University Press, 1987), 167–76.

13. For the European context see Lauren Benton, *A Search for Sovereignty: Law and Geography in European Empires, 1400–1900* (Cambridge: Cambridge University Press, 2010), 288–89.

14. Lauren Benton, *Law and Colonial Cultures: Legal Regimes in World History, 1400–1900* (Cambridge: Cambridge University Press, 2002), 27.

15. George Dargo, *Jefferson's Louisiana: Politics and the Clash of Legal Traditions* (Cambridge, MA: Harvard University Press, 1975).

16. Peter Kastor, *The Nation's Crucible: The Louisiana Purchase and the Creation of America* (New Haven, CT: Yale University Press, 2004), 12.

17. Sarah Paradise Russell, "Cultural Conflicts and Common Interests: The Making of the Sugar Planter Class in Louisiana, 1795–1853" (PhD diss., University of Maryland, 2000).

18. Jack P. Greene, "The Cultural Dimensions of Political Transfers: An Aspect of the European Occupation of the Americas," *Early American Studies* 6, no. 1 (Spring 2008): 26.

19. Julien Vernet, *Strangers on Their Native Soil: Opposition to United States' Governance in Louisiana's Orleans Territory, 1805–1809* (Jackson: University Press of Mississippi, 2013), 162; Richard W. Alstyne, *The Rising American Empire* (New York: W. W. Norton, 1960); Alexander DeConde, *This Affair of Louisiana* (New York: Charles Scribner's Sons, 1976); Thomas R. Hietala, *Manifest Design: American Exceptionalism and Empire* (Ithaca, NY: Cornell University Press, 1985); Alexander DeConde, "The Imperial Thrust," in *The Louisiana Purchase and Its Aftermath, 1800–1830*, ed. Dolores Egger Labbé, Louisiana Purchase Bicentennial Series, vol. 3 (Lafayette: Center for Louisiana Studies, University of Southwestern Louisiana, 1996), 609–19.

20. See Jack P. Greene, "Reflection on a Continuing Problem," *William and Mary Quarterly* 65, no. 2 (April 2007): 248–49.

21. Plumer, 18 February 1804, *Memorandum of Proceedings,* 145.

22. In March of 1804 the U.S. Congress established two territorial governments from the Louisiana Purchase; the southern territory became the territory of Orleans. The legislative functions of the new territory would be exercised by a Legislative Council composed of the governor and members appointed by the president.

23. *Orleans Gazette* (New Orleans), 11 June 1805; An Act for the Government of Orleans Territory, 2 March 1805, *TP,* 9:405–7; A Native, *View of the Political and Civil Situation of Louisiana from the Thirtieth of November 1803 to the First of October 1804, by a Native* (Philadelphia, 1804); Julien Paul Vernet, "'Strangers on Their Native Soil?': Opposition to United States Territorial Government in Orleans, 1803–1809" (PhD diss., Syracuse University, 2002), 127–44.

24. The county of Orleans, which contained New Orleans, elected seven representatives, seven counties had two representatives, and the four northernmost counties received one each.

25. *Constitution or Form of Government of the State of Louisiana* (New Orleans, 1812).

26. Lee Hargrave, *The Louisiana State Constitution: A Reference Guide* (New York: Greenwood, 1991), 2–3; Warren M. Billings and Edward F. Haas, eds., *In Search of Fundamental Law, Louisiana's Constitutions* (Lafayette: Center for Louisiana Studies, University of Southwestern Louisiana, 1993), 6–20.

Chapter One

1. See Jared William Bradley, "Biographical Sketches: James Workman," *IA,* 389–414; *DLB,* 2:860–61.

2. James Workman, *Liberty in Louisiana; A Comedy* (Charleston, SC: Query and Evans, 1804), 94–95, 101.

3. See Bradley, "Biographical Sketches: James Workman," *IA,* 397.

4. Francis Bailly, Thursday, 11 May 1797, *Journal of a Tour in Unsettled Parts of North America in 1796 and 1797*, ed. Jack D. L. Holmes (Carbondale: Southern Illinois University, 1969), 150.

5. James Workman, *Essays and Letters on Various Political Subjects*, 2nd American ed. (New York: Gould & Van Winkle, 1809), 109–48, 136–37(quotation).

6. See *The Trials of the Honb. James Workman and Col. Lewis Kerr before the United States' Court for the Orleans District, on a Charge of High Misdemeanor, in Planning and Setting on Foot, within the United States, an Expedition for The Conquest and Emancipation of Mexico* (New Orleans: Bradford & Anderson, 1807). Workman's indecorous language garnered him eight hours in jail and a twenty-five-dollar fine. See *The Case of Mr. Workman, On a Rule for An Alleged Contempt of the Superior Court of the Territory of Orleans* (Philadelphia: William Fry, 1809).

7. Maier, *Among Empires*, 107, 93.

8. Plumer, 3 April 1806, *Memorandum of Proceedings*, 474.

9. Peter Onuf and Nicholas Onuf, *Federal Union, Modern World: The Law of Nations in an Age of Revolutions, 1776–1814* (Madison: Madison House, 1993), 149–51.

10. Stephen Aron, *American Confluence: The Missouri Frontier from Borderland to Border State* (Bloomington: Indiana University Press, 2006), 96.

11. Patricia Nelson Limerick, *The Legacy of Conquest: The Unbroken Past of the American West* (1987; reprint, New York: W. W. Norton, 2006), 28–29.

12. Peggy K. Liss, *Atlantic Empires: The Network of Trade and Revolution, 1713–1826* (Baltimore: Johns Hopkins University Press, 1983), 2, 5, 36.

13. Jack Ericson Eblen, *The First and Second United States Empires* (Pittsburgh: University of Pittsburgh Press, 1968), 318.

14. Paul E. Hoffman, *Florida's Frontiers* (Bloomington: Indiana University Press, 2002), 209–10, 237, 244–46, 253–54, 282–83.

15. Daniel L. Schafer, *Zephaniah Kingsley Jr. and the Atlantic World* (Gainesville: University Press of Florida, 2013), 2–6, 34, 39, 52–67, 100, 148.

16. Robert V. Haynes, *The Mississippi Territory and the Southwest Frontier, 1795–1817* (Lexington: University Press of Kentucky, 2010), 33.

17. Eblen, *The First and Second United States Empires*, 45, 55, 103.

18. Utah's territorial period lasted from 1850 to 1896 and New Mexico's from 1850 to 1912.

19. Eric Hinderaker, *Elusive Empires: Constructing Colonialism in the Ohio Valley, 1673–1800* (Cambridge: Cambridge University Press, 1997), xiv, 176, 261.

20. Eblen, *The First and Second United States Empires*, 302–3.

21. Laura E. Gómez, *Manifest Destinies: The Making of the Mexican American Race* (New York: New York University Press, 2007), 48, 86–87, 64–66, 98.

22. Martín de Navarro, *Political Reflections on the Present Condition of the Province of Louisiana, c. 1785, LUR*, 1:243, 247–51.

23. Christopher Hodson, *The Acadian Diaspora: An Eighteenth-Century History* (Oxford: Oxford University Press, 2012), 6, 193–95; Gilbert C. Din, *Populating the Barrera: Spanish Immigration Efforts in Colonial Louisiana* (Lafayette: University of Louisiana at Lafayette Press, 2014), 11, 21.

24. Din, *Populating the Barrera*, 60–61, 77–78, 59.

25. Baron de Carondelet, "Military Report on Louisiana and West Florida," 24 November 1794, *LUR*, 2:301.

26. Gilbert. C. Din, *War on the Gulf Coast: The Spanish Fight against William Augustus Bowles* (Gainesville: University Press of Florida, 2012), 69–70.

27. Din, *Populating the Barrera*, 123–24.

28. M. G. de Lemos to J. V. Morales, 13 February 1799; J. V. Morales to M. G. De Lemos, 14 February 1799, in *Documents Relative to Louisiana and Florida; Received at the Department of State, From the Secretary of State of Spain, Throughout the Hon. C. P. Van Ness, Envoy Extraordinary and Minister Plenipotentiary at Madrid* (Washington, DC: Department of State, 1835), 19–21.

29. Manuel Gayoso de Lemos, "Political Condition of the Province of Louisiana," 5 July 1792, *LUR*, 1:283, 284, 288.

30. Minister Caballero to Minister Coruel, San Lorenzo, 13 November 1799, *LUR*, 1:355.

31. Din, *Populating the Barrera*, 105–8.

32. David J. Weber, *The Spanish Frontier in North America* (New Haven, CT: Yale University Press, 1992), 203.

33. W. C. C. Claiborne to James Madison, 3 January 1803, *LB*, 1:253.

34. Claiborne to Daniel Clark, 18 November 1803, *LB*, 1:287–90; Claiborne to Albert Gallatin, 18 November 1803, *LB*, 1:291–93; Claiborne to James Madison, 26 November 1803, *LB*, 1:297–98.

35. Claiborne to James Madison, 29 November 1803, *LB*, 1:299.

36. Claiborne to Robert Williams, Esqr., Governor of the Mississippi Territory, 10 October 1805, *LB*, 3:194–96.

37. James Madison to William C. C. Claiborne, 25 February 1805, *PJM:SSS*, 9:68.

38. Claiborne to Governor Folch, 31 October 1805, *LB*, 221–222.

39. Edmund P. Gaines to W. C. C. Claiborne, 15 November 1805, Claiborne (William C. C.) Letters and Depositions (1799–1846), MSS 5018, Louisiana and Lower Mississippi Valley Collections, LSU Libraries, Baton Rouge, LA.

40. Claiborne to General James Wilkinson, 10 October 1805, *LB*, 3:199–201.

41. Casa Irujo to Ceballos, "Important Reflections on the Cession of Louisiana," *LUR*, 2:69–71.

42. Casa Irujo to Ceballos, 5 November 1803, *LUR*, 2:118.

43. Casa Irujo to Ceballos, 4 November 1803, *LUR*, 2:114.

44. Casa Irujo to Ceballos, 21 February 1804, *LUR*, 2:131.

45. Casa Calvo to Ceballos, Very Secret Despatch Number 12, 18 May 1804, *LUR*, 2:187–88.

46. Vicente Folch, "Reflection on Louisiana by Vicente Folch, Number 2," *LUR*, 2:336–37.

47. See Jared William Bradley, "Biographical Sketches: Mexican Association," *IA*, 596–603. Purported members included James Workman, John Watkins, Daniel Clark, Lewis Kerr, George T. Ross, John B. Prevost, Edward Livingston, William Nott, Abraham R. Ellery, and James Alexander. An attempted break-in to Thomas Urquehart's home may have been because of his opposition to the Mexican Association. See *Louisiana Courier* (New Orleans), 15 November 1816, 20 November 1816; *Louisiana Gazette* (New Orleans), 18 November 1816; Pierre

Louis Berquin-Duvallon, *Travels in Louisiana and the Floridas in the Year 1802, Giving a Correct Picture of those Countries*, trans. John Davis (New York: I. Riley, 1806), 2–3. See also *The Case of Mr. Workman, On a Rule for an Alleged Contempt of the Superior Court of the Territory of Orleans.*

48. *Louisiana Gazette* (New Orleans), 25 October 1817.

49. Claiborne to Thomas Jefferson, 22 June 1806, *LB*, 3:342.

50. Vernet, *Strangers on Their Native Soil*, 76.

51. Characterization of New Orleans Residents, 1 July 1804, No. 3 Meyange, No. 57 Jerome Chiapella, No. 69 Antonio Argoti, *TP*, 9:249, 253, 254. Labigarre was most likely Pierre or Peter De Labigarre; the document lists him as married to a Livingston woman. A Peter De Labigarre was married to Margarett Beekman. Her sister Elizabeth was married to Peter W. Livingston. See William B. Aitken, *Distinguished Families in America Descended from Wilhelmus Beekman and Ian Thomasse Van Dyke* (New York: Knickerbocker, 1912), 112; Carl Carmer, *The Hudson* (1939; reprint, New York: Fordham University Press, 1992), 136–37.

52. Governor Claiborne to the Secretary of State, 22 October 1804, *TP*, 9:312.

53. William C. C. Claiborne to James Madison, 11 December 1804, *PJM:SSS*, 8:370.

54. Claiborne to James Madison, 6 June 1805, *LB*, 3:79.

55. James Brown to John Breckinridge, 17 September 1805, *TP*, 9:511.

56. Weber, *The Spanish Frontier in North America*, 337–41.

57. Claiborne to James Madison, 13 May 1804, *LB*, 2:146–47; Claiborne to James Madison, 25 July 1804, *LB*, 2:266–267; Claiborne to James Madison, 23 September 1804, *LB*, 2:340.

58. Governor Claiborne to the President, 15 April 1804, *TP*, 9:223.

59. Claiborne to James Madison, 14 July 1804, *LB*, 2:249. See also Claiborne to James Madison, 7 August 1805, *LB*, 3:154.

60. Claiborne selected A. D. Tureaud and Samuel Winter and instructed them to pick a third to settle the dispute. Claiborne to A. D. Tureaud and Samuel Winter, 9 February 1804, *LB*, 1:369–70. Salcedo eventually left Orleans for the Canaries; Claiborne to James Madison, 26 February 1804, *LB*, 1:387–88.

61. Gilbert C. Din has recently published a much-needed biography of Casa Calvo. See Gilbert C. Din, *An Extraordinary Atlantic Life: Sebastián Nicolás De La Puerta O'Farill Marqués De Casa Calvo* (Lafayette: University of Louisiana at Lafayette Press, 2016).

62. William C. C. Claiborne to James Madison, 27 July 1804, *PJM:SSS*, 7:529.

63. Claiborne to the Secy. of State, 31 December 1804, *LB*, 3:34.

64. Claiborne to James Madison, 25 July 1804, *LB*, 2:267; Din views much of this as paranoia and a failure to understand the complexity of the issues Casa Calvo faced, but complaints over his presence extended beyond Claiborne to other U.S. officials. Din, *An Extraordinary Atlantic Life*, 228–35.

65. James Brown to John Breckinridge, 17 September 1805, *TP*, 9:508.

66. Casa Calvo to Ceballos, 13 January 1804, *LUR*, 2:166. Casa Calvo continued to lobby for the return of Louisiana upon his return to Spain. See Din, *An Extraordinary Atlantic Life*, 267–72.

67. Casa Calvo to Ceballos, Secret Despatch Number 6, 30 March 1804, *LUR*, 2:174–75.

68. Claiborne to James Madison, 14 October 1805, *LB*, 3:198–199.

69. Governor Claiborne to the Secretary of State, 9 January 1806, *TP*, 9:562.

70. Louis Brognier Declouett, New Orleans, to Pierre-Joseph Favrot, 3 December 1804, *The Favrot Family Papers*, 6 vols., ed. Wilbur E. Meneray (New Orleans: Howard Tilton Memorial Library, 2001), 4:167.

71. Claiborne to James Madison, 26 August 1805, *LB*, 3:182.

72. Edward D. Turner to Governor Claiborne, 30 July 1804, *TP*, 9:271–73.

73. Claiborne to Capt. Edward D. Turner, 14 October 1805, *LB*, 196–98; Claiborne to James Madison, 14 October 1805, *LB*, 3:198–99; Claiborne to James Madison, 7 February 1806, *LB*, 3:261.

74. Claiborne to the Marquis of Casa Calvo, 9 August 1805, *LB*, 3:160–61.

75. Governor Claiborne to the Secretary of State, 6 August 1805, *TP*, 9:489; Governor Claiborne to the Secretary of State, 5 November 1804, *TP*, 9:320.

76. Claiborne to James Madison, 3 August 1805, *LB*, 3:145–46; Claiborne to James Madison, 5 August 1805, *LB*, 3:150–51. See also Elizabeth Urban Alexander, "Daniel Clark: Merchant Prince of New Orleans," in *Nexus of Empire: Negotiating Loyalty and Identity in the Revolutionary Borderlands, 1760s–1820s*, ed. Gene Allen Smith and Sylvia L. Hilton (Gainesville: University Press of Florida, 2010), 241–67; Andrew McMichael, "William Dunbar, William Claiborne, and Daniel Clark: Intersections of Loyalty and National Identity on the Florida Frontier," in *Nexus of Empire*, 271–97.

77. Claiborne to James Madison, 25 September 1805, *LB*, 3:190.

78. Juan Ventura Morales to Governor Claiborne, 19 August 1805, *TP*, 9:490–93; Claiborne to the Marquis of Casa Calvo, 21 August 1805, *LB*, 3:179–180.

79. Claiborne to James Madison, 8 November 1805, *LB*, 3:230.

80. Claiborne to Col. Done Jose Martinez de Orosa Sargento, *LB*, 25 January 1806, 3:248–249; To Casa Calvo, 11 February 1806, *LB*, 3:263–264.

81. Claiborne to James Madison, 6 June 1805, *LB*, 3:80–83.

82. Deposition from John Sibley Justice of the Peace, 3 October 1805, Claiborne (William C. C.) Letters and Depositions (1799–1846), MSS 5018, Louisiana and Lower Mississippi Valley Collections, LSU Libraries, Baton Rouge, LA.

83. Deposition from John Sibley, Justice of the Peace, 4 October 1805, Claiborne (William C. C.) Letters and Depositions (1799–1846), MSS 5018, Louisiana and Lower Mississippi Valley Collections, LSU Libraries, Baton Rouge, LA.

84. Claiborne to Henry Dearborn, 4 September 1806, *LB*, 3:399.

85. Armando C. Alonzo, "A History of Ranching in Nuevo Santander's Villas del Norte, 1730s–1848," in *Coastal Encounters: The Transformation of the Gulf South in the Eighteenth Century*, ed. Richmond F. Brown (Lincoln: University of Nebraska Press, 2007), 194; Daniel H. Usner Jr., *Indians Settlers, and Slaves in a Frontier Exchange Economy* (Chapel Hill: University of North Carolina Press, 1992), 179–80.

86. H. Sophie Burton and F. Todd Smith, *Colonial Natchitoches: A Creole Community on the Louisiana-Texas Frontier* (College Station: Texas A&M University Press, 2008), 20–54.

87. Philip C. Cook, "The North Louisiana Upland Frontier: The First Three Decades," in *North Louisiana: Essays on the Region and Its History*, ed. B. H. Gilley (Ruston, LA: McGinty

Trust Fund, 1984), 23.

88. Julia K. Garrett, *Green Flag over Texas,* (New York: Cordova, 1939), 11–12; Frank Lawrence Owsley Jr. and Gene A. Smith, *Filibusters and Expansionists: Jeffersonian Manifest Destiny, 1800–1821* (Tuscaloosa: University of Alabama Press, 1997), 35–36.

89. John Sibley to Claiborne, 14 October 1805, Claiborne (William C. C.) Letters and Depositions (1799–1846), MSS 5018, Louisiana and Lower Mississippi Valley Collections, LSU Libraries, Baton Rouge, LA.

90. Claiborne to James Madison, 24 October 1805, *LB,* 3:213.

91. Edward D. Turner to Governor Claiborne, 30 July 1804, *TP,* 9:272.

92. James Brown to the Secretary of the Treasury, 7 January 1806, *TP,* 9:559.

93. Donald William Meinig, *The Shaping of America: A Geographical Perspective on 500 Years of History,* vol. 2, *Continental America, 1800–1967* (New Haven, CT: Yale University Press, 1995), 36.

94. Samuel J. Watson, *Jackson's Sword: The Army Officer Corps on the American Frontier, 1810–1821* (Lawrence: University Press of Kansas, 2012), 44–45.

95. Anthony Merry to Lord Harrowby, 29 March 1805, in *Political Correspondence and Public Papers of Aaron Burr,* 2 vols., ed Mary-Jo Kline (Princeton, NJ: Princeton University Press, 1983), 2:928.

96. Anthony Merry to Lord Mulgrave, 25 November 1805, in *Political Correspondence and Public Papers of Aaron Burr,* 2:945.

97. Claiborne to Judge Hall, 2 January 1807, *LB,* 4:78–79; Claiborne to James Madison, 1 February 1808, *LB,* 4:148–55; Governor Folch to Claiborne, 11 February 1808, *LB,* 4:157–59.

98. Louis Roux, Report to the Duc de Cadore, 13 March 1810, *Political Correspondence and Public Papers of Aaron Burr,* 2:1117.

99. Claiborne to Henry Dearborn, 29 July 1806, *LB,* 3:374–75; Claiborne to Col. Freeman, 17 August 1806, *LB,* 3:377; W. C. C. Claiborne to R. Claiborne, 17 August 1806, *LB,* 3:378–81; Claiborne to Henry Dearborn, 18 August 1806, *LB,* 3:381.

100. Claiborne to Henry Dearborn, 4 September 1806, *LB,* 3:398.

101. Claiborne to Governor Folch, 21 January 1807, *LB,* 4:106.

102. Claiborne to Cowles Mead, 21 January 1807, *LB,* 4:108.

103. Claiborne to James Madison, 21 April 1807, *LB,* 4:124–25.

104. Claiborne to Robert Williams, 10 February 1807, *LB,* 4:120–121.

105. Claiborne to Henry Dearborn, 15 June 1806, *LB,* 3:330.

106. Claiborne to James Madison, 3 April 1806, *LB,* 3:283.

107. Governor Claiborne to the Secretary of State, 21 July 1806, *TP,* 9:676.

108. Claiborne to Henry Dearborn, 28 August 1806, *LB,* 3:387.

109. Claiborne to Col. Cushing, 9 September 1806, *LB,* 4:7.

110. Claiborne to Judge Collins, 24 September 1806, *LB,* 4:19

111. Claiborne to Henry Dearborn, 8 October 1806, *LB,* 4:25

112. From William Harris Crawford to James Madison, 3 March 1813, *PJM:PS,* 6:80.

113. Claiborne to Edward D. Turner, 1 August 1804, *LB,* 2:287.

114. Claiborne to Col. Hopkins, 10 November 1809, *LB,* 5:7–8.

115. Claiborne to Edward D. Turner, 13 May 1804, *LB*, 2:146.

116. Claiborne to Henry Dearborn, 24 January 1809, *LB*, 4:309.

117. Andrew McMichael, *Atlantic Loyalties: Americans in Spanish West Florida* (Athens: University of Georgia Press, 2008), 15–17.

118. The Orleans legislature in 1808 passed a Civil Digest printed in both English and French that established a bilingual court system. See Dargo, *Jefferson's Louisiana*, 156.

119. Claiborne to William Eustis, 20 July 1804, *LB*, 2:130.

120. The Secretary of the Treasury to Hore Browse Trist, 27 February 1804, *TP*, 9:194.

121. Claiborne to Jno. V. Morales, 27 January 1806, *LB*, 3:251.

122. Claiborne to Grand Prés, 8 April 1806, *LB*, 3:287; Claiborne to James Madison, 21 May 1806, *LB*, 3:305; Gov. Folch to Claiborne, 18 February 1807, *LB*, 4:139–40; Claiborne to James Madison, 17 February 1808, *LB*, 4:156–59.

123. Claiborne to James Madison, 13 May 1808, *LB*, 4:173–75.

124. Claiborne to Gov. Grand Prés, 31 August 1808, *LB*, 4:197–99.

125. Claiborne to James Madison, 27 June 1804, *LB*, 2:227–29.

126. Thomas D. Clark and John D. W. Guice, *The Old Southwest, 1795–1830* (Norman: University of Oklahoma Press, 1989), 46–47.

127. Marquis of Casa Calvo to Governor Claiborne, 11 August 1804, *LB*, 2:308–9.

128. McMichael, *Atlantic Loyalties*, 85–86.

129. William C. Davis, *The Rogue Republic: How Would-Be Patriots Waged the Shortest Revolution in American History* (Boston: Houghton Mifflin Harcourt, 2011), 88.

130. Ibid., 21.

131. Claiborne to the Marquis of Casa Calvo, 27 August 1804, *LB*, 2:310.

132. W. C. C. Claiborne to Julien Poydras, 30 August 1804, *LB*, 2:313.

133. W. C. C. Claiborne to Julien Poydras, 6 August 1804, *LB*, 2:293–95.

134. Davis, *The Rogue Republic*, 132, 141, 155; Haynes, *The Mississippi Territory and the Southwest Frontier, 1795–1817*, 253.

135. W. C. C. Claiborne to James Madison, 6 June 1805, *LB*, 3:78.

136. W. C. C. Claiborne to Colonel Freeman, 20 June 1805, *LB*, 3:100.

137. Marquis of Casa Calvo to Governor Claiborne, 13 September 1804, *LB*, 2:331–32.

138. Claiborne to James Madison, 11 December 1804, *LB*, 3:25.

139. Governor Claiborne to the President, 27 October 1804, *TP*, 9:315.

140. The Secretary of State to Governor Claiborne, 10 November 1804, *TP*, 9:332–33.

141. McMichael, *Atlantic Loyalties*, 93.

142. Secretary Graham to Governor Claiborne, 16 September 1805, *TP*, 9:505.

143. Governor Claiborne to Robert William, 24 October 1805, *LB*, 3:211–14; Claiborne to Henry Dearborn, 30 October 1805, *LB*, 3:216–17; Claiborne to James Madison, 27 August 1805, *LB*, 3:183; Claiborne to Governor Folch, 31 October 1805, *LB*, 3:221–22.

144. Claiborne to Henry Dearborn, 7 November 1805, *LB*, 3:229; Claiborne to James Madison, 5 November 1805, *LB*, 3:226.

145. Claiborne to Grand Prés, 8 April 1806, *LB*, 3:287.

146. Claiborne to James Madison, 17 February 1808, *LB*, 4:156.

147. Claiborne to James Madison, 31 August 1808, *LB*, 4:201; see also Claiborne to Thomas Jefferson, 1 September 1808, *LB*, 4:202–8.

148. Claiborne to Robert Smith, 19 March 1809, *LB*, 4:332.

149. William C. C. Claiborne to Thomas Jefferson, 17 May 1809, *PTJ:RS*, 1:203.

150. Claiborne to Robert Smith, 19 March 1809, *LB*, 4:333.

151. Claiborne to Robert Smith, 21 April 1809, *LB*, 4:342–43.

152. Claiborne to Robert Smith, 14 October 1809, *LB*, 4:353.

153. Rose Meyers, *A History of Baton Rouge, 1699–1812* (Baton Rouge: Louisiana State University Press, 1976), 81–83.

154. Virginia Lobdell Jennings, *The Plains and the People: A History of Upper East Baton Rouge Parish* (Gretna, LA: Pelican, 1998), 26, 20.

155. Feliciana was represented by John Rheas, William Barrow, John H. Johnson, and John Mills; Baton Rouge by Thomas Lilley, Philip Hicky, Edmund Hause, and Manuel Lopez; St. Helena by Joseph Thomas, John W. Leonard, William Spiller, Benjamin O. Williams, William Morgan; St. Tammany by a William Cooper and an unnamed gentleman. See Membership of the West Florida Convention, 26 July 1810, *TP*, 9:889, 895. Lopez was a native Spaniard and Leonard was a U.S. naval officer before moving to Saint Helena. See Davis, *The Rogue Republic*, 143–45.

156. *DLB*, 2:746.

157. Benjamin Henry Latrobe, *The Journal of Latrobe: The Notes and Sketches of an Architect, Naturalist and Traveler in the United States from 1796–1820* (New York: D. Appleton, 1905), 213.

158. Claiborne to Robert Smith, 1 December 1810, *LB*, 5:35.

159. Fulwar Skipwith to John H. Johnson, 6 December 1810, *LB*, 5:50–51.

160. W. C. C. Claiborne to Colonel Covington, 1 December 1810 and 2 December 1810, *LB*, 5:36–39. See also W. C. C. Claiborne to Audley L. Osborne, 5 December 1810, *LB*, 5:44–46.

161. John Ballinger to the Secretary of State, 26 December 1811, *TP*, 9:969–70. Ballinger was a Kentuckian who had served as a colonel in the U.S. Army. See Davis, *The Rogue Republic*, 148.

162. Governor Claiborne to the Secretary of the Treasury, 24 December 1810, *TP*, 9:904.

163. Audley Osborn to Claiborne, 6 December 1810, *LB*, 5:53.

164. The Governor of Mississippi Territory to the Secretary of State, 1 January 1811, *TP*, 9:913.

165. Claiborne to Robert Smith, 27 December 1810, *LB*, 5:68.

166. Claiborne to Robert Smith, 6 January 1811, *LB*, 5:89–90.

167. Claiborne to Colonel Pike, 8 February 1811, *LB*, 5:148–49.

168. Claiborne to General Thomas, 30 January 1811, *LB*, 5:136.

169. Clark and Guice, *The Old Southwest, 1795–1830*, 54.

170. Claiborne to Messrs. Shaler & Gray—Circular, 11 March 1811, *LB*, 5:178.

171. Haynes, *The Mississippi Territory and the Southwest Frontier, 1795–1817*, 277.

172. Claiborne to Robert Smith, 20 January 1811, *LB*, 5:111. Cyrus was the son of U.S. Indian agent John Sibley. See Claiborne to Doctor Sibley, 10 March 1811, *LB*, 5:176.

173. Claiborne to William Shaler, 3 March 1811, *LB*, 5:169.

174. Translation of a letter from the Captain General of Cuba, Marquis of Someruelos to Claiborne, 29 March 1811, *LB*, 5:225–26.

175. W. C. C. Claiborne to James Monroe, 26 July 1815, *LB*, 6:359–60.

176. Andrew Jackson to John Caldwell Calhoun, 28 November 1818, *PAJ*, 4:251.

177. Paul Alliot, *Historical and Political Reflections on Louisiana*, *LUR*, 1:35, 55.

178. C. C. Robin, *Voyage to Louisiana, 1803–1805*, trans. Stuart O. Landry Jr. (Gretna, LA: Firebird, 2000), 59 (quotation), 162.

179. François Marie Perrin du Lac, *Travels through the Two Louisianas and Among the Savage Nations of the Missouri, in the United States, along the Ohio and the Adjacent Provinces, in 1801, 1802 & 1803, Translated from the French* (London: J. G. Barnard, 1807), 100 (quotation), 101.

180. See Henry Clement Pitot, *James Pitot, 1761–1831: A Documentary Study* (New Orleans: Bocage Books, 1968), 23–35; see also Jared William Bradley, "Biographical Sketches: James Pitot," *IA*, 255–57.

181. Pitot, *James Pitot, 1761–1831*, 65, 79.

182. James Pitot, *Observations on the Colony of Louisiana from 1796 to 1802*, trans. Henry C. Pitot (Baton Rouge: Louisiana State University Press, 1979), 2–3 (quotation), 7–15, 23, 24, 25.

183. Laussat to Citizen Decrès, quoted in Alain Levasseur, *Moreau Lislet: The Man behind the Digest of 1808* (Baton Rouge: Claitor's, 2008), 25.

184. Laussat, April 1804, The Colonial Prefect, Commissioner of the French Republic, to the Citizen Decrès, Minister of the Navy and Colonies, quoted in Levasseur, *Moreau Lislet*, 45.

185. Duc Denis Decrès, "Secret Instructions for the Captain-General of Louisiana, Approved by the First Consul," 26 November 1802, *LUR*, 1:372.

186. Laussat to Denis Decrès, 18 July 1803, *LUR*, 2:43. This reputation largely stemmed from the massacre of Frenchmen at Bayajá by black allies of the Spanish while Casa Calvo was the military governor of the city. Casa Calvo was not present at the time, nor were the Spanish in any position to stop the incident. See Din, *An Extraordinary Atlantic Life*, 146–50.

187. Laussat to Denis Decrès, 18 July 1803, *LUR*, 2:46.

188. Laussat to Denis Decrès, 17 August 1803, *LUR*, 2:51.

189. Laussat to Denis Decrès, 7 April 1804, *LUR*, 2:53.

190. Laussat to Denis Decrès, 7 April 1804, in *LUR*, 2:55.

191. Governor Claiborne to the President, 25 November 1804, *TP*, 9:339.

192. William C. C. Claiborne to James Madison, 24 January 1804, *PJM:SSS*, 6:376. See also Governor Claiborne to the President, 15 April 1804, *TP*, 9:223.

193. Mr. Boree, Characterization of New Orleans Residents, 1 July 1804, *TP*, 9:248.

194. John W. Gurley to the Postmaster General, 14 July 1804, *TP*, 9:263.

195. William C. C. Claiborne to James Madison, 3 October 1804, *PJM:SSS*, 8:120.

196. Governor Claiborne to the Secretary of State, 13 July 1804, *TP*, 9:261.

197. See Governor Claiborne to the President, 13 September 1804, *TP*, 9:293; Governor Claiborne to the President, 4 September 1807, *TP*, 9:763; List of Civil and Military Officers, 21 April 1809, *TP*, 9:835–38; Governor Claiborne to the President, 4 March 1810, *TP*, 9:869–71; William Blackledge to the Secretary of State, 12 December 1808, *TP*, 9:810–11.

198. William C. C. Claiborne to James Madison, 15 July 1804, *PJM:SSS*, 7:457.

199. William Cooke to James Madison, 6 October 1804, *PJM:SSS*, 8:128; Claiborne to the Judge of the County of Natchitoches, 11 August 1805, *LB*, 3:161–62; The Secretary of War to Governor Claiborne, 1 July 1805, *TP*, 9:458–59; Claiborne to Henry Dearborn, 24 October 1805, *LB*, 4:215.

200. Secretary Robertson to the Secretary of State, 24 May 1809, *TP*, 9:841.

201. Claiborne to Robert Smith, 20 May 1809, *LB*, 4:365; see also Claiborne to John Graham, 19 July 1809, *LB*, 4:390–91.

202. Nathalie Dessens, *From Saint-Domingue to New Orleans: Migration and Influences* (Gainesville: University Press of Florida, 2007), 22, 33–34, 43–44, 130, 54–55, 63, 68.

203. Characterization of New Orleans Residents, 1 July 1804, *TP*, 9:253. Given the Englishman comment about an American, Julien Vernet believes this characterization most likely came from La Bigarre. Vernet, *Strangers on Their Native Soil*, 76.

204. Claiborne to Robert Smith, 4 January 1811, *LB*, 5:65; Claiborne to Paul Hamilton, 26 December 1811, *LB*, 6:20–22.

205. A Gentleman of respectability in the District of Baton Rouge to Claiborne, 22 April 1805, *LB*, 3:44–45.

206. Claiborne to the Marquis of Casa Calvo, 8 May 1805, *LB*, 3:46.

207. Claiborne to Colonel Freeman, 13 May 1805, *LB*, 3:54.

208. Claiborne to James Madison, 10 May 1805, *LB*, 3:51–52.

209. Claiborne to the Secretary of State, 26 March 1811, *LB*, 5:191.

210. W. C. C. Claiborne to W. L. Andrews, 28 July 1813, *LB*, 6:248.

211. Frank Lawrence Owsley Jr., *Struggle for the Gulf Borderlands: The Creek War and the Battle of New Orleans, 1812–1815* (Tuscaloosa: University of Alabama Press, 1981), 102, 121, 128, 168, 108–9.

212. Claiborne to Thomas Flournoy, 29 September 1813, *LB*, 6:271; Claiborne to Andrew Jackson, 24 October 1814, *LB*, 6:288.

213. Claiborne to General Armstrong, 14 April 1813, *LB*, 6:234; Angie Debo, *The Rise and Fall of the Choctaw Republic* (1934; reprint, Norman: University of Oklahoma Press, 1961), 40–41; Jesse O. McKee and Jon A. Schlenker, *The Choctaws: Cultural Evolution of a Native American Tribe* (Jackson: University Press of Mississippi, 1980), 54.

214. William Charles Cole Claiborne to Andrew Jackson, 12 August 1814, *PAJ*, 3:115.

215. Andrew Jackson to William Charles Cole Claiborne, 30 August 1814, *PAJ*, 3:126.

216. Andrew Jackson to William Charles Cole Claiborne, 30 September 1814, *PAJ*, 3:151.

217. Thomas Butler to New Orleans Citizens and Soldiers, 15 December 1814, *PAJ*, 3:204.

218. Appendix XX, Address by General Jackson to the Militia of New Orleans, 18 December 1814, in Arsène Lacarrière Latour, *Historical Memoir of the War in West Florida and Louisiana in 1814–15*, expanded ed., ed. Gene A. Smith (Gainesville: Historic New Orleans Collection and University Press of Florida, 1999), 216.

219. Daniel Walker Howe discusses the importance of artillery versus Jacksonian conceptions of the frontiersmen. See Daniel Walker Howe, *What Hath God Wrought: The Transformation of America, 1815–1848* (Oxford: Oxford University Press, 2007), 8–18.

220. Andrew Jackson to New Orleans Citizens, 16 December 1814, *PAJ*, 3:206–7.

221. Vincent Nolte, *The Memoirs of Vincent Nolte: Reminiscences in the Period of Anthony Adverse; or, Fifty Years in Both Hemispheres* (1854; reprint, New York: G. Howard Watt, 1934), 226–31; see also Watson, *Jackson's Sword*, 149.

222. Order to the French Citizens of New Orleans, 28 February 1815, *PAJ*, 3:294.

223. Andrew Jackson to the United States District Court, 27 March 1815, *PAJ*, 3:332–33.

224. Alexandre Declouet to William Charles Cole Claiborne, 6 February 1815, *PAJ*, 3:273; see also Andrew Jackson to John Reid, 13 June 1815, *PAJ*, 3:362–63.

225. Samuel Carswell to Andrew Jackson, 26 June 1815, *PAJ*, 3:367.

226. Andrew Jackson to Unknown, 31 March 1815, *PAJ*, 3:338.

227. William C. C. Claiborne to Thomas Jefferson, 4 November 1814, *PTJ:RS*, 8:64.

228. Elizabeth Trist to Thomas Jefferson, 28 February 1815, *PTJ:RS*, 8:295.

229. Thomas Jefferson to Henry Dearborn, 17 March 1815, *PTJ:RS*, 8:357.

Chapter Two

1. The Secretary of War to John Sibley, 13 December 1804, *TP*, 9:352–53.

2. Governor Claiborne to the President, 24 August 1803, *TP*, 9:16; Claiborne to the President, 29 September 1803, *TP*, 9:58; *DLB*, 2:743.

3. Penny S. Brandt, introduction to "A Letter of Dr. John Sibley, August 6, 1807," *Louisiana Historical Association* 29, no. 4 (Fall 1988): 367.

4. Governor Claiborne to the President, 30 August 1804, *TP*, 9:285. See also Joseph Briggs to the President, 17 August 1804, *TP*, 9:277.

5. The President to Governor Claiborne, 2 December 1804, *TP*, 9:343.

6. Governor Claiborne to the President, 10 January 1805, *TP*, 9:367–68.

7. Governor Claiborne to the President, 25 March 1805, *TP*, 9:424–25.

8. The President to Governor Claiborne, 26 May 1805, *TP*, 9:450–53.

9. Robert Bruce L. Ardoin, *Louisiana Census Records*, vol. 2, *Iberville, Natchitoches, Pointe Coupée, and Rapides Parish* (Baltimore: Genealogical, 1995); *DLB*, 2:743.

10. A Matthias Barker was released from jail on the word of Dr. Sibley that he would repay a debt once he sold his cargo in New Orleans, but Barker skipped town. Consequently, Claiborne ordered his arrest. Claiborne to Edward D. Turner, 6 May 1804, *LB*, 2:131–32.

11. The Secretary of War to John Sibley, 25 May 1805, *TP*, 9:449. See also The Secretary of War to John Sibley, 8 July 1805, *TP*, 9:469–70.

12. Claiborne to Amos Stoddart, 26 June 1804, *LB*, 2:222.

13. John Sibley to Governor Claiborne, 10 October 1803, *TP*, 9:76.

14. Watson, *Jackson's Sword*, 183.

15. Eblen, *The First and Second United States Empires*, 239–40, 248, 257.

16. Clark and Guice, *The Old Southwest, 1795–1830*, 134.

17. Donna Merwick, *Possessing Albany, 1630–1710: The Dutch and English Experiences* (Cambridge: Cambridge University Press, 1990), 63, 167.

18. See Sophie White, *Wild Frenchmen and Frenchified Indians: Material Culture and Race in Colonial Louisiana* (Philadelphia: University of Pennsylvania Press, 2012).

19. See Clarence Edwin Carter, *Great Britain and the Illinois Country, 1763–1774* (Washington, DC: American Historical Association, 1910), 16–17, 79.

20. Ilya Vinkovetsky, *Russian America: An Overseas Colony of a Continental Empire, 1804–1867* (New York: Oxford University Press, 2011), 20–35, 79–81, 92–93, 104, 122–24, 36–37, 112–15, 220–21, 288–90, .

21. Ibid., 119, 139.

22. Carter, *Great Britain and the Illinois Country, 1763–1774*, 23, 55–56, 61; Andrew R. L. Cayton, *Frontier Indiana* (Bloomington: Indiana University Press, 1996), 39; Vinkovetsky, *Russian America*, 56.

23. Clarence Walworth Alvord, *The Illinois Country, 1673–1818* (Chicago: Loyola University Press, 1965), 71–72, 106, 277–81.

24. James R. Gibson, *Imperial Russia in Frontier America: The Changing Geography of Supply of Russian America, 1784–1867* (New York: Oxford University Press, 1976), 13.

25. John R. Bockstoce, *Furs and Frontiers in the Far North: The Contest among Native and Foreign Nations for the Bering Strait Fur Trade* (New Haven, CT: Yale University Press, 2009), 325–26.

26. Hinderaker, *Elusive Empires*, 75, see also 118–19; Hoffman, *Florida's Frontiers*, 58.

27. Stuart Banner, *How the Indians Lost Their Land: Law and Power on the Frontier* (Cambridge: Belknap, 2005), 60, 68–74, 85–95, 135.

28. Eblen, *The First and Second United States Empires*, 242.

29. Limerick notes a similar phenomenon in Oregon in the 1850s. Limerick, *The Legacy of Conquest*, 45–46.

30. Cayton, *Frontier Indiana*, 123, 138–39.

31. For the creation of this Californian oligarchy as a performative process, see Andrew Gibb, *Californios, Anglos, and the Performance of Oligarchy in the U.S. West* (Carbondale: Southern Illinois University Press, 2018), 18–22.

32. George Harwood Phillips, *Indians and Intruders in Central California, 1769–1849* (Norman: University of Oklahoma Press, 1993), 116, 134, 151.

33. Banner, *How the Indians Lost Their Land*, 150–90.

34. Richard White, *"It's Your Misfortune and None of My Own": A New History of the American West* (Norman: University of Oklahoma Press, 1991), 64.

35. Phillips, *Indians and Intruders in Central California, 1769–1849*, 165.

36. Banner, *How the Indians Lost Their Land*, 148.

37. Reservations would be established in Texas relatively late, in 1854.

38. White, *"It's Your Misfortune and None of My Own,"* 92–93.

39. Ned Blackhawk, *Violence over the Land: Indians and Empires in the Early American West* (Cambridge, MA: Harvard University Press, 2006), 247.

40. Ibid., 114–18, 122, 208.

41. Andrés Reséndez, *Changing National Identities at the Frontier: Texas and New Mexico, 1800–1850* (New York: Cambridge University Press, 2004), 254–57.

42. F. Todd Smith, *Louisiana and the Gulf South Frontier, 1500–1821* (Baton Rouge: Louisiana State University Press, 2014), 114, 145–46.

43. John R. Swanton, *The Indians of the Southeastern United States* (1946; reprint, Washington, DC: Smithsonian Institution, 1979), 75.

44. David LaVere, *Contrary Neighbors: Southern Plains and Removed Indians in Indian Territory* (Norman: University of Oklahoma Press, 2000), 41–45.

45. Manuel Gayoso de Lemos, "Political Condition of the Province of Louisiana," 5 July 1792, *LUR*, 1:276.

46. Baron de Carondelet, "Military Report on Louisiana and West Florida," 24 November 1794, *LUR*, 1:300.

47. Pitot, *Observations on the Colony of Louisiana from 1796 to 1802*, 17 (quotation), 81.

48. Du Lac, *Travels through the Two Louisianas*, 96.

49. Duc Denis Decrès, "Secret Instructions for the Captain-General of Louisiana, Approved by the First Consul," 26 November 1802, *LUR*, 1:368, 369, 372–73.

50. Laussat to Denis Decrès, 18 July 1803, *LUR*, 2:49.

51. Haynes, *The Mississippi Territory and the Southwest Frontier, 1795–1817*, 50, 230–31.

52. Banner, *How the Indians Lost Their Land*, 143.

53. Aron, *American Confluence*, 135.

54. Cayton, *Frontier Indiana*, 211.

55. Blackhawk, *Violence over the Land*, 66.

56. Eblen, *The First and Second United States Empires*, 268.

57. Casa Calvo to Ceballos, Secret Despatch Number 13, 18 May 1804, *LUR*, 2:192.

58. Vicente Folch, "Reflection on Louisiana by Vicente Folch, Number 2," *LUR*, 2:341–42.

59. William Dunbar to the President, *TP*, 21 October 1803, 9:86.

60. Daniel Clark, "An Account of the Indian Tribes in Louisiana," 29 September 1803, *TP*, 9:64–66.

61. Daniel Clark to James Madison, 29 September 1803, *PJM:SSS*, 5:473.

62. Claiborne to James Pitot, 10 May 1805, *LB*, 3:50–51.

63. Richmond F. Brown, introduction to *Coastal Encounters*, 1.

64. Claiborne to William Eustis, 3 August 1811, *LB*, 5:323.

65. The Secretary of War to John Sibley, 25 May 1805, *TP*, 9:449; The Secretary of War to John Sibley, 17 October 1805, *TP*, 9:514–15.

66. Joseph Bowmar to Governor Claiborne, 15 April 1804, *TP*, 9:223–24.

67. Daniel Clark to the Secretary of State, 29 September 1803, "An Account of the Indian Tribes in Louisiana," *TP*, 9:63; The 1766 Census of Natchitoches Indian Tribes, in *Natchitoches Colonials: Censuses, Military Rolls and Tax Lists, 1722–1803*, ed. Elizabeth Shown Mills (Chicago: Adams, 1981), 21–22.

68. "An Account of the Indian Tribes in Louisiana," *TP*, 9:63.

69. F. Todd Smith, *The Caddo Indians: Tribes at the Convergence of Empires, 1542–1854* (College Station: Texas A&M University Press, 1995), 87; David LaVere, *The Caddo Chiefdoms: Caddo Economics and Politics, 700–1835* (Lincoln: University of Nebraska Press, 1998), 80.

70. Betty Pourciaux, *St. Martin Parish History* (Baton Rouge: Le Comité des Archives de la Louisiane, 1985), 2; Albert S. Gatschet, "The Shetimasha Indians of St. Mary Parish, South-

ern Louisiana," *Transactions of the Anthropological Society of Washington* 2 (February 7–May 15, 1882): 148–60.

71. Daniel Clark to the Secretary of State, 29 September 1803, *TP*, 9:63; Winston De Ville, *Opelousas: The History of a French and Spanish Military Post in America, 1716–1803* (Cottonport, LA: Polyanthos, 1973), 17.

72. Pekka Hämäläinen, *The Comanche Empire* (New Haven, CT: Yale University Press, 2008), 147–49.

73. Banner, *How the Indians Lost Their Land*, 193–94, 208.

74. An Act for the Organization of Orleans Territory and the Louisiana District, 26 March 1804, *TP*, 9:212–13.

75. William Jarvis to James Madison, 23 May 1803, *PJM:SSS*, 5:27.

76. See Hämäläinen, *The Comanche Empire*, 174–75.

77. John Gibson to James Madison, 17 January 1805, *PJM:SSS*, 8:482.

78. John Devereux DeLacy to James Madison, 14 October 1803, *PJM:SSS*, 5:520 (quotation), 520–24.

79. Leonard J. Sadosky, *Revolutionary Negotiations: Indians, Empires and Diplomats in the Founding of America* (Charlottesville: University of Virginia Press, 2009), 190–96.

80. Claiborne to Judge King, 1 November 1808, *LB*, 4:236.

81. Claiborne to John Sibley, 3 June 1809, *LB*, 4:377.

82. Daniel J. Usner Jr., *American Indians in the Lower Mississippi Valley: Social and Economic Histories* (Lincoln: University of Nebraska Press, 1998), 108.

83. The President to Governor Claiborne, 26 May 1805, *TP*, 9:450–53.

84. Governor Claiborne to Henry Hopkins, 22 April 1805, *TP*, 9:440. Regardless, sales continued; *Land Records of the Attakapas District*, vol. 2, part 1, *Conveyance Records of Attakapas County*, ed. Glenn R. Conrad (Lafayette: Center for Louisiana Studies, University of Southwestern Louisiana, 1992).

85. The Secretary of the Treasury to the President, 19 March 1806, *TP*, 9:612–13; An Act for the Organization of Orleans Territory and the Louisiana District, 26 March 1804, *TP*, 9:212–13.

86. The Secretary of War to John Sibley, 25 May 1805, *TP*, 9:450.

87. Judge Lewis and Secretary Robertson to the Secretary of the Treasury, 25 January 1811, *TP*, 9:920.

88. The Secretary of the Treasury to Gideon Fitz, 11 May 1810, *TP*, 9:882–83.

89. Governor Claiborne to Joseph Bowmar, 23 March 1805, *TP*, 9:421–22.

90. Governor Claiborne to the Secretary of State, 27 January 1805, *TP*, 9:383–84.

91. John Sibley to the Secretary of War, 20 March 1810, *TP*, 9:879.

92. John Sibley, *A Report from Natchitoches in 1807*, ed. Annie Heloise Abel (New York: Museum of the American Indian Foundation, 1922), 16–17 (quotation), 18.

93. Smith, *The Caddo Indians*, 106–7.

94. Hämäläinen, *The Comanche Empire*, 147–50, 189; Susan E. Dollar, "'Black, White, or Indifferent': Race, Identity and Americanization in Creole Louisiana" (PhD diss., University of Arkansas, 2004), 126. See Burton and Smith, *Colonial Natchitoches*, 105–26.

95. Claiborne to Samuel Mitchell, 4 October 1802, *LB*, 1:196.

96. Henry Dearborn to Governor Claiborne, 11 June 1802, *LB*, 1:158–59; Claiborne to Henry Dearborn, 19 August 1802, *LB*, 1:159–60.

97. William Darby, *A Geographical Description of the State of Louisiana* (Philadelphia: John Melish, 1816), 211.

98. Governor Claiborne to Judge Prevost, 2 February 1805, *TP*, 9:389. J. Paillette served as civil commandant of the county.

99. Edward D. Turner to Governor Claiborne, 21 November 1804, *TP*, 9:336.

100. John Sibley, *A Report from Natchitoches in 1807*, 41, 55 (quotation).

101. Edward D. Turner to Governor Claiborne, 21 November 1804, *TP*, 9:336.

102. Claiborne to Edward Turner, 25 February 1804, *LB*, 1:386.

103. Sibley, *A Report from Natchitoches in 1807*, 22.

104. Claiborne to Edward D. Turner, 28 September 1804, *LB*, 2:342. He expressed similar sentiments to Madison; see Claiborne to James Madison, 25 September 1804, *LB*, 2:341.

105. Claiborne to Captain Turner, 3 November 1804, *LB*, 2:390.

106. Claiborne to Edward D. Turner, 28 September 1804, *LB*, 2:342.

107. Claiborne to Henry Dearborn, 3 June 1805, *LB*, 3:70.

108. Smith, *Louisiana and the Gulf South Frontier*, 212.

109. Sibley, *A Report from Natchitoches in 1807*, 24.

110. Ibid., 57.

111. Ibid., 24 (quotation), 26–28, 29 (quotation).

112. Claiborne to James Madison, 5 October 1804, *LB*, 2:347–48.

113. The Marquis of Casa Calvo to Governor Claiborne, 7 November 1804, *TP*, 9:324–25.

114. Edward D. Turner to James Madison, 6 June 1805, *LB*, 3:81.

115. Claiborne to James Madison, 5 November 1805, *LB*, 3:225.

116. Claiborne to Doctor John Sibley, 14 November 1805, *LB*, 3:232.

117. George T. Ross to Governor Claiborne, 11 February 1806, *TP*, 9:582.

118. Claiborne to Thomas Jefferson, 18 March 1806, *LB*, 3:270; Claiborne to James Madison, 25 March 1806, *LB*, 3:281.

119. Claiborne to Henry Dearborn, 28 August 1806, *LB*, 3:389.

120. Statement of Stephen, a Free Negro, To Governor Claiborne, 23 January 1806, *TP*, 9:576.

121. Governor Claiborne to the Secretary of State, 29 March 1806, *TP*, 9:618.

122. Claiborne to Henry Dearborn, 28 August 1806, *LB*, 3:389–90. See also Claiborne to Thomas Jefferson, 14 July 1805, *LB*, 3:124–25.

123. Smith, *The Caddo Indians*, 103–9, 85–102.

124. Claiborne to Dr. John Sibley, 10 June 1805, *LB*, 3:87; LaVere, *The Caddo Chiefdoms*, 127–35.

125. John Sibley to W. C. C. Claiborne, Deposition of Julian Besson, 15 September 1805, and Deposition of Mary Louis Bruwell, 16 September 1805, Claiborne (William C. C.) Letters and Depositions (1799–1846), MSS 5018, Louisiana and Lower Mississippi Valley Collections, LSU Libraries, Baton Rouge, LA.

126. Claiborne to Cowles Mead, 5 September 1806, *LB*, 4:3, 4.

127. An Act for the Organization of Orleans Territory and the Louisiana District, 26 March 1804, *TP*, 9:213.

128. Governor Claiborne to the President, 30 August 1804, *TP*, 9:287.

129. Claiborne to Henry Dearborn, 20 October 1802, *LB*, 1:206; Claiborne to Henry Dearborn, 3 January 1803, *LB*, 1:252; Claiborne to Henry Dearborn, 7 March 1803, *LB*, 1:277–78; Claiborne to Henry Dearborn, 16 February 1804, *LB*, 1:373–74.

130. Edward Livingston to the Secretary of State, 15 September 1804, *TP*, 9:294–95.

131. Claiborne to Thomas Jefferson, 26 June 1804, *LB*, 2:220–21; Thomas Jefferson to James Madison, 14 July 1804, *PJM:SSS*, 7:450.

132. Claiborne to Thomas Jefferson, 26 June 1804, *LB*, 2:221. See also Claiborne to James Madison, 7 June 1804, *LB*, 2:196.

133. Claiborne to the Commandants of Districts, *LB*, 2:73.

134. Governor Claiborne to Joseph Bowmar, 29 January 1805, *TP*, 9:387.

135. Ibid.

136. Trading House License, 1 March 1804, *LB*, 2:1–2.

137. Claiborne to Major Rd. King, 3 May 1804, *LB*, 2:128–29.

138. Governor Claiborne to the President, 10 January 1806, *TP*, 9:563.

139. Governor Claiborne to the President, 4 June 1806, *TP*, 9:657.

140. The President to Philip Reibelt, 10 January 1806, *TP*, 9:563.

141. Richard White, "The Louisiana Purchase and the Fictions of Empire," in *Empires of the Imagination: Transatlantic Histories of the Louisiana Purchase*, ed. Peter J. Kastor and François Weil (Charlottesville: University of Virginia Press, 2009), 38. See also James E. Lewis Jr., "A Tornado on the Horizon: The Jefferson Administration, the Retrocession Crisis, and the Louisiana Purchase," in Kastor and Weil, *Empires of the Imagination*, 127.

142. Kathleen DuVal, *The Native Ground: Indians and Colonists in the Heart of the Continent* (Philadelphia: University of Pennsylvania Press, 2006), 182.

143. Anthony Glass, *Journal of an Indian Trader: Anthony Glass and the Texas Trading Frontier, 1790–1810*, ed. Dan L. Flores (College Station: Texas A&M University Press, 1985), 13–15.

144. Ibid., 23–24.

145. Hämäläinen, *The Comanche Empire*, 149, 156–57.

146. Governor Claiborne to the Secretary of State, 8 August 1808, *TP*, 9:798–801.

147. Claiborne to Martin Duralde, 29 August 1808, *LB*, 4:194–96; Claiborne to James Madison, 31 August 1808, *LB*, 4:199–202.

148. Glass, *Journal of an Indian Trader*, 28–30.

149. Glass, 6 September 1808, *Journal of an Indian Trader*, 52.

150. Glass, 28 October 1808, *Journal of an Indian Trader*, 71–72.

151. Glass, 7 December 1808, *Journal of an Indian Trader*, 73.

152. Glass, 19 December 1808, *Journal of an Indian Trader*, 73, 75.

153. Owsley and Smith, *Filibusters and Expansionists*, 45–46, 49.

154. Claiborne to Colonel Shaumburg [sic], 30 July 1811, *LB*, 5:321.

155. See H. Sophie Burton, "Spanish Bourbons and Louisiana Tobacco: The Case of Natchitoches," in Brown, *Coastal Encounters*, 167–86.

156. Smith, *The Caddo Indians*, 93; LaVere, *The Caddo Chiefdoms*, 125, 129–30.

157. *Louisiana Courier* (New Orleans), 2 August 1811.

158. *Louisiana Gazette* (New Orleans), 25 March 1812.

159. Claiborne to Paul Hamilton, 23 January 1812, *LB*, 6:38; see also Claiborne to James Monroe, 4 January 1812, *LB*, 6:39.

160. John Sibley, "Letter of Dr. John Sibley, August 6, 1807," *Louisiana History* 29, no. 4 (Fall 1988): 382–83, 381. In Penny Brandt's view (in her introduction to the published letter) this charge of Elliot's was probably why Fontenot resigned his seat in the territorial House of Representatives in 1806.

161. Ibid., 382–83. See also Sibley, *A Report from Natchitoches in 1807*, 45–46.

162. James Wilkinson, *Memoirs of My Own Times*, 4 vols. (Philadelphia: Abraham Small, 1816), 1:412–13.

163. Claiborne to Genl. Wade Hampton, 20 July 1812, *LB*, 6:34–36.

164. Claiborne to James Madison, 6 June 1805, *LB*, 3:80.

165. Claiborne to Don Benito Perez, 16 November 1809, *LB*, 5:10–11; Claiborne to Don Benito Perez, 17 July 1809, *LB*, 5:11.

166. Claiborne to Robert Smith, 31 December 1809, *LB*, 6:23.

167. *Louisiana Courier* (New Orleans), 2 August 1811.

168. Claiborne to General Wade Hampton, 20 January 1812, *LB*, 6:34–36; The Memorial of Natchitoches Merchants to Governor Claiborne, 4 January 1812, *TP*, 9:976–78.

169. Claiborne to James Monroe, 24 January 1812, *LB*, 6:39.

170. *Orleans Gazette and Commercial Advertizer* (New Orleans), 24 November 1819.

171. *Louisiana Courier* (New Orleans), 12 August 1818.

172. Claiborne to James Madison, 12 December 1801, *LB*, 1:13; Claiborne to Henry Dearborn, 8 April 1802, *LB*, 1:72–73.

173. Claiborne to Henry Dearborn, 19 April 1802, *LB*, 1:87.

174. Claiborne to John McKee, 4 June 1802, *LB*, 1:121.

175. Governor Claiborne to the Secretary of War, 25 July 1807, *TP*, 9:756; See also Sibley, *A Report from Natchitoches in 1807*, 12, 15, 19–20; and Smith, *Louisiana and the Gulf South Frontier*, 213.

176. Sibley, *A Report from Natchitoches in 1807*, 47.

177. John Sibley, "John Sibley to W. C. C. Claiborne, 6 August 1807," *Louisiana History* 29, no. 4 (Fall 1988): 379–80.

178. Governor Claiborne to the Secretary of War, 25 July 1807, *TP*, 9:756–57.

179. Governor Claiborne to the President, 28 June 1807, *TP*, 9:744–46; Governor Claiborne to the Secretary of War, 23 July 1807 *TP*, 754–55.

180. Governor Claiborne to the Secretary of War, 23 July 1807, *TP*, 9:755. See also Governor Claiborne to the Secretary of War, 25 July 1807, *TP*, 9:756.

181. Sibley, *A Report from Natchitoches in 1807*, 31, 84–85. A jury ascertained that the dead man was O'Neal most recently of Mississippi; see ibid., 38–39.

182. *Orleans Gazette* (New Orleans), 5 September 1808.

183. Claiborne to Henry Dearborn, 8 August 1808, *LB*, 4:185–86.

184. Ibid., 4:187. See also To Thomas Jefferson, 5 October 1808, *LB*, 4:223.

185. *Orleans Gazette* (New Orleans), 5 September 1808.

186. Governor Claiborne to the Secretary of War, 23 July 1807, *TP*, 9:754.

187. Sibley, *A Report from Natchitoches in 1807*, 43–44.

188. An Address from William C. C. Claiborne Governor of the Territory of Orleans to the Chactaws of the Bayou Chico Village West of the Mississippi, 28 September 1806, *LB*, 4:22.

189. Opelousas, 10 March 1807, in *Calendar of St. Landry Parish Louisiana, Civil Records*, vol. 1, *1803–1819*, ed. Judy Riffel (Baton Rouge: Le Comité des Archives de la Louisiane, 1995), 86. Earlier Thomas had been charged for assault and battery on Rolen Cason. Opelousas, July 1806, in Riffle, *Calendar of St. Landry Parish Louisiana, Civil Records*, vol. 1, *1803–1819*, 77.

190. Governor Claiborne to John Sibley, 25 July 1807, *TP*, 9:759–60; A Talk from William C. C. Claiborne Governor of the Territory of Orleans, and Commander in Chief of the Militia thereof to the Family, and Nearest Relation of the Choctaw Indian, who Was Killed by a White Man of the Name of Thomas, 25 July 1807, *TP*, 9:760.

191. Opelousas, 14 June 1806, in Riffle, *Calendar of St. Landry Parish Louisiana, Civil Records*, vol. 1, *1803–1819*, 75.

192. *Orleans Gazette* (New Orleans), 3 September 1808.

193. *Orleans Gazette* (New Orleans), 5 September 1808.

194. Claiborne to Thomas Villaneuva, 29 July 1804, *LB*, 2:277.

195. Claiborne to the Reverend Father St. Pierre Manshac, 24 May 1811, *LB*, 5:252–53.

196. Claiborne to the Reverend Father St. Pierre Manshac, 24 May 1811, *LB*, 5:253.

197. Claiborne to Pierre Lacoste, 2 November 1814, *LB*, 6:304.

198. Claiborne to Judge Collins, Address to Indians, 28 September 1806, *LB*, 4:22.

199. McKee and Schlenker, *The Choctaws*, 36–38.

200. Claiborne to General Wade Hampton, 30 December 1811, *LB*, 6:22–23.

201. Owsley, *Struggle for the Gulf Borderlands*, 11.

202. Appendix II, Anonymous Letter written from the Havana, 8 August 1814, in Latour, *Historical Memoir*, 184–85.

203. Appendix III, Proclamation by Lieutenant-Colonel Edward Nicholls, Commanding his Britannic Majesty's Forces in the Floridas, 29 August 1814, in Latour, *Historical Memoir*, 185–86.

204. Appendix XVI, Andrew Jackson, Proclamation, 21 September 1814, in Latour, *Historical Memoir*, 204–5.

205. Pierre-Joseph Favrot to Philogène Favrot, 16 September 1814, *The Favrot Family Papers*, 5:221.

206. Nathaniel Herbert Claiborne, *Notes on the War in the South* (Richmond: William Ramsay, 1819), 50.

207. Claiborne to Governor David Holmes, 29 September 1812, *LB*, 6:182.

208. Claiborne to Judge Toulmin, 6 September 1813, *LB*, 6:267.

209. Claiborne to Thomas Flournoy, 17 September 1813, *LB*, 6:268–69.

210. William C. C. Claiborne to James Madison, 9 July 1813, *PJM:PS*, 6:413.

211. Claiborne to Gentlemen of the Senate and of the House of Representatives, 30 July 1812, *LB*, 6:146.

212. A Talk from William C. C. Claiborne, Governor of the State of Louisiana & Commander in Chief of the Militia thereof, to the Chief Head Men & Warriors of the Chactaw Nation, *LB*, 6:153–55.

213. W. C. C. Claiborne to General James Wilkinson, 15 August 1812, *LB*, 6:140.

214. William C. C. Claiborne to Thomas Jefferson, 14 August 1813, *PTJ:RS*, 6:389.

215. William C. C. Claiborne to James Madison, 23 October 1813, *PJM:PS*, 6:707.

216. Claiborne to General Armstrong, 14 April 1813, *LB*, 6:233–35.

217. Claiborne to Simon Favre, 4 August 1812, *LB*, 6:139.

218. Claiborne to Gov. David Holmes, 29 September 1812, *LB*, 6:182–83; Claiborne to Simon Favre, 16 November 1812, *LB*, 6:200–201.

219. Claiborne to James Monroe, 20 December 1814, *LB*, 6:327–28; Claiborne to James Monroe, 6 January 1815, *LB*, 6:331.

220. Claiborne to Thomas Gales, 10 September 1815, *LB*, 6:362–65, 364–65 (quotation).

221. Major Amos Stoddard, *Sketches, Historical and Descriptive of Louisiana* (Philadelphia: Mathew Carey, 1812), 457.

222. Dollar, "'Black, White, or Indifferent,'", 121–30. The fort and the Indian agency remained until 1819.

223. John C. Carr to Governor Claiborne, 7 January 1812, *TP*, 9:975–78.

224. Smith, *The Caddo Indians*, 107–9.

225. Claiborne to John Jamison, 18 May 1816, *LB*, 6:400–403.

226. Claiborne to William H. Crawford, 18 May 1816, *LB*, 6:403–4.

227. Flores, *Journal of an Indian Trader*, 93.

Chapter Three

1. Evan Jones and Labigarre Characterization of New Orleans Residents, 1 July 1804, *TP*, 9:257. See also Governor Claiborne to the Secretary of State, 13 July 1804, *TP*, 9:261.

2. Jean-Noël Destréhan to Governor Claiborne, 24 May 1806, *TP*, 9:641.

3. Claiborne to James Madison, 26 May 1806, *LB*, 3:313.

4. Claiborne to Thomas Jefferson, 10 July 1806, *LB*, 3:364–65.

5. Governor Claiborne to the President, 4 March 1810, *TP*, 9:870.

6. Claiborne secured 3,757 votes to Jacques Villeré's 1,947 and Destréhan's 268. See Joseph T. Hatfield, *William Claiborne: Jeffersonian Centurion in the American Southwest* (Lafayette: University of Southwestern Louisiana, 1976), 265.

7. *DLB*, 1:242.

8. Stanley Clisby Arthur and George Campbell Huchet de Kernion, *Old Families of Louisiana* (Gretna, LA: Pelican, 1998), 414–16.

9. Claiborne to John N. Destréhan Esqr., 16 January 1811, *LB*, 5:100–101.

10. Answer, of the Legislative Council to Governor Claiborne's Speech, 31 January 1811, *LB*, 5:127–28.

11. Ibid., 5:127–28, 372–73.

12. Eblen, *The First and Second United States Empires*, 61.

13. Aron, *American Confluence*, 120–21.

14. Gómez, *Manifest Destinies*, 112.

15. Hoffman, *Florida's Frontiers*, 159, 246.

16. Vernon Valentine Palmer, *Through the Codes Darkly: Slave Law and Civil Law in Louisiana* (Clark NJ: Lawbook Exchange, 2012), 40–41, 53, 57.

17. Alliot, *Historical and Political Reflections on Louisiana*, 1:113.

18. Navarro, *Political Reflections on the Present Condition of the Province of Louisiana, c. 1785*, 1:252.

19. Duc Denis Decrès, "Secret Instructions for the Captain-General of Louisiana, Approved by the First Consul," 26 November 1802, *LUR*, 1:373.

20. Robin, *Voyage to Louisiana, 1803–1805*, 117 (quotation), 240 (quotation), 251–61.

21. Du Lac, *Travels through the Two Louisianas*, 93–96

22. John Watkins to Secretary Graham, 6 September 1805, *TP*, 9:503.

23. Claiborne to the Commandants of Districts, *LB*, 2:73; Claiborne to Julien Poydras, 6 August 1804, *LB*, 2:293–95.

24. W. C. C. Claiborne to R. Claiborne, 10 July 1806, *LB*, 3:359.

25. Claiborne to Mayor of Orleans, 8 July 1806, *LB*, 3:357.

26. Kastor, *The Nation's Crucible*, 81–85.

27. On December 21, 1814, the legislature passed legislation to go into effect three months later that required one white person for every thirty slaves; the provision specified that the owner and any sons over sixteen would qualify as part of this total. See François-Xavier Martin, *A General Digest of the Acts of the Legislatures of the Late Territory of Orleans and the State of Louisiana and the Ordinances of the Governor Under the Territorial Government*, 3 vols. (New Orleans: Peter K. Wagner, 1816), 1:674–76.

28. Martin, *A General Digest*, 1:600–691, 606 (quotation).

29. Palmer, *Through the Codes Darkly*, 62, 113, 103–5, 109.

30. Ibid., 106. Judith Schafer disagrees with Palmer over the impact of Roman law on Louisiana's legal system, but she also notes that Louisianans desired to limit the growth of the free black population and protect slavery. See Judith Kelleher Schafer, *Slavery, the Civil Law, and the Supreme Court of Louisiana* (Baton Rouge: Louisiana State University Press, 1994), 9.

31. Schafer, *Slavery, the Civil Law, and the Supreme Court of Louisiana*, 180–83.

32. Eberhard L. Faber, *Building the Land of Dreams: New Orleans and the Transformation of Early America* (Princeton, NJ: Princeton University Press, 2016), 17, 66, 105. See also Rashauna Johnson, *Slavery's Metropolis: Unfree Labor in New Orleans during the Age of Revolutions* (Cambridge: Cambridge University Press, 2016), 13.

33. Isaac Briggs to the President, 2 January 1804, *TP*, 9:148.

34. Claiborne to James Madison, 23 January 1802, *LB*, 1:39.

35. Schafer, *Slavery, the Civil Law, and the Supreme Court of Louisiana*, 153.

36. Latrobe, *The Journal of Latrobe*, 229.

37. Dr. Watkins Report, 2 February 1804, *LB*, 2:5, 5–6 (quotation).

38. Claiborne to James Madison, 31 January 1804, *LB*, 1:352–53.

39. Claiborne to Mayor Bore, 19 March 1804, *LB*, 2:51.

40. Jonathan Dayton to Aaron Burr, 18 May 1804, in *Political Correspondence and Public Papers of Aaron Burr,* 2:867.

41. Claiborne to James Madison, 31 March 1804, *LB,* 2:76–77.

42. James Madison to Governor Claiborne, 12 March 1804, *LB,* 2:93.

43. Claiborne to Mayor Bore, c. 23–25 April 1804, *LB,* 2:113.

44. Claiborne to James Pitot, 25 July 1804, *LB,* 2:264.

45. The 1804 legislation that created a territorial government barred foreign slave importations in the territory. Dargo, *Jefferson's Louisiana,* 29–31.

46. Claiborne to Col. Freeman, 17 July 1804, *LB,* 2:361–62.

47. Claiborne to Captain Johnson 1st Pilot at the Balize, 18 July 1804, *LB,* 2:256–57; Governor Claiborne to Abimael Nicoll, 9 March 1805, *TP,* 9:414.

48. Claiborne to James Madison, 12 July 1804, *LB,* 2:245.

49. Claiborne to Capt. Johnson, 18 July 1804, *LB,* 2:363–64; Claiborne to Capt. Nichols, 25 July 1804, *LB,* 2:365–66; Claiborne to the Mayor and Municipality, 25 July 1804, *LB,* 2:366–67.

50. Claiborne, A Proclamation, *LB,* 1:380.

51. Claiborne to Ferdinand L. Claiborne, 26 February 1804, *LB,* 1:388–89.

52. Claiborne to the Officer Commanding at Fort St. Philip, 27 May 1812, *LB,* 6:108.

53. Dr. Watkins Report, 2 February 1804, *LB,* 2:10.

54. Claiborne to James Madison, 1 March 1804, *LB,* 2:14.

55. Claiborne to Thomas Jefferson, 29 May 1804, *LB,* 2:175.

56. Claiborne to James Madison, 10 March 1804, *LB,* 2:25.

57. Laussat to Denis Decrès, 7 April 1804, *LUR,* 2:53.

58. Casa Calvo to Ceballos, Secret Despatch Number 13, 18 May 1804, *LUR,* 2:190.

59. Claiborne to James Madison, 16 March 1804, *LB,* 2:46.

60. Claiborne to James Madison, 5 July 1804, *LB,* 2:238. See also Governor Claiborne to the Secretary of State, 3 October 1804, *TP,* 9:304–5.

61. Governor Claiborne to the President, 15 April 1804, *TP,* 9:222.

62. Claiborne to James Madison, 12 July 1804, *LB,* 2:245.

63. Governor Claiborne to the President, 30 August 1804, *TP,* 9:285.

64. Governor Claiborne to the Secretary of State, 22 October 1804, *TP,* 9:312. See also Governor Claiborne to the President, 27 October 1804, *TP,* 9:314; Governor Claiborne to the President, 5 November 1804, *TP,* 9:320.

65. Claiborne to James Madison, 8 May 1804, *LB,* 2:134.

66. Secretary of State to Governor Claiborne, 16 May 1807, *TP,* 9:733.

67. Governor Claiborne to the President, 25 November 1804, *TP,* 9:340.

68. Governor Claiborne to the President, 25 March 1805, *TP,* 9:424–25.

69. Claiborne to James Madison, 28 October 1804, *LB,* 2:347.

70. Claiborne to Albert Gallatin, 7 June 1811, *LB,* 5:266–67; Claiborne to James Monroe 7 June 1811, *LB,* 5:268–69.

71. Secretary Robertson to the Secretary of State, 6 July 1810, *TP,* 9:888.

72. Claiborne to Commodore Shaw, 11 June 1811, *LB,* 5:273.

73. Claiborne to Paul Hamilton, 13 June 1811, *LB,* 5:274–75.

74. Claiborne to James Madison, 16 October 1804, *LB*, 2:358.

75. Claiborne to Robert Smith, 15 May 1809, *LB*, 4:354–55.

76. Claiborne to Capt. Many, 18 May 1809, *LB*, 4:358–59; Claiborne to Capt. Many, 22 May 1809, *LB*, 4:366–67; Claiborne to Capt. Many, 3 June 1809, *LB*, 4:378–79.

77. Claiborne to Robert Smith, 20 May 1809, *LB*, 4:363–64. See also Claiborne to Julian Poydras, 28 May 1809, *LB*, 4:372.

78. James Mather to Claiborne, 18 July 1809, *LB*, 4:389.

79. Claiborne to John Graham, 19 July 1809, *LB*, 4:390–91.

80. Claiborne to Robert Smith, 12 November 1809, *LB*, 5:1–2.

81. The Secretary of State to Governor Claiborne, 12 September 1809, *TP*, 9:850.

82. The slaves were Babet, Baptiste, Julie, Son Soucie (naturally), Petit Marie Venus, Milanese and LaFleur.

83. John W. Gurley to W. C. C. Claiborne, 22 July 1805, *LB*, 3:133.

84. W. C. C. Claiborne to M. Cantrelle, 23 July 1805, *LB*, 3:134.

85. Claiborne to the Officer Commanding at Bayou St. Jean, 29 February 1804, *LB*, 1:393.

86. Claiborne to James Madison, 16 July 1807, *LB*, 4:129.

87. Claiborne to the Public, 6 January 1807, *LB*, 4:84.

88. Claiborne to Daniel L. Patterson, 10 November 1815, *LB*, 6:383–85; Patterson to Claiborne, 11 November 1815, *LB*, 6:385–87.

89. W. C. C. Claiborne to Commodore Porter, 21 October 1808, *LB*, 4:229.

90. No. 1982 May 1804, St. Charles Parish Original Acts, in *The German Coast: Abstracts of the Civil Records of St. Charles and St. John the Baptist Parishes, 1804–1812*, ed. Glenn R. Conrad (Lafayette: Center for Louisiana Studies, 1981), 5.

91. James Wilkinson to Claiborne, 6 December 1806, *LB*, 4:47.

92. Natchitoches in 1810 had a population of 2,870, 51 percent of whom were slaves. By 1820 the total population increased by a factor of three to 8,653, with a slave population that was just 27 percent of that total. See the 1810 and 1820 Censuses.

93. William C. C. Claiborne to James Madison, 1 September 1804, *PJM:SSS*, 8:9–10.

94. Claiborne to Edward D. Turner, 10 August 1804, *LB*, 2:303–4.

95. Claiborne to Casa Calvo, 30 October 1804, *LB*, 2:382–83.

96. Edward D. Turner to Claiborne, 18 October 1804, *LB*, 2:385–86.

97. Claiborne to Capt. Turner, 3 November 1804, *LB*, 2:389–90.

98. Casa Calvo to the Governor of the Territory of Orleans, 6 November 1804, *TP*, 9:323.

99. Claiborne to the Marquis of Casa Calvo, 7 September 1804, *LB*, 2:326–27.

100. Governor Claiborne to the District Commandants, 8 November 1804, *TP*, 9:325.

101. Edward D. Turner to Claiborne, 27 December 1804, *LB*, 3:30.

102. Antonio Cordero to Governor Claiborne, 2 October 1806, *TP*, 9:683.

103. John Sibley to Claiborne, 8 March 1805, Claiborne (William C. C.) Letters and Depositions (1799–1846), MSS 5018, Louisiana and Lower Mississippi Valley Collections, LSU Libraries, Baton Rouge, LA.

104. Claiborne to Casa Calvo, 8 November 1804, *LB*, 3:5–6; Claiborne to James Madison, 21 June 1808, *LB*, 4:179–81.

105. Sibley, "John Sibley to W. C. C. Claiborne, 6 August 1807," 380.

106. Governor Claiborne to Governor Salcedo, 1 October 1807, *TP*, 9:764.

107. Claiborne to Edward Turner, 8 November 1804, *LB*, 3:6–7.

108. Claiborne to James Madison, 17 November 1804, *LB*, 3:7–8.

109. His Excellency Govr. Herrera, or Officer Commanding the Spanish Army at or Near the Settlement of Bayou Pierre to Claiborne, 26 August 1806, *LB*, 3:385; Claiborne to Gov. Genl. Salcedo, 22 November 1808, *LB*, 4:255.

110. From Gov. Herrera to Claiborne, 28 August 1806, *LB*, 3:393; From Gov. Salcedo to Claiborne, 2 January 1808, *LB*, 4:165.

111. Governor Claiborne to the Secretary of State, 5 October 1807, *TP*, 9:765.

112. Claiborne to James Madison, 14 March 1808, *LB*, 4:161–62.

113. Circular to Parish Judges, 22 November 1808, *LB*, 4:256.

114. Claiborne to James Madison, 19 January 1809, *LB*, 4:304–5.

115. Claiborne to Judge Carr, 8 January 1809, *LB*, 4:286–87.

116. Claiborne to his Excellency the Governor of the Province of Texas, 28 November 1811, *LB*, 5:388.

117. Gwendolyn Midlo Hall, *Africans in Colonial Louisiana: The Development of Afro-Creole Culture in the Eighteenth Century* (Baton Rouge: Louisiana State University Press, 1992), 344–74.

118. W. C. C. Claiborne to James Madison, 8 November 1804, *LB*, 2:394. Yellow fever epidemics exacerbated fears of slave revolts. Jo Ann Carrigan, *The Saffron Scourge: A History of Yellow Fever in Louisiana, 1796–1905* (Lafayette: Center for Louisiana Studies University of Southwestern Louisiana, 1994), 33, 335–37.

119. Henry Hopkins, General Orders, 7 January 1807, *TP*, 9:716.

120. Henry Hopkins, General Orders, 5 January 1807, *TP*, 9:715.

121. Petition to Governor Claiborne By Inhabitants of Pointe Coupée, 9 November 1804, *TP*, 9:326.

122. Claiborne to James Madison, 20 September 1804, *LB*, 2:337–38.

123. Governor Claiborne to the President, 18 September 1804, *TP*, 9:298.

124. Petition of the Inhabitants and Colonists of Louisiana, 17 September 1804, *TP*, 9:297.

125. See Ellen C. Merrill, *Germans of Louisiana* (Gretna, LA: Pelican, 2005), 42–43; Louis Voss, *The German Coast of Louisiana* (Hoboken, NJ: Concord Society, 1928), 17–18; Rene Le Conte, "The German in Louisiana in the Eighteenth Century," in Brasseaux, *A Refuge for All Ages: Immigration in Louisiana History,* 10:39.

126. St. Charles had more planters with larger land and slave holdings than St. John the Baptist Parish. See Merrill, *Germans of Louisiana,* 45–47. In 1810 slaves of St. John the Baptist made up approximately half of the parish's population, and in St. Charles Parish slaves accounted for approximately 70 percent of the population. See Robert Bruce L. Ardoin, *Louisiana Census Records,* vol. 3, *Ascension, Assumption, West Baton Rouge, East Baton Rouge, St. Bernard, St. Charles, St. James, and St. John the Baptist Parishes, 1810 & 1820* (New Orleans: Polyanthos, 1977).

127. W. C. C. Claiborne to James Wilkinson, 4 January 1807, *LB*, 4:80.

128. Albert Thrasher's account, *"On to New Orleans": Louisiana's Heroic 1811 Slave Revolt* (New Orleans: Cypress, 1995), includes an excellent collection of primary documents.

129. W. C. C. Claiborne to Thomas Jefferson, 24 January 1811, *PTJ:RS,* 3:326.

130. Answer of the Representatives to Governor Claiborne's Speech, *LB,* 5:129.

131. Herbert Aptheker's sentiment that the cause of slave revolts was slavery has become a nostrum, or more fully: "Yet, the fundamental factor provoking rebellion against slavery was that social system itself, the degradation, exploitation, oppression, and brutality which it created, and with which, indeed it was synonymous." Herbert Aptheker, *American Negro Slave Revolts,* 6th ed. (New York: International, 1993), 139.

132. Gwendolyn Midlo Hall confirmed that Deslondes was a Creole mulatto slave born on the Deslondes plantation. See Hall, "Franco-African Peoples of Haiti and Louisiana," *Southern Quarterly* (Spring 2007): 41–48.

133. Allegations that the weapons originated from the Burr conspiracy were put forth in the *Baltimore American and Commercial Daily Advertizer.* See Thomas Marshall Thompson, "National Newspaper and Legislative Reactions to Louisiana's Deslondes Slave Revolt of 1811," *Louisiana History* 33, no. 1 (Winter 1992): 7, 8.

134. Thrasher, *"On to New Orleans,"* 48–49.

135. Harnett T. Kane, *Plantation Parade: The Grand Manner in Louisiana* (New York: William Morrow, 1945), 128–29.

136. *Moniteur de la Louisiane* (New Orleans), 13 January 1811.

137. James H. Dormon, "The Persistent Specter: Slave Rebellion in Territorial Louisiana," *Louisiana History* 18 (1977): 394–95.

138. St. Charles Parish Original Acts, Book 41, No. 17, 22 February 1811, in Conrad, *German Coast,* 106.

139. Claiborne to Genl. Hampton, 9 January 1811, *LB,* 5:93.

140. Claiborne to Major St. Amand, 9 January 1811, *LB,* 5:94.

141. Claiborne to Major Bullingney, 9 January 1811, *LB,* 5:95. Bullingney is most likely Dominque Bouligny, who served as a major in the territorial militia. Circular Claiborne to the Several Colonels of Regiments; and the several Parish Judges on the Coast, 10 January 1811, *LB,* 5:96.

142. For extracts from Andry to Claiborne, see *Moniteur de la Louisiane* (New Orleans), 15 January 1811. See also Dormon, "The Persistent Specter," 396.

143. Faber views federal military force as largely unneeded. See Faber, *Building the Land of Dreams,* 302.

144. St. Charles Parish Original Acts Book 41, No. 2 January 1811, in Conrad, *German Coast,* 100–102, placed the total at sixty killed and seventeen missing. Andry's letters were published in *Moniteur de la Louisiane* (New Orleans), January 15, 1811. Other sources list the dead in the original incident as sixty-six rebels and sixteen prisoners. See John S. Kendall, "Shadow over the City," *Louisiana Historical Quarterly* 22 (January 1939): 145.

145. Jean-Noël Destréhan, Alexandre Labranche, Pierre Marie Cabaret de Trépy, Adélard Fortier, and Edmond Fortier, St. Charles Parish Original Acts, Book 41, No. 2, January 1811; *DLB,* 2:710–11.

146. St. Charles Parish Original Acts, Book 41, No. 2 January 1811, in Conrad, *German Coast*, 100–102.

147. Parish of Orleans City Court #215, in Thrasher, *"On to New Orleans,"* 250.

148. W. C. C. Claiborne to Judge St. Martin, 19 January 1811, *LB*, 5:104.

149. Case 192, 18 January 1811, in Thrasher, *"On to New Orleans,"* 241.

150. Pardon by William Charles Cole Claiborne Governor of the Territory of Orleans, 1 April 1811, *LB*, 5:198–99.

151. Claiborne to John M. Destréhan Esquire, 19 January 1811, *LB*, 5:107.

152. St. Charles Parish Original Acts, Book 41, No. 20, 25 February 1811, in Conrad, *German Coast*, 108.

153. W. C. C. Claiborne to Judge Moreau Lislet, 20 January 1811, *LB*, 5:112.

154. Wade Hampton to Governor Claiborne, 12 January 1811, *TP*, 9:917.

155. Claiborne to James Wilkinson, 12 October 1812, *LB*, 6:189–90.

156. Claiborne to James Wilkinson, 17 March 1813, *LB*, 6:216.

157. Claiborne, A Proclamation, 15 March 1813, *LB*, 6:232–33.

158. W. C. C. Claiborne to Col. John Ballinger, 20 January 1811, *LB*, 5:108–9.

159. Nathalie Dessens, *Creole City: A Chronicle of Early American New Orleans* (Gainesville: University Press of Florida, 2015), 154–57.

160. Speech Delivered by Governor Claiborne to both Houses of the Legislative Body of the Territory of Orleans, 29 January 1811, *LB*, 5:123.

161. *DLB*, 1:15.

162. *DLB*, 2:799. See also Arthur and de Kernion, *Old Families of Louisiana*, 92–97.

163. Arthur and de Kernion, *Old Families of Louisiana*, 44–48, 284–88.

164. Grace King, *Creole Families of New Orleans* (New York: Macmillan, 1921), 419–22.

165. Arthur and de Kernion, *Old Families of Louisiana*, 247–52.

166. *DLB*, 1:396–97, 460.

167. *DLB*, 1:118. See also Jared William Bradley, "Biographical Sketches: James Brown," *IA*, 258–65.

168. Arthur and de Kernion, *Old Families of Louisiana*, 354. See also Kane, *Plantation Parade*, 130.

169. Claiborne to Laussat, *LB*, 2:66.

170. In 1812 the city of New Orleans sentenced several slaves to death for insurrection in the year following the revolt: Isaac, Case #228, 30 October 1812; Honoré, Case #229, 30 October 1812; Joseph, Case #231, 30 October 1812; Charles, Case #232, 30 October 1812; Lindor, Case #233, 31 October 1812. See Thrasher, *"On to New Orleans,"* 251–56.

171. For the formation of a common planter elite in sugar parishes of Louisiana, see Russell, "Cultural Conflicts and Common Interests." For an examination of African ethnicities and the slave trade within Louisiana, see Gwendolyn Midlo Hall, *Slavery and African Ethnicities in the Americas: Restoring the Links* (Chapel Hill: University of North Carolina Press, 2005), 71–79.

172. Thompson, "National Newspaper and Legislative Reactions to Louisiana's Deslondes Slave Revolt of 1811," 20.

173. A Message from the Governor, making several nominations, *LB*, 6:172–73.

174. Hall, *Africans in Colonial Louisiana*, 373–74.

175. See Lawrence N. Powell, *The Accidental City: Improvising New Orleans* (Cambridge, MA: Harvard University Press, 2012), 254–56.

176. Of Brown's slaves involved in the rebellion, four had European names: Robaine, Peter, Andrew, and Robin. Kenner and Henderson's labor force contributed fifteen slaves to the rebellion with no clear place of origin, at least nine of them with names of European derivation and another that might have been either African or European: Guiau, Carracas, Charles, Smillet, Elisha, Jerry, Major, Peter, Croaker, Harry. Further, two names are not fully legible. Butler and McCutcheon owned ten slaves with no clear place of origin, eight of whom had names of European origin: Simon, Ephraim, Dausson, Daniel, Abraham, Joe Wilkes, Philippe, and Simeon; and two, Perry and Colas, that might be either of African or European origin. Israel Trask, coming from Mississippi, may have brought slaves with him from the territory, and seven of his slaves in the rebellion had no clear birthplace and European names: John, Janvier, Nestor, Louis, Cesar, and two without clearly legible names. Gwendolyn Midlo Hall, *Afro-Louisiana History and Genealogy, 1719–1820*, http://www.ibiblio.org/laslave/; Documents II: I Slave Lists of Key Plantation Owners About 1811, in Thrasher, *"On to New Orleans,"* 284–85, 292–93, 299–300; Book 41, No. 18, 20 February 1811, in Conrad, *German Coast*, 106–7.

177. George Deslondes in 1800 had a slave Robert, nationality given as Creole/Pennsylvania; Adélard Fortier and Félicité Fortier in 1806 referred to Sam, Zamora, and François as "English slaves"; Jean-François Trépagnier and his late wife Marie-Louise Labranche in 1810 had two slaves from Charleston; Jean-Barre Trépagnier possessed slaves whose nationality was given as "English negro." Documents II: I Slave Lists of Key Plantation Owners About 1811, in Thrasher, *"On to New Orleans,"* 286, 287–88, 301–2.

178. Thrasher, *"On to New Orleans,"* 72.

179. Documents II: I Slave Lists of Key Plantation Owners About 1811, in Thrasher, *"On to New Orleans,"* 288.

180. Book 41, No. 4, 28 January 1811, in Conrad, *German Coast*, 104. Pierre St. Amand and P. A. Cuvillier petitioned Saint Martin to free Bazile. Book 41, No. 6, 1 February 1811, in Conrad, *German Coast*, 104–5.

181. Book 41, No. 18, 20 February 1811, in Conrad, *German Coast*, 106–7.

182. Manuel Andry to Governor Claiborne, 11 January 1811, *TP*, 9:915.

183. Speech Delivered by Governor Claiborne to both Houses of the Legislative Body of the Territory of Orleans, 29 January 1811, *LB*, 5:124. See also Junius P. Rodriguez, "Always 'En Garde': The Effects of Slave Insurrection upon the Louisiana Mentality," *Louisiana History* 33, no. 4 (Fall 1992): 401.

184. W. C. C. Claiborne to Major St. Amand and Col. Andre, 14 January 1811, *LB*, 5:99. See also W. C. C. Claiborne to the Secretary of State, 11 January 1811, and W. C. C. Claiborne to the Secretary of State, 12 January 1811, *LB*, 5:96–97.

185. W. C. C. Claiborne to Major McRae, 24 December 1811, *LB*, 6:16–17; W. C. C. Claiborne to James Mather, 24 December 1811, *LB*, 6:18; W. C. C. Claiborne to Col. Adlard Fortier, 24 December 1811, *LB*, 6:17; W. C. C. Claiborne to Col. Manuel Andry, 24 December 1811, *LB*,

6:18. Two days later Claiborne discounted the rumors but did not abandon his precautions. See W. C. C. Claiborne to Paul Hamilton, 26 December 1811, *LB*, 6:20.

186. W. C. C. Claiborne to Major St. Amand, 20 January 1811, *LB*, 5:110.

187. W. C. C. Claiborne to the Secretary of War, 20 January 1811, *LB*, 5:110–11. These requests were not always well received. The Secretary of War to Governor Claiborne, 30 March 1811, *TP*, 9:929.

188. W. C. C. Claiborne to Major St. Amand and Col. Andre, 14 January 1811, *LB*, 5:99.

189. Thomas Jefferson to John Wayles Eppes, 6 September 1811, *PTJ:RS*, 4:133.

190. Answer of the Legislative Council to Governor Claiborne's Speech, 31 January 1811, *LB*, 5:128. Claiborne passed on the request to President James Madison. See William. C. C. Claiborne to James Madison, 8 March 1811, *PJM:PS*, 3:211; Answer of the House of Representatives to Governor Claiborne's Speech, *LB*, 5:130.

191. W. C. C. Claiborne to General Thomas, 30 January 1811, *LB*, 5:135–36.

192. W. C. C. Claiborne to Mr. Duralde Sr., 1 February 1811, *LB*, 5:142.

193. W. C. C. Claiborne Speech to Both Houses of the Legislative Council and of the House of Representatives, 29 January 1811, *LB*, 5:123; W. C. C. Claiborne, Message to the Legislative Council and House of Representatives, 12 March 1811, *LB*, 5:179; An Act Providing for Payment for Slaves Killed and Executed in the 1811 Insurrection, *Acts Passed at the Second Session of the Third Legislature of the Territory of Orleans 1811* (New Orleans: Thierry, 1811), 132–33.

194. W. C. C. Claiborne, Message to the Legislative Council and House of Representatives, 19 April 1811, *LB*, 5:214.

195. *Louisiana Gazette* (New Orleans), 15 February 1812.

196. *Louisiana Gazette* (New Orleans), 16 January 1812.

197. *Louisiana Gazette* (New Orleans), 18 January 1812.

198. *Louisiana Gazette* (New Orleans), 5 July 1811.

199. *Louisiana Gazette* (New Orleans), 21 December 1811.

200. *Moniteur de la Louisiane* (New Orleans), 6 July 1813.

201. See Alan Taylor, *The Internal Enemy: Slavery and War in Virginia, 1772–1832* (New York: W. W. Norton, 2013).

202. Nolte, *The Memoirs of Vincent Nolte*, 189 (quotation), 189–92.

203. Jane Landers, *Black Society in Spanish Florida* (Urbana: University of Illinois Press, 1999), 229–30; Frank Marotti, *The Cana Sanctuary: History, Diplomacy, and Black Catholic Marriage in Antebellum St. Augustine, Florida* (Tuscaloosa: University of Alabama Press, 2012), 117–18.

204. Latour, *Historical Memoir of the War*, 29 (quotation), 70 (quotation), 148.

205. Appendix No. III, Proclamation by Lieutenant-Colonel Edward Nicholls, Commanding his Britannic Majesty's Forces in the Floridas, 29 August 1814, in Latour, *Historical Memoir*, 185.

206. Appendix No. I-b, Copy of a Letter from the Secretary of State James Monroe to Major General Andrew Jackson, 27 September 1814, in Latour, *Historical Memoir*, 183.

207. Appendix No. XI, Militia General Orders, W. C. C. Claiborne, 8 September 1814, in Latour, *Historical Memoir*, 199.

208. Claiborne to Andrew Jackson, 31 January 1815, *LB*, 6:337.

209. Andrew Jackson to William Charles Cole Claiborne, 5 February 1815, *PAJ*, 3:270.

210. Claiborne to Genl. Lambert, 25 March 1815, *LB*, 6:352–53.

211. Answer to Claiborne from John Power in Absence of Major General Lambert, 30 May 1815, *LB*, 6:353–54.

212. Schafer, *Zephaniah Kingsley Jr. and the Atlantic World*, 143–45; Hoffman, *Florida's Frontiers*, 266–67.

Chapter Four

1. Jared William Bradley, "Biographical Sketch: Pierre Bailly," *IA*, 587–88, which notes his status as a free man of color, his military service under the Spanish and then his appointments as a commandant and then a judge of Iberville. See also Jack D. L. Holmes, *Honor and Fidelity: The Louisiana Infantry Regiment and the Louisiana Militia Companies, 1766–1821* (Birmingham: Holmes, 1965) 233.

2. Kimberly S. Hanger, *Bounded Lives, Bounded Places: Free Black Society in Colonial New Orleans, 1769–1803* (Durham, NC: Duke University Press, 1997), 80.

3. Jared William Bradley, "Biographical Sketches: Pierre Bailly," *IA*, 587–88; Roland C. McConnell, *Negro Troops of Antebellum Louisiana: A History of Free Men of Color* (Baton Rouge: Louisiana State University Press, 1968), 26–29. See also Hanger, *Bounded Lives, Bounded Places*, 150.

4. Hanger, *Bounded Lives, Bounded Places*, 151.

5. See Gilbert C. Din, *Spaniards, Planters, and Slaves: The Spanish Regulation of Slavery in Louisiana, 1763–1803* (College Station: Texas A&M University Press, 1999).

6. McConnell, *Negro Troops of Antebellum Louisiana*, 31.

7. Address from the Free People of Color, January 1804, *TP*, 9:174–75.

8. The 1810 Census lists a Pierre Belly in Iberville with eighty-five slaves, five other free persons (free people of color), three white males between sixteen and twenty-six years of age, and one white male between twenty-six and forty-five. See Ardoin, *Louisiana Census Records*, vol. 3.

9. Hanger, *Bounded Lives, Bounded Places*, 80, 106–8. See also Kimberly S. Hanger, "Patronage, Property and Persistence: The Emergence of a Free Black Elite in Spanish New Orleans," in *Against the Odds: Free Blacks in the Slave Societies of the Americas*, ed. Jane G. Landers (London: Frank Cass, 1996), 48, 82. Other sources also make no mention of the judicial appointment. See *DLB*, 1:29–30. Yet another alternative asserts that Bailly as likely from Cap-Républicain, making him a refugee from Saint-Domingue. See Gabriel Debien and René Le Gardeur, "The Saint-Domingue Refugees in Louisiana, 1792–1804," in *The Road to Louisiana: The Saint-Domingue Refugees, 1792–1809*, ed. Carl A. Brasseaux and Glenn R. Conrad (Lafayette: Center for Louisiana Studies, 1992), 208.

10. Judy Riffel, ed., *Iberville Parish History* (Baton Rouge: Le Comité des Archives de la Louisiane), 166–67. According to Riffel, Bailly left his wife one-fourth of his estate on his death, so it appears probable that she too was emancipated at some point.

11. Governor Claiborne to Monsieur Bailey, 14 March 1805, *TP*, 9:417.

12. Claiborne to Francis Connell, 3 May 1804, *LB*, 2:128.

13. Claiborne to Francis Connell, 26 July 1804, *LB*, 2:269.

14. Governor Claiborne to Monsieur Bailey, 14 March 1805, *TP*, 9:417–18.

15. Meriam would serve until 1813. See Riffel, *Iberville Parish History*, 92. Register of Civil Appointments in the Territory of Orleans, 13 February 1806, *TP*, 9:598.

16. W. C. C. Claiborne to Mr. Fromentin, 5 February 1806, *LB*, 3:258–59.

17. W. C. C. Claiborne to J. W. Gurley, 28 April 1806, *LB*, 3:292.

18. W. C. C. Claiborne to J. W. Gurley, 29 July 1806, *LB*, 3:374.

19. Martin, *A General Digest*, 2:294–96.

20. Michael Kammen, *Colonial New York: A History* (New York: Oxford University Press, 1975), 59.

21. Robert Olwell, "Becoming Free: Manumission and the Genesis of a Free Black Community in South Carolina, 1740–1790," in Landers, *Against the Odds*, 1.

22. Charleston's free black community took a careful and measured approach in negotiating their place within a slave society. See Olwell, "Becoming Free," 16.

23. Ashli White, *Encountering Revolution: Haiti and the Making of the Early Republic* (Baltimore: Johns Hopkins University Press, 2010), 149, 176–77.

24. Jane Landers examines Atlantic Creoles throughout the Gulf South whose knowledge of political currents in the revolutionary Atlantic informed their calculations in siding with the forces of British and Spanish monarchism as well as revolutionary movements. See Landers, *Atlantic Creoles in the Age of Revolutions* (Cambridge, MA: Harvard University Press, 2010), 4–6, 71, 93, 137.

25. Landers, *Black Society in Spanish Florida*, 67, 158–59.

26. Jane G. Landers, "Acquisition and Loss on a Spanish Frontier: The Free Black Homesteaders of Florida, 1784–1821," in Landers, *Against the Odds*, 89; Hoffman, *Florida's Frontiers*, 233.

27. Landers, "Acquisition and Loss on a Spanish Frontier," 90–92.

28. Landers, *Black Society in Spanish Florida*, 22.

29. Hoffman, *Florida's Frontiers*, 254.

30. Landers, *Black Society in Spanish Florida*, 101–6, 107–35.

31. Schafer, *Zephaniah Kingsley Jr. and the Atlantic World*, 105.

32. Landers, *Black Society in Spanish Florida*, 167–71.

33. Schafer, *Zephaniah Kingsley Jr. and the Atlantic World*, 177.

34. Marotti, *The Cana Sanctuary*, 49–51; Landers, *Black Society in Spanish Florida*, 203.

35. Landers, *Black Society in Spanish Florida*, 208.

36. Daniel L. Schafer, "Shades of Freedom: Anna Kingsley in Senegal, Florida and Haiti," in Landers, *Against the Odds*, 137, 139–40.

37. Landers, *Black Society in Spanish Florida*, 3.

38. Frank Marotti, *Heaven's Soldiers: Free People of Color and the Spanish Legacy in Antebellum Florida* (Tuscaloosa: University of Alabama Press, 2013), 11, 25–26, 31.

39. Schafer, *Zephaniah Kingsley Jr. and the Atlantic World*, 178–80, 182, 205–9.

40. Marotti, *Heaven's Soldiers*, 37–38, 58–59, 62–63.

41. Hanger, *Bounded Lives, Bounded Places*, 21–24, 12, 17.

42. By definition pardos were lighter skinned and morenos darker.

43. Hanger, *Bounded Lives, Bounded Places*, 135, 112, 1.

44. Du Lac, *Travels through the Two Louisianas*, 94–95.

45. Hanger, *Bounded Lives, Bounded Places*, 125.

46. Ibid., 6.

47. Paul LaChance, "The Limits of Privilege: Where Free Persons of Colour Stood in the Hierarchy of Wealth in Antebellum New Orleans," in Landers, *Against the Odds*, 68.

48. Marotti, *The Cana Sanctuary*, 151.

49. Appendix XX, Address by General Jackson to the Militia of New Orleans, 18 December 1814, in Latour, *Historical Memoir*, 217.

50. 1810 Census; 1820 Census.

51. Burton and Smith, *Colonial Natchitoches*, 88–104.

52. For Claiborne's approach, see Erin M. Greenwald, "To Strike a Balance: New Orleans' Free Colored Community and the Diplomacy of William Charles Cole Claiborne," in Smith and Hilton, *Nexus of Empire*, 113–39.

53. Benjamin Morgan to Chandler Price, 7 August 1803, *TP*, 9:7.

54. James Wilkinson to the Secretary of War, 11 January 1803, *TP*, 9:160.

55. Governor Claiborne to the President, 29 September 1803, *TP*, 9:59.

56. William C. C. Claiborne to James Madison, 27 December 1803, *PJM:SSS*, 6:230.

57. Address from the Free People of Color, January 1804, *TP*, 9:174.

58. William C. C. Claiborne to James Madison, *PJM:SSS*, 17 January 1804, 6:351.

59. Claiborne to Henry Dearborn, 22 June 1804, *LB*, 2:218. See also Jon Kukla, *A Wilderness So Immense: The Louisiana Purchase and the Destiny of America* (New York: Anchor Books, 2004), 324–25.

60. Claiborne to Henry Dearborn, 9 June 1804, *LB*, 2:200.

61. Claiborne to Major Fortier, 22 June 1804, *LB*, 2:215–16.

62. Greenwald, "To Strike a Balance," 127.

63. Governor Claiborne to Daniel Clark, 23 May 1807, *TP*, 9:738.

64. Governor Claiborne to the Secretary of State, 26 January 1805, *TP*, 9:381.

65. James Brown to the Secretary of the Treasury, 7 January 1806, *TP*, 9:559.

66. Governor Claiborne to the Secretary of State, 8 January 1806, *TP*, 9:561.

67. Governor Claiborne to the Secretary of State, 8 January 1806, *TP*, 9:561.

68. As the legislature prepared to make the free colored militia permanent once again, Major Nott was to make contact with the officers and noncommissioned officers. General Orders, 9 January 1807, *TP*, 9:717.

69. Claiborne to James Pitot, 1 July 1804, *LB*, 2:232.

70. Claiborne to James Madison, 3 July 1804, *LB*, 2:234–35.

71. Claiborne to James Madison, 5 July 1804, *LB*, 2:237.

72. Claiborne to James Madison, 12 July 1804, *LB*, 2:244–45.

73. Claiborne to James Madison, 7 July 1804, *LB*, 2:239.

74. Martin, *A General Digest,* 1:640–42 (quotation), 2:326–30.

75. Ibid., 1:648.

76. A Message from the Governor, Returning a Bill with His Objections, 2 September 1812, *LB,* 6:170–71; A Message from the Governor, Returning a Bill with His Objections, 6 September 1812, *LB,* 6:175.

77. Martin, *A General Digest,* 1:686, 620, 670.

78. Claiborne to James Madison, 12 July 1804, *LB,* 2:245.

79. Claiborne to William Savage, 10 November 1809, *LB,* 5:4.

80. Governor Claiborne to Julien Poydras, 4 June 1809, *TP,* 9:843.

81. James Mather to Claiborne, 18 July 1809, *LB,* 4:388.

82. Claiborne to James Mather, 9 August 1809, *LB,* 4:402. See also Claiborne to James Mather, 4 August 1809, *LB,* 4:403–4.

83. Martin, *A General Digest,* 2:100 (quotation), 102.

84. Claiborne to Mayor of Orleans, 8 July 1806, *LB,* 3:357.

85. Faber, *Building the Land of Dreams,* 228.

86. John Watkins to Secretary Graham, 6 September 1805, *TP,* 9:500–501, 503 (quotation).

87. Statement of Stephen, A Free Negro, To Governor Claiborne, 23 January 1806, *TP,* 9:575–76.

88. Claiborne to James Madison, 24 January 1806, *LB,* 3:248.

89. Claiborne to James Madison, 29 January 1806, *LB,* 3:252–53.

90. Claiborne to Henry Dearborn, 1 February 1806, *LB,* 3:257.

91. McConnell, *Negro Troops of Antebellum Louisiana,* 49.

92. Claiborne to Mr. Dubourg, 14 January 1811, *LB,* 5:99.

93. McConnell, *Negro Troops of Antebellum Louisiana,* 22–23. See also Holmes, *Honor and Fidelity,* 66.

94. W. C. C. Claiborne, Message to the Legislative Council and House of Representatives, 15 February 1811, *LB,* 5:163.

95. See Din, *Spaniards, Planters, and Slaves,* 223–24.

96. Thomas Jefferson to John Wayles Eppes, 6 September 1811, *PTJ:RS,* 4:133.

97. Claiborne to William Eustis, 31 August 1811, *LB,* 5:350.

98. Claiborne to James Wilkinson, 28 December 1812, *LB,* 6:204–5.

99. William Charles Cole Claiborne to Andrew Jackson, 12 August 1814, *PAJ,* 3:116.

100. Martin, *A General Digest,* 2:104–6.

101. Elizabeth Trist to Thomas Jefferson, 5 March 1814, *PTJ:RS,* 7:226.

102. McConnell, *Negro Troops of Antebellum Louisiana,* 61. For Creole contributions see Paul D. Gelpi Jr., "Mr. Jefferson's Creoles: The Battalion d'Orleans and the Americanization of Creole Louisiana, 1803–1815," *Louisiana History* 48, no. 3 (Summer 2007): 295–316.

103. McConnell, *Negro Troops of Antebellum Louisiana,* 67–68.

104. William Charles Cole Claiborne to Andrew Jackson, 17 October 1814, *PAJ,* 3:165.

105. McConnell, *Negro Troops of Antebellum Louisiana,* 70–71.

106. Claiborne to Andrew Jackson, 24 October 1814, *LB,* 6:289.

107. Claiborne to Andrew Jackson, 28 October 1814, *LB*, 6:294.

108. Claiborne to Andrew Jackson, 4 November 1814, *LB*, 6:305–9.

109. Mary Gehman, *The Free People of Color of New Orleans* (Donaldsonville, LA: Margaret Media, 2009), 65–67.

Chapter Five

1. Jared William Bradley, "Biographical Sketches: Michel Cantrelle," *IA*, 570.

2. Lillian C. Bourgeois, *Cabanocey: The History, Customs and Folklore of St. James Parish* (Gretna, LA: Pelican, 1998), 19–20; Marie McDowell Pilkington Campbell, *Nostalgic Notes on St. James Parish, Louisiana: Then and Now* (Baton Rouge: Instant Print Centers, 1981), 33.

3. Leonce Haydel, *La Paroisse de St. Jacques: A History in Words and Photographs* (Baton Rouge: Pelican Management Corporation, 1988), 5.

4. James Wilkinson to the President, Characterization of New Orleans Residents, 1 July 1804, *TP*, 9:255.

5. The President to Governor Claiborne, 30 August 1804, *TP*, 9:283.

6. See Warren M. Billings, "A Course of Legal Studies: Books that Shaped Louisiana Law," in *A Law unto Itself: Essays in the New Louisiana Legal History*, ed. Warren M. Billings and Mark F. Fernandez (Baton Rouge: Louisiana State University Press, 2001).

7. Governor Claiborne to the President, 15 July 1806, *TP*, 9:674.

8. Ibid.

9. William C. C. Claiborne to the Sheriff of Acadia County, 13 July 1806, *TP*, 9:693.

10. Hinderaker, *Elusive Empires*, 244.

11. White, *"It's Your Misfortune and None of My Own,"* 174–76.

12. Carter, *Great Britain and the Illinois Country, 1763–1774*, 25.

13. Aron, *American Confluence*, 53–68; Stuart Banner, *Legal Systems in Conflict: Property and Sovereignty in Missouri, 1750–1860* (Norman: University of Oklahoma Press, 2000), 38–43.

14. Aron, *American Confluence*, 146–47.

15. Leonard J. Arrington, *The Great Basin Kingdom: An Economic History of the Latter Day Saints, 1830–1900* (Cambridge, MA: Harvard University Press, 1958), 6–35, 45, 62, 129–30, 293–94, 321–22, 356.

16. Gustive O. Larson, *The "Americanization" of Utah for Statehood* (San Marino: The Huntington Library, 1971), 283–304, 16–17, 23–26, 33–36.

17. For instance, the Morrill Anti-Bigamy Law of 1862 made polygamy a felony and barred its practitioners from the vote and holding public office; the Edmunds Act of 1882 disenfranchised Mormons through the creation of a five-member commission, and the Edmunds-Tucker Law of 1887 allowed for the confiscation of church property. See Larson, *The "Americanization" of Utah*, 57–60, 95, 254; Arrington, *The Great Basin Kingdom*, 257–58, 358–65.

18. Larson, *The "Americanization" of Utah*, 77, 78, 221, 248–51, 272; Arrington, *The Great Basin Kingdom*, 376–79.

19. Sally Engle Merry, *Colonizing Hawai'i: The Cultural Power of Law* (Princeton, NJ: Princeton University Press, 2000), 12–16, 36–38, 84–85, 50, 81–83, 89, 23, 35, 113, 258; Merry, "Law

and Identity in the American Colony," in *Law & Empire in the Pacific: Fiji and Hawai'i*, ed. Merry and Daniel Brenneis (Santa Fe, NM: School of American Research Press, 2003), 132.

20. Eblen, *The First and Second United States Empires*, 114.

21. White, *"It's Your Misfortune and None of My Own,"* 139.

22. Hinderaker, *Elusive Empires*, 204–7, 239–41.

23. Alvord, *The Illinois Country, 1673–1818*, 417–22.

24. Cayton, *Frontier Indiana*, 118–23.

25. Hoffman, *Florida's Frontiers*, 211–12, 284–94.

26. Banner, *Legal Systems in Conflict*, 95, 125.

27. Aron, *American Confluence*, 114–21, 124–27.

28. Haynes, *The Mississippi Territory and the Southwest Frontier, 1795–1817*, 33, 57, 59–60.

29. Clark and Guice, *The Old Southwest, 1795–1830*, 208.

30. A Native, *View of the Political and Civil Situation of Louisiana*.

31. William C. C. Claiborne to James Madison, 3 June 1804, *PJM:SSS*, 7:275.

32. Claiborne to James Madison, 9 March 1804, *LB*, 2:23; Ordinance for the Establishment of a Bank, *LB*, 2:29–34.

33. Claiborne to James Madison, 16 March 1804, *LB*, 2:41.

34. Gallatin to Jefferson, 12 April 1804, *The Writings of Albert Gallatin*, 3 vols., ed. Henry Adams (New York: Antiquarian, 1960), 1:184–85; Gallatin to James Madison, 30 May 1804, *LB*, 2:178–82.

35. Claiborne to Albert Gallatin, 23 May 1804, *LB*, 2:161.

36. John G. Clark, *New Orleans, 1718–1812* (Baton Rouge: Louisiana State University Press, 1970), 287–91.

37. Benjamin Morgan to Chandler Price, 11 August 1803, *TP*, 9:8.

38. Governor Claiborne to the Secretary of State, 25 April 1804, *TP*, 9:232–33.

39. Claiborne to Albert Gallatin, 14 June 1804, *LB*, 2:204–5.

40. The President to the Secretary of State, 17 April 1804, *TP*, 9:224–25; The President to Governor Claiborne, 17 April 1804, *TP*, 9:225–26.

41. Claiborne to Thomas Jefferson, 3 June 1804, *LB*, 2:187–90.

42. Governor Claiborne to the Secretary of State, 4 January 1805, *TP*, 9:361–62.

43. Governor Claiborne to the Secretary of State, 1 January 1805, *TP*, 9:361.

44. Governor Claiborne to the Secretary of State, 13 January 1804, *TP*, 9:368; Governor Claiborne to the Secretary of State, 16 April 1805, *TP*, 9:434–35.

45. James Brown to John Breckinridge, 22 January 1805, *TP*, 9:380.

46. Speech Delivered by Governor Claiborne to Both Houses of the Legislative Body of the Territory of Orleans, 29 January 1811, *LB*, 5:124–25; By William C. C. Claiborne Governor of the Territory of Orleans, opening bank stock subscriptions, *LB*, 5:230–31.

47. Stephen A. Caldwell, *A Banking History of Louisiana* (Baton Rouge: Louisiana State University, 1935; reprint Ft. McCoy, FL: Criswell's, 1977), 28.

48. Nolte, *The Memoirs of Vincent Nolte*, 189–92.

49. Pitot, *Observations on the Colony of Louisiana from 1796 to 1802*, 112, 111 (quotation).

50. Claiborne to James Madison, 10 March 1804, *LB*, 2:24.

51. "To Thomas Jefferson from Daniel Clark, 6 February 1807," Founders Online, National Archives (https://founders.archives.gov/documents/Jefferson/99-01-02-5025). This is an early access document from the Papers of Thomas Jefferson. It is not an authoritative final version. The Secretary of the Treasury to the President, 12 March 1807, *TP*, 9:718–19.

52. "To Thomas Jefferson from William Barnwell, 15 January 1807," Founders Online, National Archives (https://founders.archives.gov/documents/Jefferson/99-01-02-4878). This is an early access document from the Papers of Thomas Jefferson. It is not an authoritative final version.

53. Governor Claiborne to the President, 16 January 1804, *TP*, 9:163.

54. Claiborne to James Madison, 28 June 1804, *LB*, 2:230–31.

55. Hore Browse Trist to the Secretary of State, 18 August 1804, *TP*, 9:278.

56. Joseph Briggs to James Madison, 25 August 1804, *LB*, 306–7.

57. Briggs died of the fever on September 16. See Claiborne to James Madison, 17 September 1804, *LB*, 2:337. Claiborne to Cato West, 29 August 1804, *LB*, 2:311–12; Governor Claiborne to the President, 29 August 1804, *TP*, 9:279–80; Claiborne to Albert Gallatin, 31 August 1804, *LB*, 2:314; Governor Claiborne to the President, 18 September 1804, *TP*, 9:298.

58. Governor Claiborne to the President, 13 September 1804, *TP*, 9:294.

59. James Wilkinson to the Secretary of War, 11 January 1804, *TP*, 9:159.

60. Claiborne to Edward D. Turner, 1 August 1804, *LB*, 2:287–88.

61. Claiborne to James Madison, 8 September 1804, *LB*, 2:328.

62. Governor Claiborne to the President, 18 September 1804, *TP*, 9:298.

63. Governor Claiborne to the Secretary of State, 27 September 1804, *TP*, 9:299.

64. Governor Claiborne to the Secretary of State, 13 October 1804, *TP*, 9:310; Governor Claiborne to the President, 4 November 1804, *TP*, 9:319.

65. Secretary Brown to the Secretary of State, 26 October 1804, *TP*, 9:313–14; Governor Claiborne to the President, 2 December 1804, *TP*, 9:344.

66. Governor Claiborne to the President, 22 October 1804, *TP*, 9:311. See also Claiborne to James Madison, 3 October 1804, *LB*, 2:345–46.

67. Claiborne thought almost all recent European arrivals had died over the same period. Claiborne to James Madison, 16 October 1804, *LB*, 2:352.

68. Governor Claiborne to the President, 5 October 1804, *TP*, 9:309.

69. Governor Claiborne to the Secretary of State, 4 January 1805, *TP*, 9:361–62.

70. Col. Bellechasse to Gov. Claiborne, 13 March 1804, *LB*, 2:48; Claiborne to the Secretary of State, 18 March 1811, *LB*, 5:183–84; Claiborne to James Monroe, 1 August 1813, *LB*, 6:251–52.

71. Claiborne to the Mayor and Municipality of New Orleans, 6 June 1804, *LB*, 2:194–95.

72. To James Madison, 21 September 1804, LB, 2:338; An Ordinance providing for the appointment of a Person to take charge of Estates belonging to certain persons dying Intestate in the City of New Orleans, *LB*, 2:332–35.

73. Governor Claiborne to the President, 30 August 1804, *TP*, 9:286–87.

74. Charles E. Gayarré, *History of Louisiana: The American Domination* (New Orleans: Armand Hawkins, 1866), 117.

75. Secretary Graham to the Secretary of State, 23 June 1805, *TP*, 9:457.

76. T. W. Prevost to the Secretary of State, 8 July 1805, *TP*: 9:470–71; James Brown to Samuel Smith, 28 November 1805, *TP*, 9:537–39; James Brown to the Secretary of the Treasury, 11 December 1805, *TP*, 545–49.

77. To James Madison, 20 August 1805, *LB*, 3:178–79. See for examples, Governor Claiborne to the President, 20 July 1806, *TP*, 9:675; Claiborne to James Madison, 30 July 1807, *LB*, 4:134; Claiborne to James Madison, 17 October 1807, *LB*, 4:135; Claiborne to Robert Smith, 18 August 1809, *LB*, 4:410; Claiborne to the Secretary of State, 25 February 1811, *LB*, 5:165.

78. See Claiborne to John Williams, 13 May 1811, *LB*, 5:239. Claiborne traveled to Baton Rouge in August for the same reason. See Governor Claiborne to the Secretary of the Treasury, 19 August 1811, *TP*, 9:944; Claiborne to Mr. Dawson, 4 July 1812, *LB*, 6:120.

79. Claiborne to James Madison, 10 November 1804, *LB*, 3:7–8.

80. Claiborne to James Madison, 13 January 1806, *LB*, 3:242.

81. Secretary of War to James Wilkinson, 30 April 1809, *ASPMA*, 1:273.

82. James Wilkinson to the Secretary of War, 29 May 1809, *ASPMA*, 1:273; James Wilkinson to the Secretary of War, 19 June 1809, *ASPMA*, 1:273–74.

83. Claiborne to Robert Smith, 14 May 1809, *LB*, 4:354; General Wilkinson to Governor Claiborne, 27 July 1809, *ASPMA*, 1:292; Governor Claiborne to General Wilkinson, 28 July 1809, *ASPMA*, 1:292.

84. Alfred Thruston, Report to General James Wilkinson, 29 July 1809, *ASPMA*, 1:293.

85. Deposition of Major Electus Backus, 5 April 1810, *ASPMA*, 1:281; Deposition of Captain John Darrington, 11 April 1810, *ASPMA*, 1:283.

86. Claiborne to Robert Smith, 29 July 1809, *LB*, 4:392–93.

87. General James Wilkinson to the Secretary of War, 23 July 1809, *ASPMA*, 1:274; General James Wilkinson to the Secretary of State, 19 August 1809, *ASPMA*, 274–75; Secretary of War to General James Wilkinson, 22 June 1809, *ASPMA*, 1:274.

88. Deposition of John Darrington, 11 April 1810, *ASPMA*, 1:283.

89. William Eustis to The Honorable Thomas Newton, 24 February 1810, *ASPMA*, 1:272; William Eustis to the Honorable Thomas Newton, 4 April 1810, *ASPMA*, 1:275.

90. Hatfield, *William Claiborne*, 205–6.

91. *ASPMA*, 1:269–72.

92. Deposition of William D. Beall, 21 March 1810, *ASPMA*, 1:279; Interrogatories put to Captain William E. Williams, 17 April 1810, *ASPMA*, 1:287.

93. Deposition of Colonel Alexander Parker, 14 April 1810, *ASPMA*, 1:286.

94. Deposition of Doctor Alexander Macauley, 21 March 1810, *ASPMA*, 1:279.

95. James Mather to Governor Claiborne, 9 September 1811, *TP*, 9:947.

96. One hundred seven Catholics (62 white, 45 people of color) and 128 Protestants as well as another 27 deaths in the Charity Hospital.

97. Governor Claiborne to the President, 8 October 1811, *TP*, 9:948; James Mather to Governor Claiborne, 12 October 1811, *TP*, 9:949–50.

98. Governor Claiborne to Thomas Jefferson, 12 January 1810, *TP*, 9:864. See also Governor Claiborne to the President, 17 December 1809, *TP*, 9:859–60; J. B. Robertson, 3 December 1809, *LB*, 5:21–22.

99. Petition to Congress by the Inhabitants of the Territory, 6 December 1808, *TP*, 9:807.

100. Claiborne to Paul Hamilton, 9 September 1811, *LB,* 5:356.

101. Claiborne to Paul Hamilton, 28 October 1811, *LB,* 5:369.

102. Claiborne to Paul Hamilton, 25 December 1811, *LB,* 6:19.

103. Petition to Congress by Physicians and Surgeons of New Orleans, 19 November 1811, *TP,* 9:955–56.

104. Isaac Briggs to the President, 27 February 1804, *TP,* 9:197.

105. Gideon Granger to Governor Claiborne, 12 April 1804, *LB,* 2:206. For similar recommendations for West Florida, see Claiborne to Gideon Granger, 3 September 1811, *LB,* 5:354–55; Claiborne to Gideon Granger, 23 November 1811, *LB,* 5:385–86; Claiborne to Abraham Bradley Jr., 4 December 1811, *LB,* 5:393–94.

106. Claiborne to Gideon Granger, 17 June 1804, *LB,* 2:212.

107. Claiborne to James Madison, 8 September 1804, *LB,* 2:328; Claiborne to Gideon Granger, 17 October 1805, *LB,* 3:202–4; Claiborne to James Madison, 5 April 1808, *LB,* 4:168–69; Claiborne to James Madison, 21 May 1812, *LB,* 6:103–5; Governor Claiborne to the Secretary of State, 18 March 1805, *TP,* 9:420–21; Governor Claiborne to John Sibley, 8 April 1805, *TP,* 9:433–34; Judge Duffield to the Secretary of State, 6 May 1805, *TP,* 9:447–48; Postmaster General to Governor Claiborne, 19 July 1805, *TP,* 9:473–74; Postmaster General to David Case, 11 March 1808, *TP,* 9:778.

108. Address of the Merchants of the City of New Orleans to the President, 30 December 1806, *TP,* 9:690–92.

109. The Postmaster General to Benjamin Morgan and Others, 28 March 1812, *TP,* 9:1013.

110. Governor Claiborne to the President, 24 August 1803, *TP,* 9:22; Daniel Clark to the Secretary of State, 8 September 1803, *TP,* 9:38.

111. John Watkins to Governor Claiborne, 2 August 1805, *TP,* 9:487–88.

112. John Watkins to Governor Claiborne, 2 April 1806, *TP,* 9:621.

113. Governor Claiborne to the President, 16 January 1804, *TP,* 9:161–62.

114. Governor Claiborne to the President, 25 March 1805, *TP,* 9:424–25.

115. Memorial to Congress by the Territorial House of Representatives, 14 November 1805, *TP,* 9:531–32; Petition to Congress by the Legislative Council, 10 December 1805, *TP,* 9:544–45; Memorial to Congress from the Regents of the University of Orleans, 9 December 1805, *TP,* 9:543–44; Memorial to Congress from the Regents of the University of Orleans, 20 April 1812, *TP,* 9:1014–16.

116. Clark, *New Orleans, 1718–1812,* 325–29.

117. Powell, *The Accidental City,* 325.

118. Claiborne to James Madison, 13 February 1804, *LB,* 1:371–73; Claiborne to James Madison, 18 February 1804, *LB,* 1:375–76; Claiborne to James Madison, 11 April 1804, *LB,* 2:91.

119. Governor Claiborne to the President, 24 August 1803, *TP,* 9:20.

120. Governor Claiborne to the President, 25 November 1804, *TP,* 9:340.

121. James Brown to Henry Clay, 18 December 1804, in *The Papers of Henry Clay,* 10 vols., ed. James F. Hopkins (Lexington: University Press of Kentucky, 1959), 1:165.

122. Governor Claiborne to the President, 24 August 1803, *TP,* 9:21.

123. Daniel Clark to the Secretary of State, 8 September 1803, *TP,* 9:38.

124. Claiborne to James Madison, 2 January 1804, *LB,* 1:323–24, 328.

125. An Act for the Organization of Orleans Territory and the Louisiana District, 26 March 1804, *TP*, 9:205, 209.

126. Governor Claiborne to the President, 15 July 1806, *TP*, 9:673.

127. W. C. C. Claiborne to Thomas Jefferson, 11 July 1806, *LB*, 3:365 (quotation), 366.

128. William C. C. Claiborne, New Orleans to Judge William Wikoff, Baton Rouge, 22 October 1808, *The Favrot Family Papers*, 4:266.

129. See Haynes, *The Mississippi Territory and the Southwest Frontier, 1795–1817*, 57–61; Claiborne to James Madison, 5 November 1802, *LB*, 1:211–21.

130. Claiborne to James Madison, Secretary of State, 20 December 1801, *LB*, 1:29.

131. Claiborne to James Madison, Secretary of State, 8 January 1802, *LB*, 1:32.

132. Claiborne to James Madison, 18 February 1804, *LB*, 1:377.

133. Governor Claiborne to the President, 24 August 1803, *TP*, 9:19.

134. Governor Claiborne to the Secretary of State, 7 September 1803, *TP*, 9:26.

135. Governor Claiborne to Daniel Clark, 7 September 1803, *TP*, 9:27.

136. Daniel Clark to Governor Claiborne, 20 September 1803, *TP*, 9:56.

137. Governor Claiborne to the Secretary of State, 30 September 1803, *TP*, 9:66–67.

138. Claiborne to James Madison, 5 August 1805, *LB*, 3:151; Claiborne to James Madison, 10 August 1805, *LB*, 3:158; Claiborne to the Marquis of Casa Calvo, 9 August 1805, *LB*, 3:160–61; Claiborne to the Marquis of Casa Calvo, 14 August 1805, *LB*, 167–68; Gov. Claiborne to the Marquis of Casa Calvo, 17 August 1805, *LB*, 3:174–76; Claiborne to James Madison, 20 August 1805, *LB*, 3:178–79.

139. An Act for the Organization of Orleans Territory and the Louisiana District, 26 March 1804, *TP*, 9:211–12.

140. An Act for the Adjustment of Land Titles, 2 March 1805, *TP*, 9:408–9.

141. Ibid., 9:408–14.

142. The Secretary of the Treasury to John W. Gurley, 30 March 1805, *TP*, 9:427.

143. Claiborne to Henry Hopkins, 31 July 1804, *LB*, 2:283–84.

144. Claiborne to James Madison, 18 May 1805, *LB*, 3:57.

145. Berquin-Duvallon, *Travels in Louisiana and the Floridas in the Year, 1802*, 160.

146. Stoddard, *Sketches, Historical and Descriptive of Louisiana*, 259.

147. Claiborne to Col. Henry Hopkins, 25 November 1805, *LB*, 3:238.

148. Governor Claiborne to the Secretary of State, 8 January 1806, *TP*, 9:560.

149. Governor Claiborne to the President, 25 July 1806, *TP*, 9:678. See also The Secretary of State to Governor Claiborne, 28 February 1807, *TP*, 9:711.

150. Claiborne to James Madison, 15 June 1806, *LB*, 3:331–32.

151. Jared William Bradley, "Biographical Sketches: Casa Calvo," *IA*, 491–92.

152. Claiborne to Thomas Jefferson, 17 June 1806, *LB*, 3:334–35.

153. William C. C. Claiborne Governor of the Territory of Orleans to the Sheriff of the County of Orleans and others whom it may concern, 16 June 1806, *LB*, 3:333–34.

154. Nolte, *The Memoirs of Vincent Nolte*, 184–85.

155. Memorial to Congress by the Territorial House of Representatives, 14 November 1805, *TP*, 9:528.

156. James Brown to the Secretary of state, 24 August 1805, *TP*, 9:495.

157. James Brown to John Breckinridge, 17 September 1805, *TP*, 9:512–13.

158. Claiborne to Thomas Jefferson, 14 July 1805, *LB*, 3:125.

159. Claiborne to John W. Gurley, 28 July 1805, *LB*, 3:140.

160. Claiborne to James Madison, 13 May 1808, *LB*, 4:174.

161. Claiborne to James Madison, 23 August 1805, *LB*, 3:181; Claiborne to Albert Gallatin, 9 September 1808, *LB*, 4:214–15; Claiborne to Judge Hubbard, 5 May 1809, *LB*, 4:349.

162. Levi Lincoln to Thomas Jefferson, 19 April 1804, *TP*, 9:229.

163. Baron de Bastrop Papers, 1795–1823, Center for American History, University of Texas at Austin.

164. Claiborne to James Madison, 18 May 1805, *LB*, 3:57.

165. Claiborne to Lieutenant Bowmar, 27 June 1804, *LB*, 2:223–27.

166. Governor Claiborne to the Secretary of the Treasury, 11 August 1806, *TP*, 9:679–81.

167. See Vernet, *Strangers on Their Native Soil*, 98–101.

168. Claiborne to James Madison, 18 February 1804, *LB*, 1:375.

169. The Secretary of the Treasury to John W. Gurley, 30 March 1805, *TP*, 9:428.

170. The Secretary of the Treasury to Thomas Worthington, 25 February 1807, *TP*, 9:708–11, 9:710 (quotation).

171. The Secretary of the Treasury to the President, 27 March 1807, *TP*, 9:722.

172. The Secretary of the Treasury to John Thompson and to John W. Gurley, 2 April 1807, *TP*, 9:727.

173. John W. Gurley to the Secretary of the Treasury, 3 June 1805, *TP*, 9:453–54.

174. John W. Gurley to Governor Claiborne, 25 July 1805, *TP*, 9:477.

175. The Secretary of the Treasury to the President, 19 March 1806, *TP*, 9:612–13.

176. James Brown to the Secretary of the Treasury, 29 May 1807, *TP*, 9:742.

177. Register of Civil Appointments, 30 June 1806, *TP*, 9:662–63.

178. The Secretary of the Treasury to Allan B. Magruder, James Brown and Felix Grundy, 8 July 1805, *TP*, 9:468–69.

179. Philip Grymes, Judge Lewis, and Secretary Robertson to the Secretary of the Treasury, 8 January 1810, *TP*, 9:862.

180. John Thompson to the Secretary of the Treasury, 1 May 1806, *TP*, 9:628–29.

181. See The Secretary of the Treasury to the President, 12 March 1807, *TP*, 9:718–19.

182. John W. Gurley to the Secretary of the Treasury, 24 July 1806, *TP*, 9:677.

183. John W. Gurley to the Secretary of the Treasury, 3 November 1807, *TP*, 9:766–67.

184. The Secretary of the Treasury to the Boards of Commissioners at St. Louis, New Orleans, and Opelousas, 24 April 1811, *TP*, 9:931.

185. The Secretary of the Treasury to Levin Wailes, William Garrard, and Gideon Fitz, 24 May 1811, *TP*, 9:936.

186. Judge Lewis and Secretary Robertson to the Secretary of the Treasury, 25 January 1811, *TP*, 9:920.

187. Gideon Fitz to Thomas Jefferson, 20 March 1816, *PTJ:RS*, 9:584–85.

188. Benedict Van Pradelles to the Secretary of the Treasury, 11 June 1808, *TP*, 9:792.

189. See Gary B. Mills, *The Forgotten People: Cane River's Creoles of Color* (Baton Rouge: Louisiana State University Press, 1977), 62–63.

190. James H. Dormon detects a split between Acadians who adapted to Creole-Anglo sugar agriculture and another group displaced by ethnic and market changes. Dormon, *The People Called Cajuns: An Introduction to an Ethnohistory* (Lafayette: Center for Louisiana Studies, University of Southwestern Louisiana, 1983).

191. Conrad, *Land Records of the Attakapas District,* vol. 1, *The Attakapas Domesday Book: Land Grants, Claims and Confirmations in the Attakapas District, 1764–1826* (Lafayette: Center for Louisiana Studies, University of Southwestern Louisiana, 1990), xvii.

192. The Secretary of the Treasury to Levin Wailes, William Garrard and Gideon Fitz, 24 May 1811, *TP,* 9:934 (quotation), 9:934–36.

193. Petition to Congress by Claimants to Lands in the Western District, 15 December 1811, *TP,* 9:959.

194. Representations to Congress of Eligius Fromentin and Allan B. Magruder, 13 March 1812, *TP,* 9:1006–7.

195. Claiborne to Albert Gallatin, 1 February 1812, *LB,* 6:45.

196. William Garrard to the President, 20 January 1812, *TP,* 9:988.

197. *Louisiana Courier* (New Orleans), 13 December 1813.

198. John Watkins to Governor Claiborne, 2 April 1806, *TP,* 9:621.

199. William C. C. Claiborne to all who shall see these presents, and more particularly, the Sheriff of Plaquemines, 24 December 1811, *LB,* 6:16.

200. Enclosures, Secretary Roberson to the Secretary of State, 18 January 1812, *TP,* 9:983; Claiborne to Abner L. Duncan, 9 April 1812, *LB,* 6:76.

201. John Ballinger to the Secretary of State, 26 December 1811, *TP,* 9:968.

202. Claiborne to Robert Smith, 2 December 1810, *LB,* 5:37–38.

203. Claiborne to the Secretary of the Treasury, 1 February 1811, *LB,* 5:140.

204. Claiborne to Robert Smith, 27 December 1810, *LB,* 5:68.

Chapter Six

1. James Brown to John Breckinridge, 17 September 1805, *TP,* 9:511, 9:511n.

2. *DLB,* 1:242.

3. Alexander Labranche was a large slaveholder deeply involved in land sales in St. Charles. See No. 54 6-15-09, No. 72 12-14-10, No. 4 1-28-11, St. Charles Parish Original Acts, in Conrad, *The German Coast,* 80, 99, 102–3. See Tableau de hypothèques qui existent sur les propriétés de la paroisse St. Charles Côte des Allemands 1806–1853, St. Charles Parish Courthouse Archives.

4. The Labranche plantation in 1804 produced 103,000 pounds of sugar, Bernoudy's plantation 50,000, Habine's 70,000, the Aimes' 8,000, and they financed mortgages in St. Charles. See No. 1982, May 1804, St. Charles Parish Original Acts, in Conrad, *The German Coast,* 5; Tableau de hypothèques qui existent sur les propriétés de la paroisse St. Charles Côte des Allemands 1806–1853, St. Charles Parish Courthouse Archives.

5. James Brown to Henry Clay, 26 February 1810, *The Papers of Henry Clay,* 1:453–54 (quotation), 454–55.

6. James Monroe's Account of a Conversation with Thomas Jefferson, 30 November 1809, *PTJ:RS*, 2:44–46.

7. James Madison to Thomas Jefferson, 17 March 1805, *PJM:SSS*, 9:140.

8. Nolte, *The Memoirs of Vincent Nolte*, 86.

9. Thomas Jefferson to James Madison, 24 March 1805, *PJM:SSS*, 9:169.

10. Kammen, *Colonial New York*, 73–99; David E. Narrett, "Dutch Customs of Inheritance, Women, and the Law in Colonial New York City," in *Authority and Resistance in Early New York*, ed. William Pencak and Conrad Edick Wright (New York: New York Historical Society, 1988), 27.

11. Christian J. Koot, *Empire at the Periphery: British Colonists, Anglo-Dutch Trade, and the Development of the British Atlantic, 1621–1713* (New York: New York University Press, 2011), 150–78.

12. Randall H. Balmer, *A Perfect Babel of Confusion: Dutch Religion and English Culture in the Middle Colonies* (Oxford: Oxford University Press, 1989), 87, 155–56, 9, 34–39; Kammen, *Colonial New York*, 124; David E. Narrett, "Dutch Customs of Inheritance, Women, and the Law in Colonial New York City," in Pencak and Wright, *Authority and Resistance in Early New York*, 29, 39; John M. Murrin, "English Rights as Ethnic Aggression: The English Conquest, the Charter of Liberties of 1683, and Leisler's Rebellion in New York," in Pencak and Wright, *Authority and Resistance in Early New York*, 57, 64–66, 76–80.

13. Balmer, *A Perfect Babel of Confusion*, 61.

14. Kammen, *Colonial New York*, 119–68.

15. Alvord, *The Illinois Country, 1673–1818*, 264–68, 293–95; Carter, *Great Britain and the Illinois Country, 1763–1774*, 53, 152–53.

16. Alvord, *The Illinois Country, 1673–1818*, 304–17, 329, 331–33, 336–37, 338–48.

17. Aron, *American Confluence*, 64–65, 77–78; Banner, *Legal Systems in Conflict*, 16–35.

18. Reséndez, *Changing National Identities at the Frontier*, 6–7.

19. Ibid.

20. Ibid.

21. Reséndez, *Changing National Identities at the Frontier*, 6–7, 37–40, 98–99, 240, 248–53.

22. Ibid., 201, 56–57, 125; Cayton, *Frontier Indiana*, 228–30.

23. Eblen, *The First and Second United States Empires*, 146–47, 152–53, 155, 161.

24. White, *"It's Your Misfortune and None of My Own,"* 58, 155.

25. Aron, *American Confluence*, 121–22.

26. Eblen, *The First and Second United States Empires*, 216–23.

27. Earl Pomeroy, *The Territories and the United States, 1861–1890* (Seattle: University of Washington Press, 1969), xii, 95, 97.

28. Eblen, *The First and Second United States Empires*, 166, 179.

29. Larson, *The "Americanization" of Utah*, 3–20, 170–74.

30. Jonathan Kamakawio'ole Osorio "Kū'ē and Kū'oko'a: History, Law, and Other Faiths," in Merry and Brenneis, *Law & Empire in the Pacific*, 214–15.

31. White, *"It's Your Misfortune and None of My Own,"* 157; Gómez, *Manifest Destinies*, 25–31.

32. Gómez, *Manifest Destinies*, 9–10, 40–41, 44–45, 82–90, 5, 9.

33. White, *"It's Your Misfortune and None of My Own,"* 165–69.

34. Ibid., 173.

35. Aron, *American Confluence*, 183–85.

36. Eblen, *The First and Second United States Empires*, 115.

37. Claiborne, *Notes on the War in the South*, 110.

38. Dessens, *From Saint-Domingue to New Orleans*, 71–73, 120; Alfred Oliver Hero Jr., *Louisiana and Quebec: Bilateral Relations and Comparative Sociopolitical Evolution* (Lanham, MD: University Press of America, 1995), 168.

39. Dessens, *From Saint-Domingue to New Orleans*, 89.

40. Nolte, *The Memoirs of Vincent Nolte*, 88.

41. White, *Encountering Revolution*, 10–50, 89, 181.

42. Levasseur, *Moreau Lislet*, 95–113, 114, 118–33. Lislet went on to serve as the state's attorney general and in both houses of the state legislature.

43. White, *Encountering Revolution*, 165–67.

44. Haynes, *The Mississippi Territory and the Southwest Frontier, 1795–1817*, 25.

45. Fulwar Skipwith to James Madison, 20 May 1803, *PJM:SSS*, 5:21–22; Ebenezer Potter to James Madison, 25 August 1803, *PJM:SSS*, 5:346; Samuel Coleman to James Madison, 26 October 1803, *PJM:SSS*, 5:577–78; Augustus B. Woodward to James Madison, 27 October 1803, *PJM:SSS*, 5:585–86; Harry Toulmin to James Madison, 20 December 1803, *PJM:SSS*, 6:190–91; Christopher Greenup to James Madison, 6 January 1804, *PJM:SSS*, 6:313; John Heath to James Madison, 10 March 1804, *PJM:SSS*, 6:578; John Thomas Ricketts to James Madison, 28 December 1803, *PJM:SSS*, 6:244; Gallatin to Jefferson, 11 August 1803, *The Writings of Albert Gallatin*, 1:136; Henry Clay to Caesar A. Rodney, 17 August 1811, *The Papers of Henry Clay*, 1:574–75; Thomas Jefferson to William C. C. Claiborne, 2 May 1812, *PTJ:RS* 5:9; John Strode to James Madison, 20 October 1809, *PJM:PS*, 2:24–25; James Turner and Jesse Franklin to James Madison, 25 November 1811, *PJM:PS*, 4:35; George Thompson to James Madison , 26 June 1811, *PJM:PS*, 3:360; Dominick A. Hall to James Madison, 18 September 1804, *PJM:SSS*, 8:68; William Herries to James Madison, 27 September 1804, *PJM:SSS*, 8:96–97.

46. John B. Prevost to James Madison, 8 August 1803, *PJM:SSS*, 5:287–88. Prevost may have broken with his step-father politically at this point, which might have helped him secure the appointment. See The Gubernatorial Election of 1804, *Political Correspondence and Public Papers of Aaron Burr*, 2:838–39n.

47. Aaron Burr to Rufus Easton, 18 March 1805, *Political Correspondence and Public Papers of Aaron Burr*, 2:918–19.

48. Daniel Clark to James Madison, 27 April 1803, *PJM:SSS*, 4:554.

49. Jared William Bradley, "Biographical Sketches: Abraham Redwood Ellery," *IA*, 539–45.

50. Samuel Stanhope Smith to James Madison, 14 April 1809, *PJM:PS*, 1:116. See also Samuel Stanhope Smith to James Madison, 23 October 1809, *PJM:PS*, 2:30–31.

51. *Louisiana Courier* (New Orleans), 27 August 1810.

52. William C. C. Claiborne to Thomas Jefferson, 30 January 1811, *PTJ:RS*, 3:344.

53. *Louisiana Gazette* (New Orleans), 12 December 1807.

54. His plantation produced 70,000 pounds of sugar in 1804. See No. 1982, May 1804, St.

Charles Parish Original Acts, in Conrad, *The German Coast,* 5. Mather served briefly in the third session, until his election was declared to be null since he had failed to meet the residency requirement. *JHR,* first legislature, third session, 9; *DLB,* 1:356–57; Ardoin, *Louisiana Census Records,* vol. 3. His son, George Mather, held eighty-eight slaves in 1820.

55. William Garrard to the President, 20 January 1812, *TP,* 9:987.

56. Daniel Clark to James Madison, 16 August 1802, *PJM:SSS,* 3:487.

57. Daniel Clark to James Madison, 12 August 1803, *PJM:SSS,* 5:299. See also Daniel Clark to James Madison, 18 August 1803, *PJM:SSS,* 5:323.

58. Daniel Clark to James Madison, 20 October 1803, *PJM:SSS:* 5:553.

59. Daniel Clark to James Madison, 3 December 1803, *PJM:SSS,* 6:138. Madison instructed Claiborne to appoint a Russian, Mr. Molier, as a notary whom Laussat recommended, lest Laussat slow the cession. See James Madison to William C. C. Claiborne, 14 November 1804, *PJM:SSS,* 6:36–37.

60. Daniel Clark to James Madison, 13 October 1803, *PJM:SSS,* 5:516.

61. Thomas Jefferson to James Madison, 9 November 1803, *PJM:SSS,* 6:30.

62. Mark F. Fernandez, *From Chaos to Continuity: The Evolution of Louisiana's Judicial System, 1712–1862* (Baton Rouge: Louisiana State University Press, 2001), 29.

63. William C. C. Claiborne to James Madison, 12 May 1804, *PJM:SSS,* 7:210.

64. William C. C. Claiborne to James Madison, 29 June 1804, *PJM:SSS,* 396.

65. Plumer, 15 December 1804, *Memorandum of Proceedings,* 222.

66. Haynes, *The Mississippi Territory and the Southwest Frontier, 1795–1817,* 80, 97–98.

67. Claiborne to John Watkins, 9 February 1804, *LB,* 1:368. See also William C. C. Claiborne to James Madison, 1 March 1804, *PJM:SSS,* 6:524–25.

68. Jared William Bradley, "Biographical Sketches: John Watkins," *IA,* 298–71.

69. Dr. Watkins' Report, 2 February 1804, *LB,* 2:3–13. See also Gilbert C. Din, *The Canary Islanders of Louisiana* (Baton Rouge: Louisiana State University Press, 1988), 85.

70. Peter Kastor, "'They Are All Frenchmen': Background and Nation in an Age of Transformation," in Kastor and Weil, *Empires of the Imagination,* 243–46.

71. William C. C. Claiborne to James Madison, 4 March 1810, *PJM:PS,* 2:261.

72. A Native, *View of the Political and Civil Situation of Louisiana,* 19.

73. Fernandez, *From Chaos to Continuity,* 30.

74. Schafer, *Slavery, the Civil Law, and the Supreme Court of Louisiana,* 13.

75. William C. C. Claiborne to James Madison, 27 October 1804, *PJM:SSS,* 8:230.

76. Cantrelle died soon after in 1814. Cantrelle held sixty slaves in St. James Parish in 1810. In 1820 Tureaud held fifteen slaves in addition to seven free persons of color in his household, while his extended family held fifty-six slaves. Ardoin, *Louisiana Census Records,* vol. 3.

77. Jared William Bradley, Letter 82, note 2, *IA,* 124. Cantrelle was a far more established figure, while Tureaud strove to acquire more land and slaves. Between 1806 and 1811 Tureaud paid land registration fees four times in the amount of $4.30, while over the same period Cantrelle paid nothing. See Acadian Parish Records, Land Registry, MSS 23 f1, 1806, 1807, 1808; MSS 23 f2 1809, 1810, 1811, Historic New Orleans Collection.

78. Din, *The Canary Islanders of Louisiana,* 81–85.

79. *DLB*, 1:480.

80. Jared William Bradley, "Biographical Sketches: Edward D. Turner," *IA*, 567–68.

81. Sidney A. Marchand, *The Flight of a Century* (Donaldsonville, LA: Marchand, 1936), 26.

82. W. C. C. Claiborne to the Sheriff of Acadia County, 15 June 1806, *LB*, 3:327–28; W. C. C. Claiborne to Cartier D'Outremer and A. D. Tureaud, 11 September 1812, *LB*, 6:177; *JS*, first legislature, first session, 3. See Marchand, *The Flight of a Century*, 18.

83. W. C. C. Claiborne to Cartier D'Outremer and A. D. Tureaud, 11 September 1812, *LB*, 6:197–98; W. C. C. Claiborne to Andrew Latour and Achille Trouard, 6 October 1812, *LB*, 6:187; W. C. C. Claiborne, Writ of Election to Andrew Latour and Achille Trouard, 6 November 1812, *LB*, 6:196–97.

84. Dr. Watkins Report, 2 February 1804, *LB*, 2:3–4.

85. W. C. C. Claiborne to Manuel Andry, 9 July 1805, *LB*, 3:118. Trouard was a large landowner; the average tax in St. John the Baptist in 1812 was $9.43 on slaves and land, and Trouard was assessed for $50.50. See État de la Louisiane Paroisse St. Jean Baptiste, MSS 22 f2, Historic New Orleans Collection. In addition, Trouard financed several mortgages in St. Charles. See Tableau de hypothèques qui existent sur les propriétés de la paroisse St. Charles Côte des Allemands 1806–1853, St. Charles Parish Courthouse Archives.

86. *DLB*, 1:15.

87. W. C. C. Claiborne to the Judge of German Coast County, 29 June 1805, *LB*, 3:106. Claiborne shortly thereafter ordered St. Amand to turn over papers in his possession. W. C. C. Claiborne to Mr. St. Amand, 9 July 1805, *LB*, 3:117–18.

88. W. C. C. Claiborne to the Judge of German Coast County, 9 July 1805, *LB*, 3:118–19.

89. Leblanc was assessed four dollars in 1812. See Etat de la Louisiane Paroisse St. Jean Baptiste, MSS 22 f2, Historic New Orleans Collection.

90. *Louisiana Courier* (New Orleans), 17 March 1813.

91. *Louisiana Courier* (New Orleans), 2 April 1813.

92. Governor Claiborne to the President, 29 September 1803, *TP*, 9:60.

93. Characterization of New Orleans Residents, 1 July 1804, *TP*, 9:254–55.

94. Jared William Bradley, Letter 40, note 2, *IA*, 69. See also Brian J. Costello, *The Life, Family and Legacy of Julien Poydras* (New Roads, LA: Costello, 2001); Costello, *A History of Pointe Coupée Parish, Louisiana* (New Roads, LA: Costello, 1999), 7, 11. Poydras became involved in at least twenty-six separate known transactions involving slaves or land in Pointe Coupée between 1762 and 1823, more than any other figure within the parish. See Winston De Ville, ed., *Slaves and Masters of Pointe Coupée, Louisiana: A Calendar of Civil Records, 1762–1823* (Ville Platte, LA: De Ville, 1988). Poydras had 122 slaves in 1810 and 141 in 1820. See Ardoin, *Louisiana Census Records*, vol. 2.

95. Judy Riffel, ed., *A History of Pointe Coupée and Its Families* (Baton Rouge: Le Comité des Archives de la Louisiane, 1983), 19.

96. W. C. C. Claiborne to Julien Poydras, 14 January 1804, *LB*, 1:333–34; W. C. C. Claiborne to Julien Poydras, 25 February 1804, *LB*, 1:384–85.

97. He served in the position until 1809, when he was elected to Congress. See Costello, *A History of Pointe Coupée Parish, Louisiana*, 9.

98. W. C. C. Claiborne to James Madison, 5 November 1804, quoting Julien Poydras, *LB*, 2:391.

99. W. C. C. Claiborne to Thomas Jefferson, 3 April 1806, *LB*, 3:284.

100. *Moniteur de la Louisiane* (New Orleans), 2 May 1810. For another portrayal of Livingston see *Louisiana Courier* (New Orleans), 19 November 1810, 22 October 1813.

101. Memorial to Congress from Inhabitants of Pointe Coupée, 9 June 1808, *TP*, 9:789–91.

102. W. C. C. Claiborne to Julien Poydras, 18 July 1811, *LB*, 5:307–8; W. C. C. Claiborne to Gideon Granger, 23 November 1811, *LB*, 5:307.

103. W. C. C. Claiborne to John H. Ludeling, 8 November 1811, *LB*, 5:373; Riffel, *A History of Pointe Coupée and Its Families*, 19.

104. Judge Ludeling mortgaged sixty-six slaves with Julien Poydras in return for $33,000; Sheriff Charles Morgan had a business connection to Poydras's nephew Benjamin, with whom he bought and sold slaves. De Ville, *Slaves and Masters of Pointe Coupée, Louisiana*, 43, 50, 54, 56, 57.

105. W. C. C. Claiborne to Judge Ludeling, 13 April 1812, *LB*, 6:79.

106. W. C. C. Claiborne to Judge Ludeiling, 22 April 1812, *LB*, 6:87.

107. W. C. C. Claiborne to Julien Poidrass [*sic*], 26 May 1806, *LB*, 3:314. Whatever the dispute, Poydras and Plauché moved beyond it. See Claiborne to Julien Poydras, 18 July 1811, *LB*, 5:307–8.

108. W. C. C. Claiborne to Charles Morgan, 6 November 1808, *LB*, 4:242.

109. Haynes, *The Mississippi Territory and the Southwest Frontier, 1795–1817*, 104.

110. W. C. C. Claiborne to Col. H. Hopkins, 8 December 1808, *LB*, 4:265.

111. W. C. C. Claiborne to Charles Morgan, 6 November 1808, *LB*, 4:242 (quotation), 243.

112. W. C. C. Claiborne to Colonel Freeman, 22 June 1805, *LB*, 3:102–3.

113. Governor Claiborne to the Secretary of War, 9 March 1808, *TP*, 9:775–77.

114. Charles Morgan to the Secretary of War, 1 September 1807, *TP*, 9:762.

115. Governor Claiborne to the Secretary of War, 9 March 1808, *TP*, 9:777.

116. Ibid.

117. Roger Baudier, *The Catholic Church in Louisiana* (New Orleans: Roger Baudier, 1939), 249–54.

118. Alvord, *The Illinois Country, 1673–1818*, 364–67.

119. Emily Clark, *Masterless Mistresses: The New Orleans Ursulines and the Development of a New World Society, 1727–1834* (Chapel Hill: University of North Carolina Press, 2007), 232–34.

120. See Baudier, *The Catholic Church in Louisiana*, 253.

121. W. C. C. Claiborne to the Parish Judge & Justices of the Peace of Point Coupée Parish, 26 May 1809, *LB*, 4:368–70.

122. Governor Claiborne to Robert Smith, 21 April 1809, *LB*, 4:344, 345.

123. Governor Claiborne to Robert Smith, 2 April 1809, *LB*, 4:341.

124. Governor Claiborne to Robert Smith, 21 April 1809, *LB*, 4:345.

125. Petition to Governor Claiborne by the Inhabitants of Pointe Coupée, 24 March 1809, *TP*, 9:831–32.

126. Governor Claiborne to Julien Poydras, 4 June 1809, *TP*, 9:843.

127. *Mississippi Messenger* (Natchez), 3 December 1805; W. C. C. Claiborne to the Sheriff of Pointe Coupée, 20 June 1806, *LB*, 3:336–37.

128. *Courier de la Louisiane* (New Orleans), 18 January 1809.

129. Governor Claiborne to the President, 4 March 1810, *TP*, 9:870; *DLB*, 1:55.

130. *JHR*, first legislature, first session, 1; *JHR*, first legislature, second session, 3.

131. Despite the memorial, the House ultimately upheld Dormenon's election. *JHR*, first legislature, first session, 9–11.

132. *JHR*, second legislature, first session, 3; *JHR*, second legislature, second session, 4.

133. Louisiana Historic Records Survey, Works Progress Administration, *Inventory of the Parish Archives of Louisiana: Number 44, Saint Bernard Parish (Saint Bernard)* (Baton Rouge: Louisiana Department of Archives, Louisiana State University, 1938), 4.

134. Darby, *A Geographical Description*, 182.

135. Claiborne to Abner L. Duncan, 15 May 1812, *LB*, 6:97.

136. William C. C. Claiborne to James Madison, 13 February 1804, *PJM:SSS*, 6:471.

137. Claiborne to Thomas Jefferson, 5 July 1806, *LB*, 3:350–53. See also Jared William Bradley, "Biographical Sketches: James Carrick," *IA*, 575–77.

138. Civil Appointments 1807, *LB*, 4:147.

139. Who the former priest was is unclear; the parish had been served by Father Domingo Joachin Solano, a Spanish friar, from 1802 to 1803, but the position stood vacant until 1805 when Rochanson was appointed. See Baudier, *The Catholic Church in Louisiana*, 252–53.

140. Governor Claiborne to Judge Prevost, 23 March 1805, *TP*, 9:423.

141. Claiborne to James Madison, 24 March 1805, Letter 167, *IA*, 201.

142. *Louisiana Courier* (New Orleans), 13 December 1813; *JHR*, first legislature, third session, 77; List of Civil and Military Officers, 21 April 1809, *TP*, 9:835. See also Arthur and de Kernion, *Old Families of Louisiana*, 408–10.

143. Shaumberg was a U.S. Army officer who settled in Orleans after taking part in the cession. Watson, *Jackson's Sword*, 241.

144. *JHR*, first legislature, third session, 80, 87.

145. Claiborne to Antonio Mendez, 6 October 1812, *LB*, 6:185.

146. *Louisiana Courier* (New Orleans), 14 April 1817.

147. John Pintard to the Secretary of the Treasury, 14 September 1803, *TP*, 9:53. Claiborne also complained of Fort St. Philip's condition. See Governor Claiborne to the Secretary of War, 21 April 1808, *TP*, 9:782.

148. Latrobe, 9 January 1819, *The Journal of Latrobe*, 159.

149. Paul A. Wallace, *The Muhlenbergs of Pennsylvania* (Philadelphia: University of Pennsylvania Press, 1950), 144, 288–89.

150. James Wilkinson to the Secretary of War, 3 January 1803, *TP*, 9:151, 152–53.

151. A Register of Civil Appointments, 30 June 1807, *TP*, 9:749; List of Civil and Military Officers, 21 April 1809, *TP*, 9:835.

152. Claiborne to Geo. W. Morgan, 13 April 1812, *LB*, 6:81, 82 (quotation).

153. Louisiana Historic Records Survey, Works Progress Administration, *Inventory of the Parish Archives of Louisiana: Number 38, Plaquemines Parish (Pointe à la Hache)* (Baton Rouge:

Louisiana Department of Archives, Louisiana State University, 1938), 92. A Gilbert Leonard had served as an army treasurer in Louisiana for Spain, but this is probably not the same man, as he left the territory earlier. See the Marquis of Casa Calvo to Governor Claiborne, List of the Persons Employed by his Catholic Majesty who are to depart as soon as their business shall be terminated, 30 July 1805, *TP*, 9:485. See also Safe Conduct for Gilberto Leonard, 27 January 1806, *TP*, 9:665.

154. See *Mississippi Messenger* (Natchez), 3 December 1805; *Courier de la Louisiane* (New Orleans), 18 January 1809.

155. *JHR*, first legislature, first session, 25–26 (quotation), 39.

156. *JHR*, first legislature, second session, 3, 13–14; *JHR*, first legislature, third session, 8.

157. *JHR*, third legislature, first session, 3, 9; *JHR*, third legislature, second session, 3, 58; *JHR*, fourth legislature, first session, 3–4; *JHR*, fourth legislature, second session, 3.

158. Dr. Watkins Report, 2 February 1804, *LB*, 2:6–7.

159. Joseph Briggs to the President, 17 August 1804, *TP*, 9:278.

160. W. C. C. Claiborne to Robert Smith, 1 June 1809, *LB*, 4:376.

161. Elizabeth Kellough and Leona Mayeux, *Chronicles of West Baton Rouge* (Kennedy Print Shop, 1979).

162. James Wilkinson to the President, Characterization of New Orleans Residents, 1 July 1804, *TP*, 9:255.

163. G. P. Whittington, *Rapides Parish, Louisiana: A History* (Alexandria, LA: National Society of the Colonial Dames in the State of Louisiana, 1955), 47; Meullion continued to serve as the county treasurer under his son-in-law. See Register of Civil Appointments in the Territory of Orleans, 13 February 1806, *TP*, 9:598–602.

164. Meullion held thirty-one slaves in 1810, and his son-in-law Miller held eight in both 1810 and 1820, while Miller and his brother-in-law through his wife's family, Hatch Dent, held forty-eight. See Ardoin, *Louisiana Census Records*, vol. 2.

165. Whittington, *Rapides Parish, Louisiana*, 55, 58.

166. A Register of Civil Appointments, 30 June 1807, *TP*, 9:749.

167. Return of Proclamations, Pardons, and Appointments, 30 June 1808, *TP*, 9:796.

168. Jared William Bradley, "Biographical Sketches: Major Richard D. Claiborne," *IA*, 546–52.

169. Richard Claiborne to John Graham, 10 November 1811, *TP*, 9:953–54.

170. Jared William Bradley, "Biographical Sketches: Major Richard D. Claiborne," *IA*, 550.

171. *DLB*, 1:327–28, 2:833–34. Wells served in the Territorial Legislature after J. B. Plauché resigned. See Governor Claiborne to Judge Claiborne, 4 April 1812, *LB*, 6:67.

172. Dent served as a clerk of court and directly owned only one slave, but with his brother-in-law owned another forty-eight in 1810. See Ardoin, *Louisiana Census Records*, vol. 2.

173. *DLB*, 1:237; Register of Civil Appointments in the Territory of Orleans, 13 February 1806, *TP*, 9:598–602.

174. Whittington, *Rapides Parish, Louisiana*, 55–59.

175. Governor Claiborne to Judge Claiborne, 6 April 1812, *LB*, 6:68.

176. W. C. C. Claiborne to Colonel F. L. Claiborne, 11 September 1808, *LB*, 4:216–17.

177. W. C. C. Claiborne to Colonel F. L. Claiborne, 14 October 1808, *LB*, 4:228.

178. Governor Claiborne to Judge Claiborne, 8 November 1808, *LB*, 4:246–47.

179. Governor Claiborne to Judge Claiborne, 15 November 1811, *LB*, 5:381–82.

180. Whittington, *Rapides Parish, Louisiana*, 59.

181. Claiborne to Edward Menillon [*sic*], 9 April 1804, *LB*, 2:87.

182. Claiborne to Edmund Merrilon [*sic*], 9 June 1804, *LB*, 2:200–201. Though the crime was not listed, they had been accused of some sort of favoritism within Rapides, possibly in the collection of the liquor tax, which the commandant solved by eliminating the tax.

183. Governor Claiborne to the President, 12 November 1806, *TP*, 9:687. For Jeffersonian patronage, see Sidney H. Aronson, *Status and Kinship in the Higher Civil Service: Standards of Selection in the Administrations of John Adams, Thomas Jefferson, and Andrew Jackson* (Cambridge, MA: Harvard University Press, 1964), 13.

184. Governor Claiborne to the President, 8 December 1808, *TP*, 9:808.

185. Governor Claiborne to the President, 3 May 1807, *TP*, 9:729.

186. Return of Proclamations, Pardons, and Appointments, 30 June 1808, *TP*, 9:796. Oliver came from Massachusetts. See Corinne L. Saucier, *History of Avoyelles Parish, Louisiana* (Gretna, LA: Firebird, 1998), 127; List of Civil and Military Officers, 21 April 1809, *TP*, 9:835. In 1810 Oliver held six slaves. See Robert Bruce L. Ardoin, *Louisiana Census Records*, vol. 1, *Avoyelles and St. Landry Parish, 1810 & 1820* (Baltimore: Genealogical, 1995).

187. A Message from the Governor, Making Several Nominations, *LB*, 6:172.

188. Parish Records, *Biographical and Historical Memoirs of Louisiana* (Shreveport: J. & W. Enterprises, 1892), 9.

189. These land deals often involved the sale of mortgages with Julien Poydras as the lender. See William Nelson Gremillion Sr. and Loucille Edwards Gremillion, *Some Early Families of Avoyelles Parish, Louisiana: Genealogical Studies of the Early Generations of 36 Families* (Eunice, LA: Hebert Publications, 1980), 318–19. Claiborne to Julien Poydras, 18 July 1811, *LB*, 5:307–8. See also Arthur and de Kernion, *Old Families of Louisiana*, 421–25.

190. Daniel Clark to James Madison, 20 October 1803, *PJM:SSS*, 5:554.

191. Hints of Evan Jones: Administration of Justice, *TP*, 9:83.

192. H. M. Brackenridge, *Views of Louisiana; Containing Geographical, Statistical and Historical Notices of the Vast and Important Portion of America* (Baltimore: Schaeffer & Maund, 1817), 298–99.

193. Darby, *A Geographical Description*, 73.

194. De Ville, *Opelousas*, 37; Mariette Marie LeBreton, "A History of the Territory of Orleans, 1803–1812" (PhD diss., Louisiana State University, 1969), 21–22.

195. Glenn R. Conrad, *Land Records of the Attakapas District*, vol. 2, part 2, *Attakapas—St. Martin Estates, 1804–1818* (Lafayette: Center for Louisiana Studies, University of Southwestern Louisiana, 1993.), x–xii. Though Non-Acadian French had fewer holdings, they had larger estates on average.

196. Glenn R. Conrad, "Some Observations on Anglo-Saxon Settlers in Colonial Attakapas," in *Louisiana Purchase Bicentennial Series*, vol. 10, *A Refuge for All Ages: Immigration in Louisiana History*, 10:231–38.

197. Robin, *Voyage to Louisiana, 1803–1805*, 262–63 (quotation), 264–66.

198. Claiborne to James Madison, 9 August 1804, *LB*, 2:298–99.

199. *IA*, 196n4.

200. W. C. C. Claiborne to Henry Hopkins, 22 April 1805, *IA*, 236.

201. Governor Claiborne to Henry Hopkins, 22 April 1805, *TP*, 9:440.

202. Register of Civil Appointments in the Territory of Orleans, 13 February 1806, *TP*, 9:602; *DLB*, 1:223.

203. Claiborne to Henry Hopkins, 1 August 1804, *LB*, 2:283.

204. Claiborne regularly intervened to secure clemency. When Agricole Landry had been convicted of an assault and battery charge and fined fifty dollars, Claiborne instructed the sheriff to pardon him and remit the fee. See Pardon of Agricole Landry, 24 May 1806, *TP*, 9:667. In a similar crime in Attakapas the governor pardoned Robert Armstrong, sentenced to imprisonment and a fifty-dollar fine for assault. See Pardon of Robert Armstrong, 29 September 1806, *TP*, 9:694.

205. Claiborne to Henry Hopkins, 20 January 1804, *LB*, 1:336–38; Claiborne to James Madison, 24 January 1804, *LB*, 1:344–49; Claiborne to Lewis Deblanc, 5 February 1804, *LB*, 1:362–63.

206. Robin, *Voyage to Louisiana, 1803–1805*, 209, 209.

207. Gertrude C. Taylor, "War Clouds: The St. Julien-DeClouet Affair," *Attakapas Gazette* 22, no. 2 (Summer 1987): 52.

208. Robin, *Voyage to Louisiana, 1803–1805*, 210.

209. Louis St. Julien, "Against His Enemies, His Accusers, His Assassins," trans. and ed. Robert St. Julien and Lou Ann St. Julien, *Attakapas Gazette* 22, no. 2 (Summer 1987): 59.

210. Robin, *Voyage to Louisiana, 1803–1805*, 211.

211. Ibid., 211–12; Taylor, "War Clouds," 52n5.

212. Robin, *Voyage to Louisiana, 1803–1805*, 212.

213. See Julien Vernet, "Citizen Laussat and the St. Julien Case: Royalists and Revolutionaries in Early Nineteenth Century Louisiana," *Louisiana History* 51, no. 2 (2010): 195–214.

214. Robin, *Voyage to Louisiana, 1803–1805*, 213, 213–14 (quotation), 212–13.

215. For an analysis of the revolutionary challenge individuals like St. Julien could pose to the Spanish empire see Vernet, "Citizen Laussat and the St. Julien Case," 195–214.

216. Robin, *Voyage to Louisiana, 1803–1805*, 214–18, 224–30.

217. Laussat to Denis Decrès, 18 July 1803, *LUR*, 2:46.

218. Quoted in Robin, *Voyage to Louisiana, 1803–1805*, 71.

219. Robin, *Voyage to Louisiana, 1803–1805*, 214.

220. Ibid., 214n1; Alexandre Barde, *The Vigilante Committees of the Attakapas: An Eyewitness Account of Banditry and Backlash in Southwestern Louisiana* (Lafayette: Acadiana, 1981), 277; Faber, *Building the Land of Dreams*, 106–7. Barière was a Frenchman. See Donald J. Hébert, *Southwest Louisiana Records: Church and Civil Records*, vol. 1-B, *(1801–1810)* (Rayne, LA: Hébert, 1996), 781.

221. St. Julien, "Against His Enemies, His Accusers, His Assassins," 60 (quotation), 67–70.

222. Robin, *Voyage to Louisiana, 1803–1805*, 214; Baudier, *The Catholic Church in Louisiana*, 251.

223. St. Julien, "Against His Enemies, His Accusers, His Assassins," 61.

224. W. C. C. Claiborne to Henry Hopkins, 20 January 1804, *LB*, 1:336–38.

225. W. C. C. Claiborne to James Madison, 24 May 1805, *LB*, 2:165.

226. James Madison to Governor Claiborne, 19 June 1804, *LB*, 2:278–79; James Madison to William C. C. Claiborne, 19 June 1804, *PJM:SSS*, 7:331.

227. William C. C. Claiborne to James Madison, 24 May 1804, *PJM:SSS*, 7:250.

228. Louis Declouet, "Translation of Declouet's Memorial, 7 December 1814," in *Archivo General de Indias, Indiferente, General Legajo 146-3-8, Declouet to Cevallos, Madrid, Louisiana Historical Quarterly* 22, no. 3 (July 1939): 13–26.

229. Marquis of Caso Calvo to Governor Claiborne, *LB*, 2:156.

230. Thomas Jefferson to James Madison, 5 July 1804, *PJM:SSS*, 7:420.

231. W. C. C. Claiborne grants permission to St. Julien to return to the Attakapas, 24 January 1804, *LB*, 1:349.

232. Claiborne to the Marquis of Caso Calvo, 22 May 1804, *LB*, 2:158–59.

233. Claiborne to James Madison, 9 August 1804, *LB*, 2:299–301.

234. Claiborne to James Madison, 29 May 1804, *LB*, 2:170–71.

235. James Madison to William C. C. Claiborne, 10 July 1804, *PJM:SSS*, 7:436.

236. Claiborne to Henry Hopkins, 29 May 1804, *LB*, 2:169–70. Barière was a Frenchman. See Hébert, *Southwest Louisiana Records*, 781. See also *DLB*, 2:822.

237. Claiborne to Henry Hopkins, 28 July 1804, *LB*, 2:275. The following year Walsh made himself rector of St. Louis Cathedral, aggravating Father Antonio de Sedella and requiring Casa Calvo and the mayor of New Orleans to intervene. Walsh died in 1806, but this failed to resolve Sedella's discontent.

238. Thomas Jefferson to James Madison, 5 July 1804, *PJM:SSS*, 7:420.

239. Robin, *Voyage to Louisiana, 1803–1805*, 215.

240. Claiborne to Henry Dearborn, 7 July 1804, *LB*, 2:240.

241. Claiborne to Colonel Freeman, 16 June 1804, *LB*, 2:209; Claiborne to General Wilkinson, 10 August 1804, *LB*, 304–6.

242. W. C. C. Claiborne to Henry Hopkins, 22 April 1805, *IA*, 238.

243. Register of Civil Appointments in the Territory of Orleans, 13 February 1806, *TP*, 9:598–600; Pourciaux, *St. Martin Parish History*, 10–14.

244. *DLB*, 2:602–3.

245. Edward C. Nichols to James Madison, 12 January 1804, *PJM:SSS*, 6:338–39. Tax records in 1808 show Nichols with seven slaves and eleven arpents of land, and the tax records from 1810 show an E. Nicholas with five slaves and seven arpents of land. Attakapas County Papers, Attakapas Tax Rolls 1808–1810, Mss. 10 A:17, Louisiana and Lower Mississippi Valley Collection, LSU Libraries, Baton Rouge, LA.

246. Governor Claiborne to the President, 30 August 1804, *TP*, 9:286.

247. Governor Claiborne to the Secretary of State, 4 December 1805, *TP*, 9:540–41.

248. James Brown to the Secretary of the Treasury, 11 December 1805, *TP*, 9:547.

249. Louis Brognier Declouet to Pierre-Joseph Favrot, 15 June 1805, *The Favrot Family Papers*, 4:201.

250. Robin, *Voyage to Louisiana, 1803–1805*, 219, 220, 222.

251. The letter is unsigned, and while the finding aid lists the author as possibly Judge John Prevost, the context of the letter makes it more likely that Nichols was the author. Unsigned, 29 December 1805, Claiborne (William C. C.) Letters and Depositions (1799–1846), MSS 5018, Louisiana and Lower Mississippi Valley Collections, LSU Libraries, Baton Rouge, LA.

252. *DLB*, 2:840–41, 1:512. See also Darby, *A Geographical Description*, 106.

253. For a brief overview of St. Mary's history, see Bernard Broussard, *A History of St. Mary Parish* (Franklin, LA: Broussard, 1977).

254. Claiborne to Judge Lewis, 19 April 1811, *LB*, 5:213–14; Claiborne to Henry Johnson Esqre., 1 May 1811, *LB*, 5:222; Return of Civil Appointments made in the Territory of Orleans from the 1st January 1811 to the 31 December of the same year, *TP*, 9:984.

255. *DLB*, 1:437. Johnson was not among the economic elite of the parish. See Mary Elizabeth Sanders, comp., St. Mary Parish 1813 Tax List, in *Records of Attakapas District, Louisiana 1739–1811*, ed. Mary Elizabeth Sanders (Franklin, LA: Sanders, 1962), 92–93.

256. Broussard, *A History of St. Mary Parish*, 13.

257. Clarisse Duralde Claiborne died in 1808. Claiborne married Sophronia Bosque in 1812. See Arthur and de Kernion, *Old Families of Louisiana*, 146–47.

258. Claiborne to Judge Johnson, 26 May 1812, *LB*, 6:106–8.

259. Wilkinson held property but was not one of the larger landholders of the parish. See St. Mary Parish 1813 Tax List in Sanders, *Records of Attakapas District*, 92–93.

260. A Message from the Governor, Making Several Nominations, 4 September 1812, *LB*, 5:172.

261. The average slaveholder in St. Martin in 1812 had 3.88 slaves. In 1812 Ransom Easton held none. Attakapas County Papers, St. Martin Tax List 1812, Mss. 13 A:17, Records, Louisiana and Lower Mississippi Valley Collection, LSU Libraries, Baton Rouge, LA.

262. *DLB*, 1:109–10. Attakapas County Papers, St. Martin Tax List 1812, Mss. 13 A:17, Records, Louisiana and Lower Mississippi Valley Collection, LSU Libraries, Baton Rouge, LA.

263. *Mississippi Messenger* (Natchez), 3 December 1805.

264. *DLB*, 2:754–55, 1:31, 2:676, 1:456.

265. Governor Claiborne to John Bowyer, 23 March 1805, *TP*, 9:422; Opelousas, 5 July 1806, in Riffle, *Calendar of St. Landry Parish Louisiana, Civil Records*, vol. 1, *1803–1819*, 77, 79. Rogers possessed a bit of a temper, as he assaulted a James Reed the same year.

266. Governor Claiborne to John Bowyer, 19 April 1805, *TP*, 9:437.

267. Register of Civil Appointments in the Territory of Orleans, 13 February 1806, *TP*, 9:598–99.

268. *DLB*, 1:465; List of Civil and Military Officers, 21 April 1809, *TP*, 9:835.

269. *JHR*, third legislature, first session, 35.

270. Claiborne to Judge King, 17 May 1811, *LB*, 5:243; Harry Lewis Griffin, *The Attakapas Country* (Gretna, LA: Firebird Press, 1999), 195–96. Though an American, King had married

into a prominent local Italian family, the Gradenigos. His removal did not prevent Voorhies from serving in similar posts; Voorhies needed to explain his conduct to the governor, and the state legislature kept apprised of his lack of action. *JHR*, first legislature, first session, 16.

271. Governor Claiborne to the President, 30 August 1804, *TP*, 9:285.

272. Winston De Ville, ed., *Southwest Louisiana in 1807: The Land and Slave Tax of Landry Parish in the Territory of Orleans* (Ville Platte, LA: De Ville, 1993); Darby, *A Geographical Description*, 89.

273. James Wilkinson to the President, 1 July 1804, *TP*, 9:256.

274. Persons Recommended by Governor Claiborne for Members of the Legislative Council of the Orleans Territory in Joseph Briggs to the President, 17 August 1804, *TP*, 9:277; The President to Governor Claiborne, 30 August 1804, *TP*, 9:283. See also Register of Civil Appointments in the Territory of Orleans, 13 February 1806, *TP*, 9:601.

275. *JS*, first legislature, first session, 4; *JS*, first legislature, second session, 3; *JS*, first legislature, third session, 43; *JS*, second legislature, first session; *JS*, second legislature, second session, 8; *JS*, third legislature, first session, 3; *JS*, third legislature, second session, 3; *JS*, fourth legislature, first session, 13.

276. *DLB*, 1:336.

277. Dr. Watkins Report, 2 March 1804, *LB*, 2:6; W. C. C. Claiborne to Francis Rivas, 20 April 1804, *Letter Books*, 2:106–7.

278. Claiborne to Pierre Bailly, 14 March 1805, *IA*, 193.

279. Meriam differed substantially from his predecessor; while Bailly had eighty-five slaves in 1810, Meriam had three. See Ardoin, *Louisiana Census Records*, vol. 2, *Iberville, Natchitoches, Pointe Coupée and Rapides Parishes, 1810 & 1820*; Riffel, *Iberville Parish History*, 300.

280. Claiborne named Bush and Landry as justices of the peace and Brown as sheriff. See W. C. C. Claiborne to Judge Meriam, 22 November 1811, *LB*, 5:384.

281. W. C. C. Claiborne to James Monroe, 28 February 1812, *LB*, 6:61; W. C. C. Claiborne to Mr. Smith, Collector of the Revenue, *LB*, 6:361–62; W. C. C. Claiborne to Daniel L. Patterson, 25 October 1815, *LB*, 6:387. Claiborne's journeys to Iberville became a subject of discussion for those in New Orleans. See W. C. C. Claiborne to James Madison, 17 October 1807, *LB*, 4:135.

282. Meriam was elected as president of the Senate at the second legislature's second session and again for the third and fourth, though he lost the presidency of the Senate to Julien Poydras at the second session of the fourth legislature, See *JS*, first legislature, first session, 3; *JS*, first legislature, second session, 50; *JS*, first legislature, third session, 43; *JS*, second legislature, first session, 3; *JS*, second legislature, second session, 3; *JS*, third legislature, first session, 3; *JS*, third legislature, second session, 3; *JS*, fourth legislature, first session, 3; *JS*, fourth legislature, second session, 3–4; *JHR*, third legislature, first session, 3; *JHR*, third legislature, second session, 3, 7; *JHR*, fourth legislature, first session, 3, 7; *JHR*, fourth legislature, second session, 3.

283. W. C. C. Claiborne to Judge Meriam, 6 April 1812, *LB*, 6:69.

284. W. C. C. Claiborne to the Gentlemen of the Senate, 4 September 1812, *LB*, 6:172.

285. Ardoin, *Louisiana Census Records*, vol. 2, *Iberville, Natchitoches, Pointe Coupée and Rapides Parishes, 1810 & 1820*.

286. Ouachita had 1,077 people in 1810, 26 percent of them slaves. By 1820 the population increased to 2,967, with 28 percent slaves. See 1810 and 1820 Censuses.

287. In 1807 Vidal was the largest single taxpayer on land that year, and his extended family had still larger holdings; in 1811 he had 4,800 acres, taxed at $58.60; in 1812 the tax was $38.88, but Vidal remained the largest taxpayer on land for the county. See Concordia Parish Collection, Concordia Tax Rolls 1807, 1811, 1812, MSS 5579 U:26 or F:12, Calhoun Collection, LSU Hill Memorial Library, Baton Rouge, LA.

288. Governor Claiborne to Ferdinand L. Claiborne, 29 January 1805, *TP*, 9:386–87.

289. Claiborne to Major Claiborne, 4 May 1805, *LB*, 3:36–37; Register of Civil Appointments in the Territory of Orleans, 13 February 1806, *TP*, 9:598–603; Register of Civil Appointments, 30 June 1806, *TP*, 9:662–63.

290. In the House he served on the select committee on divorce and alimony. See Samuel S. Mahon, "A Discourse on Divorce: Orleans Territorial Legislature, 1806," ed. W. Magruder Drake, *Louisiana History* 22, no. 4 (Fall 1981): 434–37.

291. A Register of Civil Appointments, 30 June 1807, *TP*, 9:749–52. See also Jared William Bradley "Biographical Sketches: George T. Ross," *IA*, 447 n. 2.

292. Bradley, "Biographical Sketches: George T. Ross," *IA*, 451.

293. Claiborne to Doctor D. Lattimore, 10 October 1808, *LB*, 4:224; Claiborne to Dr. David Lattimore, *LB*, 4:241; Secretary Robertson to the Secretary of State, Civil Appointments, 17 January 1809, *TP*, 9:824.

294. List of Civil and Military Officers, 21 April 1809, *TP*, 9:835.

295. Return of Civil Appointments Made in the Territory of Orleans from the 1st January 1811 to the 31st December of the Same Year, *TP*, 9:984–86.

296. Norman E. Gillis, *Early Inhabitants of the Natchez District* (Greenville, SC: Southern Historical Press, 1999), 41, 89.

297. *DLB*, 1:643, 581.

298. In 1811 Concordia was briefly split into two parishes with the creation of Warren Parish, which would be subsumed into Concordia and Ouachita again in 1814. The first judge of Warren Parish was William Lindsey, who recommended lesser appointees. See Claiborne to William Lindsey Esqre., 28 March 1811, 29 March 1811, *LB*, 5:195–96, 198. Lindsey in turn selected a Mr. Patterson as the sheriff of Warren Parish. See Claiborne to William Lindsay Esqre., 26 April 1811, *LB*, 5:220.

299. Robin, *Voyage to Louisiana, 1803–1805*, 136, 160 (quotation), 164, 262 (quotation).

300. Register of Civil Appointments in the Territory of Orleans, 13 February 1806, *TP*, 9:598–603. The House of Representatives recommended Danemours as a nominee for the Legislative Council. See Governor Claiborne to the President, 13 November 1805, *TP*, 9:525–26.

301. Register of Civil Appointments, 30 June 1806, *TP*, 9:662–63. See also Donna Rachal Mills, *Some Southern Balls: From Valentine to Ferdinand and Beyond* (Orlando: Mills Historical, 1993), 116, 122.

302. A Register of Civil Appointments, 30 June 1807, *TP*, 9:749.

303. Governor Claiborne to the President, 4 March 1810, *TP*, 9:871.

304. *DLB*, 1:123. Bry was a relation of Albert Gallatin. See Marshall Scott Legan, "Judge Henry Bry: Genevan on the Ouachita," *North Louisiana Historical Association Journal* 3, no. 3, 81.

305. List of Civil and Military Officers, 21 April 1809, *TP*, 9:835.

306. *Ouachita Telegraph* (Monroe), 19 November 1870.

307. Darby, *A Geographical Description*, 198, 121; Brackenridge, *Views of Louisiana*, 302–3. See also Louisiana Historic Records Survey, Works Progress Administration, *Inventory of the Parish Archives of Louisiana: Number 29, Lafourche Parish (Thibodeaux)* (Baton Rouge: Louisiana Department of Archives, Louisiana State University, 1942), 16–17.

308. In 1810 Lafourche's slave population was just under 15 percent and its free black population less than 1 percent, while Assumption's slave population was just over 22 percent and its free black population likewise under 1 percent. By 1820 the slave population in Lafourche had increased to just under 25 percent, while in Assumption the slave population had increased to just under 31 percent. See 1810 and 1820 Censuses.

309. Dr. Watkins Report, 2 February 1804, *LB*, 2:4, 4–5 (quotation), 3–4.

310. Register of Civil Appointments, 13 February 1806, *TP*, 9:598; *DLB*, 1:557.

311. Claiborne to the Commandant of La Fourche, 13 July 1805, *LB*, 3:124. Villanueva became the first treasurer of the county. See Register of Civil Appointments, 13 February 1806; Register of Civil Appointments, 1 January–30 June 1806, *TP*, 9:600, 663.

312. Civil Appointments, 31 December 1806, *TP*, 9:701.

313. Return of Civil Appointments, Pardons &c. from the 1st of July 1807, to the 31st Decr. 1807 inclusive, *LB*, 4:146. A Register of Civil Appointments, 30 June 1807, *TP*, 9:749; List of Civil and Military Officers, 21 April 1809, *TP*, 9:835.

314. Return of Proclamations, Pardons, and Appointments, 30 June 1808, *TP*, 9:796.

315. List of Civil and Military Officers, 21 April 1809, *TP*, 9:835.

316. Kenneth B. Toups, *Assumption Parish, LA, Original Cahier Records Books 1 thru 5, 1786–1813* (Thibodaux, LA: Audrey B. Westerman, 1991), 48.

317. *Mississippi Messenger* (Natchez), 3 December 1805.

318. *DLB*, 2:786.

319. Return of Civil Appointments, Pardons &c. from the 1st of July 1807, to the 31st Decr. 1807 inclusive, *LB*, 4:145.

320. Return of Proclamations, Pardons, and Appointments, 30 June 1808, *TP*, 9:796.

321. *Courier de la Louisiane* (New Orleans), 18 January 1809.

322. Carla Gerona, "With a Song in Their Hands: Incendiary *Décimas* from the Texas and Louisiana Borderlands during a Revolutionary Age," *Early American Studies* 12, no. 1 (Winter 2014): 102–3, 106.

323. Claiborne to Edward Turner, 25 February 1804, *LB*, 1:386.

324. Edward Turner to Claiborne, 5 April 1805, Claiborne (William C. C.) Letters and Depositions (1799–1846), MSS 5018, Louisiana and Lower Mississippi Valley Collections, LSU Libraries, Baton Rouge, LA.

325. John Sibley to Claiborne, 8 January 1805, Claiborne (William C. C.) Letters and Depositions (1799–1846), MSS 5018, Louisiana and Lower Mississippi Valley Collections, LSU Libraries, Baton Rouge, LA.

326. Edward Turner to Claiborne, 5 May 1805, Claiborne (William C. C.) Letters and Depositions (1799–1846), MSS 5018, Louisiana and Lower Mississippi Valley Collections, LSU Libraries, Baton Rouge, LA.

327. Claiborne to Colonel Cushing, 9 September 1806, *LB*, 4:6–7; Claiborne to Henry Dearborn, 12 October 1806, 4:29.

328. Claiborne to Captain Turner, 7 May 1805, *LB*, 3:41–42; Register of Civil Appointments in the Territory of Orleans, *TP*, 9:598–602.

329. Claiborne to John W. Alexander, 7 May 1805, *LB*, 3:42–43.

330. Register of Civil Appointments, 1 January–30 June 1806, *TP*, 9:662–63.

331. Register of Civil Appointments, 30 June 1807, *TP*, 9:749–51.

332. List of Civil and Military Officers, 21 April 1809, *TP*, 9:835.

333. J. C. A. Stagg, *Borderlines in Borderlands: James Madison and the Spanish-American Frontier* (New Haven, CT: Yale University Press, 2009), 149.

334. A Message from the Governor, Making Several Nominations, 4 September 1812, *LB*, 6:172.

335. *DLB*, 2:666–67.

336. List of Civil and Military Appointments, 21 April 1809, *TP*, 9:835.

337. Samuel C. Hyde Jr., *Pistols and Politics: The Dilemma of Democracy in Louisiana's Florida Parishes, 1810–1899* (Baton Rouge: Louisiana State University Press, 1996), 3–10, 23–36, 65–67.

338. Claiborne to Robert Smith, 3 January 1811, *LB*, 5:70.

339. *Time Piece* (St. Francisville), 23 May 1811.

340. Memorial to Congress from Inhabitants of Feliciana County, 17 March 1812, *TP*, 9:1007–12.

341. Claiborne to the Secretary of State, 22 March 1811, *LB*, 5:187–88.

342. Claiborne to Genl. Thomas, 9 April 1811, *LB*, 5:209.

343. Claiborne to Biddle Wilkinson, 4 April 1811, *LB*, 5:204.

344. Claiborne to Robert Smith, 24 December 1810, *LB*, 5:62.

345. Claiborne to Judge Mather, 19 January 1811, *LB*, 5:105; Claiborne to Doctor Steele, 27 February 1811, *LB*, 5:166.

346. *Louisiana Courier* (New Orleans), 26 February 1813. A Sergeant Wilkinson from the fort at Baton Rouge discharged one of the guns.

347. Return of Civil Appointments made in the Territory of Orleans from the 1st January 1811 to the 31st December of the Same Year, *TP*, 9:984.

348. East Baton Rouge Parish, Judge Books.

349. Haynes, *The Mississippi Territory and the Southwest Frontier, 1795–1817*, 78.

350. Claiborne to John Rhea, 19 January 1811, *LB*, 5:105; Return of Civil Appointments Made in the Territory of Orleans from the 1st January 1811 to the 31st December of the Same Year, *TP*, 9:984.

351. *DLB,* 1:680; H. Skipwith, *East Feliciana, Louisiana, Past and Present: Sketches of the Pioneers* (New Orleans: Hopkins, 1892), 6.

352. Claiborne to James Monroe, 2 September 1811, *LB,* 5:353.

353. Claiborne to Judge Rhea, 20 December 1811, *LB,* 6:14.

354. Gurley attended Williams College just three years before, and he went on to be a congressman, a prominent Whig, and judge in Baton Rouge. *DLB,* 1:367.

355. For a survey of the first printers in the city, see Douglas C. McMurtrie, *Early Printing in New Orleans, 1764–1810, with a Bibliography of the Issues of the Louisiana Press* (New Orleans: Searcy & Pfaff, 1929).

356. *DLB,* 1:102–3.

357. Claiborne to James Monroe, 2 September 1811, *LB,* 5:352.

358. Claiborne to John Rhea, 1 February 1812, *LB,* 6:47.

359. Claiborne to Thomas Butler, 1 February 1812, *LB,* 6:48; *DLB,* 1:136–37; *Louisiana Gazette* (New Orleans), 25 March 1812; Claiborne to John P. Hampton, 24 February 1812, *LB,* 6:59.

360. Claiborne to John Rhea, 24 February 1812, *LB,* 6:60.

361. Claiborne to James M. Bradford, 22 December 1812, *LB,* 6:204.

362. *DLB,* 1:439.

363. Claiborne to Robert Smith, 24 December 1810, *LB,* 5:62.

364. Claiborne to Audley L. Osborne, 14 January 1811, *LB,* 5:98; Return of Civil Appointments Made in the Territory of Orleans from the 1st January 1811 to the 31st December of the Same Year, *TP,* 9:984. Claiborne also recommended Osborne to Secretary of the Treasury Albert Gallatin as a land registrar for West Florida. Claiborne to Albert Gallatin, 2 July 1812, *LB,* 6:131.

365. Donna Burge Adams, *Officials of the Florida Parishes of Louisiana* (Baton Rouge: D. B. Adams, 1992), 15, 17.

366. Claiborne to Gentlemen of the Senate & of the House of Representatives, 14 August 1812, *LB,* 6:161–62.

367. Frederick S. Ellis, *St. Tammany Parish: L'Autre Côté du Lac* (Gretna, LA: Pelican, 1998), 85.

368. *DLB,* 1:362, 2:788.

369. In addition, he was purportedly the first planter to own a sugar mill in the parish. *DLB,* 1:401–2.

370. *JS,* second legislature, first session, 3; *JS,* second legislature, second session, 3; *JS,* third legislature, first session, 18; *JS,* third legislature, second session, 4.

371. *DLB,* 2:817. Waggaman's father had served as the first attorney general of Maryland.

372. *JS,* fourth legislature, first session, 3, 10–11; *JS,* fourth legislature, second session, 3. Gurley won with four ineligible voters casting ballots for him, but his opponent still fell short.

373. *DLB,* 1:531, 301, 2:867.

374. Adrian D. Schwartz, *Sesquicentennial in St. Tammany* (Covington, LA: Parish Typewriter Service, 1963), 18.

375. J. Bushnell, who represented St. Helena and St. Tammany at the second session of the

first state Senate, resigned over questions as to whether he had resided in the district prior to annexation. *JS,* first legislature, second session, 3, 11.

376. Governor Claiborne to Robert Smith, 21 April 1809, *LB,* 4:345. Claiborne frequently differentiated between original Creole inhabitants and the foreign French, but here he noted the American/Francophone divide.

377. *Louisiana Gazette* (New Orleans), 1 June 1812, 3 June 1812, 5 June 1812.

378. *Louisiana Gazette* (New Orleans), 16 June 1812.

379. *Louisiana Gazette* (New Orleans), 22 June 1812.

380. James Madison to William Jones, 11 October 1813, *PJM:PS,* 6:689.

381. Isaac Lewis Baker to Andrew Jackson, 7 April 1819, *PAJ,* 4:281–82.

Conclusion

1. Paul A. Rahe, *Republics Ancient & Modern: New Modes & Orders in Early Modern Political Thought* (Chapel Hill: University of North Carolina Press, 1994), 36.

2. John W. Gurley to Gideon Granger, 14 July 1804, *TP,* 9:264.

3. *L'Ami des Lois* (New Orleans), 27 June 1816.

4. Darby, *A Geographical Description,* 263–65, 266.

5. Latrobe, *The Journal of Latrobe,* 169, 173.

Bibliography

Primary

Archival Collections

CENTER FOR AMERICAN HISTORY, UNIVERSITY OF TEXAS

Baron de Bastrop Papers, 1795–1823, Center for American History, University of Texas at Austin.

HISTORIC NEW ORLEANS COLLECTION

Acadian Parish Records, Mss. 23, Historic New Orleans Collection.

St. John the Baptist Records, État de la Louisiane Paroisse St. Jean Baptiste Recensement Général de l'année 1813, Mss. 22, Historic New Orleans Collection.

LOUISIANA STATE ARCHIVES

St. Landry 1805 and 1806 Tax Lists.

LOUISIANA STATE UNIVERSITY

Attakapas County Papers, Attakapas Tax Rolls 1808–1810, Mss. 10 A:17, Louisiana and Lower Mississippi Valley Collection, LSU Libraries, Baton Rouge LA.

Claiborne (William C. C.) Letters and Depositions (1799–1846), MSS 5018, Louisiana and Lower Mississippi Valley Collections, LSU Libraries, Baton Rouge LA.

Concordia Parish Collection, Concordia Tax Rolls 1807, 1811, 1812, MSS 5579 U:26 and F:12, Calhoun Collection, LSU Libraries, Baton Rouge LA.

Natchitoches Parish Records, Notarial Acts to 1820, Louisiana and Lower Mississippi Valley Collections, LSU Libraries, Baton Rouge, LA.

PARISH ARCHIVES

Ascension Parish Conveyance Records, 1807–1820.
Assumption Parish Conveyances, 1813–1820.
Assumption Parish Sheriff sales start, 1816–1820.
Assumption Parish Original Acts.
Avoyelles Parish Conveyance Records, 1808–1820.
Catahoula Parish Conveyance Records, 1808–1820.
Concordia Parish Conveyance Records, 1804–1820.
East Baton Rouge Parish, Judge Books.
East Baton Rouge Parish, Sheriff Sales, 1813–1820.
East Baton Rouge Parish, Notarial Acts, 1812–1813.
Iberville Parish Conveyance Records.
Lafourche Parish Conveyance Records, 1808–1820.
Lafourche Parish Original Acts.
Natchitoches Parish Conveyance Records, 1812.
Natchitoches Succession Records, 1813–1816.
Pointe Coupée Parish Conveyances, 1810–1820.
St. Charles Parish Original Acts.
Tableau de hypothèques qui existent sur les propriétés de la Paroisse St. Charles Côte des Allemands 1806–1853, St. Charles Parish Courthouse Archives.
St. James Parish Conveyance Records, 1809–1820.
St. James Parish Acts, 1808–1820.
St. John the Baptist Parish Original Acts.
St. Martin Parish Conveyances Records, 1806–1820.
St. Martin Parish Sheriff's Book, 1814–1820.
St. Mary Parish Conveyances, 1807–1820.
St. Mary Parish Mortgages, 1811–1820.
St. Mary Parish Minute Books, 1811–1820.
St. Tammany Conveyance Records, 1810–1827, New Orleans Public Library.
West Baton Rouge Conveyance Records.
West Feliciana Inventory Book, 1815–1820.
West Feliciana Inventory Record Book, 1815–1819.
West Feliciana Notarial Records, 1818–1820.
West Feliciana Probate Sales Book, 1815–1820.

Published Works

Acts Passed at the Second Session of the Third Legislature of the Territory of Orleans 1811. New Orleans: Thierry, 1811.

Aggregate Amount of Persons Within the United States in the Year 1810. Washington, DC: Census Office, 1811.

American State Papers: Military Affairs. 38 vols. Washington, DC: Gales and Seaton, 1832–61.

Assumption Parish Louisiana Original Cahier Records Books 1 thru 5, 1786–1813. Thibodaux, LA: Audrey B. Westerman, 1991.

Bailly, Francis. *Journal of a Tour in Unsettled Parts of North America in 1796 and 1797.* Edited by Jack D. L. Holmes. Carbondale: Southern Illinois University, 1969.

Berquin-Duvallon, Pierre Louis. *Travels in Louisiana and the Floridas in the Year 1802, Giving a Correct Picture of those Countries.* Translated by John Davis. New York: I. Riley, 1806.

Brackenridge, H. M. *Views of Louisiana; Containing Geographical, Statistical and Historical Notices of the Vast and Important Portion of America.* Baltimore: Schaeffer & Maund, 1817.

Brand Book for the Attakapas and Opelousas District 1739 to 1888.

Burr, Aaron. *Political Correspondence and Public Papers of Aaron Burr.* 2 vols. Edited by Mary-Jo Kline. Princeton, NJ: Princeton University Press, 1983.

The Case of Mr. Workman, On a Rule for an Alleged Contempt of the Superior Court of the Territory of Orleans. Philadelphia: William Fry, 1809.

Census for 1820. Washington, DC: Gales & Seaton, 1821.

Claiborne, Nathaniel Herbert. *Notes on the War in the South.* Richmond: William Ramsay, 1819.

Claiborne, W. C. C. *Official Letter Books of W. C. C. Claiborne, 1801–1816.* 6 vols. Edited by Dunbar Rowland. Jackson: Mississippi State Department of Archives and History, 1917.

———. *Interim Appointment: W. C. C. Claiborne Letter Book, 1804–1805.* Edited by Jared William Bradley. Baton Rouge: Louisiana State University Press, 2002.

Clay, Henry. *The Papers of Henry Clay.* 10 vols. Edited by James F. Hopkins. Lexington: University Press of Kentucky, 1959–1991.

Conrad, Glenn R., ed. *The German Coast: Abstracts of the Civil Records of St. Charles and St. John the Baptist Parishes, 1804–1812.* Lafayette: Center for Louisiana Studies University of Southwestern Louisiana, 1981.

———. *Land Records of the Attakapas District.* Vol. 1, *The Attakapas Domesday Book: Land Grants, Claims and Confirmations in the Attakapas District, 1764–1826.*

Lafayette: Center for Louisiana Studies, University of Southwestern Louisiana, 1990.

———. *Land Records of the Attakapas District*. Vol. 2, part 1, *Conveyance Records of Attakapas County, 1804–1818*. Lafayette: Center for Louisiana Studies, University of Southwestern Louisiana, 1992.

———. *Land Records of the Attakapas District*. Vol. 2, part 2, *Attakapas—St. Martin Estates, 1804–1818*. Lafayette: Center for Louisiana Studies, University of Southwestern Louisiana, 1993.

Constitution or Form of Government of the State of Louisiana. New Orleans, 1812.

Darby, William. *A Geographical Description of the State of Louisiana*. Philadelphia: John Melish, 1816.

Declouet, Louis. "Translation of Declouet's Memorial, 7 December 1814." In *Archivo General de Indias, Indiferente, General Legajo 146-3-8, Declouet to Cevallos, Madrid, Louisiana Historical Quarterly* 22, no. 3 (July 1939).

"Despatches from the United States Consulate in New Orleans, 1801–1803." *American Historical Review* 32, no. 4. (July 1927).

De Ville, Winston, ed. *Slaves and Masters of Pointe Coupée, Louisiana: A Calendar of Civil Records, 1762–1823*. Ville Platte, LA: De Ville, 1988.

———, ed. *Southwest Louisiana in 1807: The Land and Slave Tax of St. Landry Parish in the Territory of Orleans*. Ville Platte, LA: De Ville, 1993.

Documents Relative to Louisiana and Florida; Received at the Department of State, From the Secretary of State of Spain, Through the Hon. C. P. Van Ness, Envoy Extraordinary and Minister Plenipotentiary at Madrid. Washington, DC: Department of State, 1835.

Du Lac, François Marie Perrin. *Travels through the Two Louisianas and Among the Savage Nations of the Missouri, in the United States, along the Ohio and the Adjacent Provinces, in 1801, 1802 & 1803, Translated from the French*. London: J. G. Barnard, 1807.

The Favrot Family Papers. 6 vols. Edited by Wilbur E. Meneray. New Orleans: Howard-Tilton Memorial Library, 1988–2012.

Gallatin, Albert. *The Writings of Albert Gallatin*. 3 vols. Edited by Henry Adams. New York: Antiquarian, 1960.

Glass, Anthony. *Journal of an Indian Trader: Anthony Glass and the Texas Trading Frontier*. Edited by Dan L. Flores. College Station: Texas A&M University Press, 1985.

Jackson, Andrew. *The Papers of Andrew Jackson*. Edited by Harold D. Moser et al. 9 vols. to date. Knoxville: University of Tennessee Press, 1980–.

Jefferson, Thomas. *Papers of Thomas Jefferson: Retirement Series*. Edited by J. J. Looney et al. 8 vols. to date. Princeton, NJ: Princeton University Press, 2004–.

Journal of the House of Representatives of the State of Louisiana. New Orleans: Thierry, Baird & Wagner, Peter K. Wagner, J. C. de St. Romes, 1812–20.

Journal of the Senate of the State of Louisiana. New Orleans: Thierry, Baird & Wagner, Peter K. Wagner, J. C. de St. Romes, 1812–20.

Latour, Arsène Lacarrière. *Historical Memoir of the War in West Florida and Louisiana in 1814–1815.* Expanded ed. Edited by Gene A. Smith. Gainesville: Historical New Orleans Collection and University Press of Florida, 1999.

Latrobe, Benjamin Henry. *The Journal of Latrobe: The Notes and Sketches of an Architect, Naturalist and Traveler in the United States from 1796–1820.* New York: D. Appleton, 1905.

Louisiana under the Rule of Spain, France, and the United States, 1785–1807. Edited by James Alexander Robertson. 2 vols. Freeport, NY: Books for Libraries, 1969.

Madison, James. *Papers of James Madison: Secretary of State Series.* Edited by Robert J. Brugger et al. 9 vols. to date. Charlottesville: University Press of Virginia, 1986–.

———. *Papers of James Madison: Presidential Series.* Edited by Robert A. Rutland et al. 7 vols. to date. Charlottesville: University Press of Virginia, 1986–.

Mahon, Samuel S. "A Discourse on Divorce: Orleans Territorial Legislature, 1806." Edited by W. Magruder Drake. *Louisiana History* 22, no. 4 (Fall 1981).

Martin, François-Xavier. *A General Digest of the Acts of the Legislatures of the Late Territory of Orleans and the State of Louisiana and the Ordinances of the Governor Under the Territorial Government.* 3 vols. New Orleans: Peter K. Wagner, 1816.

Mills, Elizabeth Shown, ed. *Natchitoches Colonials: Censuses, Military Rolls and Tax Lists, 1722–1803.* Chicago: Adams, 1981.

A Native. *View of the Political and Civil Situation of Louisiana from the Thirtieth of November 1803 to the First of October 1804, by a Native.* Philadelphia, 1804.

Nolte, Vincent. *The Memoirs of Vincent Nolte: Reminiscences in the Period of Anthony Adverse; or, Fifty Years in Both Hemispheres.* 1854. Reprint, New York: G. Howard Watt, 1934.

Plumer, William. *William Plumer's Memorandum of Proceedings of the United States Senate, 1803–1807.* Edited by Everett Somerville Brown. New York, 1923.

Pitot, James. *Observations on the Colony of Louisiana from 1796 to 1802.* Translated by Henry C. Pitot. Baton Rouge: Louisiana State University Press, 1979.

Riffel, Judy, ed. *Calendar of St. Landry Parish Louisiana, Civil Records.* Vol. 1, 1803–1819. Baton Rouge: Le Comité des Archives de la Louisiane, 1995.

———, ed. *Iberville Parish Records.* Vols. 1–2. Baton Rouge: Riffel, 1981.

Robin, C. C. *Voyage to Louisiana, 1803–1805.* Translated by Stuart O. Landry Jr. Gretna, LA: Firebird, 2000.

St. Julien, Louis. "Against His Enemies, His Accusers, His Assassins." Translated and edited by Robert St. Julien and Lou Ann St. Julien. In *Attakapas Gazette* 22, no. 2 (Summer 1987).

Sanders, Mary Elizabeth, comp. *Records of Attakapas District, Louisiana 1739–1811.* Franklin, LA: Sanders, 1962.

———, comp. *Annotated Abstracts of the Successions of St. Mary Parish, LA., 1811–1834.* Franklin, LA: Sanders, 1972.

———, comp. *An Index to the 1820 Census of Louisiana's Florida Parishes and 1812 St. Tammany Tax List.* Baton Rouge: Le Comité des Archives de la Louisiane, 1972.

Sibley, John. "John Sibley to W. C. C. Claiborne, 6 August 1807." *Louisiana History* 29, no. 4 (Fall 1988).

———. "Letter of Dr. John Sibley, August 6, 1807." *Louisiana History* 29, no. 4 (Fall 1988).

———. *A Report from Natchitoches in 1807.* Edited by Annie Heloise Abel. New York: Museum of the American Indian, Heye Foundation, 1922.

Stoddard, Major Amos. *Sketches, Historical and Descriptive of Louisiana.* Philadelphia: Mathew Carey, 1812.*The Territorial Papers of the United States.* Vol. 9, *The Territory of Orleans, 1803–1812.* Edited by Clarence Edwin Carter. Washington, DC: Government Printing Office, 1940.

The Trials of the Honb. James Workman and Col. Lewis Kerr, Before the United States' Court, for the Orleans District, on a Charge of High Misdemeanor, in Planning and Setting on Foot, within the United States, an Expedition for the Conquest and Emancipation of Mexico. New Orleans: Bradford & Anderson, 1807.

Wilkinson, James. *Memoirs of My Own Times.* 4 vols. Philadelphia: Abraham Small, 1816.

Workman, James. *Liberty in Louisiana: A Comedy, Performed at the Charleston Theater.* Charleston: Query and Evans, 1804.

———. *Essays and Letters on Various Political Subjects.* 2nd American ed. New York: Gould & Van Winkle, 1809.

Newspapers

Courier de la Louisiane / Louisiana Courier (New Orleans).

L'Ami des Lois (New Orleans).

Louisiana Gazette (New Orleans).

Louisiana Gazette and Mercantile Advertiser (New Orleans).

Louisiana Herald (New Orleans).

Louisianian (St. Francisville).

The Mississippian (Natchez).

Mississippi Messenger (Natchez).

Moniteur de la Louisiane (New Orleans).

Orleans Gazette (New Orleans).

Orleans Gazette and Commercial Advertizer (New Orleans).

Ouachita Telegraph (Monroe)

Time Piece (St. Francisville).

Census Transcriptions

Ardoin, Robert Bruce L. *Louisiana Census Records.* Vol. 1, *Avoyelles and St. Landry Parish, 1810 & 1820.* Baltimore: Genealogical, 1970.

———. *Louisiana Census Records.* Vol. 2, *Iberville, Natchitoches, Pointe Coupée and Rapides Parishes, 1810 & 1820.* Baltimore: Genealogical, 1972.

———. *Louisiana Census Records.* Vol. 3, *Ascension, Assumption, West Baton Rouge, East Baton Rouge, St. Bernard, St. Charles, St. James, and St. John the Baptist Parishes, 1810 & 1820.* New Orleans: Polyanthos, 1977.

Secondary

Books

Abernethy, Thomas Perkins. *The Burr Conspiracy.* New York: Oxford University Press, 1954.

Adams, Donna Burge. *Officials of the Florida Parishes of Louisiana.* Baton Rouge: D. B. Adams, 1992.

Aitken, William B. *Distinguished Families in America Descended from Wilhelmus Beekman and Ian Thomasse Van Dyke.* New York: Knickerbocker, 1912.

Alstyne, Richard W. *The Rising American Empire.* New York: W. W. Norton, 1960.

Alvord, Clarence Walworth. *The Illinois Country, 1673–1818.* Chicago: Loyola University Press, 1965.

Aptheker, Herbert. *American Negro Slave Revolts.* 6th ed. New York: International, 1993.

Aron, Stephen. *American Confluence: The Missouri Frontier from Borderland to Border State.* Bloomington: Indiana University Press, 2006.

Aronson, Sidney H. *Status and Kinship in the Higher Civil Service: Standards of Selection in the Administrations of John Adams, Thomas Jefferson, and Andrew Jackson.* Cambridge, MA: Harvard University Press, 1964.

Arrington, Leonard J. *The Great Basin Kingdom: An Economic History of the Latter Day Saints, 1830–1900.* Cambridge, MA: Harvard University Press, 1958.

Arthur, Stanley Clisby, and George Campbell Huchet de Kernion. *Old Families of Louisiana.* 1931. Reprint, Gretna, LA: Firebird, 1998.

Balmer, Randall H. *A Perfect Babel of Confusion: Dutch Religion and English Culture in the Middle Colonies.* Oxford: Oxford University Press, 1989.

Banner, Stuart. *How the Indians Lost Their Land: Law and Power on the Frontier.* Cambridge, MA: Harvard University Press, 2005.

———. *Legal Systems in Conflict: Property and Sovereignty in Missouri, 1750–1860.* Norman: University of Oklahoma Press, 2000.

Barde, Alexandre. *The Vigilante Committees of the Attakapas: An Eyewitness Account of Banditry and Backlash in Southwestern Louisiana.* Lafayette: Acadiana, 1981.

Baudier, Roger. *The Catholic Church in Louisiana.* New Orleans: Roger Baudier, 1939.

Benton, Lauren. *Law and Colonial Cultures: Legal Regimes in World History, 1400–1900.* Cambridge: Cambridge University Press, 2002.

———. *A Search for Sovereignty: Law and Geography in European Empires, 1400–1900.* Cambridge: Cambridge University Press, 2010.

Billings, Warren M., and Mark F. Fernandez, eds. *A Law unto Itself: Essays in the New Louisiana Legal History.* Baton Rouge: Louisiana State University Press, 2001.

Billings, Warren M., and Edward F. Haas, eds. *In Search of Fundamental Law: Louisiana's Constitutions.* Lafayette: Center for Louisiana Studies, University of Southwestern Louisiana, 1993.

Biographical and Historical Memoirs of Louisiana. Shreveport: J. & W. Enterprises, 1892.

Blackhawk, Ned. *Violence over the Land: Indians and Empires in the Early American West.* Cambridge, MA: Harvard University Press, 2006.

Bockstoce, John R. *Furs and Frontiers in the Far North: The Contest among Native and Foreign Nations for the Bering Strait Fur Trade.* New Haven, CT: Yale University Press, 2009.

Bourgeois, Lillian C. *Cabanocey: The History, Customs and Folklore of St. James Parish.* Gretna, LA: Pelican, 1957.

Brasseaux, Carl A. *The Founding of New Acadia: The Beginnings of Acadian Life in Louisiana, 1765–1803.* Baton Rouge: Louisiana State University Press, 1987.

———, ed. *A Refuge for All Ages: Immigration in Louisiana History.* Louisiana Purchase Bicentennial Series in Louisiana History, vol. 10. Lafayette: Center for Louisiana Studies, University of Southwestern Louisiana, 1996.

Brasseaux, Carl A., and Glenn R. Conrad, eds. *The Road to Louisiana: The Saint-*

Domingue Refugees, 1792–1809. Lafayette: Center for Louisiana Studies, University of Southwestern Louisiana, 1992.Broussard, Bernard. *A History of St. Mary Parish.* Franklin, LA: Broussard, 1977.

Brown, Richmond F., ed. *Coastal Encounters: The Transformation of the Gulf South in the Eighteenth Century.* Lincoln: University of Nebraska Press, 2007.

Burbank, Jane, and Frederick Cooper. *Empires in World History: Power and the Politics of Difference.* Princeton, NJ: Princeton University Press, 2010.

Burton, H. Sophie, and F. Todd Smith. *Colonial Natchitoches: A Creole Community on the Louisiana-Texas Frontier.* College Station: Texas A&M University Press, 2008.

Caldwell, Stephen A. *A Banking History of Louisiana.* Baton Rouge: Louisiana State University Press, 1935. Reprint, Ft. McCoy, FL: Criswell's, 1977.

Campbell, Mary McDowell Pilkington. *Nostalgic Notes on St. James Parish Louisiana: Then and Now.* Baton Rouge: Instant Print Centers, 1981.

Carmer, Carl. *The Hudson.* 1939. Reprint, New York: Fordham University Press, 1992.

Carrigan, Jo Ann. *The Saffron Scourge: A History of Yellow Fever in Louisiana, 1796–1905.* Lafayette: Center for Louisiana Studies, University of Southwestern Louisiana, 1994.

Carter, Clarence Edwin. *Great Britain and the Illinois Country, 1763–1774.* Washington, DC: American Historical Association, 1910.

Cayton, Andrew R. L. *Frontier Indiana.* Bloomington: Indiana University Press, 1996.

Clark, Emily. *Masterless Mistresses: The New Orleans Ursulines and the Development of a New World Society, 1727–1834.* Chapel Hill: University of North Carolina Press, 2007.

Clark, John G. *New Orleans, 1718–1812.* Baton Rouge: Louisiana State University Press, 1970.

Clark, Thomas D., and John D. W. Guice. *The Old Southwest, 1795–1830.* Norman: University of Oklahoma Press, 1983.

Conrad, Glenn R. *The First Families of Louisiana.* 2 vols. Baton Rouge: Claitor's Publishing Division, 1970.

———, ed. *A Dictionary of Louisiana Biography.* 2 vols. Lafayette: Louisiana Historical Association, 1988.

Costello, Brian J. *A History of Pointe Coupée Parish Louisiana.* New Roads, LA: Costello, 1999.

———. *The Life, Family and Legacy of Julien Poydras.* New Roads, LA: Costello, 2001.

Daniels, Christine, and Michael V. Kennedy, eds. *Negotiated Empires: Centers and Peripheries in the Americas, 1500–1820.* New York: Routledge, 2002.

Dargo, George. *Jefferson's Louisiana: Politics and the Clash of Legal Traditions*. Cambridge, MA: Harvard University Press, 1975.

Davis, William C. *The Rogue Republic: How Would-Be Patriots Waged the Shortest Revolution in American History*. Boston: Houghton Mifflin Harcourt, 2011.

Debo, Angie. *The Rise and Fall of the Choctaw Republic*. 1934. Reprint, Norman: University of Oklahoma Press, 1961.

DeConde, Alexander. *This Affair of Louisiana*. New York: Charles Scribner's Sons, 1976.

Deiler, J. Hanno. *The Settlement of the German Coast of Louisiana and the Creoles of German Descent*. Philadelphia: American Germanica, 1909.

Dessens, Nathalie. *Creole City: A Chronicle of Early American New Orleans*. Gainesville: University Press of Florida, 2015.

———. *From Saint-Domingue to New Orleans: Migration and Influences*. Gainesville: University Press of Florida, 2007.

De Ville, Winston. *First Settlers of Pointe Coupee: A Study, Based on Early Louisiana Church Records*. New Orleans: Polyanthos, 1974.

———. *Opelousas: The History of a French and Spanish Military Post in America, 1716–1803*. Cottonport, LA: Polyanthos, 1973.

———. *The Parish of St. James in the Province of Louisiana: Genealogical Abstracts from the Spanish Census of 1777*. Ville Platte, LA: Provincial, 1987.

Din, Gilbert C. *The Canary Islanders of Louisiana*. Baton Rouge: Louisiana State University Press, 1988.

———. *An Extraordinary Atlantic Life: Sebastián Nicolás De La Puerta O'Farill Marqués De Casa Calvo*. Lafayette: University of Louisiana at Lafayette Press, 2016.

———. *Populating the Barrera: Spanish Immigration Efforts in Colonial Louisiana*. Lafayette: University of Louisiana at Lafayette Press, 2014.

———. *Spaniards, Planters, and Slaves: The Spanish Regulation of Slavery in Louisiana, 1763–1803*. College Station: Texas A&M University Press, 1999.

———. *War on the Gulf Coast: The Spanish Fight against William Augustus Bowles*. Gainesville: University Press of Florida, 2012.

Dormon, James H. *The People Called Cajuns: An Introduction to an Ethnohistory*. Lafayette: Center for Louisiana Studies, University of Southwestern Louisiana, 1983.

DuVal, Kathleen. *The Native Ground: Indians and Colonists in the Heart of the Continent*. Philadelphia: University of Pennsylvania Press, 2006.

Eblen, Jack Ericson. *The First and Second United States Empires: Governors and Territorial Government, 1784–1912*. Pittsburgh: University of Pittsburgh Press, 1968.

Ellis, Frederick S. *St. Tammany Parish: L'Autre Côté du Lac*. Gretna, LA: Pelican, 1998.

Faber, Eberhard L. *Building the Land of Dreams: New Orleans and the Transformation of Early America*. Princeton, NJ: Princeton University Press, 2016.

Fernandez, Mark F. *From Chaos to Continuity: The Evolution of Louisiana's Judicial System, 1712–1862*. Baton Rouge: Louisiana State University Press, 2001.

Garrett, Julia K. *Green Flag over Texas*. New York: Cordova, 1939.

Garrigoux, Jean. *A Visionary Adventurer: Arsène Lacarrière Latour, 1778–1837: The Unusual Travels of a Frenchman in America*. Translated by Gordon S. Brown. Lafayette: University of Louisiana at Lafayette Press, 2017.

Gayarré, Charles E. *History of Louisiana: The American Domination*. New Orleans: Armand Hawkins, 1866.

Gehman, Mary. *The Free People of Color of New Orleans*. Donaldsonville, LA: Margaret Media, 2009.

Gibb, Andrew. *Californios, Anglos, and the Performance of Oligarchy in the U.S. West*. Carbondale: Southern Illinois University Press, 2018.

Gibson, James R. *Imperial Russia in Frontier America: The Changing Geography of Supply of Russian America, 1784–1867*. New York: Oxford University Press, 1976.

Gilley, B. H., ed. *North Louisiana: Essays on the Region and Its History*. Ruston, LA: McGinty Trust Fund, 1984.

Gillis, Norman E. *Early Inhabitants of the Natchez District*. Greenville, SC: Southern Historical Press, 1999.

Gitlin, Jay. *The Bourgeois Frontier: French Towns, French Traders, and American Expansion*. New Haven, CT: Yale University Press, 2010.

Gómez, Laura E. *Manifest Destinies: The Making of the Mexican American Race*. New York: New York University Press, 2007.

Gremillion, William Nelson, Sr., and Loucille Edwards Gremillion. *Some Early Families of Avoyelles Parish, Louisiana: Genealogical Studies of the Early Generations of 36 Families*. Eunice, LA: Hebert Publications, 1980.

Griffin, Harry Lewis. *The Attakapas Country*. Gretna, LA: Firebird, 1999.

Hall, Gwendolyn Midlo. *Africans in Colonial Louisiana: The Development of Afro-Creole Culture in the Eighteenth Century*. Baton Rouge: Louisiana State University Press, 1992.

———. *Slavery and African Ethnicities in the Americas: Restoring the Links*. Chapel Hill: University of North Carolina Press, 2005.

Hämäläinen, Pekka. *The Comanche Empire*. New Haven, CT: Yale University Press, 2008.

Hanger, Kimberly S. *Bounded Lives, Bounded Places: Free Black Society in Colonial New Orleans, 1769–1803*. Durham, NC: Duke University Press, 1997.

Hardin, J. Fair. *Northwestern Louisiana: A History of the Watershed of the Red River.* 3 vols. Shreveport: Historical Record Association, 1939.

Hargrave, Lee. *The Louisiana State Constitution: A Reference Guide.* New York: Greenwood, 1991.

Hatfield, Joseph T. *William Claiborne: Jeffersonian Centurion in the American Southwest.* Lafayette: University of Southwestern Louisiana, 1976.

Haydel, Leonce. *La Paroisse de St. Jacques: A History in Words and Photographs.* Baton Rouge: Pelican Management Corporation, 1988.

Haynes, Robert V. *The Mississippi Territory and the Southwest Frontier, 1795–1817.* Lexington: University Press of Kentucky, 2010.

Hébert, Donald J. *Southwest Louisiana Records,* vol. 1-B, *Church and Civil Records (1801–1810).* Rayne, LA: Hébert, 1996.

Hero, Alfred Olivier, Jr. *Louisiana and Quebec: Bilateral Relations and Comparative Sociopolitical Evolution.* Lanham, MD: University Press of America, 1995.

Hietala, Thomas R. *Manifest Design: American Exceptionalism and Empire.* Ithaca, NY: Cornell University Press, 1985.

Hinderaker, Eric. *Elusive Empires: Constructing Colonialism in the Ohio Valley, 1673–1800.* Cambridge: Cambridge University Press, 1997.

Hodson, Christopher. *The Acadian Diaspora: An Eighteenth-Century History.* Oxford: Oxford University Press, 2012.

Hoffman, Paul E. *Florida's Frontiers.* Bloomington: Indiana University Press, 2002.

Holmes, Jack D. L. *Honor and Fidelity: The Louisiana Infantry Regiment and the Louisiana Militia Companies, 1766–1821.* Birmingham: Holmes, 1965.

Holt, Michael F. *The Rise and Fall of the American Whig Party: Jacksonian Politics and the Onset of the Civil War.* New York: Oxford University Press, 1999.

Howard, Perry H. *Political Tendencies in Louisiana.* Rev. ed. Baton Rouge: Louisiana State University Press, 1971.

Howe, Daniel Walker. *What Hath God Wrought: The Transformation of America, 1815–1848.* Oxford: Oxford University Press, 2007.

Hyde, Samuel C., Jr., ed. *A Fierce and Fractious Frontier: The Curious Development of Louisiana's Florida Parishes, 1699–2000.* Baton Rouge: Louisiana State University Press, 2004.

—— *Pistols and Politics: The Dilemma of Democracy in Louisiana's Florida Parishes, 1810–1899.* Baton Rouge: Louisiana State University Press, 1996.

Jennings, Virginia Lobdell. *The Plains and the People: A History of Upper East Baton Rouge Parish.* Gretna, LA: Pelican, 1998.

Johnson, Rashauna. *Slavery's Metropolis: Unfree Labor in New Orleans during the Age of Revolutions.* Cambridge: Cambridge University Press, 2016.

Kammen, Michael. *Colonial New York: A History.* New York: Oxford University Press, 1975.

Kane, Harnett T. *Plantation Parade: The Grand Manner in Louisiana.* New York: William Morrow, 1945.

Kastor, Peter J. *The Nation's Crucible: The Louisiana Purchase and the Creation of America.* New Haven, CT: Yale University Press, 2004.

Kastor, Peter J., and François Weil, eds. *Empires of the Imagination: Transatlantic Histories of the Louisiana Purchase.* Charlottesville: University of Virginia Press, 2009.

Kellough, Elizabeth, and Leona Mayeux. *Chronicles of West Baton Rouge.* Kennedy Print Shop, 1979.

King, Grace. *Creole Families of New Orleans.* New York: Macmillan, 1921.

Koot, Christian J. *Empire at the Periphery: British Colonists, Anglo-Dutch Trade, and the Development of the British Atlantic, 1621–1713.* New York: New York University Press, 2011.

Kukla, Jon. *A Wilderness So Immense: The Louisiana Purchase and the Destiny of America.* New York: Random House, 2003.

Labbé, Dolores Egger, ed. *The Louisiana Purchase and Its Aftermath.* Louisiana Purchase Bicentennial Series in Louisiana History, vol. 3. Lafayette: Center for Louisiana Studies, University of Southwestern Louisiana, 1998.

Landers, Jane G., ed. *Against the Odds: Free Blacks in the Slave Societies of the Americas.* London: Frank Cass, 1996.

——. *Atlantic Creoles in the Age of Revolutions.* Cambridge, MA: Harvard University Press, 2010.

——. *Black Society in Spanish Florida.* Urbana: University of Illinois Press, 1999.

Larson, Gustive O. *The "Americanization" of Utah for Statehood.* San Marino, CA: Huntington Library, 1971.

LaVere, David. *The Caddo Chiefdoms: Caddo Economics and Politics, 700–1835.* Lincoln: University of Nebraska Press, 1998.

——. *Contrary Neighbors: Southern Plains and Removed Indians in Indian Territory.* Norman: University of Oklahoma Press, 2000.

Levasseur, Alain. *Moreau Lislet: the Man behind the Digest of 1808.* Baton Rouge: Claitor's, 2008.

Lewis, James E., Jr. *The American Union and the Problem of Neighborhood: The United States and the Collapse of the Spanish Empire, 1783–1829.* Chapel Hill: University of North Carolina Press, 1998.

——. *The Burr Conspiracy: Uncovering the Story of an Early American Crisis.* Princeton, NJ: Princeton University Press, 2017.

Limerick, Patricia Nelson. *The Legacy of Conquest: The Unbroken Past of the American West*. New York: W. W. Norton, 1987.

Liss, Peggy K. *Atlantic Empires: The Network of Trade and Revolution, 1713–1826*. Baltimore: Johns Hopkins University Press, 1983.

Louisiana Historic Records Survey, Works Progress Administration. *Inventory of the Parish Archives of Louisiana: Number 4, Assumption Parish (Napoleonville)*. Baton Rouge: Louisiana Department of Archives, Louisiana State University, 1942.

———. *Inventory of the Parish Archives of Louisiana: Number 29, Lafourche Parish (Thibodeaux)*. Baton Rouge: Louisiana Department of Archives, Louisiana State University, 1942.

———. *Inventory of the Parish Archives of Louisiana: Number 38, Plaquemines Parish (Pointe à la Hache)*. Baton Rouge: Louisiana Department of Archives, Louisiana State University, 1938.

———. *Inventory of the Parish Archives of Louisiana: Number 44, Saint Bernard Parish (Saint Bernard)*. Baton Rouge: Louisiana Department of Archives, Louisiana State University, 1938.

Maier, Charles S. *Among Empires: American Ascendancy and Its Predecessors*. Cambridge, MA: Harvard University Press, 2006.

Marotti, Frank. *The Cana Sanctuary: History, Diplomacy, and Black Catholic Marriage in Antebellum St. Augustine, Florida*. Tuscaloosa: University of Alabama Press, 2012.

———. *Heaven's Soldiers: Free People of Color and the Spanish Legacy in Antebellum Florida*. Tuscaloosa: University of Alabama Press, 2013.

Martin, François-Xavier. *The History of Louisiana, from the Earliest Period*. 1827. Reprint, New Orleans: Pelican, 1963.

McCaleb, Walter Flavius. *The Aaron Burr Conspiracy*. New York: Wilson-Erickson, 1936.

McConnell, Roland C. *Negro Troops of Antebellum Louisiana: A History of Free Men of Color*. Baton Rouge: Louisiana State University Press, 1968.

McKee, Jesse O., and Jon A. Schlenker. *The Choctaws: Cultural Evolution of a Native American Tribe*. Jackson: University Press of Mississippi, 1980.

McMichael, Andrew. *Atlantic Loyalties: Americans in Spanish West Florida*. Athens: University of Georgia Press, 2008.

McMurtrie, Douglas C. *Early Printing in New Orleans, 1764–1810, with a Bibliography of the Issues of the Louisiana Press*. New Orleans: Searcy & Pfaff, 1929.

McNeill, J. R. *Mosquito Empires: Ecology and War in the Greater Caribbean, 1620–1914*. Cambridge: Cambridge University Press, 2010.

Meinig, Donald William. *The Shaping of America: A Geographical Perspective on 500 Years of History*. Vol. 2, *Continental America, 1800–1967*. New Haven, CT: Yale University Press, 1995.

Merrill, Ellen C. *Germans of Louisiana*. Gretna: Pelican, 2005.

Merry, Sally Engle. *Colonizing Hawai'i: The Cultural Power of Law*. Princeton, NJ: Princeton University Press, 2000.

Merry, Sally Engle, and Daniel Brenneis, eds. *Law & Empire in the Pacific: Fiji and Hawai'i*. Santa Fe, NM: School of American Research Press, 2003.

Merwick, Donna. *Possessing Albany, 1630–1710: The Dutch and English Experiences*. Cambridge: Cambridge University Press, 1990.

Meyers, Rose. *A History of Baton Rouge, 1699–1812*. Baton Rouge: Louisiana State University Press, 1976.

Mills, Donna Rachal. *Some Southern Balls: From Valentine to Ferdinand and Beyond*. Orlando: Mills Historical, 1993.

Mills, Gary B. *The Forgotten People: Cane River's Creoles of Color*. Baton Rouge: Louisiana State University Press, 1977.

Nardini, Louis Raphael, Sr. *My Historic Natchitoches, Louisiana and Its Environment*. Natchitoches: Nardini, 1963.

Onuf, Peter, and Nicholas Onuf. *Federal Union, Modern World: The Law of Nations in an Age of Revolutions, 1776–1814*. Madison: Madison House, 1993.

Owsley, Frank Lawrence, Jr. *Struggle for the Gulf Borderlands: The Creek War and the Battle of New Orleans, 1812–1815*. Tuscaloosa: University of Alabama Press, 1981.

Owsley, Frank Lawrence, Jr., and Gene A. Smith. *Filibusters and Expansionists: Jeffersonian Manifest Destiny, 1800–1821*. Tuscaloosa: University of Alabama Press, 1997.

Palmer, Vernon Valentine. *Through the Codes Darkly: Slave Law and Civil Law in Louisiana*. Clark, NJ: Lawbook Exchange, 2012.

Pencak, William, and Conrad Edick Wright, eds. *Authority and Resistance in Early New York*. New York: New York Historical Society, 1988.

Phillips, George Harwood. *Indians and Intruders in Central California, 1769–1849*. Norman: University of Oklahoma Press, 1993.

Pitot, Henry Clement. *James Pitot (1761–1831): A Documentary Study*. New Orleans: Bocage Books, 1968.

Pomeroy, Earl. *The Territories and the United States, 1861–1890*. Seattle: University of Washington Press, 1969.

Pourciaux, Betty. *St. Martin Parish History*. Baton Rouge: Let Comité des Archives de la Louisiane, 1985.

Powell, Lawrence N. *The Accidental City: Improvising New Orleans.* Cambridge, MA: Harvard University Press, 2012.

Rahe, Paul A. *Republics Ancient & Modern: New Modes & Orders in Early Modern Political Thought.* Chapel Hill: University of North Carolina Press, 1994.

Rasmussen, Daniel. *American Uprising: The Untold Story of America's Largest Slave Revolt.* New York: Harper Collins, 2011.

Reséndez, Andrés. *Changing National Identities at the Frontier: Texas and New Mexico, 1800–1850.* New York: Cambridge University Press, 2004.

Riffel, Judy, ed. *A History of Pointe Coupee Parish and Its Families.* Baton Rouge: Le Comité des Archives de la Louisiane, 1981.

———, ed. *Iberville Parish History.* Baton Rouge: Le Comité des Archives de la Louisiane, 1985.

Robichaux, Albert J., Jr. *German Coast Families: European Origins and Settlement in Colonial Louisiana.* Rayne, LA: Hebert, 1997.

Sacher, John M. *A Perfect War of Politics: Parties, Politicians, and Democracy in Louisiana, 1824–1861.* Baton Rouge: Louisiana State University Press, 2003.

Sadosky, Leonard J. *Revolutionary Negotiations: Indians, Empires, and Diplomats in the Founding of America.* Charlottesville: University of Virginia Press, 2009.

Saucier, Corinne L. *History of Avoyelles Parish, Louisiana.* Gretna, LA: Firebird, 1998.

Schafer, Daniel L. *Zephaniah Kingsley Jr. and the Atlantic World.* Gainesville: University Press of Florida, 2013.

Schafer, Judith Kelleher. *Slavery, the Civil Law, and the Supreme Court of Louisiana.* Baton Rouge: Louisiana State University Press, 1994.

Schwartz, Adrian D. *Sesquicentennial in St. Tammany.* Covington, LA: Parish Typewriter Service, 1963.

Skipwith, H. *East Feliciana, Louisiana, Past and Present: Sketches of the Pioneers.* New Orleans: Hopkins, 1892.

Smith, F. Todd. *The Caddo Indians: Tribes at the Convergence of Empires, 1542–1854.* College Station: Texas A&M University Press, 1995.

———. *Louisiana and the Gulf South Frontier, 1500–1821.* Baton Rouge: Louisiana State University Press, 2014.

Smith, Gene Allen, and Sylvia L. Hilton, eds. *Nexus of Empire: Negotiating Loyalty and Identity in the Revolutionary Borderlands, 1760–1820s.* Gainesville: University Press of Florida, 2010.

Stagg, J. C. A. *Borderlines in Borderlands: James Madison and the Spanish-American Frontier, 1776–1821.* New Haven, CT: Yale University Press, 2009.

Swanton, John R. *The Indians of the Southeastern United States.* 1946. Reprint, Washington, DC: Smithsonian Institution, 1979.

Taylor, Alan. *The Internal Enemy: Slavery and War in Virginia, 1772–1832*. New York: W. W. Norton, 2013.

Thompson, Leonard, ed. *The Frontier in History: North America and Southern Africa Compared*. New Haven, CT: Yale University Press, 1981.

Thrasher, Albert. *"On to New Orleans": Louisiana's Heroic 1811 Slave Revolt*. New Orleans: Cypress, 1995.

Tregle, Joseph G., Jr. *Louisiana in the Age of Jackson: A Clash of Cultures and Personalities*. Baton Rouge: Louisiana State University Press, 1999.

Toups, Kenneth B. *Assumption Parish, LA, Original Cahier: Record Books 1 thru 5, 1786–1813*. Thibodeaux, LA: Audrey B. Westerman, 1991.

Turner, Frederick Jackson. *The Frontier in American History*. New York: Henry Holt, 1920.

Usner, Daniel H., Jr. *Indians, Settlers, and Slaves in a Frontier Exchange Economy: The Lower Mississippi Valley before 1783*. Chapel Hill: University of North Carolina University Press, 1992.

———. *American Indians in the Lower Mississippi Valley: Social and Economic Histories*. Lincoln: University of Nebraska Press, 1998.

Vernet, Julien. *Strangers on Their Native Soil: Opposition to United States' Governance in Louisiana's Orleans Territory, 1803–1809*. Jackson: University Press of Mississippi, 2013.

Vinkovetsky, Ilya. *Russian America: An Overseas Colony of a Continental Empire, 1804–1867*. New York: Oxford University Press, 2011.

Voss, Louis. *The German Coast of Louisiana*. Hoboken, NJ: Concord Society, 1928.

Wallace, Paul A. *The Muhlenbergs of Pennsylvania*. Philadelphia: University of Pennsylvania Press, 1950.

Watson, Samuel J. *Jackson's Sword: The Army Officer Corps on the American Frontier, 1810–1821*. Lawrence: University Press of Kansas, 2012.

Weber, David J. *The Spanish Frontier in North America*. New Haven, CT: Yale University Press, 1992.

White, Ashli. *Encountering Revolution: Haiti and the Making of the Early Republic*. Baltimore: Johns Hopkins University Press, 2010.

White, Richard. *"It's Your Misfortune and None of My Own": A New History of the American West*. Norman: University of Oklahoma Press, 1991.

White, Sophie. *Wild Frenchmen and Frenchified Indians: Material Culture and Race in Colonial Louisiana*. Philadelphia: University of Pennsylvania Press, 2012.

Whittington, G. P. *Rapides Parish, Louisiana: A History*. Alexandria, LA: National Society of the Colonial Dames in the State of Louisiana, 1955.

Williamson, Frederick William, and George T. Goodman. *Eastern Louisiana: A History of the Watershed of the Ouachita River and the Florida Parishes.* 3 vols. Louisville: Historical Record Association, 1939.

Womack, Annette Carpenter. *Captain Edward D. Turner's Company of the 2nd Regiment of the United States Army, Stationed in the Territory of Orleans of the Louisiana Purchase, 1802–1805.* Bowie, MD: Heritage Books, 2000.

Yoes, Henry E., III. *Louisiana's German Coast: A History of St. Charles Parish.* Lake Charles, LA: Racing Pigeon Digest, 2005.

Theses and Dissertations

Buman, Nathan A. "To Kill Whites: The 1811 Louisiana Slave Insurrection." Master's thesis, Louisiana State University, 2008.

Dollar, Susan E. "'Black, White, or Indifferent': Race Identity and Americanization in Creole Louisiana." PhD diss., University of Arkansas, 1994.

Kastor, Peter J. "'An Apprenticeship to Liberty': The Incorporation of Louisiana and the Struggle for Nationhood in the Early American Republic, 1803–1820." PhD diss., University of Virginia, 1999.

LeBreton, Marietta Marie. "A History of the Territory of Orleans." PhD diss., Louisiana State University, 1969.

Newton, Lewis William. "The Americanization of French Louisiana: A Study of the Process of Adjustment between the French and the Anglo-American Populations of Louisiana." PhD diss., University of Chicago, 1929.

Roberts, Kevin David. "Slaves and Slavery in Louisiana: The Evolution of Atlantic World Identities, 1791–1831." PhD diss., University of Texas, 2003.

Russell, Sarah Paradise. "Cultural Conflicts and Common Interests: The Making of the Sugar Planter Class in Louisiana, 1795–1853." PhD diss., University of Maryland, 2000.

Thomas, David Yancey. "A History of Military Government in Newly Acquired Territory of the United States." PhD diss., Columbia University, 1904.

Toups, Gerard J. "The Provincial, Territorial, and State Administrations of William C. C. Claiborne, Governor of Louisiana, 1803–1816." PhD diss., University of Southwestern Louisiana, 1979.

Townes, J. Edward. "Invisible Lines: The Life and Death of a Borderland." PhD diss., Texas Christian University, 2008.

Tregle, Joseph G. "Louisiana in the Age of Jackson, A Study in Ego-Politics." PhD diss., University of Pennsylvania, 1954.

Vernet, Julien Paul. "'Strangers on Their Native Soil?': Opposition to United States Territorial Government in Orleans, 1803–1809." PhD diss., Syracuse University, 2002.

Articles

Adelman, Jeremy, and Stephen Aron. "From Borderlands to Borders: Empires, Nation-States, and Peoples in Between in North American History." *American Historical Review* 104 (June 1999).

Baum, Michiel, and Willem van Schendel. "Towards a Comparative History of Borderlands." *Journal of World History* 8 (Fall 1997).

Dormon, James H. "The Persistent Specter: Slave Rebellion in Territorial Louisiana." *Louisiana History* 18, no. 4 (Fall 1977).

Everett, Donald E. "Emigres and Militiamen: Free Persons of Color in New Orleans, 1803–1815." *Journal of Negro History* 37, no. 4 (January 1916).

Gatschet, Albert S. "The Shetimasha Indians of St. Mary Parish, Southern Louisiana." *Transactions of the Anthropological Society of Washington* 2 (February 7–May 15, 1882): 148–60.

Gelpi, Paul D., Jr. "Mr. Jefferson's Creoles: The Battalion d'Orleans and the Americanization of Creole Louisiana, 1803–1815." *Louisiana History* 48, no. 3 (Summer 2007).

Gerona, Carla. "With a Song in Their Hands: Incendiary *Décimas* from the Texas and Louisiana Borderlands during a Revolutionary Age." *Early American Studies* 12, no. 1 (Winter 2014).

Greene, Jack P. "The Cultural Dimensions of Political Transfers: An Aspect of the European Occupation of the Americas." *Early American Studies* 6, no. 1 (Spring 2008).

———. "Reflection on a Continuing Problem." *William and Mary Quarterly* 64, no. 2 (April 2007).

Hall, Gwendolyn Midlo. "Franco-African Peoples of Haiti and Louisiana." *Southern Quarterly* (Spring 2007).

Kendall, John S. "Early New Orleans Newspapers." *Louisiana Historical Quarterly* 10, no. 3 (July 1927).

———. "Shadow over the City." *Louisiana Historical Quarterly* 22, no. 1 (January 1939).

Legan, Marshall Scott. "Judge Henry Bry: Genevan on the Ouachita." *North Louisiana Historical Association Journal* 3, no. 3.

Nicholas, Roy F. "Challenge and Stimulus to American Democracy." *Louisiana Historical Quarterly* 38, no. 2 (April 1995).

Rodriguez, Junius P. "Always 'En Garde': The Effects of Slave Insurrection upon the Louisiana Mentality, 1811–1815." *Louisiana History* 33, no. 4 (Fall 1992).

Taylor, Gertrude C. "War Clouds: The St. Julien-DeClouet Affair." *Attakapas Gazette* 22 (Summer 1987).

Thelen, David. "Of Audiences, Borderlands and Comparisons: Toward the Internationalization of American History." *Journal of American History* 79 (September 1992).

Thompson, Thomas Marshall. "National Newspaper and Legislative Reactions to Louisiana's Deslondes Slave Revolt of 1811." *Louisiana History* 33, no. 1 (Winter 1992).

Vernet, Julien. "Citizen Laussat and the St. Julien Case: Royalists and Revolutionaries in Early Nineteenth Century Louisiana." *Louisiana History* 51, no. 2 (Spring 2010).

Weber, David J. "Turner, the Boltonians, and the Borderlands." *American Historical Review* 91 (January 1986).

Index

CPSIA information can be obtained
at www.ICGtesting.com
Printed in the USA
LVHW101932280422
717218LV00027B/74

9 780807 174289